REVISED EXPANDED EDITION

ABRAHAM DIVIDED

AN LDS PERSPECTIVE ON THE MIDDLE EAST

Daniel C. Peterson

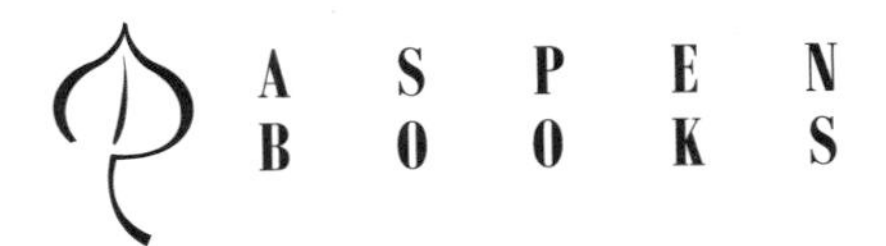

Abraham Divided: An LDS Perspective on the Middle East
by Daniel C. Peterson

Library of Congress Cataloging-in-Publication Data

Peterson, Daniel C.
Abraham divided: an LDS perspective on the Middle east / by Daniel C. Peterson. -- Rev. ed.
p. cm.
Includes bibliographic references (p.) and index.
ISBN 1-56236-224-0
1. Middle East. I. Title.
DS44.P48 1995 95-40429
956--dc20 CIP

Printed in the United States of America.

First Printing: February 1992
Second Printing: October 1995

Cover Art: Mark Robison
Cover Design: Brian Bean

Author's Note

There is no clear distinction anymore—if ever there really was—between the terms "Near East" and "Middle East." I tend to use them interchangeably, here and in my other speech and writing. No significance should be read into this.

There are at least two competing systems for numbering the verses of the Qur'an—the older one of G. Flügel and the increasingly dominant one of the Cairo edition. My quotations and citations follow the latter system. However, owing to the disagreement here, some readers who want to look up my references may have difficulty finding them. I can only advise persistence. The difference between the Flügel and Cairo numerations is seldom more than a few verses one way or the other.

Having disposed of those necessary remarks, it is my pleasure to thank some of those who helped in the production of this book.

My wife, Deborah, spent many patient hours checking the majority of my footnotes. She has worked alongside me at every stage of my career—this is only one instance among many—and my debt to her is beyond my ability ever to pay her back. (For several days, too, my mother and father, Berniece and Carl Peterson, of Whittier, California, were also pressed into service—during what they had vainly imagined would be simply a pleasant visit.) Curtis Taylor of Aspen Books was unfailingly pleasant and helpful during the writing of the first edition; waiting for completion of the second edition, Paul Rawlins was more than patient. Cheryl Hall, then of the Jerusalem Center office at BYU Travel Study, went beyond duty to help out at a crucial moment during the composition of the first edition, as she had done several times before. My friend and colleague, Dr. William J. Hamblin, furnished the photographs that appear at the beginning of each chapter. Additionally, he and his research assistant John Hamer designed and produced the book's two maps. Dr. Stephen D. Ricks, my department colleague and former missionary companion, read a late draft of several of the chapters and offered useful comments. My colleagues Dr. James A. Toronto and Dr. David B. Galbraith also gave me helpful advice toward the second edition, as did, most especially, my student and research assistant Amy Livingstone. Needless to say, however, nobody other than myself is responsible for the final results here.

Finally, I wish to dedicate this book to the memory of

Joseph Wilford Booth.

Since the time, during my own mission, when I first heard of his long and dedicated ministry as a missionary in the Near East, I have felt strongly that he deserves to be better remembered by members of the Church he so loyally served.

A Political Map of the Middle East Today

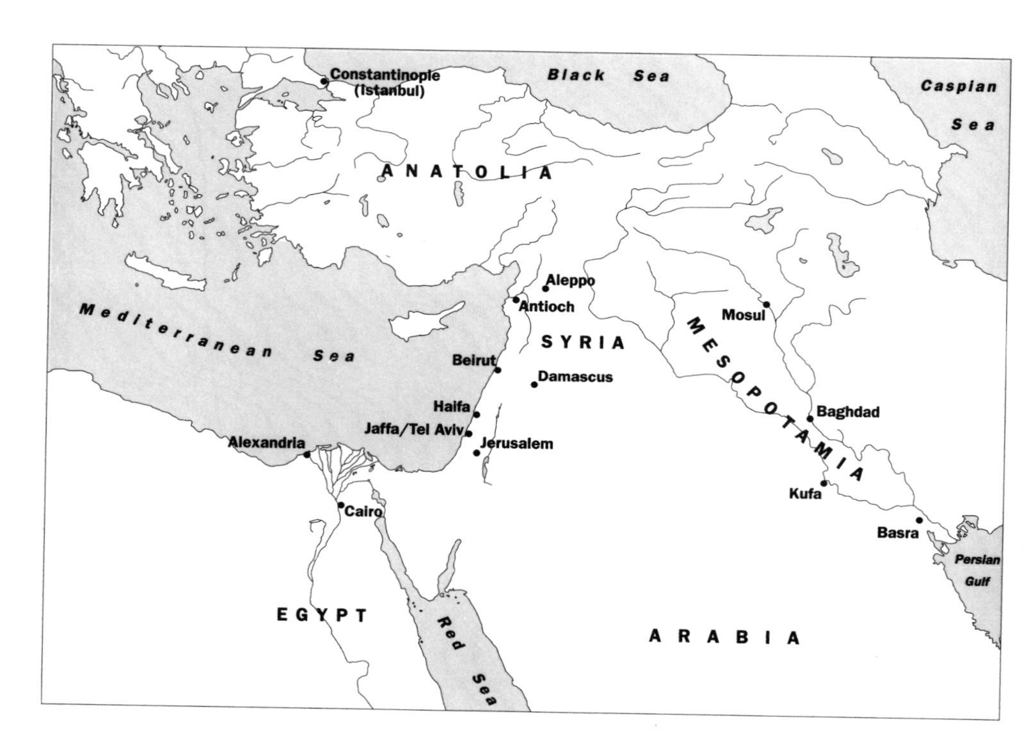

Prominent Locations of the Middle East Through History

Contents

ABRAHAM DIVIDED

The Mount of Olives, where Elder Orson Hyde offered his dedicatory prayer, looms behind the seventh-century Muslim Dome of the Rock.

Prologue

Before dawn on the morning of Sunday, 24 October 1841, a Connecticut Yankee in his mid-thirties climbed out of his bed in Jerusalem's Latin Convent and walked to one of the city's gates. When the gate was opened, he crossed the Kidron Valley, much as David and Jesus and other biblical figures had crossed it centuries before.[1] He made his way up the Mount of Olives, and there, sitting silent and alone on the crest of the hill, he took out pen and paper and began to write. After a considerable time spent thus writing and thinking, he knelt in prayer, reading from the papers on which he had been working. After his prayer, the man erected a pile of stones there on the mount, as a witness and a testimony of what he had done. Finally, he descended the rocky slope and returned across the dusty brook of Kidron to his lodgings in Jerusalem.

Who was this man? His name was Orson Hyde, and he was an apostle of The Church of Jesus Christ of Latter-day Saints, a small and controversial group that had been driven from one American state to another (and would be again). At the time of his visit to Jerusalem, the Church's headquarters were in an Illinois town on the banks of the Mississippi River. The town's name was Nauvoo, from a Hebrew root meaning "beautiful." What was Orson Hyde doing in Palestine, so alone and so far from his home? The answer to that question demands, perhaps, a more complicated answer.

---

1. See 2 Samuel 14:23 and John 18:1.

From its establishment in 1830, The Church of Jesus Christ of Latter-day Saints had shown deep interest in the Near East. At first, this was simply because the Near East was the place from which much of Latter-day Saint scripture had come and the place in which virtually all of the most beloved Jewish and Christian stories found their setting. But the biblical and Book of Mormon texts upon which the new Church was founded also foresaw an important future role for the Near East in the divine plan. For one thing, it was foretold clearly in the scriptures that the Jews would someday return from their *diaspora*, their dispersion or scattering.

> And it shall come to pass in that day, that the Lord shall set his hand again the second time to recover the remnant of his people, which shall be left, from Assyria, and from Egypt, and from Pathros, and from Cush, and from Elam, and from Shinar, and from Hamath, and from the islands of the sea. And he shall set up an ensign for the nations, and shall assemble the outcasts of Israel, and gather together the dispersed of Judah from the four corners of the earth.[2]

This would be part of a general gathering both of the Jews and converted Gentiles to two great world centers, as is made clear by a revelation to Joseph Smith, the founder of the Church, late in 1831:

> Let them, therefore, who are among the Gentiles flee unto Zion. And let them who be of Judah flee unto Jerusalem, unto the mountains of the Lord's house. Go ye out from among the nations, even from Babylon, from the midst of wickedness, which is spiritual Babylon.[3]

In a revelation granted on 7 March 1831, the Lord repeated teachings that he had earlier given to his disciples in Palestine. He told them of the destruction of the temple at Jerusalem and predicted the desolation of that city and the dispersion of the Jews among all nations. "But they shall be gathered again; but they shall

---

2. Isaiah 11:11-12; compare 1 Nephi 22:25; 3 Nephi 16:5.
3. Doctrine and Covenants 133:12-14.

remain until the times of the Gentiles be fulfilled."[4] This delay of their redemption until after the fulfillment of "the times of the Gentiles" is borne out, too, by the Lord's statement to the Nephites that, after the non-Jews "shall have received the fulness of [his] gospel," he will give to his people again "the land of their fathers for their inheritance, which is the land of Jerusalem."[5]

Sometime in 1832, the Prophet Joseph Smith laid his hands upon the head of a new convert by the name of Orson Hyde and told him, "In due time thou shalt go to Jerusalem, the land of thy fathers, and be a watchman unto the house of Israel; and by thy hands shall the Most High do a great work, which shall prepare the way and greatly facilitate the gathering together of that people."[6]

On the sixth of August, 1833, the Lord spoke to Joseph Smith in a revelation and commanded him to take the gospel to the Jewish people, to "seek diligently to turn...the hearts of the Jews unto the prophets...lest I come and smite the whole earth with a curse, and all flesh be consumed before me."[7] This matter was still much on the mind of both the Lord and his prophet when the Kirtland Temple was dedicated on 27 March 1836. In his dedicatory prayer for that first Latter-day Saint temple, revealed to him from heaven, the Prophet reminded the Lord of his

> great love for the children of Jacob, who have been scattered upon the mountains for a long time, in a cloudy and dark day. We therefore ask thee to have mercy upon the children of Jacob, that Jerusalem, from this hour, may begin to be redeemed; and the yoke of bondage may begin to be broken off from the house of David; and the children of Judah may begin to return to the lands which thou didst give to Abraham, their father.[8]

---

4. Doctrine and Covenants 45:24-25.
5. 3 Nephi 20:28-29; compare 3 Nephi 21:22-29; also the remarks of Elder Charles W. Penrose, given on 18 May 1883, *Journal of Discourses*, 24:215.
6. This incident is recalled in a letter from Elder Orson Hyde to Rabbi S. Hirschell, dated approximately 15 June 1841. The letter is reproduced in *History of the Church*, vol. 4, pp. 374-78; the relevant passage is on page 375.
7. Doctrine and Covenants 98:16-17.
8. Doctrine and Covenants 109:61-64.

An important step toward the fulfillment of this prophetic request occurred within days, when Moses, appearing in the Kirtland Temple on 3 April 1836, bestowed "the keys of the gathering of Israel from the four parts of the earth" upon Joseph Smith and Oliver Cowdery.[9] This was the same day on which the prophet Elijah appeared to Joseph and Oliver and committed to them the keys of this last dispensation of the gospel. A recent examination of the appearance of Elijah in the Kirtland Temple has demonstrated that he came during the Passover season, at just the time that Jews around the world were putting out chairs and table settings for his coming. "Elijah did come at Passover time—as pious Jews had long hoped he would—although he did not avail himself of the hospitably opened door of a faithful Jewish family but came to the House of the Lord in Kirtland."[10] That it was the Passover season on which these visions occurred is also relevant to the appearance of Moses (who is, of course, closely linked with the institution of the Passover itself)[11] and to his restoration of "the keys of the gathering of Israel." For it was at the Passover that Jews throughout the diaspora vowed to celebrate that festival "next year in Jerusalem." It is doubtful that Joseph Smith even *knew* it was Passover, but the bestowal of the keys for gathering at this very time is highly significant.

Thereafter, Elder Hyde spent his efforts almost entirely among the Gentiles. But in the early part of March 1840, after he had gone to bed, a vision opened itself to him in which he saw in succession the cities of London, Amsterdam, Constantinople, and Jerusalem. A voice came to him, saying, "Here are many of the children of Abraham whom I will gather to the land that I gave to their fathers; and here also is the field of your labors...Go ye forth to the cities which have been shown you, and declare these words unto Judah...Speak ye comfortably to Jerusalem, and cry unto her, that her warfare is accomplished—that

---

9. Doctrine and Covenants 110:11.

10. Stephen D. Ricks, "The Appearance of Elijah and Moses in the Kirtland Temple and the Jewish Passover," *Brigham Young University Studies* 23 (Fall 1983), 483-86. The quotation is from page 486.

11. Ricks, "The Appearance of Elijah and Moses," 485-86, finds it highly significant that Moses and Elijah are linked on this important occasion.

her iniquity is pardoned, for she hath received of the Lord's hand doubly for all her sins."[12] At the Church's April conference of that year, held in Nauvoo, Elder Hyde stood before the Saints and told them of his vision, as well as of the prophecy which had been made to him about the work he was to do among the Jewish people. The conference unanimously voted to approve his mission. Elder John E. Page, also of the Council of the Twelve, then arose and spoke of Elder Hyde's mission, of "the gathering together of the Jews, and the restoration of the house of Israel." He declared to the assembled Saints "that these things must take place and that the time had now nearly arrived for their accomplishment." On the next day, the Prophet Joseph Smith related to the conference the impression he had received that Elder Page should accompany Elder Hyde to Jerusalem. This was approved by all. The authorities then composed a certificate authorizing Elders Hyde and Page to serve as representatives of the Church in the nations of the Mediterranean and the Middle East. It declared, in part, that "the Jewish nation have been scattered abroad among the Gentiles for a long period; and in our estimation, the time of the commencement of their return to the Holy Land, has already arrived."[13]

Wasting no time, the two apostles left Nauvoo on the 15th of April, on their way to Jerusalem. A month later, the Prophet wrote a letter of encouragement and counsel to them. "It is a great and important mission," he told them,

> and one that is worthy [of] those intelligences who surround the throne of Jehovah to be engaged in. Although it appears great at present, yet you have but just begun to realize the greatness, the extent and glory of the same... Brethren, you are in the pathway to eternal fame, and immortal glory: and inasmuch as you feel interested for the covenant people of the Lord, the God of their fathers shall bless you. Do not be discouraged on account of the greatness of the work; only be humble and faithful.[14]

---

12. Letter of Orson Hyde to S. Hirschell, *History of the Church* 4:375–76.
13. For the conference minutes, see *Times and Seasons* 1 (April 1840), 91–95. The certificate of authority granted to Elders Hyde and Page is found in the same number of the *Times and Seasons*, on pp. 86–87.
14. Joseph Smith letter of 14 May 1840, reprinted in *History of the Church* 4:128–29.

At some point, however, Elder Page lost the spirit of his mission. He and his companion separated at Dayton, Ohio, and he remained in North America.[15] But Orson Hyde continued onward, in faithful obedience to the visions and inspiration he had received and under the authority of the Lord's modern prophet. It was not easy going. He made his way to New York and waited in vain for Elder Page to catch up with him. Eventually realizing that he must go on alone, but not having the money to buy passage across the Atlantic, he went south to Pennsylvania and tried to find some way to continue his mission. Fortunately, there were those who were prepared to help. After a meeting of the Saints in the city of Philadelphia, a stranger came forward and offered a purse of gold in support of the assignment, with the simple request that Elder Hyde remember him when he prayed at the holy city of Jerusalem.[16]

Shortly after receiving this act of kindness, Elder Hyde was able to embark for Liverpool, England. There, he met with Brigham Young and the other apostles who were there on their historic mission. Also, while he was in England, he wrote a letter to the chief rabbi of England, Samuel Hirschell, whom he had been unable to visit personally. In that letter, Elder Hyde recounted the vision he had received in March of 1840 and assured the rabbi and his people that "the time has arrived when the day-star of your freedom already begins to dispel the dark and gloomy clouds which have separated you from the favor of your God."[17]

15. This was an ominous portent of things to come. John E. Page was excommunicated in 1846.

16. Elder Hyde would do so faithfully. "Do Thou also look with favor," he prayed from the Mount of Olives, "upon all those through whose liberality I have been enabled to come to this land; and in the day when Thou shalt reward all people according to their works, let these also not be passed by or forgotten, but in time let them be in readiness to enjoy the glory of those mansions which Jesus has gone to prepare. Particularly do Thou bless the stranger in Philadelphia, whom I never saw, but who sent me gold, with a request that I should pray for him in Jerusalem. Now, O Lord, let blessings come upon him from an unexpected quarter, and let his basket be filled, and his storehouse abound with plenty, and let not the good things of the earth be his only portion, but let him be found among those to whom it shall be said, 'Thou hast been faithful over a few things, and I will make thee ruler over many.'" *History of the Church*, 4:458.

17. Letter of Orson Hyde to S. Hirschell, *History of the Church* 4:377.

He continued his journey across the continent of Europe and into Asia Minor, the first Latter-day Saint missionary to proclaim the gospel in those then-distant lands. He worked in Rotterdam, in the Netherlands, as well as in Frankfurt-am-Main in Germany. He traveled through Vienna to Romania and on to Istanbul, the capital of the vast Ottoman Empire that had previously served, under the name of Constantinople, as the imperial capital of the Byzantines. From there, he traveled by sea to Smyrna (the modern Izmir) and from Smyrna to Beirut. The voyage was not entirely pleasant. It took longer than planned and, since the captain had not loaded enough food, Elder Hyde was obliged for a number of days to live on snails gathered from the coastal rocks. (His major regret about the snails was that he could never find enough of them, so that he was always hungry and grew progressively weaker.)

Finally, in late October of 1841, Elder Hyde's ship dropped anchor in the harbor at Jaffa. It had been more than a year and a half since he had left Nauvoo, but, finally, he was within a few miles of the holy city of Jerusalem. Still, the journey that remained before him was anything but routine. For one thing, the area through which he had to pass was a lawless one, and there was a very real possibility that he would be killed or robbed by marauding bedouins. Fortunately, though, he was able to travel with a group of English gentlemen, who went accompanied by a large number of well-armed servants.

When he arrived at Jerusalem, he was not especially impressed by the sight. The city held about twenty thousand inhabitants in the early 1840s, and they were surrounded by a strong wall that varied from about twelve to thirty feet high and was between five and ten feet thick. The hills among which the city rested were bare, denuded of crops and vegetation, and covered with rocks. The heat was oppressive, even in October, and he found many of the customs of the local people not merely foreign and exotic but irritating. He could see little or nothing desirable in the place. Nevertheless, it was the city of the great King, and it was the site of innumerable stories held sacred by himself and by Christians and Jews around the world. It was the city to which he had been called by divine vision.

> My natural eyes, for the first time, beheld Jerusalem; and as I gazed upon it and its environs, the mountains and hills by which it is surrounded, and considered, that this is the stage upon which so many scenes of wonders have been acted, where prophets were stoned, and the Saviour of sinners slain, a storm of commingled emotions suddenly arose in my breast, the force of which was only spent in a profuse flow of tears...As I stood upon this almost sacred spot and gazed upon the surrounding scenery, and contemplated the history of the past in connection with the prophetic future, I was lost in wonder and admiration, and felt almost ready to ask myself—Is it a reality that I am here gazing upon this scene of wonders? or, am I carried away in the fanciful reveries of a night vision? Is that city which I now look down upon really Jerusalem, whose sins and iniquities swelled the Saviour's heart with grief, and drew so many tears from his pitying eye? Is that small enclosure in the Valley of Kedron, where the boughs of those lonely olives are waving their green foliage so gracefully in the soft and gentle breeze, really the Garden of Gethsemane, where powers infernal poured the flood of hell's dark gloom around the princely head of the immortal Redeemer? Oh, yes! The fact that I entered the garden and plucked a branch from an olive, and now have that branch to look upon, demonstrates that all was real. [This] is the place where the Son of the Virgin bore our sins and carried our sorrows.[18]

Elder Hyde was able to secure lodging for a few nights at the Latin Convent in the old city.[19] He toured the city, visiting the pool of Bethesda and bathing in the pool of Siloam. He marvelled, as many tourists have in the years since his visit, at the continuity of ancient customs. Biblical images, previously only imagined, came to literal life before his eyes. Walking outside the walls of the city, for example,

---

18. Orson Hyde, *A Voice from Jerusalem* (Liverpool: Millennial Star Office, 1842), 7, 17.

19. He may have inscribed his last name on one of the doors of the Convent, where it was customary for pilgrims to do so. The name "Hyde" has been found carved there. See Steven W. Baldridge, *Grafting In: A History of the Latter-day Saints in the Holy Land* (Jerusalem: Jerusalem Branch, 1989), 64. A picture of this door is found following p. 98 of the same book.

he saw two women who were grinding wheat at a small hand mill. One of the women would grind the wheat for a while, and then, when she needed a break from the tiresome work, the other would take over. He thought of the Savior's prophecy concerning the suddenness of his second coming, when "two women shall be grinding at the mill; the one shall be taken, and the other left."[20] After his walk in and around the city, he returned to his room at the Latin Convent completely coated with the fine powdery dust of Palestine in the dry season, and he remembered the Lord's command to his disciples that they should "shake off the dust of [their] feet" when they departed from an unreceptive house or city.[21]

We have a letter sent by Elder Hyde from Alexandria, Egypt, on 22 November 1841. In it, he gives the first details of his mission to Palestine, which he had by then successfully completed. "I have only time to say that I have seen Jerusalem precisely according to the vision which I had. I saw no one with me in the vision; and although Elder Page was appointed to accompany me there, yet I found myself there alone."[22] Before dawn on the morning of Sunday, 24 October 1841, as Elder Hyde records it, "I arose from sleep, and went out of the city as soon as the gates were opened, crossed the brook Kedron, and went upon the Mount of Olives, and there, in solemn silence, with pen, ink, and paper, just as I saw in the vision, offered up the following prayer to Him who lives forever and ever."[23]

There follows in Elder Hyde's letter the complete text of his prayer, which occupies three full pages of small print in the History of the Church by Joseph Smith. A few selections will be sufficient for our purposes here:

> Now, O Lord! Thy servant has been obedient to the heavenly vision which Thou gavest him in his native land; and under the

---

20. Matthew 24:41.

21. Matthew 10:14. Perhaps he thought, too, of the Savior's washing of the apostles' feet (John 13:4–17), an ordinance that probably had its origins in the practical realities of life in such a place.

22. The letter from Orson Hyde to Parley P. Pratt, dated 22 November 1841, is reproduced in *History of the Church*, 4:454–59.

23. Letter of O. Hyde to P. P. Pratt, *History of the Church*, 4:456.

shadow of Thine outstretched arm, he has safely arrived in this place to dedicate and consecrate this land unto Thee, for the gathering together of Judah's scattered remnants, according to the predictions of the holy Prophets—for the building up of Jerusalem again after it has been trodden down by the Gentiles for so long, and for rearing a Temple in honor of Thy name . . .

Grant, therefore, O Lord, in the name of Thy well-beloved Son, Jesus Christ, to remove the barrenness and sterility of this land, and let springs of living water break forth to water its thirsty soil. Let the vine and olive produce in their strength, and the fig-tree bloom and flourish. Let the land become abundantly fruitful when possessed by its rightful heirs; let it again flow with plenty to feed the returning prodigals who come home with a spirit of grace and supplication; upon it let the clouds distil virtue and richness, and let the fields smile with plenty. Let the flocks and the herds greatly increase and multiply upon the mountains and the hills; and let Thy great kindness conquer and subdue the unbelief of Thy people. Do thou take from them their stony heart, and give them a heart of flesh; and may the Sun of Thy favor dispel the cold mists of darkness which have beclouded their atmosphere. Incline them to gather in upon this land according to Thy word. Let them come like clouds and like doves to their windows. Let the large ships of the nations bring them from the distant isles; and let kings become their nursing fathers, and queens with motherly fondness wipe the tear of sorrow from their eye.

Thou, O Lord, did once move upon the heart of Cyrus to show favor unto Jerusalem and her children. Do Thou now also be pleased to inspire the hearts of kings and the powers of the earth to look with a friendly eye towards this place, and with a desire to see Thy righteous purposes executed in relation thereto. Let them know that it is Thy good pleasure to restore the kingdom unto Israel—raise up Jerusalem as its capital, and constitute her people a distinct nation and government, with David Thy servant, even a descendant from the loins of ancient David, to be their king.[24]

---

[24] Letter of O. Hyde to P. P. Pratt, *History of the Church*, 4:456-57.

At the time that Orson Hyde offered this prayer on the Mount of Olives, there were approximately ten thousand Jews living in Palestine. Most of these were elderly people who had come to the sacred land of their ancestors to die, hoping for burial in its holy soil. (Indeed, the lower slope of the Mount of Olives itself is covered with Jewish burial grounds.) "Their object," as Ivan J. Barrett memorably puts it, "was not to write a new chapter in the land of their forefathers, but to live out the final chapter of their own lives."[25] This hardly looked like a promising start to the prophesied return of the Jews to Palestine.

Nonetheless, for those with their ears to the ground, there were stirrings. When Mehmet Ali, the viceroy of Egypt, overran Syria in 1832, political leaders in both the Near East and Europe began to seriously consider what ought to be the future of the Holy Land. One of the suggestions made was the establishment of a Jewish buffer state in Palestine, situated neatly between Turkey and Egypt. This idea received some favorable response. In 1838, just two years after the "the keys of the gathering of Israel from the four parts of the earth" had been restored to earth in the Kirtland Temple, the Jewish philanthropist Sir Moses Montefiore submitted a plan for Jewish colonization in Palestine to the Egyptian viceroy. However, these ideas died essentially stillborn. Or, at least, it seemed so at the time. There was no Jewish organization capable of carrying out so ambitious a plan as the restoration of the Jews to Palestine. And this was a plan that definitely required organization on a massive scale. The Jews were a scattered people, in many countries, speaking many languages. They were, or they seemed to be, deeply rooted in their homelands. Many of them were relatively comfortable. Many, for the first time, were beginning to feel themselves full citizens of their respective nations. Why should they leave now, and for such a desolate and forbidding place as Palestine? Certainly they retained a spiritual affinity for the land of their fathers, but wasn't that enough?

---

25. Ivan J. Barrett, *The Story of the Mormons in the Holy Land* (unpublished manuscript), 9c.

Elder Hyde's mission was complete. Only time would tell if his prayer had been heard and if his prophecies would be fulfilled. But, although he was finished with the work he had been summoned by vision to do, there remained before him a long and arduous journey homeward. After embarking from the Egyptian port of Alexandria, bound for northern Italy, he survived the worst storm at sea he had ever experienced. And then, upon his arrival at Trieste on 22 December 1841, the Italian authorities quarantined him for four full weeks, with the crew of his ship and his fellow passengers. Sitting in Italian quarantine, he had time to think and worry about his family, from whom he had not heard in nearly a year.[26] Later, on 30 January 1842, having received a letter from his wife dated the previous 14 November, he said that he "laughed and cried together." It was not, however, until the end of 1842 that Elder Hyde would be able to see his family again. His path homeward led across the Alps, in mid-January, and included a prolonged sojourn in Germany, where he published one of the most important early Latter-day Saint pamphlets. At length, after a prolonged stay in England, he departed for North America.[27]

When, on 7 December 1842, Orson Hyde arrived in Nauvoo and was reunited with his wife, his children, and the Saints, he had completed the longest, and almost certainly the most dangerous, mission in the history of the Church to that time. Indeed, there have been few even in the years since who have travelled further

---

[26]. That the Lord and the Lord's prophet shared his concern is evident in a revelation received by Joseph Smith on 2 December 1841: "Verily thus saith the Lord unto you my servant Joseph, that inasmuch as you have called upon me to know my will concerning my handmaid Nancy Marinda Hyde—behold it is my will that she should have a better place prepared for her, than that in which she now lives, in order that her life may be spared unto her; therefore go and say unto my servant, Ebenezer Robinson, and to my handmaid his wife—Let them open their doors and take her and her children into their house and take care of them faithfully and kindly until my servant Orson Hyde returns from his mission, or until some other provision can be made for her welfare and safety. Let them do these things and spare not, and I the Lord will bless them and heal them if they do it not grudgingly, saith the Lord God; and she shall be a blessing unto them." *History of the Church*, 4:467.

[27]. The pamphlet was *Ein Ruf aus der Wüste, eine Stimme aus dem Schoose der Erde* (Frankfurt: Orson Hyde, 1842), one of the most important sources for early information on Joseph Smith's First Vision.

and longer and under more adverse conditions than he did. He had covered nearly twenty thousand miles in an age before automobiles, steamships, and aircraft. He had proclaimed the gospel for the first time in this dispensation in continental Europe, in Turkey, in Palestine and Egypt. He had been away from his wife and family for nearly three exhausting years.

Today, a garden of five and a quarter acres commemorates Orson Hyde's visit to the Near East in late 1841. It covers part of the Mount of Olives across the Kidron Valley from the east wall of the Old City, not far from the Garden of Gethsemane. Paths meander through indigenous trees and other vegetation typical of Palestine, leading eventually to a 150-seat amphitheatre that features a large brass plaque. On this plaque are passages from Elder Hyde's dedicatory prayer in both English and Hebrew.[28] This garden was dedicated by a prophet of God (Spencer W. Kimball), a direct successor of the prophet who had sent Elder Hyde to the Near East in the first place. It is a symbol, as Elder Hyde himself is a symbol, of the importance that the Lord continues to place on this relatively barren and often troublesome part of the world. It raises many questions.

Why was it necessary to send Orson Hyde to the Near East? Why and how had the Jews been scattered, dispersed from the land in which their history, as recorded in the Bible, had occurred? Who had occupied the country in the meantime? What religion did those people bring with them? How is that religion similar to Judaism and to Christianity? How does it differ? Was Elder Hyde's mission a success? Why do many in the Near East today object to the state of Israel, and why are many hostile to the West and to the United States? These are some of the questions I shall attempt to answer in the following pages.

---

28. It was decided not to include a translation of the prayer into Arabic, out of the obvious desire not to offend Arabs.

The so-called "Wailing Wall" is all that remains of the great Jewish temple at Jerusalem. It takes its name from the sorrowful prayers and lamentations that generations of Jews have recited at its foot, but legend says that the wall itself weeps over the temple's destruction.

After the Testaments

I have a little book in my home library that I treasure. I love it for its impressive title: *The History of the World in Two Hundred and Forty Pages*.[1] In many ways, although I am about to use it as a bad example, it isn't really a bad book. But I confess that I actually bought it for its table of contents, which is highly instructive. Here is a list of the book's chapter headings:

1) Prehistoric Man
2) The Ancient World
3) The Age of Greece
4) The Thousand Years of Rome
5) The Thousand Years of Christendom
6) The Awakening of the West
7) The Age of Italy
8) The Age of Spain
9) The Centuries of France
10) The Anglo-Saxon Centuries

These chapter headings tell us something important about a certain view of the world. In *The History of the World in Two Hundred and Forty Pages*, the first twenty-two pages are actually taken up by the title page, the table of contents, and a chapter on

---

1. René Sédillot, *The History of the World in Two Hundred and Forty Pages*, translated from the French by Gerard Hopkins (New York: The New American Library, 1951).

prehistory. Thus, a more accurate— and even more impressive—title might have been "The History of the World in Two Hundred and Eighteen Pages." History proper begins only with the second chapter, which discusses the great civilizations that grew up around the Nile, Tigris, Euphrates, Indus, and Yellow Rivers. With its discussion of Egypt, Mesopotamia, India, and China, this chapter really does look like an attempt at world history. But there is little effort at world coverage after Chapter Two. It seems, in fact, that the great river-based civilizations of the ancient world existed only to give rise to Greece, the subject of the third chapter. There are nods toward India and China, but as far as this book is concerned their central role in world history is essentially past. Greece, in its turn, sparks the rise of Rome and then vanishes from the stage. Rome is important for its role in the rise of Christianity, which receives a chapter. Eventually, Italy reappears as the cradle of the Renaissance, but it is soon replaced at center stage by Spain and its conquest of the New World. The chapter on Spain is followed by a chapter on "The Centuries of France" and then by a concluding chapter on "The Anglo-Saxon Centuries."

The most noticeable thing about this list of chapter headings is that eight of the nine historical chapters in *History of the World* deal primarily with the history of Europe. And seven of those eight chapters, in turn, are focused primarily or even entirely on the history of western Europe. But Europe is only a peninsula on the western end of the Eurasian landmass. A pygmy among continents, it doesn't even have a clear geographical boundary that defines it in the way North and South America can be distinguished from one another, or, to choose an even clearer example, in the way Australia and Africa are unmistakably distinct. It is, from a certain perspective, a continent by courtesy. Certainly it seems strange that so small an area should so dominate a book on "world history." Certainly, too, it is noteworthy that all of world history culminates in France and England. It reminds me a bit of the comment I heard many years ago to the effect that the nineteenth century liked Darwin's theory of evolution so very much because it seemed to say that all of the history of the globe, all the struggles of the reptiles and the dinosaurs, the primitive gropings of the cavemen and the slow progress of civilization through the centuries of history, had culminated in...the enlightened thinkers of the nineteenth century, the crown of creation.

Yet this small book, while extreme, is not really very unusual. My own high school studies in history—and probably yours as well—were similarly focused. We nodded in the direction of India and China and Mesoamerica; we drowsed through five or six pages on the medieval Near East; but we spent the bulk of our time on Europe. And not on all of Europe. How many high school students ever learn much about Poland or the fascinating history of Hungary or the Balkans? What do we ever learn about the Byzantine Empire? We limit our attention to a few nations in the western part of the European peninsula. We study England, France, Spain, and Italy—countries with cultures and religions very close to our own—and we call it world history. This is, frankly, scandalous.

Post-biblical Judaism

There is a similar gap—not scandalous, but still more than a bit unfortunate—in our knowledge of the history of religion. For most Latter-day Saints, and for most Christians generally, the history of Israel ends with Malachi. There is a blank space of a few centuries, and then the New Testament opens. But the New Testament covers the events of only a few decades. In it, the Sadducees and Pharisees strut briefly on stage, then are gone. This poses a problem. The Bible and the other standard works of the Church contain enough material to guide us on the path to salvation, which is obviously the most important information we could possibly desire, but if we want to understand the world of today, neither the Bible nor any other book of scripture is enough by itself. And this is true even in the area of religion. Surely Latter-day Saints, of all people, will understand that it is impossible to fully understand modern Christianity on the basis of the Bible alone. Too much change has occurred—much of it of the kind that we would recognize as part of the "great apostasy." By the same token, the Bible does not account for Judaism as it exists today. Yet few of us know much about Judaism beyond the Old Testament, the Sadducees, and the Pharisees. If we want to understand the Judaism of today, we have to learn something of its development during the nearly twenty centuries between the crucifixion of Christ and our own time. And, as will become clear, we especially need to learn something about the six centuries between the death of Jesus and the coming of Islam.

The most striking fact about Judaism during the past twenty centuries is its survival. By all reasonable expectations, Judaism should have disappeared long ago, as many other ancient religions have done. Sometimes I think that a powerful argument for the existence of God could be constructed solely on the fact that Judaism exists to this day, and, perhaps even more impressively, on the fact that, two thousand years after its destruction, a Jewish state has been reestablished in the Near East. "The Jews," writes the brilliant British historian Paul Johnson with considerable reason, "are the most tenacious people in history."[2]

Most of us know something of the history of Israel—which, of course, originally included more tribes than merely Judah, or the Jews—from the Old Testament. Even so, it is important to remember two central ideas from the ancient teachings because they continue to be fundamental to Judaism in the centuries after the close of the Bible. These ideas, which have their origins in Abraham himself, are the covenant with God and the attachment to the Land of Israel.

The covenant suggests a special relationship between God and those with whom he has made the covenant. It does not mean that they are necessarily better than others, nor that their souls are worth more than the souls of the Father's other children. It does, however, mean that they are called to be "a chosen generation, a royal priesthood, an holy nation, a peculiar people; that [they] should shew forth the praises of him who hath called [them] out of darkness into his marvellous light."[3] Just before the revelation of the Ten Commandments, the Lord told Moses to inform the people that they were to be "a kingdom of priests, and an holy nation."[4] Even earlier, God spoke to Abraham, saying, "I will make of thee a great nation, and I

---

2. Paul Johnson, *A History of the Jews* (New York: Harper and Row, 1987), 3.
3. 1 Peter 2:9.
4. Exodus 19:6.

will bless thee, and make thy name great; and thou shalt be a blessing…and in thee shall all families of the earth be blessed."[5] The prophets of Israel liked to compare the covenant between Jehovah and his people to the marriage contract between a husband and his wife. The people's unfaithfulness was like a wife's adultery. The unfortunate prophet Hosea, for instance, was directed by the Lord to make his own family life a symbol of the relationship between God and Israel: "Go, take unto thee a wife of whoredoms and children of whoredoms: for the land hath committed great whoredom, departing from the Lord."[6] As Hosea's wife strayed, so too did Israel stray from its promise of faithfulness. The Savior himself denounced "an evil and adulterous generation [that] seeketh after a sign."[7] Through Isaiah, God announced that if there was going to be a divorce, it would come because of Israel's transgressions, not his.[8] But in the last days, Isaiah declared, the Lord would take his "wife" back, and her tent would be so full of children that its stakes would have to be moved further out and the tent expanded just to hold them.[9]

Second, the covenant implies a demand for better behavior. It requires not just accurate notions about God and not just "faith without works." It requires action, a certain kind of conduct. If other nations are not holy, still Israel is to be holy. If most of us in modern Israel are not quite saints, still we are called "Saints" and are called to become such in full reality. "For," says the Lord, "of him unto whom much is given much is required."[10]

The second principle is just as essential to understanding Judaism. From its earliest days, Israel has felt itself linked to a particular piece of land. This is important for many reasons. For one thing, much of the story of Israel recounts its efforts to acquire the

---

5. Genesis 12:2-3; compare Abraham 2:8-11.
6. Hosea 1:2.
7. Matthew 12:39.
8. Isaiah 50:1; compare Doctrine and Covenants 82:10.
9. Isaiah 54:1-10. It is this image of the bedouin tent—or, more precisely, of the tabernacle in the wilderness, which was a special kind of bedouin tent—that gives us our modern word "stake" for an administrative unit of the Church. The "center stake of Zion" is the pole that holds the tent up in the center.
10. Doctrine and Covenants 82:3.

land in the first place, along with the warnings of the prophets about losing it and the dream after one exile or another of returning to it. Many of the messages of the prophets deal with Israel's worthiness or lack of worthiness to possess the land, as well as with the future of the land—whether that future was darkened in the short term by the wickedness of the people or glorious in the long term because of the mercy and power of Jehovah. This relationship between land and people helped to form Israel in many ways. I think it is important, too, to notice which land it was that God appointed for his covenant people. He could have given them a nicer place.

For all the talk of a land "flowing with milk and honey," Palestine is a relatively difficult place to eke out a living. Tahiti might have been nice, with fruit just waiting to be picked. Switzerland is far prettier. Even in the Near East, there are places where it would have been much easier to live a peaceful life. Take Egypt, for instance. With a regular and predictable river running gently through it, separated from would-be enemies by harsh deserts but itself enjoying the lushness of the Nile Valley, Egypt was a wonderful place by the standards of the ancient Near East. Palestine, on the other hand, was the highway that nearly every Near Eastern conqueror took to get to his next trophy. President Gordon B. Hinckley has called it, quite accurately, "the bloody doormat of the eastern world."[11] Why did God put his people there? I think it has to do with the development of character. Goethe noted that, while talent is developed in stillness and quiet, character is developed in the stream, or torrent, of everyday events. Today the Lord asks us to be in the world, while not of it—to be actively involved in making a living, in raising a family, in marriage—and does not allow us the sometimes tempting alternative of withdrawal to a nice, quiet monastery. So did the Lord plant his people in Palestine, rather than in some more peaceful and pleasant land. We humans seem to need some discomfort to prod us to great achievements; neither Tahiti nor Switzerland has yet produced a great literature.

---

11. Cited by Truman G. Madsen, in his foreword to Baldridge, *Grafting In*, i.

God's concern with the literal soil of Palestine was also reflected in his concern for the way the people behaved on it and in regard to it. It strengthened the concern of the Israelite prophets for proper behavior, for righteousness. Judaism was to be a religion interested in this world, not just in the next. Unlike Buddhism and Hinduism, which encourage us to escape this world, Judaism teaches that this world is—or, at least, can be—sanctified. "And God saw every thing that he had made, and, behold, it was very good."[12] Righteousness could dwell upon this earth; a sanctified society could be built here. It would be a literal place, with physical structures of brick and stone, not merely a spiritual abstraction.[13] Someday, the Messiah would purify Israel and glorify Jerusalem. The prophets sought, not escape, but the blessing of the Lord upon them and their people in this world as well as in the next. Far from seeking a timeless Nirvana, the Hebrew scriptures pronounced time to be holy. "And God blessed the seventh day, and sanctified it."[14]

Their very positive attitude toward the world, and toward time, almost guaranteed that the Hebrews would take history seriously. God, they were convinced, revealed himself in this world and acted

---

12. Genesis 1:31. It is beyond the scope of this book, but I would like to suggest, even if I cannot develop the thought here, that Latter-day Saints share this positive evaluation of the world. We do not dream of "escaping the body," and we are not inclined to asceticism. There are no Mormon monks. See Daniel C. Peterson and Huston Smith, "Purpose of Earth Life: Comparative Perspective" in Daniel H. Ludlow, ed., *Encyclopedia of Mormonism* (New York: Macmillan, 1992), 3:1181–83.

13. Latter-day Saints too have their attachment to a land. There is Utah, "sacred home of the prophets of God" in the words of the hymn. Even more, there is the New Jerusalem, someday literally to be built of actual brick, steel, glass, boards and stone. It is not a mere spiritual abstraction. And if Zion means "the pure in heart," as it does (Doctrine and Covenants 97:21), it also signifies a literal place. Interestingly, some nineteenth-century critics of the Church thought it too concerned with fields and barns and fences to be truly "spiritual." Nowadays, one occasionally hears the criticism from liberal Protestant and Catholic theologians that Mormonism is too concerned with the next life; they themselves, having often abandoned their belief in transcendent matters such as life after death, now focus on religion as a tool for social reform. Amidst the fashions of the world, however, the Church goes on its way. It sanctifies the world of work and everyday life, teaching that cleaning one's yard can be an act of worship, while at the same time it regards the life to come as a literal reality. Like their predecessors, modern prophets teach a balance between this life and the next. The two are, after all, not so very different.

14. Genesis 2:3.

in this time. And it was their religious duty to record those revelations and mighty acts. As Paul Johnson points out, the Jews

> were the first to create consequential, substantial and interpretative history... [T]hey were fascinated by their past from very early times. They knew they were a special people who had not simply evolved from an unrecorded past but had been brought into existence, for certain definite purposes, by a specific series of divine acts. They saw it as their collective business to determine, record, comment and reflect upon these acts. No other people has ever shown, particularly at that remote time, so strong a compulsion to explore their origins. The Bible gives constant examples of the probing historical spirit: why, for instance, was there a heap of stones before the city gate at Ai? What was the meaning of the twelve stones at Gilgal? This passion for aetiology, the quest for explanations, broadened into a more general habit of seeing the present and future in terms of the past. The Jews wanted to know about themselves and their destiny. They wanted to know about God and his intentions and wishes. Since God, in their theology, was the sole cause of all events—as Amos put it, 'Does evil befall a city unless Yahweh wills it?'—and thus the author of history, and since they were the chosen actors in his vast dramas, the record and study of historical events were the keys to the understanding of both God and man. Hence the Jews were above all historians, and the Bible is essentially a historical work from start to finish.[15]

> The people of Israel were not great craftsmen, or painters, or architects. But writing was their national habit, almost their obsession. They probably produced, in sheer quantity, the greatest literature of antiquity, of which the Old Testament is only a small fragment... [They] saw literature as a didactic activity, with a collective purpose. It was not an act of personal self-indulgence.[16]

The records that the Hebrews had so laboriously created would eventually prove to be of great worth to their descendants, helping

---

15. P. Johnson, *History of the Jews*, 91-92.
16. P. Johnson, *History of the Jews*, 88.

them understand their own uniqueness and special covenant relationship with God.[17] New challenges were arising, and these records became invaluable. In the late fourth century B.C., the landscape of the Near East was dramatically changed by the invasion of Alexander the Great. Alexander, descendant of a royal family in the relatively uncultured area of Macedonia, north of Greece, was a pupil of the great philosopher Aristotle and, with all the fervor of a convert, brought a form of Greek civilization with him wherever he went.[18] His armies pushed into Asia and Africa, establishing Greek colonies such as Alexandria in Egypt. After a few years of what has come to be known as the Hellenistic Age, much of the eastern Mediterranean world was tied together in an unprecedented way by links of culture, common learning, and shared knowledge of the Greek language.[19] People were able to move around now. A new international society was created in which Jews could, and did, spread out to fill much of the eastern Mediterranean. Large Jewish colonies were established in many areas, most notably in the new city of Alexandria. (This merely continued a process of dispersal which had begun with the Babylonian captivity. Many Jews, having grown wealthy and comfortable, had simply stayed in Babylonia when the captivity came to an end.)

Alexander's successors—he died at a very young age—were his generals, who carved out empires for themselves. Notable among these were Ptolemy in Egypt, and Seleucus in Syria and Mesopotamia (modern Iraq). The Jews were ruled first by the Ptolemies and then, after 200 B.C., by the Seleucids. These new Hellenistic rulers brought Greek institutions with them. The most prominent of

---

17. The Book of Mormon furnishes a splendid example, in the Mulekites, of a people who lacked such records and who consequently lost their identity and even their language. See Omni 1:17. This situation, which comports so well with what scholars know today about linguistic evolution and the development of cultures, seems to me utterly beyond the capacity of an uneducated 1820s New York farmboy to have made up on his own.

18. Aristotle, in his turn, had studied under Plato, who had been a disciple of Socrates. There is probably no more distinguished lineage of teachers and students anywhere in the history of education.

19. Words like "Hellenistic" and "Hellene" come from the Greeks' word for their own homeland, "Hellas."

these institutions was the *gymnasium*, whose functions were far broader than the name suggests to modern hearers. It was not only an athletic center where, to the horror of pious Jews, men and sometimes women competed in the nude, but a community center. Furthermore, it was the main educational institution of Greek culture.

That culture held tremendous attraction. People who wanted to be sophisticated—like Philip of Macedon, who hired Aristotle to tutor his son Alexander—were eager to learn from the Greeks. Moreover, they were often eager to be Greeks. Or, at least, they tried to imitate them to the extent of their ability. The best science and philosophy of the period were Greek. The most prosperous people of the new period were either Greeks or imitators of Greeks. They were phenomenal traders and merchants, with networks across the Mediterranean world. Owing to such trade and learning, the eastern Mediterranean coast was soon heavily Hellenized. And the Greek cities of the coast established satellite towns on the interior. Soon, the mountainous regions of Judea and Samaria seemed rustic and backward by contrast.

But adaptation to the world comes at a price. At the least, it presents considerable risks. Greek culture was the passport to sophistication, to social advancement. Those who rejected it were likely to be mocked by their more up-to-date neighbors.[20] Some Jews, therefore, and especially the upper classes, the rich, and the chief priests, wanted to be like their Hellenized overlords. If their Jewishness got in the way, well, they were prepared to abandon it, or better yet, to redefine it so that it was no longer an obstacle. A number even wanted to push the pace of Hellenization—some for selfish, materialistic interests and others because they were genuinely attracted to Hellenistic ideas (which were, it must constantly be stressed, genuinely attractive). Consequently, there was, among many Jews, a secularizing and materialistic tendency to the age.

Reactions varied. Many Jews, probably the majority, resisted. Some withdrew into an ever more rigorous adherence to the old traditions. The Essene community at Qumran, from whom we have

20. See 1 Nephi 8:26–28.

received the Dead Sea Scrolls, seems to have originated in the third century B.C. as a reaction to what it perceived as the "corruption" brought in by the Greeks. Other pious Jews sought to adapt to the new world without giving up their principles. They learned Greek, they lived in Hellenized cities (many in Alexandria), and they translated their scriptures into Greek, giving us the famous Septuagint, the Greek version of the Old Testament that is still an important document to this day. (The New Testament figure of Apollos is a good illustration of this middle tendency to neither withdraw from the "modern" world nor totally surrender to it. We are told of him that he was a Jew and that he was "mighty in the scriptures" even before his conversion to Christianity. Yet he was "born at Alexandria," and there can hardly be a more perfectly Greek name than "Apollos.")[21]

But the resources available to Judaism for resistance and adaptation were fairly limited by now. By 200 B.C., the idea of a Jewish canon was beginning to take shape. This had the effect of discouraging additions. Prophecy was discouraged and began to die out. Even the Jews themselves realized that something was missing. The First Book of Maccabees, for example, was written in the century before Christ. Speaking of one difficult period for the Jews, it declares that "there had been nothing like it since the disappearance of prophecy among them."[22] Later on, during another period of stress and confusion, "the Jews and the priests...agreed that Simon [Maccabeus] should be their perpetual leader and high priest until a trustworthy prophet should arise."[23] Clearly, just when a new living prophet was needed, no prophet was found.

In 175 B.C., aggressive Jewish reformers found an enthusiastic but dangerous ally in a new Seleucid monarch who called himself Antiochus Epiphanes. Antiochus believed in Hellenism, yes, but he also thought that Hellenism would provide him with higher tax revenues—revenues that he desperately needed in order to keep his

---

21. Acts 18:24-25. Apollos became a very important missionary ally of Paul's. See 1 Corinthians 1:12; 3:4-6, 22; 16:12; Titus 3:13.
22. 1 Maccabees 9:27 (Jerusalem Bible translation).
23. 1 Maccabees 14:41 (Jerusalem Bible translation).

many wars going. Casting his eyes around the empire for money, he found a promising source of untapped cash. The vast funds of the temple at Jerusalem were simply too much to pass up. Fortunately for him, the militant Hellenizers in Jerusalem, who were his natural allies, had gained control of the office of high priest. They had also published a decree recognizing the divinity of Olympian Zeus. "Zeus" was just another name for Jehovah, after all, and they couldn't see that it was worth quibbling over names in this new age of cosmopolitan sophistication. More important still, from Antiochus's perspective, the Hellenizers were busily downgrading what they saw as the absurd rituals of the temple. No use spending all that good money on sacrifices when you could divert it to really useful things like athletic competitions and drama festivals or, as their boss Antiochus chimed in, like military equipment and naval vessels. So he began to dip into the temple treasuries to further his international adventures, with the aid and connivance of Hellenizing Jews.

The outcry from the people was deafening. Probably even Antiochus could hear it, far away in his Syrian palace. The Hellenizers were now revealed to be not only enemies of Jehovah but willing tools of a greedy, tax-happy foreign imperialist. There was tremendous popular resistance, and there were many martyrs. Open revolution broke out in the small town of Modin, located not far from the site of the modern Tel Aviv airport, when one of the "reformers," an agent of the Hellenizing government, was killed by an aged priest named Matthias Hasmon. The old man's five sons, led by Judah the Maccabee ("the Hammer"), perhaps knowing that they now had very little to lose, launched an astonishing guerrilla campaign that crushed the Hellenizers and won the Jews' virtual independence. (However, in the course of their long and difficult campaign, the Hasmoneans, as the Maccabees were sometimes called, turned to a rising Italian city-state for help. A place called Rome. As can be imagined, this step had important consequences down the road.) A priestly family, the Maccabees stood for strict allegiance to the Law. Their prestige after a successful rebellion against one of the world's leading powers merely reinforced the tendency toward reverence for the Law, or the Torah, that had already begun to characterize Judaism since at least the days of Ezra and Nehemiah. It would mark Judaism ever afterwards.

As part of this return to the Law, a national education system began to evolve in which, theoretically, all Jewish boys were taught the Torah. This education was entirely religious, rejecting—for reasons that ought to be obvious—anything foreign or nonreligious. The Hellenizers had discredited themselves within Palestine by their alliance with a foreign tyrant, as well as by their willingness to abandon important aspects of the Jewish religion. The new form of education that arose upon their downfall had the benefit of avoiding the dangers of contact with corrupt foreign ideas and of strict focus upon scripture. As such, it had a great deal to do with the later rise of rabbinic Judaism. However, in trying to steer clear of ideas from outside, it tended to make Judaism narrow and xenophobic. This was an opposite but equally dangerous error.

John Hyrcanus, a grandson of Matthias Hasmon who reigned over the Jews from 134 to 104 B.C., maintained his line's reputation for zeal by setting out to conquer the entire land of Palestine, which the Bible told him was rightfully his as ruler of the Jewish state. It was his duty to eliminate foreign religions and unorthodox sects and, if necessary, to slaughter those who hesitated to give them up. He massacred entire towns whose only crime, as far we can determine, was speaking Greek. He conquered the province of Idumea and forcibly converted the inhabitants of its chief cities to Judaism, butchering those who refused to convert. This was bad enough, but the Hasmonean dynasty, which had at least begun in an outburst of pious heroism, ultimately ended in impiety and oppression. The later members of the family, rich and corrupt, were a disgrace to their name. It is from this time of deep disappointment in the nation's leaders that we first hear of a faction known as the "Perushim," the Pharisees, who rejected the royal religious establishment and emphasized personal righteousness as the way to salvation. In a sense, they represented a popular revolt against the aristocracy. The temple, the Pharisees were willing to admit, might well be corrupt, or at least administered by corrupt men, but it was still possible for each individual Jew, regardless of class, to live the laws of purity and to study the Torah within his own home. The Sadducees, on the other hand, represented the rich and were more closely affiliated with the ruling class.

In 63 B.C., Judea became a client-state of the new superpower, Rome. Thus, as the Christian era dawned, the vast majority of the Jewish population—in Palestine and in other centers such as Alexandria—lived in areas under Roman control. At first, the Romans did not rule Palestine directly. They preferred rule through locals, such as the infamous Herod.

Herod saw himself as something of a reformer, dragging a backward people kicking and screaming into the modern age. He sought to weaken the power of rigorist Judaism by separating church and state. One of his first acts upon coming to power in 37 B.C. was to execute forty-six leading members of the Sanhedrin, whose chief sin was seeking to uphold the law of Moses in secular matters. Largely for reasons of personal interest, he wanted the Sanhedrin to be a religious court only. Herod did not seek to become high priest, but he made it an appointed post to which he could name virtually anybody he liked, any time he liked. He favored the Jews of the diaspora—that is, those who lived abroad, or were "dispersed"—and he was their greatest patron, endowing charities, synagogues, and libraries in Alexandria, Rome, Babylon, and throughout the world wherever Jews were to be found. But his sense of Jewish destiny also allowed him to rebuild the temple of Apollo at Rhodes and to single-handedly save the Olympic games, which earned him great popularity beyond the Jewish community. On the coast, he created the new port city of Caesarea, in honor of his patron, Augustus. In Jerusalem, after he had established a firm grip on power, he founded both a theatre and an amphitheatre—among the most Greek of institutions. He thought diaspora Jews were more sophisticated, more open, than the benighted inhabitants of Judea, so he brought them in to fill many of the municipal offices in Jerusalam and throughout the area. He even favored diaspora Jews for the office of high priest. The construction of a massive new temple was part of his modernizing plan to make

Jerusalem not merely the provincial capital of Judea but the capital of Jews worldwide. The temple was to be—and indeed was—a spectacle famous the world over, one that made his name and the name of Jerusalem itself well known.

Herod's temple became a repository of riches. Even Gentiles and foreigners offered gifts and sacrifices. Kings like Artaxerxes and Augustus donated golden vessels to it, which were stored in its treasuries. And Jews throughout the world were hardly behind in their generosity. Josephus says the temple became "the general treasury of all Jewish wealth."[24]

We know a great deal about the temple of Herod. Its platform covered thirty-five acres and was a mile in circumference. Those who have been to Jerusalem and have had the opportunity to stand beneath the platform are often struck by its height, but it was actually twice as high then as it is now, since 2,000 years of rubbish have covered up many of the lower courses of stone. It was an immense structure, and it was clearly designed to impress. Gates and decorations were covered in gold and silver. An unusually white stone was used for its walls, which gleamed for miles in the bright Palestinian sun. (Very little money was spent on the actual interior of the temple, which was relatively plain. After all, Herod was not from a priestly family and thus could not even enter the inner court. So why spend valuable resources on it? And, anyway, the chief aim of the building was to impress mortal human beings, and the overwhelming majority of those who were to be impressed also could not enter the most sacred sanctuaries. This says much of Herod's motives.)

However, if buildings, even impressive ones, do not last forever—and we all know that the temple of Herod did not last beyond the first century after Christ—their builders certainly do not live forever. Just before his death, Herod ordered a great golden eagle to be placed above the entrance to the temple. Pious Jews at Jerusalem were outraged, and a group of Torah students managed to climb up and smash the eagle to pieces. Sick as he was, Herod responded

---

24. Josephus, *Wars of the Jews*, 6:282 (6:5:2 in the Whiston translation).

with his typical cruelty. According to most modern scholars, he passed to his eternal reward in the spring of the year 4 B.C., shortly after having the students burned to death. (It was a typical action for the man who, according to the gospel of Matthew, had killed all of the infant children in Bethlehem and surrounding areas just a short while before.)

The death of Herod the Great marked the end of the last period of stable Jewish rule in Palestine until, in the middle of the twentieth century, David Ben Gurion proclaimed the state of Israel. True, Herod had sons, but they proved unworthy and incompetent. Archelaus, to whom Herod left Judea, was deposed by the Romans in 6 A.D. For several decades afterwards, the province of Judea and its major city, Jerusalem, were ruled directly by a Roman procurator from his headquarters in Caesarea on the coast. (Pontius Pilate was one of these.) It seems, however, that the Romans really didn't want to rule Judea directly. In 37 A.D., they returned the province to the family of Herod the Great, appointing his grandson, Herod Agrippa, to rule the area. Agrippa seems to have been a competent ruler, but he died relatively young in 44 A.D., and the Romans saw themselves with no choice but to impose direct rule again. And that, effectively, was the end of any real possibility for Jewish self-government in Palestine.

But many Jews continued to hope for independence and self-rule, and there were many rebellions. The Zealots, for example, carried out street assassinations. The so-called Essenes, gathered on the barren shores above the Dead Sea, dreamed of apocalyptic violence and produced military training manuals such as the one entitled "The War of the Children of Light Against the Children of Darkness." (It doesn't take much imagination to realize which side they saw themselves on.) But these revolutionaries had little chance of success, and they were crushed every time the Romans could catch them. Rome must have been rather puzzled by Jewish discontent. Most Roman provinces prospered and were largely content. In fact the majority of the Jews was satisfied, if the truth were known. Rome was liberal and tolerant by ancient standards; its governors were usually competent, and its laws were just.

The Romans' image as something like ancient Nazis, standard in Hollywood movies for many years, is undeserved. But the Jews were different, and Judea was a constant source of trouble and torment for its Roman rulers.

In 66 A.D., the "Great Revolt," as it is known, of the Jews against Rome broke out in Caesarea. It started with a riot in which Greeks began to kill Jews while the Greek-speaking Roman garrison of the town stood by with its hands in its pockets. A massacre ensued, and the news spread to Jerusalem where more riots broke out. The situation was made worse by the fact that the Roman occupation government, needing money, had decided (like Antiochus before them) to dip into the temple treasury. Radical Jewish nationalists saw this as their opportunity to throw the Romans out once and for all. They also turned their attention to the Jewish upper classes, to the Hellenizers, whom they identified with the evil Greeks and who had identified themselves so completely with Roman rule. ("We have no king but Caesar," the chief priests had told Pilate when seeking Christ's death.)[25] We know that the aristocratic rich were a target of the radicals because one of the radicals' first acts, when trouble broke out in Jerusalem, was to seize and burn the temple archives, which housed all records of debts.

The rebels also attacked and massacred the Roman garrison in Jerusalem. Such an act, of course, could not possibly go unpunished. The Roman legate in Syria, who bore overall responsibility for the entire region, thereupon gathered a large force and marched unsuccessfully on the city. At this, Rome itself took over. An enormous force of four Roman legions, under the command of a highly experienced general named Titus Flavius Vespasian, moving at a careful pace, cleared the coast, seized virtually every fortress held by Jewish forces, and pacified the countryside. It was a smooth, professional operation. And it was noticed by those who counted. In 69 A.D., Vespasian was chosen emperor of Rome, and he departed for Italy after leaving his son Titus, a future emperor

25. John 19:15. In so saying, in proclaiming their sole loyalty to an earthly monarch, the chief priests rejected their heavenly king—in more ways than one. Contrast 1 Samuel 8:6-7; Judges 8:22-23.

himself, in charge of the army during the final phase of the campaign, which centered on the siege of Jerusalem.

The siege lasted from April to September of 70 A.D. Titus had 60,000 men under his command, highly disciplined and well trained in the use of the latest and most modern siege equipment. The Jewish defenders of the city, by contrast, were only about 25,000 in number and were divided bitterly among themselves. The outcome was never really in doubt, although it was hard work for the Romans at every step. By the end of the siege, the temple had been burned to the ground, and those of the Jews who had not been killed had either been sent off as slaves or to die in the gladiatorial arenas of Caesarea, Antioch, or Rome itself. Titus's triumphal arch still stands in Rome where it was erected to commemorate his victory, and on it, carved in stone and still clearly visible, is the great menorah, the lampstand of the temple that he captured and carried off.

The last Jewish stronghold was the spectacular mountain fortress-palace of Masada, 1300 feet above the barren wilderness of the Dead Sea. It is still possible today to stand upon Masada and see the outlines of the siege walls left behind by Flavius Silva and his Tenth Legion in the arid, hot soil. The Romans must have wondered just who was besieging whom. (Occasionally, the Jewish garrison on Masada would open up one of the cisterns of the fortress and let a cascade of water run down the side of the massive rock. This showed their enemies that they were comfortable and well supplied.) Still, while the Jews survived for a while and even thumbed their noses for a season at the Roman soldiers, time was again on Rome's side.

The siege of Masada called for exactly the kind of military engineering at which the Romans were expert. With the forced assistance of thousands of Jewish prisoners of war, the Romans built an immense ramp to the top of Masada, which is still there today. The defenders of the fortress, unable to stop the ramp—and reluctant to fire upon their captive countrymen, who were building it—knew the end was near. So, in a final act of defiance, they committed suicide. Nearly a thousand Jewish rebels died, including, perhaps, the last residents of the Essene community at Qumran. The Essenes had evidently sealed up their sacred records in the caves there and had retreated southward for a final stand against the Romans at Masada. Nearly two thousand years later, their documents would be discovered and become known to the world as the Dead Sea Scrolls. Thus, too, the Nephite practice of sealing up important documents during periods of impending military disaster to come forth at a later time—a practice much ridiculed when Joseph Smith revealed it to the modern world—came to seem authentically ancient and Near Eastern.

At the end of the revolt, the land was in ruins. Villages and cities were destroyed. Vast numbers of Jews were dead. Palestinian agriculture had suffered severely. The orchards of the hills and plains had been laid waste, sometimes by deliberate Roman policy and sometimes by the Jews themselves. Palestine's persimmon groves, the only ones in the world, were uprooted by Jewish rebels to prevent them from falling into the hands of the Romans.

However, this cataclysmic revolt that left Jerusalem destroyed and the holy temple in ruins—just as Jesus had said it would soon be—was not the last Jewish rebellion against Rome. A revolt in Egypt lasted from 115 to 117 A.D. and crippled the Jewish community there. Jews were never again to be an important element in the life of the great ancient city of Alexandria. But Palestine, too, would see one more revolt. Astonishingly, the economy and the population of the Holy Land were able to bounce back by the end of the first century, so much so that the Jews were soon able to launch yet another suicidal war against the Roman Empire. This revolt broke out around 132 A.D. under the leadership of a guerrilla leader generally known as Simon bar Kokhba.[26] He enjoyed considerable early success. Simon drafted the local population into his army and gained control of the whole province of Judea, including Jerusalem. He even managed to secure much of the rest of the Holy

26. There is some dispute about Simon's name, but "Bar Kokhba" is the title by which he is most widely known. It means "Son of the Star" and is related to the words "Kokob" and "Kokaubeam" occurring in Abraham 3:13. Ancient Christian sources thought the title was given to Simon for its alleged messianic implications.

Land. One entire Roman legion, the 22nd, from Egypt, was annihilated. But, once again, the revolt's ultimate fate was never really in question. Rome summoned its legions from as far away as Britain and the Danube frontier and concentrated them around Judea. As in the earlier revolt, the Romans—eventually there were a full twelve legions of them, three times as many as Vespasian and Titus had commanded—proceeded slowly, methodically, through the countryside, destroying outlying points of resistance, dividing and conquering, using siege warfare to starve holdouts into submission. Galilee was lost to the Jews early on. From that point, the destruction and ruin of war were concentrated almost entirely on Judea itself. Some Jewish rebels attempted to hold Jerusalem, but it was hardly defensible because its walls had not been rebuilt since the last insurrection against Rome. Gradually, although they inflicted heavy losses upon their adversaries, the Jewish rebels were pushed back into the town of Betar in the Judean hills southwest of Jerusalem, where they fell to Roman forces in the summer of 135 A.D.

The Romans were much harsher this time than they had been in the Great Revolt of 66-70 A.D. Simon was killed in the siege of Betar, and the great Rabbi Akiva ben Joseph, the most illustrious scholar of his time, was tortured to death. (Rabbinic lore indicates that Akiva had not only supported Simon's revolt but had pronounced Simon to be the Messiah.) Ancient sources speak of Jewish deaths numbering well above half a million, of nearly a thousand towns and villages being utterly destroyed. Unnumbered Jews were sold into slavery, and nearly all of Judea was left a wasteland. But the Romans' losses had been heavy too, and when the emperor Hadrian reported to the Senate, he omitted the customary introductory phrase, "I trust you and your children are well; I and my troops are well."[27]

In fact, Hadrian was furious. Personally hostile to Judaism because he found practices like circumcision disgusting and barbaric, he ordered the transformation of Jerusalem into a Greek-style

---

27. Dio Cassius, *Roman History*, 59.

pagan city, or *polis*. He used the debris of the old city to fill up the hollows and ravines of the site and to create a level platform upon which to build his new creation, which he named not Jerusalem but Aelia Capitolina, after his own family name and the name of the tutelary god of Rome. Hadrian transferred a population of Greek-speakers into the new city and forbade Jews to enter it on pain of death. The old official name of "Judea" was abolished and was replaced by the new name "Syria-Palestina."[28] Thus ended what was definitively the last Jewish revolt against Rome.[29]

Paul Johnson well summarizes the catastrophic changes in the fortunes of world Jewry:

> In the short-term perspective of the second century AD, the Jews appeared to have been a powerful national and religious group which had courted ruin, and achieved it. During most of the first century, the Jews not only constituted a tenth of the empire, and a much higher proportion in certain big cities, but were expanding. They had the transcendent new idea of the age: ethical monotheism. They were almost all literate. They had the only welfare system that existed. They made converts in all social groups, including the highest. One or more of the Flavian emperors might easily have become a Jew, just as Constantine was to become a Christian 250 years later. Josephus was entitled to boast: "There is not one city, Greek or barbarian, nor a single nation where the custom of the seventh day, on which we rest from all work, and the fasts and the lighting of the candles, are

28. This new name represented a lingering memory of the ancient Philistines and may have been especially galling to the Jews.

29. In 1961, the great Israeli archaeologist Yigael Yadin found a land deed connected with the Bar Kokhba revolt in a place not far from the Dead Sea called the Cave of Letters. See Yigael Yadin, *Bar-Kokhba* (New York: Random House, 1971), 176. This document is of considerable interest for Latter-day Saints, since it was signed by one "Alma the son of Judah." The Nephite masculine name "Alma" has occasioned much ignorant laughter among anti-Mormons, but it is now known to be authentically ancient and authentically Jewish. How, though, could Joseph Smith have known that? See Hugh Nibley, *The Prophetic Book of Mormon*, Volume 8 in the Collected Works of Hugh Nibley (Salt Lake City and Provo: Deseret Book and the Foundation for Ancient Research and Mormon Studies, 1989), 281-82. Nibley offers a discussion of Bar Kokhba at pp. 274-88 of the same volume in a book review that originally appeared in *Brigham Young University Studies* 14 (Autumn 1973), 115-26.

> not observed...and as God permeates the universe, so the Law has found its way into the hearts of all men." A century later, the whole process had been reversed. Jerusalem was no longer a Jewish city at all. Alexandria, once 40 percent Jewish, lost its Jewish voice completely. The huge casualty figures cited by such authors as Josephus, Tacitus and Dio for the two revolts (Tacitus said 1,197,000 Jews were killed or sold as slaves in the 66-70 struggle alone) may be exaggerated but it is clear that the Jewish population of Palestine fell rapidly at this time. In the diaspora, the expanding Christian communities not only purloined the best Jewish theological and social ideas, and so the role of "light to the gentiles," but made increasing inroads into the Jewish masses themselves, diaspora Jews forming one of the chief sources of Christian converts.[30]

It would have seemed, with the temple gone, with all the old priesthood organizations destroyed and the rituals no longer able to be performed, with the people scattered and leaderless, that Judaism was finished. Other religions, after all, had vanished from the face of the earth before. Nobody worshipped Babylonian Marduk any more. The gods of ancient Egypt were dead or dying. So, too, were the gods of ancient Greece. And, truly, this was a traumatic period. A vacuum appeared at the center of Judaism. There can be no doubt that Jews everywhere were depressed and demoralized. The zeal of the first revolt and the messianic fervor of Bar Kokhba's rebellion were succeeded by doubt and despair. Gloom, as we can well understand, was pervasive, and the next five centuries would be a time of agonized adjustment to the new and harsh reality of exile. But Judaism was different. It survived.

One of the forms in which it survived is scarcely noticed by us today, so familiar are we with it. In the midst of all of the political agitation and instability, amid the wars and the massacres and the exiles, a movement had arisen that would prove far more important than any of the political revolutionaries and their plots. A man by the name of Jesus of Nazareth had taught for a few years in Palestine

[30] P. Johnson, *History of the Jews*, 147-48.

and had then been put to death by the Romans. This was done at the request of the Jewish leadership, ostensibly because they feared that he was preparing yet another rebellion against Rome, but more precisely because his teachings undercut their own authority among their people. The trouble, of course, was that Jesus did not stay dead. His followers, energized by their conviction of his triumph over the grave, as well as by the outpouring of the Holy Ghost upon them, began to spread his teachings with more vigor than ever. The worst fear of the chief priests and Pharisees had come horribly true: Please, they had begged Pilate, please assign a guard to Jesus' tomb, "lest his disciples come by night, and steal him away, and say unto the people, He is risen from the dead: so the last error shall be worse than the first."[31]

New believers flocked to the standard of Christianity, including a diaspora Jew by the name of Saul of Tarsus who was transformed from persecutor to convert by a direct appearance of the risen Christ. Saul's family was originally from Galilee, and although he had been raised in Cilicia, in what is today Turkey, he had returned to Palestine to study under the great rabbi Gamaliel the Elder. Convinced by his vision of the divinity of Christ, Saul devoted his life to preaching the gospel to the Jews of the diaspora and even to the Gentiles. It was a mission for which he was perfectly suited. He was fully Jewish. As he himself said, he was "circumcised the eighth day, of the stock of Israel, of the tribe of Benjamin, an Hebrew of the Hebrews; as touching the law, a Pharisee."[32] Yet he also had a good secular education, including a command of Greek and of gentile culture. He could quote their own poets to the Athenians on Mars Hill, trying to convince them to listen to his message.[33] Furthermore, Saul held Roman citizenship, something that was comparatively rare out in the provinces, and he used it and its privileges on more than

31. Matthew 27:64.

32. Philippians 3:5.

33. Acts 17:28 features references to at least two Greek philosopher-poets. Epimenides of Cnossos, who wrote in the sixth century B.C., used language very much like Paul's "in him we live, and move, and exist." The statement "We are all his children" is a direct quotation from the *Phainomena* of Aratus, a third-century pagan poet from Saul's own native Cilicia.

one occasion to further his mission.[34] In fact, he soon began to go by his Roman name, Paul, rather than by his Jewish name.

The new gospel preached by Jesus and Paul and the other apostles was, in a certain sense, the universal reformed Judaism of which Hellenistic reformers—at least those of the better sort—had long dreamed. The blessings of Abraham were now available to all, provided only that they accepted Jesus and his teachings. "There is," wrote Paul, "neither Jew nor Greek...for ye are all one in Christ Jesus. And if ye be Christ's, then are ye Abraham's seed, and heirs according to the promise."[35] But we should not mistake the situation and begin to think of the early Hellenizers as forerunners of the religion of Jesus. Christianity is a voluntary, almost democratic, form of religion, quite unlike the aristocratic religion that the Hellenizers had tried to force upon their people by means of power and wealth and through the use of military force and the extortions of tax-collectors.

Paul's audience was immense. There were millions of people throughout the Mediterranean who were ready for the message of Christianity. First of all, there were the Jews of the diaspora, of whom he himself was one. There were a million of them in Egypt alone, and they outnumbered Gentiles in two of the five "quarters" of Alexandria, which was the second city, after Rome itself, in the

---

34. In Acts 22:24-30, he used his citizenship to avoid a scourging. It may also have helped him to escape a lynch mob, according to Acts 23:27. Faithful to the command given him at Acts 23:11 to go and preach the gospel at Rome, Paul managed, by appealing to Caesar (Acts 25:9-12), to get the Roman government to pay his mission expenses. It is a bit reminiscent of Parley P. Pratt's experience while a missionary in western Ohio. He was arrested on a baseless charge and hauled off to court, where he preached and sang to the judge. Such behavior did not amuse the court officials, and Brother Pratt spent the night in jail. However, on the next morning he was in the mood to continue his missionary labors and had no interest in further imprisonment. At a certain point while standing in the public square, he turned to his jailor, a Mr. Peabody, and said, among other things, "You have given me an opportunity to preach, sing, and have also entertained me with lodging and breakfast. I must now go on my journey...I thank you for all your kindness—good day, sir." At which, he escaped by running into the nearby forest, which is a hilarious story in its own right. See *Autobiography of Parley Parker Pratt*, edited by Parley P. Pratt, Jr., 6th ed. (Salt Lake City: Deseret Book, 1966), 48-51.

35. Galatians 3:28-29.

ancient world. There was a substantial colony of them in Rome, as well as in major cities like Damascus and Antioch and Ephesus. They were in Gaul (today's France) and in Spain and northwest Africa. Many of them, however, found that it was very difficult to live according to the rules of Judaism in these far-off areas. They did not want to abandon their religion, but they felt themselves hemmed in by the details and minutiae of the Mosaic law and by the practice of circumcision. For many of them, Christianity seemed to be precisely what it was—a heaven-sent deliverance. The same was true for the large number of pious Gentiles throughout the Mediterranean basin who sympathized with Judaism, who accepted its basic teachings on the nature of God and the ethical demands he makes of his followers, but who were reluctant to undergo circumcision and to bind themselves to the hundreds of rules that accompanied the religion. The Christians now offered what could be considered a form of Judaism, but one stripped of unpalatable aspects—including its sometimes obnoxious ethnocentrism and intolerance and its insistence that Gentiles were ritually unclean and should be avoided—that had made Judaism unaccetable to otherwise sympathetic outsiders.

Thus, a form of what can be considered Judaism not only survived, but as every reader of this book well knows, spread throughout the entire world. On the other hand, Judaism itself survived too.

Originally, most Christians had been Jews. After a point early in Christian history, however, it had become clear that the vast majority of members of the Church were not Jews and had, in fact, had no prior contact with Judaism at all. The huge success of Christian missionary efforts among the Gentiles, accompanied by the destruction of the Jewish homeland in Palestine, left Jewish Christians in the minority and made certain that there would be little confusion between Judaism and Christianity in the future. Furthermore, the triumph of Hellenistic Christianity, and the demise of Jewish Christians, made it even easier for Jews to denounce and castigate Christianity. Wasn't it just another form of the old enemy, Hellenism? In a sense, that is precisely what Christianity was becoming, since, with the rise to dominance within the Church of converted Hellenistic pagans, numerous pagan ideas began to enter the Christian church. Christianity was losing touch with its Jewish roots. By the end of the first century or the beginning of the second, formal prayers against heretics, including Christians, had become a part of the Jewish daily service. By the time of the second Jewish revolt against Rome, in 132 A.D., the Christians were seen as open enemies, and early Christian writers report that Simon bar Kokhba massacred Christian communities as well as pagan Greek ones. As Paul Johnson writes,

> The Jews could not concede the divinity of Jesus as God-made-man without repudiating the central tenet of their belief. The Christians could not concede that Jesus was anything less than God without repudiating the essence and purpose of their movement. If Christ was not God, Christianity was nothing. If Christ was God, then Judaism was false. There could be absolutely no compromise on this point. Each faith was thus a threat to the other.[36]

Meanwhile, Judaism itself was undergoing major changes. The cataclysmic end of the Bar Kokhba rebellion guaranteed that Judaism would no longer be a national religion, since no nation was left. The rituals of the temple had already vanished, along with the temple itself, in the first revolt against Rome. Thus, Judaism became a religion focused almost entirely on the study and observance of the Torah. There had long been a tendency in this direction. The reforms of King Josiah, the career of Ezra the scribe, the advent of the synagogue as another place of meeting beside the temple, the rise of the Pharisees, the revolt of the Maccabees, all of these developments had emphasized the importance of the Torah. But now there was nothing else. The temple was gone, and the state was no more. The Jews were scattered, and they had only one thing that they could carry with them—the Law.

Furthermore, the ruling classes of Jewry, including the chief families of hereditary priests, had perished along with the temple

---

36. P. Johnson, *History of the Jews*, 144-45.

and the state they had served. Roman administrators were busily monitoring, harrassing, and persecuting descendants of the Davidic line, including the leaders of the Sanhedrin, in order to prevent them from serving as the nucleus of any new revolt. The prophets were long gone. Only the rabbis were left to become the leaders of a new Torah-centered Judaism. And, of course, since the Torah was their specialty and since their knowledge of it was the source of their authority, they were uniquely qualified to take over. Jewish tradition records that the great rabbi Johanan ben Zakkai, deputy head of the Sanhedrin, was smuggled out of the city of Jerusalem in a coffin just before it fell to the Romans in 70 A.D., not for fear of the besieging armies but because his fellow Jews, the Zealots, were guarding all exits to prevent anybody from escaping the doomed city. Rabbi Johanan, a priest and a Pharisee, was a realist. He favored peace and rejected fanaticism. He had opposed the revolt and, in fact, had long felt that Judaism would actually do better without the corruption and the distraction that seemed necessary accompaniments to a Jewish state. Thus, when the state disappeared, he was spiritually and intellectually prepared to go on and, more importantly, to help his people to go on.

Rabbi Johanan sought and received permission from the victorious Roman authorities to set up a Jewish religious center at Jabneh, or Jamnia, to the west of Jerusalem. There, with the Jewish state gone and its traditional leadership destroyed, an assembly of rabbis met and, still under the title of "Sanhedrin," set about to answer the questions that arose among Jews from the radically new conditions in which they found themselves. There were many of these questions. Jews had been accustomed to praying toward the temple, for example.[37] Now, with it gone, where should they pray? The Sanhedrin had always met within the temple precincts. How could it function now? The tithes and dues and offerings that were so important to Jewish practice were almost all tied up with Jerusalem and the temple. What now? Could Passover still be celebrated with the sacrificial lamb? These questions had to be

---

37. This practice was attested to in Daniel's day (Daniel 6:10).

answered, and in order to do so, the rabbis had to create or discover new resources among the treasures of their ancient heritage. Rabbi Johanan and his associates took decisive steps in this direction. To his disciples and to the Jewish people in general, who were dismayed by the fall of the temple and wondered where the sins of Israel could now find atonement, he taught: "My son, do not distress yourself, we have another atonement that is like it; and what is it? Charity: 'For charity I desire, not sacrifice.'"[38]

It was under Johanan ben Zakkai that the process of canonizing the Psalms and the so-called "wisdom books" of the Hebrew Bible was completed. Previously, while all Jews had agreed to accept the so-called "five books of Moses," the Pentateuch, some—notably the Sadducees—had refused to recognize the other books of our Old Testament as canonical. It is noteworthy, in fact, that the old sectarian divisions among Jews—between Zealots, Essenes, Sadducees, various schools of Pharisees, and the like—virtually disappeared. Only rabbinic Judaism survived, focused intensely on the Law and sustained by a consensus among Jews that this, and this alone, was or should be the true center of a pious Jewish life for both the individual and the community. As time passed, the new Sanhedrin at Jabneh took on most of the functions of the old one that had operated when the temple was still in place. The Sanhedrin became the executive body within Jewish community life, as well as the interpreter of the Law and an academy for training new generations in the intricacies of the Torah.

The scholars now reigned supreme within Palestinian Judaism. Family, social standing, and wealth no longer mattered. All that mattered was learning. Study, the scholars said, was even more important than keeping the commandments.[39] They did not claim revelation themselves, and they did not recognize revelation to others. This is well illustrated by the excommunication of Rabbi Eliezer ben Hyrcanus, a conservative scholar who followed the

---

38. Cited by Shmuel Safrai, in H. H. Ben-Sasson, *A History of the Jewish People* (Cambridge: Harvard University Press, 1976), 321. Rabbi Johanan is himself citing the great statement of Hosea 6:6.

39. Shmuel Safrai, in Ben-Sasson, *A History of the Jewish People*, 327.

earlier Rabbi Shammai and who, it seems, was something of an individualist. When the Sanhedrin ruled against him on a point relating to ritual purity, he nonetheless insisted that his interpretation was correct. He said he had received a revelation to this effect. So what? said the scholars. The Torah is "not in heaven," they said, but has been given to man on earth and is to be interpreted by men. At the very time of Rabbi Eliezer's excommunication, the leader of the Sanhedrin, the great rabbi Gamaliel, was on a ship at sea.[40] A terrible storm arose, and Rabbi Gamaliel feared that he was about to be drowned. Realizing that he was being punished by God for the injury that he and his associates had inflicted upon Rabbi Eliezer, he still refused to back down. Jewish tradition represents him standing on the ship and arguing with the Almighty, contending that the treatment meted out to Rabbi Eliezer had not been done in his own self-interest, but "only for Thine honour, that there shall not be divisions in Israel."[41]

But even if, from the perspective of the restored gospel, this fixation on the interpretation of past revelations seems to have blinded Jewish leaders to the possibility of ongoing communication with heaven, it nonetheless served a useful function. The Law, in fact, was the Jews' earthly salvation. It was the Law that allowed them to survive, unlike many other ancient nations whose names are today known only to scholars. Intense concentration on the Torah helped them to maintain their separateness during their dispersion to the four quarters of the earth. Still, such intense concentration on one thing also noticeably narrowed their intellectual horizon. Where Jews had once produced psalms, allegories, apocalyptic books, and a rich literature of proverbs and wisdom, from this point on, under the dominion of the rabbis and the Torah, they would limit themselves for centuries to writing commentaries and supercommentaries on the Law. The ancient people that had, in a sense, invented the writing of history, now turned their back on such things, perhaps feeling that history had turned its back

40. He is not to be confused with the Gamaliel of Acts 5:34-40, who had been dead for many years.
41. Cited by Shmuel Safrai, in Ben-Sasson, *A History of the Jewish People*, 324.

on them. As a result, it is difficult to piece together the events of the early centuries after the two disastrous revolts, for there is virtually no Jewish historical and biographical writing from the period.

An example will serve to make the new situation clear: At roughly the time of Christ, a great Jewish thinker by the name of Philo Judaeus lived in Egyptian Alexandria. Philo was thoroughly at home in Greek literature and wrote excellent Greek himself. His attempts to harmonize Judaism with Platonic philosophy put him in the vanguard of the intellectual life of his day. (He is, in my opinion, a highly important figure for the understanding of the Great Apostasy, for he seems to have been the first to apply the tool of allegorical interpretation to the scriptures in order to ensure that they taught philosophy and that they never ever taught anything embarrassing such as the doctrine of an embodied God.) By the middle of the second century A.D., however, a figure like Philo would have been unthinkable within Judaism. And, indeed, it is very striking that, while early Christian thinkers like Origen and Clement of Alexandria carried on the kind of allegorical reconciliation of scripture with Greek philosophy that had been Philo's chief interest, he had no successors at all within Judaism itself. In fact, Judaism appears to a large extent to lack much of anything that can strictly be called "theology." The Christians worked up doctrines like that of the "Trinity," which proved fertile ground for heresies and disagreements, and what Paul Johnson calls "the professional Christian intelligentsia" became preoccupied with disputes over theology and dogma and have remained so down to the present day. The leading thinkers of Judaism, by contrast, were preoccupied with behavior, with the way life should be lived in this world. As Johnson puts it, "Judaism is not so much about doctrine—that is taken for granted—as behaviour; the code matters more than the creed."[42] Indeed, although Christian theologians began producing creeds from quite an early period, the first Jewish creed was not composed until the Egyptian Saadya Gaon, under influence from Greek philosophy, issued his ten articles of faith in the tenth century A.D. Jewish doctrine was relatively simple—God was

---

42. P. Johnson, *History of the Jews*, 161, 162.

one, for instance, not three-in-one-and-one-in-three—and did not call forth the kinds of disagreements that would divide Christendom into innumerable warring factions.

What really interested the earliest rabbis was the collection and organization of the so-called "oral law," the traditions that had been gathering about the text of the Torah for centuries already. This was the next layer, the next level of sediment in the mounting deposit of what would come to be modern rabbinic Judaism. It culminated in the completion of the Mishnah, around the year 200 A.D. This important text, collected and edited by the illustrious Rabbi Judah the Prince, is one of the earliest documents of what can properly be called Judaism in the modern sense. It remains one of Judaism's greatest classics and, after the Bible itself, is the foundation of the Jewish religion. The term "mishnah" comes from a Hebrew word meaning "to repeat" or "to study," which points to the way in which it was originally studied—by memorization. The Mishnah is organized by topics and is comprised of sixty-two sections known as "tractates." These tractates are divided into six principal parts, dealing with (1) agriculture, and also the portions of various crops that are to be set aside for the temple, the priests, and Israel's poor; (2) sabbaths and festivals; (3) women, property, marriage, and divorce; (4) civil and criminal law, including torts and the law of witnesses; (5) conduct of the cult or sacrificial liturgy of the temple; and (6) the preservation of purity in the temple and, in certain specific circumstances, in the home. Noteworthy is the continuing emphasis on the temple. At least two of the six principal parts of the Mishnah deal with that building, which is not surprising since much of the oral law had probably begun to take shape during the period when it was still standing. But it is impressive that successive generations of Jews have continued to study the Mishnah, including the substantial portions of it that would train them to conduct the sacrifices and other rites of the temple should it ever return. And it must be assumed that, at the early time when the Mishnah was compiled, the hope that the temple would soon be rebuilt still burned bright in the hearts of many scattered Jews. The lack of a temple, they were certain, would only be temporary.

Indeed, for a brief period in the fourth century, the Roman emperor Julian (360-63)—known to Christian sources as "Julian the Apostate," but in Jewish tradition under the more neutral nickname of "Julian the Hellene"—raised hopes for the Jews of Palestine and the rest of the empire. Quite understandably unimpressed by the behavior of his supposedly Christian imperial family, which included murders and cruelties of astonishing variety, Julian had renounced Christianity. A highly intelligent man, he had accepted in its stead a philosophical version of the old Greek religion and had set out to reduce the power of the Christian church and its bishops. As part of his policy, he announced in 362 that he would sponsor the rebuilding of "Holy Jerusalem," including its temple. By restoring the Jews to their ancient capital and by reestablishing their great shrine, Julian knew he would score a major propaganda victory against the Christian church, which had based much of its propaganda on the destruction of Jerusalem as a sign of God's curse upon the Jewish people and the transfer of his blessing to the Christians.[43] He was also motivated, it seems, by genuine sympathy with Jewish doctrine and by a deep interest in religious ritual generally. The Christian reaction to Julian's plans was, predictably, furious—and apparently violent. Thus, when Christian legends report miraculous fireballs that destroyed everything the Jews had built on the temple mount, we can probably infer from this that pious arsonists set fire to the construction site. And when Julian was stabbed to death by a devout Christian Arab soldier among his troops, the dream of a restored Jewish temple died with him.

There still existed a large Jewish colony in Mesopotamia, in the area to which the Jews had been carried off in the so-called "Babylonian captivity." As already mentioned, the captives had prospered there, and most of them had chosen to remain in comfortable exile even when the road to return was entirely open. They enjoyed a flourishing intellectual life and maintained relatively close contact with their fellow-believers in and around Palestine. Soon, the

---

[43] For some interestingly similar modern views on the matter, see Thomas L. Friedman, *From Beirut to Jerusalem* (New York: Farrar Straus Giroux, 1989), 430-31.

Mishnah reached them there. But the rabbis did not, at first, occupy the first rank among Babylonian Jewry. Surprisingly enough, these exiles enjoyed a kind of quasi-political autonomy later than the Jews of Palestine did. For a time, their leader, who was known as the "exilarch," functioned as a kind of prince—he claimed to be descended from the king Zedekiah who had been carried away into captivity just after Lehi's departure from Jerusalem in the sixth century B.C.—and served as a high official in the Parthian state that ruled the area. However, when the fervidly Zoroastrian Sasanian Dynasty came to power early in the third century, the privileged role and the political powers of the exilarch were curtailed. But as the political elite of Babylonian Jewry lost power and prestige, the influence of the rabbis expanded to fill the vacuum. Thus, just as in Palestine, the scholars took over. Jesus' words, spoken more than two centuries before, were now truer than ever: "The scribes and the Pharisees," he had said, "sit in Moses' seat."[44]

Given the new Jewish focus on the writing of commentaries, it is not to be wondered that scholars immediately began to comment upon the Mishnah. Both the rabbis of Palestine and the rabbinic academies of Mesopotamia thus produced editions of what is known as the "Talmud." (The name comes from a Hebrew word meaning "study," or "learning.") This represents the third layer of Judaism as we know it. The Talmud grew out of lectures and discussions on the Mishnah, which was the core of the curriculum. The Jerusalem Talmud, or Talmud of the West, was complete by the end of the fourth century A.D. Most of the work on it was actually done in the city of Tiberias, on the sea of Galilee. It represents the thought and the decisions of the Palestinian rabbis and scholars during the two centuries that had passed since the compiling of the Mishnah. In fact, although it is presented in the form of a commentary, it actually goes beyond the Mishnah and includes material on issues the Mishnah had not touched at all. Work on the Babylonian Talmud took somewhat longer and was finished a century later. Although the Babylonian is the more detailed of the two Talmuds,

---

44. Matthew 23:2.

both are in substantial agreement. Both are mostly in Hebrew, with passages in "western" Aramaic and a sprinkling of Greek loan words in the Jerusalem Talmud, and passages in "eastern" Aramaic and a few Persian loan words in the Babylonian Talmud. Together, they form an admirable foundation for a unified body of religious law and practice.

The Babylonian Talmud became, by a considerable distance, the more important of the two works, partly because Palestinian Jewry was steadily on the wane while the Jews of Babylon were relatively well organized and prosperous. "It became," as Israeli historian Shmuel Safrai observes,

> the basic—and in many places almost the exclusive—asset of Jewish tradition, the foundation of all Jewish thought and aspirations and the guide for the daily life of the Jew... In almost every period and community until the modern age, the Talmud was the main object of Jewish study and education; all the external conditions and events of life seemed to be but passing incidents, and the only true, permanent reality was that of the Talmud.[45]

In 313 A.D., however, the Emperor Constantine officially recognized Christianity, and within a remarkably short time the new religion had become the official faith of the empire. The Jews now faced a twofold threat. Besides the paganism they had opposed for centuries, they now had to deal with their far more zealous and far more dangerous religious cousins, the self-proclaimed disciples of Jesus of Nazareth. Christianity was considerably less tolerant than paganism had been; unlike pagans, the monotheistic Christians could not accept the legitimacy and truth of other, contradictory faiths. By at least the end of the fourth century, the continued existence of this obstinate people, the Jews, had become an irritation that pious Christians could not overlook. Jews were seen, as the Emperor Constantius put it, as nothing but a "pernicious" or "despicable sect," meeting not for worship so much as to carry out what he termed "sacrilegious assemblies." "The Church," writes Shmuel

---

45. Shmuel Safrai, in Ben-Sasson, *A History of the Jewish People*, 379.

Safrai, "consistently fostered hatred and contempt for all that was Jewish."[46] As bigoted preachers constantly reminded their Christian neighbors, the Jews were the "murderers of Christ." In Palestine, entire Jewish villages—the majority of the province was still held by Jewish landowners until the beginning of the century—were burned to the ground by devout followers of Jesus. These Christians reasoned that—since they were the new Israel, having replaced the old Israel that had forfeited its blessings and its covenant through its rejection of the Messiah—the Holy Land was theirs. Besides, didn't Palestine contain the site of the Crucifixion of Christ and the Holy Sepulchre? (That Palestine also included sites holy in Jewish history was not of great importance to the new masters of the empire. Among other things, Christian government officials seem to have banned Jewish pilgrimages to Jerusalem.)

Such treatment merely accelerated a process of de-Judaization that had been going on in Palestine since the Great Revolt of 66-70 A.D. Gradually, despite the efforts of the rabbis to preserve Jewish landholdings in Palestine, and indeed to encourage foreign Jews to return to the Holy Land, small farmers had found themselves unable to retain their lands. The process was painful and humiliating. And it was all the worse because it represented the seemingly final and decisive loss of Jewish land to foreign oppressors. (The Roman government eventually began to offer incentives to its retiring soldiers to settle in Palestine. This led to a surge in the Christian population there, but, this time around, these were not Jewish but gentile Christians.) Taxes on Palestinian Jews grew and grew, often as punishment for their rebelliousness and their "obstinacy." The pagan Romans had resented the difficulty that Judea had given them and were angered by their own heavy losses in putting down what they regarded as wholly unjustifed rebellions against their own competent and fair-minded administration of the province. It is not to be wondered at, therefore, that they decided to make the Jews pay. Sometimes this even involved *literal* payment. From the

---

46. Shmuel Safrai, in Ben-Sasson, *A History of the Jewish People*, 349. Constantius's language—which, incidentally, is not unlike the language of some modern anti-Mormons—is cited by Safrai on p. 350.

time of the Great Revolt in the first century, for instance, Jews were taxed more heavily than others in the empire in order to pay for the larger Roman garrisons and bureaucracies that were dispatched to Palestine to keep them under control. Their small holdings were gobbled up by ever larger and larger estates, and, now propertyless, the Jews turned to commerce and trade. (In the third century, Roman taxes were relatively light on city dwellers—in Palestine, since the Jews had been expelled from the cities, these were mostly Gentiles—but they were oppressively heavy on agriculturalists, who, in Palestine, were mostly Jews.) Then, detached from the land, unable to make ends meet, they emigrated. And as its population declined, the influence of Palestinian Judaism over world Jewry declined correspondingly. Sometimes, even under the pagan Romans, there was open persecution of the Jews on religious grounds, although it was undoubtedly given impetus by anger over the two rebellions.

> Rabbi Nathan says: "They who love and keep my commandments"—those are the Jews who live in the Land of Israel and give their lives for the sake of the commandments. Why were you killed? For having circumcised my son. Why were you burned? For having studied the Torah. Why were you crucified? For having eaten unleavened bread. Why were you flagellated? For having blessed the lulav.[47]

Some Jews were martyred, some hid in caves and deserts in order to continue to live the commandments, some—perhaps (understandably) questioning the point of remaining faithful—apostatized. Many simply left, hoping to get away. The dispersion of the Jews, their *diaspora*, had now begun in earnest. Some of Hadrian's successors relaxed official measures against Judaism. The situation was not always desperate; there were even times of relative prosperity among the Jews in the Holy Land. For many reasons, however, Jewish emigration from Palestine continued. Yet conditions were often no better elsewhere. And as Christianity gained

---

47. *Mekhilta* on *Jethro*, cited by Shmuel Safrai, in Ben-Sasson, *A History of the Jewish People*, 334.

power within the Roman government, it set about to make sure that Judaism would remain the religion of a second-class people. Throughout the empire, the Jews were deprived of many of the rights of citizenship and were forbidden to proselyte or to intermarry with Christians. Christian mobs, often encouraged by their bishops, harassed and persecuted Jews and destroyed their synagogues.

Things were especially rough for Jews during the fifth and sixth centuries. The office of the Jewish patriarch, for instance, who had presided over the Sanhedrin in the north of Palestine since the fall of Jerusalem, was abolished early in the fifth century. Abolition of the office had been an important aim of Christian persecutors of the Jews for many years, since, as a descendant of David, the patriarch represented both the memory of Jewish nationhood and a hope for its restoration. Anti-Jewish laws were passed in large numbers. Christian mobs attacked Jews and burned their synagogues for the "greater glory" of God and his church, while the government forbade the Jews to rebuild the synagogues that had been destroyed. Even when local governors protested, they were powerless to stop the clergy and the mobs. (Sometimes even the emperor had to back down before the zeal of the bishops.) By the early sixth century, with the coming of the code of Justinian, the bishops actually shared in the legal authority of the civil authorities, and the law directed them to appeal to the emperor if a local governor showed insufficient enthusiasm for persecuting Jews. The Christian population of Palestine surged, while, demoralized, abused, and humiliated, the Jewish population dwindled.

But if Christians seemed to be triumphant in the land of Christ's birth, their triumph would be short-lived. By the seventh century, the Byzantine Empire had weakened itself to the point of seeming feebleness by endless theological disputes and by the kind of political infighting and treachery that has come to be described in modern times, no matter where it occurs, as "Byzantine intrigue." It presented an inviting target to ambitious and greedy neighbors that was not lost on the Sasanian Persian Empire.

At the beginning of the seventh century, the Persians set out on a series of conquests in the Near East. They invaded the province of

Palestine in 611 A.D. and their approach ignited a messianic fire among the persecuted Jews of the Holy Land. (From the Jewish perspective, rule by Zoroastrians could hardly be any worse than the reign of Christians.) The Jews rose enthusiastically to assist the non-Christian invaders, who took the city of Jerusalem in 614. As a reward, when the Persians took the city of Jerusalem they turned it over to Jewish control. This did not last, however, for when the Persian Empire made peace with the Byzantines, the Jews did not. The Persians were therefore obliged to fight against their erstwhile allies, and many Jews died. It seemed that they just could not win.

In the meantime, the Persians had carried off the "True Cross" of the crucifixion from the Church of the Holy Sepulchre in Jerusalem. This was one of the holiest relics of Christendom—discovered by St. Helena, the mother of Constantine, after strenuous torture of the local rabbis—and its theft as a Persian trophy virtually guaranteed a Byzantine response, peace treaty or no peace treaty. Sure enough, a new Byzantine emperor by the name of Heraclius soon embarked upon a military buildup with the intention of renewing war against the Persians. In the spring of 622, he launched a new campaign to retake the territory that had been lost. He was largely successful, and in 629 A.D. he reentered the holy city of Jerusalem. The Persians had by now surrendered to Heraclius the remnants of the "True Cross," and the high point of his visit to Jerusalem was to be the ceremonial restoration of those relics to their original resting place. The Jews, terrified at the possibility of retribution for their collaboration with the Persians, begged Heraclius for mercy. To his credit, he granted it. To their eternal shame, however, the local clergy demanded that Heraclius punish the Jews, and, when he protested that he had promised mercy, they told him that perjury in cases like this was no sin. Indeed, the priests assumed responsibility for any sin that might be involved and declared a special fast to atone for it in advance.[48] On the advice of the clergy, therefore, the emperor ordered the expulsion of Jews from Jerusalem and its

48. Compare Matthew 27:25, where the Jews, seeking the death of Jesus, cry out, "His blood be on us." The Coptic church of Egypt continued to celebrate this fast for several centuries afterward.

surrounding areas. Many Jews were executed, and others fled to the desert or into the territory of the relatively tolerant Persians. A campaign was even launched to convert the Jews by force to the religion of Jesus.

But the Christians were not to savor their victory for long. The Persians were not, it turned out, the greatest threat to Christian dominance in the Holy Land. Another power was rising that would destroy the Persian Empire, deal a critical blow to Zoroastrianism, and seriously wound the Byzantines within only a few years. A vast transformation was underway that would give almost all of the world's Jews the chance to live under non-Christian rule. A virtually irresistible religious and political force would seize control of many of the Christian world's greatest centers of thought and piety. It would permanently remove such illustrious cities as Alexandria and Aleppo, Antioch and Jerusalem from Christian control and would make into foreign territory the regions of North Africa that had produced Tertullian, Augustine, and others among the greatest thinkers of the early Latin Church. Yet the new empire that was taking initial shape in distant, forgotten Arabia was one that nobody had anticipated. It was one that few, if any, were likely even to have imagined. Until some time after the Arabs had taken their first unplanned steps toward world empire, leaders of the great powers quite pardonably took no notice. If they had looked in that direction—from which, as they thought, nothing important had yet come—they would, like Elijah's servant, have seen on the horizon only "a little cloud...like a man's hand."[49] Nothing to worry about.

---

[49] 1 Kings 18:44.

This pre-Islamic stone carving shows a fight between two camel-mounted Arab warriors.

The Arabs before Islam

The first question that comes up when we begin to discuss "the Arabs" is what, exactly, we mean by the term "Arab." As the word is used today, it refers to people whose primary language is Arabic. This Semitic language, a relative of Hebrew, is spoken by well over a hundred million people and is the official tongue of countries from Iraq in the East to Morocco in the West. The largest Arabic-speaking country is Egypt. Even in Israel, Arabic is, along with Hebrew, one of the official languages of the nation. This linguistic definition means that many Arabs are Christians. There is no religious requirement, no necessity of being a Muslim, in order to be an Arab. It also means that most of the world's Muslims are not Arabs. The Persians, for instance, who are better known to us today as Iranians, are devout Muslims but are not Arabs in any sense. In fact, their language is distantly related to English. (The Persian word for "bad," for instance, is *bad*, which seems rather closely related. The Persian word for "father" is *padar*; the word for "mother" is *madar*; and "brother" is *biradhar*.)[1] The Turks are Muslims but are not Arabs. Neither are the large Muslim populations of Pakistan, China, Nigeria, Kenya, India, the former Soviet Union, and many other nations. The largest Muslim country in the world is Indonesia, which is not Arab at all.

---

1. On the other hand, the Persian word for "sister" is *khwahar*. We're talking about a foreign language, after all.

The important thing to note here is that calling someone an "Arab" today does not necessarily say a great deal about his or her lineage. The Arabs of northwest Africa, presumably, have a far different genealogy than do the Arabs of Yemen or of Syria, a continent away. No genealogical significance at all to the term "Arab" would come as something of a shock to many Latter-day Saints, who have been raised on the notion that the Arabs are the descendants of Abraham's son Ishmael. The answer is that, yes, there is a genealogical aspect of the word "Arab." There is a connection between the Arabs and Ishmael. But we must be precise in the way we talk about it.

The Egyptians, as I have already noted, represent the largest national population of Arabs in the world. Yet the Egyptians of today are virtually all direct descendants of the ancient people who built the pyramids and the great temples at Luxor and Karnak, and those people were not Arabs. How we account for this fact will help to explain what I mean when I say that the Arabs' descent from Ishmael must be carefully qualified. The original home of the Arabs is the area known as the Arabian Peninsula, occupied today by such states as Saudi Arabia, Yemen, the United Arab Emirates, and Oman. While the Arabs remained in their original homeland, the Egyptians remained clearly non-Arab, as did the populations of Iraq and Morocco. It was when the Arabs, inspired by the call of Islam, poured out of the peninsula, across North Africa, and up into Mesopotamia, when they occupied those lands and began to intermarry with the local populations, and when their Arabic began to be the language of everyday speech in the conquered territories that those areas beyond the peninsula came to be "Arab" in the modern sense.

A useful way of distinguishing between the original more-or-less pure Arabs of the peninsula and the Arabs of today is to call the former peoples "Arabian." These are the people who actually lived in the Arabian Peninsula. The subsequent conquests and intermingling, which shall be discussed more fully, mean that there is Arabian blood throughout the Arab world. But it also means that, for many areas, and especially for the outlying ones, the lineage of Ishmael is probably not the dominant bloodline in the general population.

Arabia is the largest peninsula in the world, covering almost a million square miles, which makes it roughly one third the size of the continental United States. It is a rectangle, bound on the west by the Red Sea, on the south by the Gulf of Aden and the Indian Ocean, and on the east by the Gulf of Oman and the Persian Gulf (which the Arabs generally refer to as the *Arabian* Gulf). On the north, the geographical boundary is less decisive, merely the Euphrates River, and there Arabia meets the modern states of Jordan, Syria, and Iraq. Since it is bound on three sides by seas and on the north by a river, the peninsula is known to the Arabs themselves as "the Island of the Arabs."

Talk of an island should not, of course, mislead anybody into thinking that Arabia is moist or green. The area in the southern portion of the peninsula known as "the empty quarter" is the largest continuous area of sand in the world. Parts of it receive rain only once every ten years. To the north is another great sandy desert, the Nufud, which some readers will remember from the movie *Lawrence of Arabia*. When we say that most of Arabia is desert, we mean that it is truly, absolutely desert. The dry areas of the United States sometimes look like tropical rain forests by comparison. This astonishing desolateness, coupled with the area's remoteness—which is still the case today, as we learned in the difficult process of trying to get men and material into Saudi Arabia just before the recent war in the Persian Gulf—meant that the Arabs had the peninsula pretty much to themselves. Occasionally, outsiders would try to take control of a part of the area, but they were virtually never successful. A Roman expedition, for example, met with disaster in Arabia under the command of Aelius Gallus in 25 B.C.[2]

But why would anybody *want* to take over so inhospitable a place? An understanding of the area is necessary before the answer is clear.

A rim of mountains runs along the western side of the peninsula. These mountains are cut by many valleys, each of which is known as a *wadi* (pronounced *wah*-dee), and many of these *wadis* serve as caravan routes. Plains, usually narrow, are found along the

---

2. Strabo, *Geographica*, 16:4:22-24. Treachery and the harsh environment both played a role in this situation. Among other things, the Romans were looking for "aromatics."

coasts. Oases, where a spring furnishes enough water for at least some vegetation, are found especially along the caravan routes in northern Arabia. No large lakes exist in Arabia, and there is only one short river, in the south, that manages to flow year round. On the other hand, after occasional cloudbursts, temporary freshets may rush down the valleys. But these torrents soon vanish, and they cannot serve as dependable sources of water to travellers. (See, for instance, Job 6:15-20, which refers to known locations in the Nufud desert and in the south of the peninsula). It was probably one of these "rivers of water" that Nephi saw as he and his family made their way down the coast of Arabia toward the land of promise.[3] Even the "filthy" river observed by Lehi and Nephi in their visions of the Tree of Life sounds like one of these torrents, hurtling down the valleys with a load of dirt and sand and rocks. Like flash floods in the deserts of western North America, these "rivers" would disappear as suddenly as they had appeared. So the people in the peninsula have had to be resourceful, and, since water sometimes remains in the subsoil of the wadis, the Arabians have learned to dig wells to find it.

It was not, however, only the Arabians who had to put up with the harsh climate of their land. Sometimes that climate visited surrounding lands. The east wind, for example, which came from the deserts to the south and southeast of Palestine, carried dry, dusty, hot air—to the immense discomfort of both men and animals. It blasted vegetation, as in Pharaoh's dream of the seven thin ears of corn. It could become a tempest, destroying ships at sea. It was an east wind that drove back the waters of the Red Sea, permitting the children of Israel to pass over on dry ground. It was the east wind that brought Moses' locust plague to Egypt and the prophet Joel's plague to Palestine.[4]

---

3. 1 Nephi 2:6-9, 16:12. See Hugh Nibley's discussion in *Lehi in the Desert/The World of the Jaredites/There Were Jaredites*, Volume 5 in the Collected Works of Hugh Nibley (Salt Lake City and Provo: Deseret Book and the Foundation for Ancient Research and Mormon Studies, 1988), 79-83.

4. On the east wind, see Genesis 41:6-7; Exodus 10:13; 14:21; Job 27:20-21; Psalm 48:7; Isaiah 27:8; Ezekiel 17:10; 27:26; Jonah 4:8. So powerful was the image of the east wind as an agent of destruction and divine wrath that the peoples of the Book of Mormon continued to use it, even if it was perhaps not strictly applicable to their different geographical situation: King Limhi quotes the Lord as saying, "If my people shall sow filthiness they shall reap the east wind, which bringeth immediate destruction" (Mosiah 7:31; compare 12:6).

So, why would anybody want to control so inhospitable a place as Arabia? The answer is that it was a crossroad of world trade. Whoever controlled it, controlled the trade. Oil had not yet assumed any importance, but there were many other commodities that moved across Arabian sands on their way to the wealthy cities of the eastern Mediterranean. "Almug trees," to choose just one such commodity, were brought by the Arabian queen of Sheba to king Solomon and are commonly thought to have been red sandalwood, brought originally from India and Ceylon.[5] Ebony seems to have been imported by early Arabian merchants from Africa.[6] Dates and date palms, such as those found by the wandering children of Israel at Elim, were also an important part of the Arabian economy.[7] To this day, they are known as "bedouin bread."

But the most important commercial products freighted across ancient Arabia were, beyond doubt, frankincense and other perfumes. Arabia and the Arabians are often associated with spices in the Bible. Thus, Joseph's brothers, for instance, sold him to "a company of Ishmeelites," who had come "from Gilead with their camels bearing spicery and balm and myrrh, going to carry it down to Egypt."[8] And the queen of Sheba, visiting Solomon, "came to Jerusalem with a very great train, with camels that bare spices, and very much gold, and precious stones... And she gave the king an hundred and twenty talents of gold, and of spices very great store, and precious stones: there came no more such abundance of spices as these which the queen of Sheba gave to king Solomon."[9] Even in prophecy, this is the image of Arabia: "The multitude of camels shall cover thee," says Isaiah, "the dromedaries of Midian and Ephah; all they from Sheba shall come: they shall bring gold and incense; and they shall shew forth the praises of the Lord."[10]

---

5. 1 Kings 10:11-12.
6. See, for example, Ezekiel 27:15.
7. Exodus 15:27
8. Genesis 37:25.
9. 1 Kings 10:2, 10; compare 2 Chronicles 9:1, 9. The queen's visit to Solomon was almost certainly part of a trade mission.
10. Isaiah 60:6.

Frankincense is a fragrant gum resin consisting of small white chunks and beads that can easily be ground into a powder. When burned, this powder gives off a pleasant odor like that of balsam. The resin, milky white in color, was probably produced in the central district of Hadramawt, along the Indian Ocean coast of southern Arabia. From there, it was imported to Palestine and other parts of the Mediterranean world. The caravan routes for transporting Arabian incense and the products of Africa and India began in Sheba, the modern Yemen. The main route went north via the valleys and oases of the peninsula, through Mecca, and to Ma'an, where it split into two branches. One of these went west to Gaza and Egypt and the other north to Damascus.

The importance of this trade cannot be overestimated. The temples, and later the churches, of the eastern Mediterranean were hungry for frankincense, as were upper-class private dwellings. (The prophet Ezekiel, for instance, condemns a rich and unrighteous woman who sat "upon a stately bed, and a table prepared before it, whereupon thou hast set mine incense and mine oil.")[11] Frankincense was used extensively in the rituals of the temple at Jerusalem.[12] It was a major and essential ingredient of the incense which was holy to the Lord, and the use of this incense for any unauthorized purpose was expressly forbidden in the law of Moses.[13] Such incense was burned on a specially dedicated and

---

11. Ezekiel 23:41.

12. Also at the derivative Jewish temple at Elephantine in Egypt. On this, see "Advice of the Governors of Judah and Samaria to the Jews of Elephantine," in James B. Pritchard, ed., *Ancient Near Eastern Texts Relating to the Old Testament*, 2d ed. (Princeton: Princeton University Press, 1955), 492. Many critics of the Book of Mormon, incidentally, have ridiculed the idea that a pious Jew, such as Nephi is alleged to have been, would ever have dreamed of building a temple outside of Jerusalem (2 Nephi 5:16). The Elephantine temple, however, near Aswan in upper Egypt, shows that the Book of Mormon is plausible on this point, and that its critics are incorrect. It was probably constructed at almost exactly the same time that Nephi built his temple in the Americas and functioned with the apparent approval of the authorities at Jerusalem. See Hayim Tadmor, in H. H. Ben-Sasson, *A History of the Jewish People* (Cambridge: Harvard University Press, 1976), 179-80; also Bezalel Porten, "Did the Ark Stop at Elephantine?" *Biblical Archaeology Review* 21/3 (May/June 1995): 54-67, 76-77. Later, yet another Jewish temple, that of Onias, was built at Leontopolis.

13. Exodus 30:9, 34-38; Leviticus 10:1-3.

designed altar of incense by the high priest each morning and evening.[14] That altar stood just before the veil of the holy of holies in the temple, flanked on one side by the altar of "the bread of the presence" and on the other by the seven-branched candelabra.[15] Once a year the high priest was directed to carry a censer of burning incense as he entered the holy of holies and approached the mercy seat.[16] But the substance also played a role in the ordinary daily service of the temple. Of the Levites, the Old Testament says, "They shall teach Jacob thy judgments, and Israel thy law: they shall put incense before thee, and whole burnt sacrifice upon thine altar."[17] Frankincense and oil were added to the cereal offerings.[18] Frankincense was placed with the "bread of the presence" before the holy of holies.[19] Such extensive use required large amounts of the precious material. In Herod's day, we know that the temple consumed more than 600 pounds of incense each year, specially prepared according to a secret formula. Huge stores of the substance were kept in the temple treasury.[20]

The fragrance of the incense symbolized the prayers of God's people, ascending upward to the divine throne. "Let my prayer be set forth before thee as incense," says the Psalmist, "and the lifting

---

14. Exodus 30:1-10. Luke 1:8-11 reflects this practice, although it suggests that, by the time of Christ, other priests were permitted to officiate in this service in place of the high priest.

15. K. Galling, "Incense Altar," in George Edward Buttrick, et al., eds., *The Interpreter's Dictionary of the Bible*, 4 vols. and a supplement (Nashville: Abingdon, 1962-1976), 2:699-700, supplies references for the idea that at least one type of Israelite incense altar was itself borrowed from Arabia.

16. Leviticus 16:12-13. The censers of ancient Israelite temple worship were of an interesting form, with the incense itself often resting in a "hand," carved in cupping shape, at the end of a long handle which had been hollowed out to allow air to pass through in order to keep the incense burning. See L. E. Toombs, "Incense, Dish for," in George Edward Buttrick, et al., eds., *The Interpreter's Dictionary of the Bible*, 4 vols. and a supplement (Nashville: Abingdon, 1962-1976), 2:698-99, for a very brief article on the subject, with further references. The angel of Revelation 8:3-4 stands at the altar with a censer from which the prayers of the Saints ascend, mingled with incense. An intriguing image, I think, for Latter-day Saint temple-goers.

17. Deuteronomy 33:10.

18. Leviticus 2:1-2, 14-16; 6:14-18; compare Isaiah 43:23; Jeremiah 17:26; 41:5.

19. Leviticus 24:7.

20. 1 Chronicles 9:29; Nehemiah 13:5, 9.

up of my hands as the evening sacrifice."[21] This notion continued into New Testament times. John the Revelator saw the four beasts and the twenty-four elders of his vision fall down before the Lamb of God, "having every one of them harps, and golden vials full of odours, which are the prayers of saints."[22] When, however, the worship of the temple or the Church became merely an empty form, when the people lacked the proper spirit of sincere worship and devotion, the prophets were there to relate the Lord's condemnation. Thus, in the days of Lehi, the prophet Jeremiah lashed out against such empty and meaningless worship: "To what purpose cometh there to me incense from Sheba?...your burnt offerings are not acceptable, nor your sacrifices sweet unto me."[23]

It was not only in the divinely revealed ordinances of the temple that frankincense played a central role. Incense was an important part of the worship of other deities as well,[24] and it had other functions besides worship in the strictest sense. In Israel, incense helped to purify from the plague, and it may have been thought to have a sanitary influence in places of slaughter and sacrifice.[25] Certainly its aroma must have been preferable to the smell that would otherwise have filled the temple, which, for all its holiness, was like a huge slaughterhouse. But even if it served such a prosaic function as covering up the stench of the sacrifices, the offering of incense is always portrayed as a very holy ritual wherever it occurs in the Old Testament.[26]

In Babylon, frankincense was offered to highly esteemed mortal men as a token of respect and goodwill.[27] (Its high price alone would make sure that it was not offered to just anybody.) In Israel,

---

21. Psalm 141:2. Anciently, it was common to raise the hands heavenward as a gesture of prayer, as we today fold our hands or our arms. Some may find this significant. I do.

22. Revelation 5:8; compare 8:3-4; also Luke 1:10. The marginal note in the KJV to the word "odours" suggests "incense" as an alternate reading, which is precisely correct.

23. Jeremiah 6:20.

24. Leviticus 26:30-31; 1 Kings 11:7-8; 2 Kings 22:17; 23:5; 2 Chronicles 34:25; Jeremiah 1:16; 7:9; 11:13; 19:13; 32:29; 44:15-30; 48:35; Ezekiel 6:13.

25. Numbers 16:46-48.

26. The offering of incense could serve as an occasion of revelation, as is shown in the well-known story of Zacharias (Luke 1:5-23) and in the lesser-known account of John Hyrcanus, related in Josephus, *Antiquities of the Jews*, 13:282-83 (13:10:3 in the Whiston translation).

27. Daniel 2:46.

frankincense was offered to the Lord by private people for the same reason—when, of course, they could afford it. Thus, offerings of frankincense were made to the tabernacle in the wilderness and to the temple. And, as everyone knows, the wise men offered "gold, and frankincense, and myrrh" to the infant Jesus.[28]

Obviously, any substance as valuable as frankincense would generate a lucrative trade. When John the Revelator described the wealth of Babylon, frankincense was one of the commodities he listed to give his readers an idea of the almost unbelievable extent of Babylon's riches.[29] King Solomon, who was also famous for his wealth and glory, profited specifically from his trade with Arabia.[30] This was a very active trade, requiring a great deal of travel through difficult territory, and it is noteworthy that the Old Testament seems to have a fairly detailed knowledge of Arabian geography.[31] (Such biblical place names as Dedan, Bumah, Ephah, Midian, Ophir, Sheba, Tema, and Uz are either known or widely thought to be located in Arabia.) The classical geographer Strabo writes of caravan traders "in such numbers of men and camels that they differ in no way from an army."[32]

But Solomon, the Greeks, the Romans, and the Babylonians were at the outer ends of the frankincense trade routes. What of the people actually living in Arabia? The great wealth of Arabian merchants is mentioned at several places in the Bible. "Who is this that cometh out of the wilderness like pillars of smoke, perfumed with myrrh and frankincense, with all powders of the merchant?" asks the Song of Solomon.[33] Ezekiel refers to "Sabaeans from the wilderness, which put bracelets upon their hands, and beautiful crowns upon their heads."[34] Arabian merchants are routinely linked by the Old Testament with gold and silver, incense, spices, and precious stones.[35]

---

28. Numbers 7:14, 20; Jeremiah 17:26; Matthew 2:11.
29. Revelation 18:13.
30. 1 Kings 10:15.
31. J. A. Thompson, "Arabia," in George Edward Buttrick, et al., eds., *The Interpreter's Dictionary of the Bible*, 4 vols. and a supplement (Nashville: Abingdon, 1962-1976), 1:181.
32. Strabo, *Geographica*, 16:4:23.
33. Song of Solomon 3:6; compare 4:6, 14. Compare Ezekiel 38:10-13.
34. Ezekiel 23:42.
35. 2 Chronicles 9:14; Isaiah 60:6; Jeremiah 6:20; Ezekiel 27:22.

From a Latter-day Saint perspective, the most interesting thing about the frankincense trail that ran along the Red Sea coast of the Arabian peninsula is that it seems to have been followed by the prophet Lehi during his flight from Jerusalem. The account in 1 Nephi is astonishingly accurate in its depiction of both the manner of the Lehi party's travel and the route they took.[36] Even "Nahom," mentioned in the Book of Mormon as the burial place of Ishmael—which is, by the way, a highly appropriate name for someone traveling through the Arabian desert—has recently shown up in Arabia in just the right place.[37]

It was at Nahom, incidentally, that Lehi and his party abruptly turned due east after their long period of travel along the coast of

---

36. Some interesting Latter-day Saint studies of this question have appeared. Hugh Nibley's discussion in *Lehi in the Desert/The World of the Jaredites/There Were Jaredites* is a superb starting point. Lynn M. and Hope Hilton actually traveled through Arabia in search of Lehi's trail and published a highly interesting and well-illustrated account of that journey in a book of the same name, published by Deseret Book in 1976. In my judgment, their proposed route for Lehi seems to be fundamentally correct. Eugene England's article "Through the Arabian Desert to a Bountiful Land: Could Joseph Smith Have Known the Way?" in *Book of Mormon Authorship: New Light on Ancient Origins*, edited by Noel B. Reynolds (Provo: Religious Studies Center, Brigham Young University, 1982), 143-56, argues that the Book of Mormon account of Lehi's journey across the Arabian peninsula has to have been written by an eyewitness and that the detailed knowledge of the ancient frankincense trail that it reveals was unavailable to outsiders in the 1820s. William J. Hamblin, "Pre-Islamic Arabian Prophets," in *Mormons and Muslims: Spiritual Foundations and Modern Manifestations*, edited by Spencer J. Palmer, (Provo: Religious Studies Center, Brigham Young University, 1983), 85-104, surveys the nonbiblical prophets connected by the Qur'an with pre-Islamic Arabia and speculates that one of these may have been Lehi himself. Warren P. and Michaela J. Aston have plausibly refined the Hiltons' findings in two papers, published by the Foundation for Ancient Research and Mormon Studies and entitled, respectively, "And We Called the Place Bountiful" (Provo: F.A.R.M.S., 1991) and "The Place Which Was Called Nahom" (Provo: F.A.R.M.S., 1991) and, most recently, in their book *In the Footsteps of Lehi: New Evidence for Lehi's Journey across Arabia to Bountiful* (Salt Lake City: Deseret Book, 1994). Some critics have objected that 1 Nephi mentions no camels. But this represents no serious problem, since the use of camels to cross Arabia would have been so obviously necessary that it would hardly have required mention. When I say to someone today that I plan to drive to Denver, he is unlikely to ask me *what* I'm going to drive. The answer to that question is clearly understood. Significantly, the common Arabic verb *rahala*, which today means simply "to depart," or even "to travel," and which can be applied to travel by airplane, by boat, and by automobile, originally meant specifically "to saddle [a camel]." It would not have been necessary to mention camels any more than, when we speak of baptism, to specify water as opposed to gasoline or molten lead.

37. 1 Nephi 16:34.

Arabia in a southeasterly direction. A glance at the map shows that by doing so, they missed the area of what is today called Yemen. Instead, they moved along behind the mountains that form the natural division between Yemen and the rest of the Arabian peninsula. (Most of Yemen is mountainous. The tallest measured peak is 12,336 feet high.) This may or may not have been deliberate. But I suspect that it was, for several reasons. First of all, whether they knew it yet or not, they needed to find a place in which they could find ship-building materials. Few such places exist, so the direction of their travel had to be quite deliberately chosen. (Whether it was chosen by the travelers themselves or by the Lord for them is immaterial.) But Lehi may well have wanted to avoid the relatively civilized area of Yemen, the ancient Sheba. For one thing, it would have constituted a real temptation to his sons Laman and Lemuel, for whom he still had some faint hopes. For another, Yemen represented the Arabian end of the major frankincense trail. There would have been Jewish merchants there, and, if Hugh Nibley is correct in asserting that Lehi himself came from a merchant background, there might have been people in the towns of Yemen who would actually have known him.[38] Given the circumstances of his escape from Palestine, including the death of Laban, it might have been unwise to have met such people. Even Lehi's vision of the Tree of Life may suggest something of the image that wealthy, mercantile Yemen could well have had in his mind. The "great and spacious building," standing "as it were in the air, high above the earth" and "filled with people...[whose] manner of dress was exceedingly fine," seems very like the ancient "skyscraper" architecture of Yemen. These multistory Yemeni buildings, many of which still stand, have no windows on the ground floor, so as to be less vulnerable to thieves and robbers. At night, or in the "mist of darkness" reported by the prophet, it would indeed seem that the people who leaned out of the windows "in the attitude of mocking and pointing

---

38. In the period just prior to the rise of Islam, a Jewish kingdom was actually established for a brief time in southern Arabia. And persecuted Jews often fled to Arabia even at that relatively late time. See Shmuel Safrai, in Ben-Sasson, *A History of the Jewish People*, 358–59, 380.

their fingers" were in a building that floated "as it were in the air, high above the earth."[39]

Thus, Arabia and the Arabs play an important role in the early portion of the Book of Mormon. They figure prominently in the other scriptures as well. Some of the mountains of northwest Arabia, for example, are volcanoes which are now reckoned to be extinct (although eruptions are recorded into medieval times). Certain scholars have seen in the smoke and fire and earthquake of Mount Sinai a description of a volcanic eruption (Exodus 19:18) and have argued that Moses' reception of the stone tablets of the law actually took place in what is today Saudi Arabia, rather than at the traditional site in the Sinai Peninsula.[40]

It is not certain just when the Arabian peoples first appear in history. As early as 854 B.C., an inscription of Shalmaneser III mentions "Gindibu the Arabian," who had assembled a camel corps to oppose the Assyrians. In the very south of the Arabian Peninsula, an advanced civilization seems to have developed as early as 1200 B.C., although we are only now beginning to have some idea about it. The island of Bahrayn, off the eastern coast of Arabia in the Persian Gulf, may be the ancient Sumerian Dilmun. The genealogical tables in the Old Testament include recognizably Arabian groups among the children of Cush, Aram, and Eber, as well as among the children of Abraham by Keturah and by Hagar.[41] The complexity of the situation is increased by Arabian peoples being known throughout the Old Testament by a number of different (and occasionally puzzling) names, including, most prominently, Ishmaelites, Midianites, Dedanites, and Sabeans. It is not easy in the present state of our knowledge to reconcile all of these accounts, but we know that they contain truth because many of the names can be plausibly related to known peoples and places in Arabia.

The Hebrew word *Arab* properly means "nomad," which tells us a great deal about these early people.[42] The description of Ishmael

---

39. 1 Nephi 8:23, 26-27.
40. Galatians 4:25 places Mount Sinai in "Arabia." But, since even the traditional Sinai falls within the biblical definition of that term, this probably means nothing.
41. Genesis 10:7, 23, 25-30; 25:1-4, 13-16.

in Genesis 16:12 as "a wild man," whose "hand will be against every man, and every man's hand against him," well describes the life of the nomad, who has been famous from the beginning of history for his raids against settled folk.[43] It was a group of Sabeans—listed above as an Arabian people—who raided Job's lands, killing his herdsmen and riding off with his cattle as booty.[44] This is the kind of life (though possibly without the thievery) that Ishmael seems to have led, wandering the desert and dwelling in a tent. "And God was with the lad; and he grew, and dwelt in the wilderness."[45]

From the earliest times, the people of Arabia, though dominantly nomadic, have also included seminomadic and even fully settled groups. Sedentary life was overwhelmingly concentrated in the south, with the inhabitants of north and central Arabia being largely nomadic. The two classes of Arabs seldom got along with one another. Arabic literature is full of references to the contempt felt by nomads for settled folk and to the scorn of the people of the settlements for the nomads of the desert.[46] Such desert nomads, or bedouins, roam the Arabian wastelands in units known as tribes. These tribes are really just large extended families, although they also function much like a government in that they preserve order, take care of the poor and the orphans and widows, and even occasionally negotiate with one another in much the same way as modern nation-states. Each group possesses, for instance, a recognized pastureland in which to wander. (They don't just wander *anywhere*.) But, especially in premodern

---

42. Later, in the Arabic language itself, the Qur'an contrasts the settled peoples of the oases with the nomads, whom it terms "Arabs."

43. The Amalekite raid on Ziklag recorded in 1 Samuel 30 is a good example of this, as is the Arabian raid that carried off Jehoram's family and possessions, mentioned in 2 Chronicles 21:16-17, 22:1. (In Psalm 83, the Ishmaelites and the Hagarenes are depicted as the hereditary enemies of Israel.) Such raiding provoked pursuit, and the oracle of Isaiah 21:13-17 seems to be addressed to a group of fleeing Arabs.

44. Job 1:15.

45. Genesis 21:20.

46. This is not altogether unlike the relationship between Nephites and Lamanites in much of the Book of Mormon. Some writers on Mormonism have argued that, in the friction depicted between urban Nephites and wandering Lamanites, the Book of Mormon reflects early American feeling for the "yeoman farmer." But in this these writers only reveal their lack of acquaintance with ancient history and the Near East. The dispute between "ranchers" and "farmers" is not merely American. It goes back to Cain and Abel.

times, the boundary lines were fluid and were changed constantly by intertribal conflict. Each tribe was sovereign—again, in much the same way that a nation is sovereign—and was led by a chief, or *shaykh*, who was chosen partly on the basis of descent and partly on the basis of proven valour and wisdom.[47] In theory, at least, tribes were made up of blood relatives and were named after a common ancestor—either real or fictional. Thus, a tribe known as the Banu Murra would believe themselves to be the sons of someone called "Murra."

The nomads' seasonal migrations are dictated by the necessities of water and pasturage. They have to go where the water and the grass are. In this harsh land, the camel is far and away the most important animal, and the Bible often connects it with the Arabs.[48] The head of David's camel keepers, for instance, was an Ishmaelite.[49] Indeed, even in modern times the camel continues to be the main beast of burden and means of transport for these nomadic tribes. But sheep and goats were also important to ancient Arabs.[50] And the horse, which is not nearly so well suited to life in the desert as the camel, was a highly-esteemed luxury.[51] The most common nomadic dwelling—useful because it is mobile—was and is a tent. (When Nephi, in the shortest verse in the Book of Mormon, records that his father "dwelt in a tent," he tells us volumes, I think, about the lifestyle that he and his family had adopted while in the desert en route to the land of promise.[52] Tents are a prominent part of the

---

47. The work *shaykh*—sometimes spelled "sheik" and "sheikh," and often mispronounced as if it were the French word "chic"—means "elder." Someday, when Latter-day Saint missionaries take the gospel to the Arabs, we will have Mormon shaykhs. *Shaykh* is also often used by Arab newspapers to translate the title "senator," since that English word too was originally connected with the idea of age. (Think of "senile"!)

48. As in Genesis 37:25; Judges 6:5; 7:12; 8:26; 1 Samuel 15:3; 30:17; 1 Kings 10:2; 1 Chronicles 5:21; 27:30; 2 Chronicles 9:1; Jeremiah 49:29, 32.

49. 1 Chronicles 27:30.

50. Ezekiel 27:21.

51. See the admiring words of Job 39:19-25. A. J. Arberry, *Aspects of Islamic Civilization* (Ann Arbor: University of Michigan Press, 1967), 19-31, furnishes specimens of pre-Islamic Arabic poetry in excellent translation. Several passages are in praise of the nomads' horses and camels.

52. 1 Nephi 2:15. The tents of the ancient Arabs, sometimes associated with camels, are mentioned in the Bible at places like Judges 8:11; Psalms 83:6; 120:5; Jeremiah 49:29, 31-32; Ezekiel 38:11.

first chapters of 1 Nephi.) Pictorial representations of these tents on ancient Assyrian monuments show them to have been much the same in ancient times as they are today. Modern bedouin women, like their ancient counterparts, do the domestic work around the tent, of which half is considered "women's quarters." They tend to the small animals, prepare food, and weave. The males, on the other hand, take care of the camels and the horses, hunt, and, of course, raid. Judges 8:21-26 mentions a style of ornamentation of men and camels that remains common today. And the nose ring and bracelets given to Rebekah are still the ornaments given to a bedouin girl.[53]

The "sons of Heth" from whom Abraham bought a burial ground for his family in Hebron, and among whom Esau found wives, seem to have been Arabs.[54]And, intriguingly, the "ravens" who fed Elijah "by the brook Cherith" in the wilderness may well have been the bedouin Arabs of the region. According to this view, which remains rather speculative, 1 Kings 17:4 should read "I have commanded the Arabs to feed thee there." (The Hebrew words for "raven" and "Arab" are quite similar and could easily have been confused with one another over the many centuries of the transmission of the biblical text.)[55] If such an interpretation is true, we see an early instance of Arabians as agents of God, receiving revelation or inspiration from him.

The Midianites are an Arabian group of bedouins who play an important role in the scriptures. They were Ishmaelite traders who took caravans to Egypt, as mentioned in the story of Joseph.[56] The prophet Isaiah speaks of their "multitude of dromedaries [camels]" and of their great wealth in gold and incense, brought up from

---

53. Genesis 24:22, 47.

54. Genesis 26:34; 27:46; 36:2. They were almost certainly not the same people as the more famous "Hittites" of Anatolia, whose Indo-European language, like modern Persian, is (very) distantly related to English.

55. 1 Kings 17:4, 6. See A. Jeffery, "Arabians," in Buttrick, et al., eds., *The Interpreter's Dictionary of the Bible*. 1:182; John Gray, *I and II Kings: A Commentary* (Philadelphia: The Westminster Press, 1963), 338-39.

56. Genesis 37:24-36. Judges 8:22-27 also links the Midianites with Ishmael (and with camels).

Sheba in South Arabia.[57] In the story of Gideon, "the Midianites came up, and the Amalekites, and the children of the east…with their cattle and their tents, and they came as grasshoppers for multitude; for both they and their camels were without number" (Judges 6:3, 5).

Some Midianites, at least, seem to have been a pastoral people, a people of shepherds. It was among them that Moses found his wife after he had fled from before the pharaoh, and it was to them that he led the children of Israel after their exodus from Egypt.[58] In at least one case, a Midianite appears to have served as an authorized agent of the Lord: According to Doctrine and Covenants 84:6-7, Jethro, the Midianite chief, held the priesthood and conferred it upon Moses. This goes considerably beyond what the Bible says about him. But it may receive some support from Arabic tradition, which seems to know Jethro under the name of Shu'ayb, whom it views as a great prophet and preacher who spoke with authority from God.[59]

When the Jewish exiles returned from the Babylonian captivity and under the leadership of Nehemiah began to rebuild Jerusalem, they found Arabs among those who sought to hinder them.[60] These may have been the Nabateans, who were the only northern Arabians to establish a civilization comparable to that of South Arabia in the period before Islam. (In fact, some think that they were actually of South Arabian origin; trading colonies from the south are well known in the north during this and earlier periods.) When the Nabateans first appeared in history, they were still nomads. However, by the fourth century B.C. they had managed to take the ancient city of Sela away from the Edomites. This would become Petra, the famous city carved in the red rocks of what is today Jordan.[61] From this, their capital, they would build up a kingdom that

---

57. Isaiah 60:6.

58. Exodus 2-3, 17.

59. See, in the Qur'an, 7:85-93.

60. Nehemiah 2:19; 4:7; 6:1-6.

61. Some readers will have seen Petra in the film *Indiana Jones and the Last Crusade*, where it appears (under a different name) as the repository of the Holy Grail.

stretched from the Red Sea to a point beyond Damascus, penetrating deeply into Arabia itself.

The first recorded king of the Nabateans bore the name or title of Harethath I, and many of his successors bore the same name or title, which seems to be the same as the modern Arabic name Harith. Harethath IV, who ruled from 9 B.C. to 40 A.D., is called Aretas in the King James New Testament and plays a role in the story of the apostle Paul.[62] (And that apostle, it will be remembered, fled into "Arabia" immediately after his miraculous conversion on the road to Damascus.)[63] The Arabians present at Jerusalem on the day of Pentecost were apparently Jews from some Nabatean settlement.[64]

The society of Arabia in the period immediately before the rise of Islam was tribal and egalitarian. What the latter term means is that everybody was on virtually the same level. On the same level of bare survival, one might say in some cases. (The famous Arabian wealth, so frequently mentioned in the Bible, was probably enjoyed by only a few in the earliest days and then only by those on the fringes of Arabia who came into frequent contact with settled peoples who were willing to pay high prices for the goods they brought.) The chief loyalty of any Arab was to his tribe. In some ways, in fact, it was his only loyalty. It was much like the kind of patriotism that says "My country, right or wrong." Thus, the poet Durayd ibn Simma once said of his tribe, Ghaziyya,

> I am of Ghaziyya: if she be in error, then I will err;
> And if Ghaziyya be guided right, I go right with her.[65]

Apart from devotion to one's tribe, the virtues most highly prized among the Arabians before Islam included bravery in battle, patience in misfortune, persistence in revenge, protection of the weak, defiance of the strong, and honor and generosity. These

---

62. 2 Corinthians 11:32.
63. Galatians 1:17.
64. Acts 2:11.
65. Cited by Reynold A. Nicholson, *A Literary History of the Arabs* (Cambridge: Cambridge University Press, 1962), 83.

are often called the "heroic virtues," and they are not far different from the virtues extolled by other societies—Homeric Greece, for example—at a similar stage of development.

The idea of protecting the weak also frequently led to an attitude toward women that could be called "chivalrous." Pre-Islamic Arabian women inspired the poet to sing and the warrior to fight and, indeed, were often present at battles.[66] (Some will remember the scene in the film *Lawrence of Arabia* where, as the army rides out to fight, the women, perched high up on the walls of a narrow valley, give out their characteristic loud trill, urging the men on to heroic battle.) R. A. Nicholson may be right when he declares that "the chivalry of the [European] Middle Ages is, perhaps, ultimately traceable to heathen Arabia." If so, it probably entered into Europe via the Muslim occupation of Spain, which lasted from the early 700s to 1492. "Knight-errantry, the riding forth on horseback in search of adventures, the rescue of captive maidens, the succour rendered everywhere to women in adversity—these were essentially Arabian ideas, as was the very name of *chivalry*, the connection of honourable conduct with the horse-rider, the man of noble blood, the cavalier."[67]

Nomadic life breeds hardiness, frugality, eagerness for material things, fortitude, and hospitality. Such qualities are essential to survival. Furthermore, the nomad was and is an individualist, impatient of discipline, reluctant to submit to restraint or authority. (In early Islam, it was always wondered whether the bedouins could ever be real Muslims.) This trait had interesting consequences. With a few exceptions where they came in contact with the Romans

---

[66] Sometimes, women themselves composed poetry. Several prominent examples of this are known from pre-Islamic Arabia. Their specialty was elegiac poetry, the poetry of mourning and lament. This is because, in their society, ostentatious mourning was first and foremost a woman's job. In many areas of the Middle East, I can testify from first-hand observation, it still is.

[67] Nicholson, *A Literary History of the Arabs*, 88. The Arabic word *furusiyya*, which primarily means "horsemanship," can also mean "chivalry," "knighthood," "heroism," and "valor." The same connection between horsemanship and a certain noble kind of behavior is made, of course, in various languages of western Europe. We speak of "chivalry," "cavalry," "caballeros," and "a cavalier attitude."

or the Persians, or in Yemen to the far south, no authoritarian political forms developed among the pre-Islamic Arabs. In fact, no political institutions arose at all, in the sense we generally view such things. Bedouin culture has always been much less stratified, less divided into classes, less complex (in a way) than societies based on agriculture. There were transient concentrations of wealth, perhaps, but there was little lasting class stratification among the Arabs before Islam. In a sense, life was very democratic. Indeed, it was virtually anarchic. (Quite the opposite of, say, the Sasanian Persians and their "king of kings.") Society was based on individual prowess and prestige, as well as on close lineage and group loyalties. The chief had no authority to coerce. Herdsmen or nomads could not be exploited like the rooted peasant. They had pride. Every man was free to depart with his dependents. (Late in the 1970s, I encountered a group of bedouins in the Sinai. That area had recently reverted from Israeli to Egyptian control, and I asked them if they were happy to be back under the rule of fellow Arabs. They looked at me as if I were crazy. "We are bedouins," they said. What did they care who ran the government?)

At this point, some readers will no doubt wonder how the tribes held together at all, if individual Arabs and their families were constantly setting out on their own. How can a society exist without some controls? A good question. In fact, while there was a certain freedom to depart, there were also constraints that would make people want to stay with their tribes and work things out. I have said that there were no political institutions throughout most of pre-Islamic Arabia. That is true, but the practice of blood feud maintained a certain intertribal peace. Blood feuds maintained the peace in the same way that the threat of war maintains a fragile peace in today's international relations. It worked as follows: If someone from Tribe A killed someone from Tribe B, Tribe B would feel itself justified in killing someone from Tribe A. If the actual perpetrator of the original murder could be caught and punished, that would be wonderful. But if not, just about *anybody* from Tribe A would do—provided he or she were of the same social status. If not, Tribe A would feel itself victimized and would set out to get somebody else from Tribe B. And on and on, much like the famous Hatfields and McCoys. Sometimes a feud would go on for so long that nobody could remember the original offense, only that they had gotten the short end of the stick on the last exchange and that the other tribe was going to have to pay before things were over. This may not seem a very promising way to keep the peace, but it was. Blood feuds were costly. So if Tribe A found that it had a member who was likely to get the tribe into trouble, they would often find a way to deal with him on their own before he acted out his violent intentions. And it was in the interest of every individual Arab to maintain his links to a tribe because without such tribal affiliation, he was vulnerable to anybody who wanted his horse or didn't like his face. There was no government to protect him. If a tribe did find itself involved in a dispute, it would try long and hard to buy its way out of the situation or in some other way to find a peaceful solution.

Virtue, to the ancient Arab, was *muruwwa*, or "manliness." (This is not far different from the original meaning of our own English word "virtue": *Vir*, in Latin, is the word for "man." Related to this is the term "werewolf," for a supposedly half-wolf half-human creature.)[68] This "manliness" expressed itself in a number of ways that we would perhaps not find admirable, although "manly" bravery and honor certainly have something to be said for them. The general spirit of the pre-Islamic Arabian ideal is that of Tennyson's hero: "To strive, to seek, to find, and not to yield."[69]

That spirit was not precisely Christian. Revenge, for instance, was considered a virtue, indeed a duty, among the Arabians of the century or so prior to Islam. "When wrong befalls me," exclaimed a pre-Islamic Arabian Jew by the name of Samawal ibn Adiya, expressing a widely felt idea, "I endure not tamely."[70] There was, of course,

---

68. I once gave this explanation to a Gospel Doctrine class and then left the words "virtue" and "werewolf" on the blackboard. I was told later that the Relief Society of another ward, meeting in the same classroom afterward, had a vigorous discussion trying to determine what my lesson had been about.
69. This is the last line of Tennyson's "Ulysses"—written, appropriately enough, about a Homeric hero.
70. Nicholson, *A Literary History of the Arabs*, 88.

some good reason for this: To fail to avenge an injury was to invite another one, either to yourself or to your kinfolk. There was no government, no police force to prevent such injuries. It was up to you. Thus, we have preserved the lament of an Arab whose kin refused to help him against a group of raiders who had stolen his camels. In the final line of the lament, we can almost hear the poet's disgusted disbelief in the weakness of his relatives:

> For all their numbers, they are good for naught,
> My people, against harm however light:
> They pardon wrong by evildoers wrought,
> Malice with loving kindness they requite.[71]

The story of Shanfara, a poet and outlaw of the tribe of Azd, will also illustrate something of the ideal Arabian hero. The story is told that when he was just a young child, he was kidnapped by another tribe known as the Banu Salaman. ("Banu," here, means "sons [of].") He was brought up among them and for many years had no idea that he was not actually one of them. However, when he grew up and learned the truth he vowed that he would avenge the injury done to him and his tribe by killing a hundred warriors of the Banu Salaman. Preparing his revenge, he left the Banu Salaman, and went back to his real kinfolk, the Banu Azd. Over the next several years, he did indeed manage to kill ninety-eight of the Banu Salaman, but then they managed to ambush him, and it looked as if he would fail to fulfill his vow. However, in the fierce fight of the ambush one of his hands was chopped off by the stroke of a sword. Shanfara grabbed the amputated hand with his other hand and threw it as hard as he could in the face of one of his attackers and killed him. Furious, the ambushers overpowered him and hacked him to death, leaving his body to rot on the desert sand. The total of the Banu Salaman that he had slain came to ninety-nine, one short of fulfilling his vow. He had failed, or so one might have thought. However, many days after the death of Shanfara, one of the Banu Salaman was passing by and paused to look at the bones of

71. Nicholson, *A Literary History of the Arabs*, 92.

their late enemy as they lay there, bleaching in the intense desert sun. To show his contempt, the man gave a powerful kick to Shanfara's skull, sending it bouncing across the sand. But a splinter of bone from the skull pierced his foot. The wound festered, and the man died. Shanfara had fulfilled his vow. And his persistence in revenge—a persistence that endured beyond his death—makes him a great hero of pre-Islamic Arabia.

Honor was another pre-Islamic virtue. A couple of stories will illustrate something of what it meant to the early Arabians.

The first, and the shortest, is connected with a famous pre-Islamic poet by the name of Tarafa. Tarafa had a problem, perhaps not an unexpected one, considering that he made his living by words. He could not keep his mouth shut. He showed great impertinence toward Amr ibn Hind, who reigned as king of Hira between 554 and 568 A.D. On one occasion, for instance, finding himself seated opposite the king's beautiful sister at a banquet, he exclaimed:

> Behold, she has come back to me,
> My fair gazelle whose ear-rings shine;
> Had not the king been sitting here,
> I would have pressed her lips to mine!

This was not the kind of outburst that was likely to win favor with the princess's royal brother. But the impertinence was nothing compared to the insult that Tarafa had earlier directed at the king himself:

> Would that we had instead of Amr
> A milch-ewe bleating round our tent!

Fed up with such behavior from a mere poet, Amr sent Tarafa and a friend (who must have been similarly offensive) to Bahrayn, carrying sealed letters to that island's governor. En route, however, the friend began to grow suspicious and opened his letter. Sure enough, he found that it contained orders to bury him alive. He threw his letter into the stream and advised Tarafa to do likewise. Tarafa, however, would not. He felt himself honor-bound to carry his letter to Bahrayn and to deliver it unopened, as he had promised to do. When he arrived in Bahrayn, he was executed. According to some sources, he was not yet twenty years old.

The next story relates to the pre-Islamic Arabian Jew Samawal, whom we have briefly met. He lived in a castle some distance to the north of an oasis called Yathrib, a place that will take on considerable importance in the next chapter. One day, the great pre-Islamic poet Imru al-Qays is said to have taken refuge with Samawal when fleeing from some of his enemies (of whom he had many) in the direction of Syria. Before the poet departed from the castle, he left five coats of mail armor with Samawal for safe-keeping, items that had been handed down from generation to generation as heirlooms within his family. Imru al-Qays then continued on his journey toward Syria. Eventually, he went on to Constantinople, where he sought help from the Byzantine emperor in regaining his kingdom, which had been stolen from him. The appeal found sympathy, but Imru al-Qays died on his way home.

Meanwhile, his enemy, the king of Hira, sent an army against Samawal, demanding the five coats of mail that Imru al-Qays had deposited with him. But Samawal had given a solemn promise to take care of the armor, and he refused to yield it up. So the army of Hira besieged his castle. The siege went on and on, and Samawal was unbending. Finally, the besiegers were able to capture Samawal's son, who had gone out to hunt.

"Do you know this boy?" the commander of the besieging forces asked.

"Yes," replied Samawal. "He is my son."

"Then will you deliver up the things you have in your possession, or should I kill him?"

"Do with him as you will," replied Samawal. "I will never break my oath, nor will I give up the property of my guest."

The general then drew his sword and hacked the boy to death before the eyes of his father, Samawal. Immediately afterwards, the army of Hira raised the siege and went home, knowing that Samawal would never yield up what they wanted.

As in the case of Shanfara, the devotion to one's oath is striking. This was perhaps characteristic of the ancient Semitic peoples, who saw words themselves as sacred, as containing a power of their own, independent of the intentions of those who utter them. (We ourselves still speak of "casting a spell.") The story of Isaac's blessing of Jacob, which could not be undone even though it was given to the wrong person, illustrates this.[72] So, too, does the story of Zoram in 1 Nephi. Zoram had every reason to be afraid of Nephi and his brothers: They had killed his master, had "stolen" the brass plates, had lured him beyond the city walls after dark, and were going about in disguise. And they had good reason to mistrust him. Had he not been the trusted servant of the evil Laban? Might he not escape and inform the authorities of their activities? Weren't the people of Jerusalem already seeking to kill Lehi? The obvious course would have been to kill him on the spot to prevent him from escaping or at least to bind him hand and foot and never let him out of their sight. But Zoram, after hearing their explanation of what they had done, and after hearing Nephi swear an oath that he could go with them and be a free man like themselves, himself swore an oath that he would stay with them and not attempt to flee. So confident were they that he would hold his word sacred, Nephi later recorded, "that when Zoram had made an oath unto us, our fears did cease concerning him."[73]

So seriously did the ancient Hebrews take the notion of keeping one's solemn oath that it was included in the requirements for admission to the temple-shrine of God.

> Who shall ascend into the hill of the Lord? or who shall stand in his holy place? He that hath clean hands, and a pure heart; who hath not lifted up his soul unto vanity, nor sworn deceitfully.[74]

Another list, even more complete, of those who "shall dwell in [the] tabernacle [and]...in the holy hill," identifies among them "he that sweareth to his own hurt, and changeth not." That is, whoever has made an oath when it seemed easy to carry out and then, later, discovers that fulfilling it will cost him substantially more than he

72. Genesis 27.
73. 1 Nephi 4:37.
74. Psalm 24:3-4.

had anticipated, or cause him pain, or put him at risk, but still does it, will be admitted to the Lord's temple. Implicitly, too, that person of integrity will be admitted to the Lord's presence in the life to come, which is what the temple symbolizes. (Another of the categories of people who are to be admitted to the temple is described here as "he that putteth not out his money to usury." This principle as it relates to Islam will be discussed in a later chapter.)[75]

Another feature of the story of Samawal worthy of note is his remarkable devotion to his guest, to the extent that he will sacrifice his son rather than yield up the armor that his guest entrusted to him. This, too, has its analogy in the rather horrifying story of Lot and his angelic visitors, told in the nineteenth chapter of Genesis. Lot, it will be recalled, offered his two daughters for the abuse of the men of Sodom, rather than allow his two guests—whom he apparently did not know to be angels—to be abused while under his protection. It should not be thought that Lot made this offer (which, fortunately, was not accepted by the Sodomites) out of a lack of respect for women or some such motive. That would be to read twentieth-century concerns back into a very ancient story. The real reason was the sacredness, as the ancient Semites saw it, of the relationship between host and guest. The host should allow nothing bad to happen to his guests, no matter what it cost him to ensure their safety and security. This relationship even overcame the traditional demands of vengeance: One story from pre-Islamic Arabia tells of a man who had vowed to avenge the murder of his son and then, to his shock, discovered that a man he had accepted as his guest was the murderer. He took no action against the man, although the man did not realize who his host was and that he was completely within the power of his host. Instead, he declared, he

---

75. Psalm 15:4–5. This idea of "swearing to one's own hurt" shows up in an interesting way in the Old Testament books of Ruth, Samuel, and Kings. There, a formula running roughly as follows occurs several times: "The Lord do so to me, and more also, if I do not do x, y, and z." Edward F. Campbell, Jr., a non-Mormon biblical scholar, offers some insights into these passages that many Latter-day Saints will find intensely interesting. See Edward F. Campbell, Jr., *Ruth*, The Anchor Bible, Vol. 7 (Garden City, N.Y.: Doubleday, 1975), 74.

76 Nicholson, *A Literary History of the Arabs*, 87.

would wait until the murderer had left his castle and was no longer under his sacred protection. Then, although it would be far more difficult, the father would feel that he could legitimately seek his vengeance.

Closely related to the obligations felt by a host toward his guests is the notion of generosity, which was one of the leading virtues of a pre-Islamic Arabian hero. And of all those heroes, there is one whose name became virtually synonymous with the idea of generosity in subsequent Arab tradition—Hatim of Tayyi. He is once reputed to have said to his wife Mawiyya,

> The guest's slave am I, it's true, as long as he stays with me,
> Although in my nature otherwise no trait of the slave is shown.[76]

Once again, a story will give a clearer idea of the early Arabian idea of generosity.

It is told that Hatim's mother, when she was pregnant with him, dreamed that someone asked her, "Which would you prefer—a generous son named Hatim, or ten sons like those of other people, lions in the hour of battle, brave young men, strong limbed?" Attractive as the second choice was—what pre-Islamic mother would not have been pleased with ten heroic warrior sons?—she answered without hesitation that she would prefer the generous son, Hatim. And she received what she desired. As Hatim grew up, he developed the habit of taking his food and going out into the roads, looking for travellers to share his food. If he found someone he could share with, he would eat. If he did not, he would throw his food away and fast.

Hatim's father (who seems not to have been consulted about the kind of son *he* wanted) was displeased with this wasteful behavior. Food didn't exactly grow on trees in the Arabian desert, after all. So, as some kind of cure, he gave Hatim a slave girl, a mare, and a foal and sent him out into the middle of nowhere to herd the family camels.

---

[76]. Nicholson, *A Literary History of the Arabs*, 87.

On reaching the place where he was supposed to pasture the camels—who were, as one can imagine, a large portion of any well-to-do desert Arab's treasure—Hatim went out, as was his habit, to find somebody to share his food with. But, search as he might, he could find nobody. Finally, off in the distance, he spotted a party of riders coming toward him. He hurried out to meet them, and it turned out that the riders were three extremely famous Arabian poets, riding together to the court of Hira.

"Young man," they called out. "Do you have anything that we can eat?"

"How can you ask me a question like that," Hatim replied, "when you can see all these camels I have?" And he slaughtered three camels for them.

"You shouldn't have gone to such trouble," said one of the travelling poets. "We didn't really need anything more than a little milk. Even if you felt yourself obliged to give us more than that, a single young she-camel would have been plenty."

"Oh," said Hatim, "I knew that well enough. But, looking at you, I noticed that you were dressed in different fashions and that you look unrelated, so I figured that you must be from three different places. And I wanted to do something for you that would be so striking that you would each mention it when you got back to your home."

At that, the poets complied with his wishes, and each recited a verse in praise of Hatim's generosity. This might have been expected to please him, but it did not.

"I wanted to do something kind for you, but now, with your verses, you have been more generous with me than I was with you. I am in your debt, and that is not what I had in mind. I swear a solemn oath to God that I will hamstring every camel in the herd unless you step forward and divide the entire herd among yourselves."

Having heard this solemn oath, and knowing full well that—as we ourselves have learned—Hatim was bound to fulfill it, the three poets did indeed divide the herd up among themselves. Each of the three received ninety-nine camels. (Making a neat total of three hundred camels in the original herd, when the three that Hatim had slaughtered are figured in. A bit too neat, perhaps, but old stories are often like this.) Then they proceeded on to Hira.

Not long after this, Hatim's father began to overhear disquieting rumors about his camel herd and came to investigate. What he saw—or, rather, what he didn't see—infuriated him. "Where...are ...the...*camels*?" he asked, measuring his words carefully and struggling to maintain self-control.

"O my father," Hatim replied brightly, "by means of those camels I have conferred upon you everlasting fame and honor. That fame and honor will stick to you always, just like the ring of the ringdove sticks to its neck, and men will always be hearing some verse or other of poetry in which our family is praised. This is your reward for the camels!"

Perhaps it was a joke. Perhaps, the father thought, perhaps I just didn't hear it quite right. "Did you actually do with my camels what I just heard you say you did?"

"Yes."

"By God," said the father, "I will never live with you again."

So Hatim's father took his family and moved away, and Hatim was left in the desert with his slave girl and his mare and the mare's foal.

Poetry and Poets

Poetry was the sole medium of literary expression in pre-Islamic Arabia. In a real sense, it was the only form of art. This is related at least partially to the high Semitic reverence for the word that we have already mentioned. It is also undoubtedly related to the fact that nomads, constantly on the brink of starvation and always on the move, are hardly likely to produce great architecture or monumental sculpture.They have to be able to carry their art, such as it is, with them. So women's dresses and camel bags come in for some attention. But the lightest-weight form of art anywhere is the memorized word.

The period from which come the pre-Islamic Arabic poems that we possess today extends back to only about a century before the rise of Islam—that is, to about 500 A.D. But the Arabs were known even in biblical times for their poetry and for what the scholars sometimes call "gnomic wisdom."[77] In 1 Kings 44:30, Solomon's wisdom is said to have been so great that it surpassed that of "all the children of the east country." And Job's wise friends, it is clear, come from north Arabian groups.[78] (Indeed, the book of Job as a whole has been argued by some commentators to have an Arabian origin.)

It is perhaps hard for us in the English-speaking world to picture a society in which poetry was not just for the cultured élite, but for everyone. Nevertheless, this is the picture we get of early Arabia. Poetry was a matter of passionate interest, in much the way, perhaps, that sports captures the attention of many modern men. It was one of the few things that unified the Arabs. Throughout the peninsula, the same Arabic dialect was used for poetry, and the same rules of composition were followed. This made poetry a powerful public relations tool. (We have seen to what lengths Hatim of Tayyi was willing to go in order to get three famous poets to praise his family.) In fact, the poet's usual job was to praise his tribe and to vilify the tribes of others. If he was good at his job, if he composed memorable lines, his praise (or his satire) could stick for years and even for generations. As one ancient Arab writer put it, already looking back on the pre-Islamic period,

> When there appeared a poet in a family of the Arabs, the other tribes round about would gather together to that family and wish them joy of their good luck. Feasts would be got ready, the women of the tribe would join together in bands, playing upon lutes, as they were wont to do at bridals, and the men and boys would congratulate one another; for a poet was a defence to the honour of them all, a weapon to ward off insult from their good name, and a means of perpetuating their glorious deeds and of

---

77. From the Greek word *gnosis*, or "knowledge," from which we also get the terms "gnosticism" and "gnostic"—to say nothing of the common word "agnostic" for someone who does not know.

78. A. Jeffery. "Arabians." In George Arthur Buttrick, et al. eds. *The Interpreter's Dictionary of the Bible*. 1:184.

> establishing their fame for ever. And they used not to wish one another joy but for three things—the birth of a boy, the coming to light of a poet, and the foaling of a noble mare.[79]

A couple of stories will make clear the power that poets were thought to enjoy.

The first concerns a man by the name of Maymun ibn Qays, who is generally known by the name of al-Asha. He was a professional troubadour, to borrow a later term. He traveled from one end of the Arabian peninsula to the other, harp in hand, singing the praises of those wise enough to reward him. He was also famous as a satirist, and a person to whom he offered his services would have to be very brave indeed to refuse him the reward he sought. For if al-Asha thought himself slighted, the person at whose hands the offense came was likely to wake up one morning as the butt of a stinging song or versified joke that would soon be on everyone's lips across the peninsula. Al-Asha survived into the days of the Prophet Muhammad, and it is during this time, late in his life, that the story I will now tell occurs:

Al-Asha set out to visit Muhammad.[80] He had composed an ode in honor of the Prophet and wanted to recite it in the Prophet's presence. When Muhammad's enemies, the Quraysh, heard about this, they were terrified that their enemy's prestige would be significantly enhanced by his being praised by so famous and popular a poet. So they intercepted him on his journey and politely asked him where he was headed.

"To your relative, Muhammad," he said. "I intend to accept Islam."

"Oh no," they replied. "You don't really want to do that! Don't you realize that Muhammad will forbid you to do certain things that you like to do?"

---

79. Ibn Rashiq, cited in the translation of Sir Charles Lyall, by Nicholson, 71.

80. A word about the name "Muhammad": Over the years, it has been variously spelled by English writers. "Mahomet," "Mohammed," "Muhammed," and even the disrespectful "Mahound" are all forms of the same proper name. "Muhammad," however, represents the Arabic most faithfully and is beginning to become the standard transliteration.

"Like what?" al-Asha inquired.

"Like fornication," they said.

"Oh," he replied. "That's no big deal. I have not abandoned it, but it has certainly abandoned me! What else?"

"Gambling. Muhammad won't allow you to gamble."

"That's fine. Maybe he'll give me something that will compensate me for the loss of gambling. What else?"

"Usury. He won't permit you to lend money out at interest."

"I've never borrowed or lent anyway. What else?"

"Wine."

"I'll drink water."

Seeing that al-Asha could not be talked out of going to Muhammad and accepting Islam, the representatives of Quraysh changed their approach. They offered him a hundred camels if he would simply go home and wait for a while, to see what the outcome would be of the struggle they were waging against Muhammad. If they won, which they had every intention of doing, there would soon enough be no Islam for him to accept and no danger if he did. And if they lost...well, they had no intention of losing.

"I agree," said al-Asha.

"O Quraysh," cried the leader of the men, "this is al-Asha, and I promise you that if he becomes a follower of Muhammad he will inflame the Arabs against you by his poetry. Therefore, hurry and collect a hundred camels for him. It is a small enough price to pay!"

Camels, of course, were among the pre-Islamic Arabs' most valued possessions. They carried him, along with his family and his property. They gave him milk and, sometimes, meat. They were an emblem of his pride. Yet, threatened by the damage that a poet's words might do them, the Quraysh hastened to buy that poet off with a large herd of camels.

The second story that will illustrate the power of poets among the pre-Islamic Arabs occurs a few decades after the rise of Islam. But the figures involved are agreed by virtually everyone to reflect accurately the attitudes of Arabian paganism, so I use it nonetheless. It involves two famous poets by the name of Jarir and Farazdaq, who carried on a literary feud over the entire course of their lives.[81] Many other people, poets and nonpoets, became involved in the feud from time to time, taking sides in the dispute over which one was the most brilliant.

My story, however, focuses on a rather minor poet who was known as the Camel-herd. This man, the Camel-herd, had loudly expressed his opinion to anybody who would listen that Farazdaq was a better poet than Jarir. This was bound to draw the attention of Jarir, especially since the Camel-herd's attacks smelled somewhat of disloyalty; Jarir, after all, had written verses in praise of the Banu Numayr, the Camel-herd's tribe, while Farazdaq had composed poetry that made fun of them. Why would the Camel-herd prefer a poet who had attacked his own tribe to one who had praised it?

One day, Jarir ran into the Camel-herd and his son, who were mounted on mules. Offended by the Camel-herd's ingratitude, he argued with him but got no satisfactory reply. Meanwhile, the Camel-herd's son, an obnoxious young man by the name of Jandal, was watching with mounting impatience. Finally, he could bear it no longer. Referring to Jarir's tribe, he cried out, "Why do you halt before this dog of the Banu Kulayb, as though you had anything to hope or fear from him?" Then he gave his mule a sharp lash with his whip, meaning to leave Jarir in the dust. But the animal started violently and kicked Jarir, who was standing by it, knocking his hat to the ground. The Camel-herd pretended not to notice and rode to catch up with his son.

Jarir bent over, picked up the hat, carefully brushed it off, and put it back on his head. Then he exclaimed in verse:

> O Jandal! What will Numayr say of you
> When my dishonouring shaft has pierced your father?[82]

Furious, he returned home. After the evening prayer—he was a pious Muslim, after his own slightly weird fashion—he called for a jar of date wine and a lamp and set to work on a new poem. After a

---

81. Jarir's name is pronounced with the emphasis on the second syllable (Juh-*reer*).

82. Cited at Nicholson, *A Literary History of the Arabs*, 245. I have modified the translation slightly.

while, an old woman who was in the house heard his muttering, and climbed the stairs to see if he was all right. She found him crawling naked on his bed as if he were possessed. Astonished, she ran down the stairs yelling, "He is mad!" She described what she had seen to the other people who were in the house. "Don't be concerned," they told her. "We know what he is up to."

By sunrise the next morning, Jarir had composed a satire, eighty verses long, against the tribe of the Banu Numayr. When he had finished the poem to his satisfaction, he shouted out in triumph *Allahu akbar*! ("God is most great!") and rode off to the place where he expected to find the Camel-herd, along with Farazdaq and other friends of the Numayr tribe. Arriving there, he did not waste time greeting anybody, but immediately began to recite the poem he had composed.

It was devastating. As he spoke, Farazdaq and the Camel-herd bowed their heads, and the other tribesmen of Banu Numayr sat in silent mortification at what they were hearing. Finally, Jarir spoke the last words of his poem:

> Cast down your eyes for shame! For you are of
> Numayr—no equal of Kaab nor even of Kilaab.[83]

At that, the Camel-herd jumped up and hurried to his tent as fast as his mule could carry him. "To the saddle! To the saddle!" he called out to his comrades. "You cannot stay here any longer! Jarir has disgraced you all!"

They left Basra immediately and went out into the desert to rejoin the rest of their tribe, who bitterly scolded the Camel-herd for stupidly drawing the fire of Jarir upon them. By his rashness, and that of his son, the entire tribe of Numayr had been shamed. And even hundreds of years afterwards, the lines of Jarir were remembered, and the name of the Camel-herd was a hiss and a byword among his people.

Several observations can be made about this story. First of all, like the story before it, it illustrates the power of the pre-Islamic

---

83. Kaab and Kilaab were other tribes of pre-Islamic Arabia.

Arabian poet. But it also says a great deal about primitive Arab notions of where poetry comes from. The image of Jarir writhing upon his bed, and the old woman's judgment that he was mad, are extremely significant. For the word "mad" in Arabic is *majnun* (pronounced maj-noon). Although, today, it has generally come to mean "mad" or "crazy," it originally meant "*jinn*-possessed" or, literally, "*jinn*ed." Poetry was thought to be a genuine inspiration from the *jinn*. Who were the *jinn*? People in the West know them better as "genies," from the Arabic singular *jinnee*. (They should not, however, be confused with Barbara Eden, who was—how can I put this gently?—not entirely authentic in her television show of the 1960s.)

The premier collection of pre-Islamic poetry is an anthology known since early times as the *Mu'allaqat*. And the oldest and most famous of the pieces included in the *Mu'allaqat* is a poem attributed to Imru al-Qays. Imru al-Qays is almost universally considered the greatest of the pre-Islamic poets. Muhammad, too, recognized his eminence, if in a rather unusual way: He is said to have described Imru al-Qays as "their leader to hellfire." According to tradition, Imru al-Qays was the son of Hujr, the ruler of the tribe of Banu Asad in Central Arabia. Tradition says that he was banished by his father, who despised him for being a poet—hardly a princely way of life!—but it seems more plausible that he was driven away on account of his scandalous love affairs. (Imru al-Qays seems to have been ahead of his time, leading the life of a Bohemian artist long before there was a Bohemia.) When he left home, his wild life continued and even intensified. He took up wandering with other outcasts and became known as "the Vagabond Prince." But then his father was murdered, and he found himself under the sacred Arabian obligation to avenge him.

This was a duty, not a passion with him. In fact, he resented it. "My father wasted my youth," he was heard to complain, "and now that I am old he has laid upon me the burden of blood-revenge. Wine today, business tomorrow!" Still, he seems to have been in no great hurry to get to it. For seven nights he caroused in wild parties, and then, at the end of the seventh day, he swore neither to eat meat, nor to drink wine, nor to use ointment, not to wash his head or touch a woman, until he had extracted vengeance.

But before he actually carried out his vengeance, Imru al-Qays visited the oracle-idol of Dhu al-Khalasa, in the valley of Tabala, north of Najran. There was a receptacle at this oracle-idol holding three arrows, marked, respectively, "The Commanding," "The Forbidding," and "The Waiting."[84] The person seeking guidance was supposed to draw one of the arrows and then to obey its advice. (That, after all, was what he had come for.) Imru al-Qays drew the second, the one marked "The Forbidding." At that, he broke all three of the arrows and dashed them in the face of the idol, yelling (with an unrepeatable oath), "If *your* father had been slain, you would never have hindered me!"

Imru al-Qays went to Constantinople for help, and the Emperor Justinian received him well and, for his own political reasons, offered to assist him. Indeed, the emperor is supposed to have appointed him phylarch of Palestine. But the poet died en route home, at a place called Angora, somewhere around 540 A.D. (Yes, it is the same place that Angora cats are named after. It is also the same place as the modern capital city of Turkey, Ankara.) He is said to have perished by putting on a poisoned robe sent to him as a gift from Justinian, whose daughter he had seduced.[85]

Arabia on the Eve of Islam

The vast majority of the Arabs on the eve of the rise of Islam were pagans. But this statement, true though it is, requires some careful explanation. Not *all* Arabs were pagans. There were Christians and Jews in some parts of the peninsula who had considerable influence.

---

84. Hugh Nibley has linked this sort of Arabian arrow divination with the Book of Mormon's Liahona. See *Since Cumorah*, 2d ed., Volume Seven of the Collected Works of Hugh Nibley, edited by John W. Welch (Salt Lake City and Provo: Deseret Book and the Foundation for Ancient Research and Mormon Studies, 1988), 251-63.

85. Unfortunately, it is this last detail, seemingly so true to the character of Imru al-Qays, that casts doubt upon the whole story. Justinian had no daughter. For this and other reasons, some scholars have argued that the poet Imru al-Qays did not really exist, that he is a bit of early Arabian fiction. This may be true, of course, but his poem exists, whether he did or not, and it needs some sort of explanation.

Furthermore, the paganism of the majority was clearly an apostate remnant of earlier revelations.

For example, the pre-Islamic Arabs knew of a being they called Allah.

This word, familiar to many in the West but widely misunderstood, needs explanation. There are many in the Church and elsewhere who think that "Allah"—the emphasis in this word is properly given to the second syllable (Ahl-*lah*)—is the name of some funny godling worshipped by the Islamic heathens. Nothing could be more wrong. "Allah" is not a name at all. It is a title. It is formed from two words, the Arabic article *al-*, meaning "the," and the word *ilah*, meaning "god." The resultant blending of the two words thus means "the god"—or, to place the emphasis where it ought to be placed, "*the* god." (As opposed to other, lesser gods, or—in Islam—to false gods.) To put it another way, "Allah" is simply the Arabic equivalent of the English word "God," with a capital "g." It is the word used for "God" in Arabic translations of the Bible and, for that matter, in the Arabic translation of the Book of Mormon. It is related to another word that should be familiar to most readers, "Elohim." (When the masculine plural ending *-im* is removed, the word's kinship with "Allah" is clear: Hebrew *eloh* is related to the Arabic *ilah* in much the same way that the German *Gott* is related to the English "God." Arabic and Hebrew are cousins, just as English and German are.)

Although the Arabs knew of a being called Allah, they were still considered pagans. How can that be? It's quite elementary; they knew of Allah, but they paid little or no attention to him. Instead, they had a host of lesser beings, sprites and demons and goddesses, to whom they gave their worship, such as it was, and from whom they sought favors. Allah was too far away, too distant, too intimidating.

There were other connections between Arabian paganism and the religion of the biblical peoples. The pre-Islamic Arabs thought of themselves as the descendants of Ishmael. Beyond that, they seem to have been familiar with a story according to which both Ishmael and his father Abraham had come to central Arabia and had constructed a shrine in the town of Mecca, known as the "Ka'ba." The Qur'an, the holy book of Islam, refers to this story as something already familiar to its audience. It never needs to argue for it. "Children of Israel," the Qur'an says, addressing Arabian Jews,

> remember...when We appointed the House to be a place of visitation for the people, and a sanctuary, and [said]: "Take to yourselves Abraham's station for a place of prayer." And We made covenant with Abraham and Ishmael: "Purify My House for those that shall go about it and those that cleave to it, to those who bow and prostrate themselves"... And when Abraham, and Ishmael with him, raised up the foundations of the House: "Our Lord, receive this from us . . ."[86]

No discussion of Ishmael and the Arabs that is intended for a Latter-day Saint audience can avoid the question of who it was, in the Arab view, that Abraham nearly sacrificed on Mount Moriah. Many people, Arabs and Westerners alike, think that Muslims believe it was Ishmael, and not—contrary to the Bible—Isaac. But nearly everybody is wrong. Classical Muslim writers are evenly divided on the question, for although the story is known to the Qur'an, the Muslim scripture never identifies which son it was.

> So We gave him tidings of a gentle son. And when [his son] was old enough to walk with him, [Abraham] said: O my dear son, I have seen in a dream that I must sacrifice thee. So look, what thinkest thou? He said, O my father! Do that which thou art commanded. Allah willing, thou shalt find me of the stedfast. Then, when they had both surrendered [*aslamaa*; i.e. to Allah], and he had flung him down upon his face, We called unto him: O Abraham! Thou hast already fulfilled the vision. Lo! thus do We reward the good. Lo! that verily was a clear test. Then We ransomed him with a tremendous victim.[87]

But, whatever the identity of the nearly-sacrificed son, the descent of Muhammad and the Arabs from Ishmael is of fundamental

---

86. Qur'an 2:122, 127; A. J. Arberry's translation.
87. Qur'an 37:101–7; M. M. Pickthall's translation.

importance. They saw it as such, and so did Elder George A. Smith of the Council of the Twelve Apostles of The Church of Jesus Christ of Latter-day Saints. Speaking to the Saints in 1855, Elder Smith noted that

> this Mahometan race, this dominant power of the 7th and 8th centuries, were the descendants of Abraham, which Mahometan records show in a straight-forward genealogy, from the family of Mahomet direct to that of Abraham, through the loins of Ishmael, the son of Abraham; and in this dominion there certainly was a recognition of the dominion of the sons of Abraham.[88]

The blessings of Abraham are not restricted solely to the line of Isaac. Speaking to that great prophet of Hagar and her son Ishmael, the Lord declared, "And also of the son of the bondwoman will I make a nation, because he is thy seed."[89] Perhaps—despite the widespread ignorance of his life and work in the West, and despite centuries of prejudice against him among Christians—these blessings are reflected even in the career of Muhammad, a man who, in Elder Smith's opinion, "descended from Abraham and was no doubt raised up by God on purpose to scourge the world for their idolatry."[90] It is Muhammad we must consider next.

---

88. *Journal of Discourses* 3:34.
89. Genesis 21:13.
90. *Journal of Discourses* 3:32.

The Muslim call to prayer goes out today to hundreds of millions of the faithful, from minarets like this one in Cairo, Egypt.

Muhammad

On 23 September 1855, Elder George A. Smith of the Council of the Twelve stood up in the Bowery in Great Salt Lake City—the Tabernacle had not yet been built—and delivered what was, for the time and place, a very well informed and astonishingly positive sermon on Islam. "I am aware," he said, "that it is a difficult matter to get an honest history of Mahometanism translated into any of the Christian languages." He was reminded, when he read about Islam as portrayed by Western writers, of ex-Governor Thomas Ford's biased *History of Illinois*, which managed to put the governor in a good light, and the persecuted and abused Latter-day Saints in quite a bad one.[1] "It is a hard matter, as I have said, to get an honest history of any nation or people by their enemies." So he thereupon proceeded to give to his audience what was, as I say, a remarkably friendly account of Islam.

Concluding his remarks, though, and perhaps just a little bit embarrassed for having spoken in a Christian religious service on so unusual a topic, he asked his listeners to "excuse me for my Mahometan narrative."[2] At that, though, Elder Parley P. Pratt jumped to his feet and approached the pulpit. "My brother, George A. Smith," he remarked, "has wished us to excuse his Mahometan narration, but I would feel more like giving a vote of thanks to the

1. *Journal of Discourses* 3:35.
2. *Journal of Discourses* 3:37.

Almighty and to His servant for so highly entertaining and instructing us."[3]

Such instruction may well have been entertaining. Today, when we have more thrilling modes of entertainment than the spoken word of preaching, we may find it harder to regard instruction on a foreign culture as entertainment. But, if anything, knowledge of other cultures and civilizations is a far more pressing necessity today, than it ever was in the remote mountain valleys of mid-nineteenth century Deseret. It is especially pressing for us as we pursue our divinely-given mandate to take the gospel of Jesus Christ to the entire world.

As Marxism crumbles, one great ideology remains as an alternative to the liberal humanism that characterizes much of today's West. That is Islam. And in Islam, perhaps more than in any other religion or ideology, it is the past that determines the present. We cannot understand today's Islam without understanding events of the seventh century A.D., for it is through those events as well as through certain events of the intervening years, that Muslims understand themselves. In the next few chapters, therefore, I will offer a capsule history of the rise of Islam and a survey of the immense and wonderful civilization that emerged from it. I do not apologize for doing so. Failure to understand the religion of Islam and its seventh century roots has created many problems for the West. We owe it to ourselves—to say nothing of our obligation to our Muslim brothers and sisters—to overcome our misperceptions and our ignorance.

Mecca and the Quraysh

In the period immediately before the rise of Islam, a tribe known as Quraysh had assumed a special place in Arabian society. It had done so by taking control of the town of Mecca, a town that sat astride the major caravan route, dividing the route almost equally midway down the coast of Arabia.

Mecca was an important shrine center. It was built around a structure known as the Ka'ba, which Arabian legend said had been

---

3. *Journal of Discourses* 3:38.

erected by Abraham and his son Ishmael. The Ka'ba stood as it stands today, in an enclosure known as the *haram*.[4] At certain times of the year, pilgrims came to the *haram*, in the thousands, from around the peninsula. This was a major source of revenue for the town, which had few natural resources of its own. But Mecca had also become, probably in the century or so preceding the rise of Islam, an important center of commerce. This was not unrelated to the town's position as a center for pilgrimage. Central markets had been set up, and objects representing the gods of the entire peninsula had been placed in the Ka'ba. (If that structure ever *had* been Abraham's, it was certainly pagan now.) Fighting was banned during the market and pilgrimage times, and was always banned within the *haram* precincts. This created an international marketplace.

It is not possible to reconstruct with certainty the process by which Mecca transformed itself into a center for caravan trade as well as a marketplace, but it may have run something along the following lines: Caravans, as we know, had been running up and down the Arabian coast for centuries. The residents of Mecca, with their central position in the peninsula, and with their knowledge of the terrain and, most importantly, of where the few crucially important water holes were, had managed to establish themselves as guides to the caravans. They made a reasonably adequate living from such service. (They may also have run something of a protection racket: "Gee, that's a nice caravan you have there. Lots of nice stuff. You sure are alone out here, though. It'd be a pity if something were to happen to you around these parts, what with nobody to help you and all. You know—just thinking, of course—for a nominal fee we could make it a whole lot less likely that something nasty would happen to you. What do you say?") At some point in the sixth century, someone seems to have realized that it would make great sense, not to mention great profit, if the Meccans simply took over the trade themselves. Without their cooperation, nobody could

4. The root idea behind the Arabic root *hrm* is "to forbid" or "to be forbidden." Most Westerners will be familiar with the word "harem" (Arabic *harim*; pronounced "ha-*reem*"), signifying a place for women, off-limits to all but certain men.

compete with them, and they would be able to take all of the profits instead of just a fee and perhaps some protection money.

Mecca was roughly equidistant from both the Sasanian Persian empire and the Byzantine empire, which is to say from both the Christians and the Zoroastrians. This was fitting, since Mecca was pagan, and was thus, so to speak, neutral in the conflict between the two great religions. As we have seen, there were Christians and Jews in the Arabian peninsula, but their influence was quite limited in Mecca.

Another religious possibility, however, became available in and around the area of Mecca. A number of men known as *hanifs*—it would be claiming too much to describe them as a group, or as a movement—were growing dissatisfied with Arabian paganism.[5] In the increasingly sophisticated merchant society of Mecca, they were undoubtedly aware of the advanced religions of the Byzantines and the Persians, and they knew something of the Jews. They were puzzled that God appeared to have spoken to other peoples, but not to them. (The Arabic *hanif* could perhaps be loosely translated as "generic monotheist," in contrast to the "brand name" monotheists of the great religious traditions.)[6] They were also dissatisfied with what was happening to their society.

Part of their dissatisfaction was based on the changing economics of Mecca. As residents of the city became involved in international caravan trade, it was predictable that some would grow wealthier than others. Whether for reasons of intelligence or diligence or sheer dumb luck, some people will always prosper more than others. But the rise of social and economic classes in a town which had really never known these classes was bound to have some effects. The old tribal values, under which people were responsible for their kinfolk, and especially for widows and orphans, began to break down. It had been easier, oddly enough, to live according to such values when everyone was on more or less

---

5. The singular of the Arabic word *hanif* is pronounced "ha-*neef*."

6. I once thought that this suggestion was original with me. I have since found out, however, that Professor Marilyn Waldman of Ohio State University, an eminent American Islamicist, makes precisely the same comparison. So I must be right.

the same level of poverty, than it was proving to be when some were growing rich.[7] The temptation to plow one's money right back into the business, or at least to spend it on some well-earned luxuries, and not to "waste" it on unproductive people, was just too strong.[8]

The problem, in the eyes of the *hanifs*, seems to have been that the tribal paganism of the Arabs did not oblige them to do any better than that. It had no ethical code to speak of, and suggested few standards of moral behavior. Allah was a distant being, too far away in the eyes of the pagans to be of any practical significance in everyday life. As for the *jinn*, well, they weren't always so good themselves and could probably be bought off with a small offering every now and then. The *hanifs* were aware of the higher religions elsewhere, religions that made real moral demands upon their adherents and hence made a moral contribution to society. But those religions were the religions of other people. The *hanifs*, for some reason, could not—or at least did not—bring themselves to accept either Christianity or Judaism or Zoroastrianism.

Several reasons may be offered for this. For one thing, the Jews of Arabia seemed not to encourage conversions. For another, given the political climate of the period, to have accepted either Christianity or Zoroastrianism might have implied that one was joining up with either the Byzantine or the Persian party, in much the same way that joining the Communist Party in the Congo would—at one time, at least—have aligned someone, like it or not, with the Soviet Union. Finally, there was an expectant air in the Arabia of the period. If God had so far not seen fit to reveal himself to the Arabs, some seem to have felt, perhaps he soon would. (In this respect, the situation in Arabia may recall the mood in upstate New York, where many people were anticipating some sort of restoration, some kind of American revelation. Many of the early converts and future leaders of the Church came from a background of what is often called "Restorationism.")

---

7. The Book of Mormon, of course, illustrates such a tendency at numerous points in Nephite history.
8. See King Benjamin's remarks at Mosiah 4:16–26.

Muhammad in Mecca

Within a few years of his birth at Mecca in 570 A.D., Muhammad, the future prophet of Islam, became an orphan. He had been born into an important clan of the Quraysh, known as the Banu Hashim. (That is why Jordan, whose king claims descent from the Prophet, is even today officially known as "The Hashemite Kingdom of Jordan.") But, though the Banu Hashim were important, by this point they had also fallen on somewhat hard times. They were like the proverbial penniless aristocrat: they had a rich heritage but no cash. Muhammad clearly could not relax with inherited wealth, so he had to seek some way of making a living. In Mecca, the most promising way to make a living for anyone with ambition and ability—both of which, as later events clearly demonstrate, Muhammad had in abundance—was in caravan trade, and it was into caravan trading that the young man went.

His capacities were apparent to outsiders. Even if we strip away the layers of accumulated legend that attach to his figure, Muhammad emerges from the past as a man of great talent and integrity. By his early 20s, he was managing camel caravans for a rich Meccan widow by the name of Khadija (pronounced "Kha*dee*ja"). In this role, he made a considerable impression. In fact, she was so impressed with him and his abilities that she soon asked him to marry her. According to tradition, she was forty years old, and he was twenty-five.

It was a happy marriage. While Khadija lived, she was Muhammad's most loyal supporter, and he took no other wife. The marriage gave him freedom from the financial worries that must otherwise have occupied much of the time and attention of a poor young orphan, and he could now direct his focus to the things that really interested him. And what was it that most deeply occupied his interest? Clearly, it was religion. Muhammad should almost certainly be classed among the people we have met as the *hanifs*. But he was now in exceptionally good circumstances. With money and security, he now had leisure to ponder the weighty issues of life.

When he was about forty—approximately 610 A.D.—mainstream Islamic tradition represents Muhammad as meditating and praying in a cave of a mountain called Hira, located near Mecca. According to tradition, the angel Gabriel appeared to Muhammad and commanded him to read, or (the words are identical in Arabic) to recite:

> Recite: In the Name of thy Lord who created,
> created Man of a blood-clot.
> Recite: And thy Lord is the Most Generous,
> who taught by the Pen,
> taught Man that which he knew not.[9]

Thus began the revelation of the Qur'an. Sometimes known in English as the "Koran," this is the holy book of the Islamic religion.[10] It was, in many ways, an answer to the religious yearnings long felt by the *hanifs*. For those who wondered why no revelation had come to the Arabs, it announced "There has now come to you a Messenger of your own."[11] It pointedly identified itself as "an Arabic Qur'an."

Muhammad's reception of the Qur'an would continue from this time to nearly the day of his death, twenty-two years later. Its messages were orally delivered and memorized; only later were they written down by Muslims.

The form of the Qur'an is rhymed prose, but it is not and must not be confused with poetry. The *Fatihah* or "Opener," which is the first *sura* or chapter of the Qur'an, will suffice to make this clear:

---

9. 96:1-5; Arberry. Almost all of the quotations from the Qur'an in this book are taken from the translation of N. J. Dawood. Those taken from that of A. J. Arberry, or from M. M. Pickthall, or translated by myself, will be so marked. Where a reference is given in the footnotes to chapter and verse, but without an identifying book (e.g. "Mosiah," or "Genesis"), it is to be understood that the reference is to the Qur'an. I have not infrequently made slight modifications to the translations I have used, for clarity and consistency. (Thus, for example, Dawood's "Allah" is routinely changed to "God," both in order to match Arberry's usage and to accord with my own preferences.)

10. "Qur'an" is the most accepted spelling of the word among modern authorities because it makes clear the derivation of the title from the verb *qara'a*, meaning "to read" or "to recite." Thus, "Qur'an" could be translated approximately as "Reading" or "Recitation."

11. Qur'an 1; Arberry. The phrase, "In the name of God, the Merciful, the Compassionate," occurs at the beginning of every chapter of the Qur'an but one. Only the ninth chapter lacks it, for no obvious reason.

In the name of God, the Merciful, the Compassionate.
Praise belongs to God, the Lord of all Being,
the All-merciful, the All-compassionate,
the Master of the Day of Doom.

Thee only we serve; to Thee alone we pray for succour.
Guide us in the straight path,
the path of those whom Thou hast blessed,
not of those against whom Thou art wrathful,
nor of those who are astray.

I have told you that this is rhymed prose, but you can only *know* that if you read Arabic, or if you are very trusting. I shall therefore try to help you read it yourself. In my very unscientific transliteration—where, as before, italicized syllables receive the emphasis—this chapter sounds something like the following:[12]

Bismee *laah* irah*maan* ira*heem*
Al-*ham*doo li *laa*hee rabb al-aala*meen*
Irah*maan* ira*heem*
*Maa*lik eeyom id*deen*
Ee*yaa*ka *na*boodoo wa ee*yaa*ka nasta'*een*
Ih*di*naas si*raat* al-musta*keem*
Si*raat* ala*thee*na an'*um*ta a*lay*him wa laa *daaleen*. *Ameen*.[13]

Several things can be noted about the Arabic original of this chapter, things which are for the most part also true of the other chapters of the Qur'an that were revealed in Mecca. First, each line of the transliteration represents a verse. Thus, it can be seen that the

---

12. I offer my apologies to any Arabist who might be reading these lines. I have made an effort here to transliterate the Arabic in such a way that non-Arabists, who will make up the overwhelming majority of this book's readers, will have an approximate idea of how to pronounce it. I am aware that the results look a bit silly—especially, perhaps, in this instance. I can only say that they hurt my eyes, too. Incidentally, the "th" in "*alatheena*" is to be pronounced like the "th" in "that," rather than like the "th" in "thing."
13. The final "Ameen"—which is simply "Amen," and which often shows up in Arabic and other Muslim proper names, in the meaning of "faithful" or "true," as "Amin"—does not actually occur in the text, but is routinely added by reciters at the conclusion of a chapter of the Qur'an. I like to add it here since it matches the rhyme scheme of the chapter. Of course, not all chapters of the Qur'an have this particular rhyme.

verses are quite short. This is typical of chapters revealed in Mecca; they are always relatively short and made up of short individual verses. But it will also be noted that the verses are of widely varying lengths. The third verse, for instance, contains only six syllables, while the last, even omitting the "Ameen," comprises sixteen.[14] Therefore, although the verses of the Qur'an have rhyme, they do not have meter. Thus, strictly speaking, they are not to be considered poetry.

Muslims and Western scholars agree upon a division of the *suras* or chapters of the Qur'an between those received at Mecca, and those later received at the oasis town of Medina. There are differences between the two groups that go considerably beyond the mere time of the reception, extending to questions of theme, style, and content. I shall examine the two groups in order.

The revelations of the earliest (Meccan) period of the Prophet's career have certain recurring themes. One of them is the imminent end of this world. These early revelations are, to use a marvelous, hundred-dollar word, *eschatological.* The hundredth chapter of the Qur'an is a typical example of the vigorous, poetic quality of its language during this period and, even more, of the apocalyptic themes which characterize many of the earliest revelations:

> By the snorting war steeds, which strike fire with their hoofs as they gallop to the raid at dawn and with a trail of dust split the foe in two; man is ungrateful to his Lord! To this he himself shall bear witness.
>
> He loves riches with all his heart. But is he not aware that when the dead are thrown out from their graves and men's hidden thoughts are laid open their Lord will on that day know all that they have done?

Another representative passage occurs in the eighty-second chapter, entitled *Infitaar* or "The Splitting":

> When heaven is split open,
> when the stars are scattered,

14. 9:128.

when the seas swarm over,
when the tombs are overthrown,
then a soul shall know its works, the former and the latter.[15]

Another theme is the denunciation of the wealthy for their greed and selfishness.[16] Using the mercantile language of Mecca, it describes them as "those that barter guidance for error and forgiveness for punishment."[17] The wealthy were always so, the Qur'an informs Muhammad,[18] and it quotes God as addressing them directly:

You honour not the orphan,
and you urge not the feeding of the needy,
and you devour the inheritance greedily,
and you love wealth with an ardent love.[19]

Muhammad was directed always to remember his own humble origins and to recall the grace of God in delivering him from them:

Did He not find thee an orphan, and shelter thee?
Did He not find thee erring, and guide thee?
Did He not find thee needy, and suffice thee?[20]

His rocky reception at the hands of his Meccan neighbors probably helped to keep him humble, too. There were a number of things about Muhammad and his teaching that the Meccans and others in the audience found extremely difficult to take seriously. "When we

---

15. 82:1-5; Arberry.
16. For example, at 70:11-18; 104:1-3.
17. 2:175. The notion that Islam is somehow a religion of the desert is, on the whole, false. Much nonsense has been written on this theme, trying, for instance to derive the alleged "harshness" of the religion from the severity of the Arabian desert, or to deduce its strict monotheism from the simplicity of Arabian sand and sky. In reality, Islam was born in a commercial center and constantly uses commercial language, in much the same way that Jesus tended to use the language of sheep herding and agriculture, in order to make its points understandable to its audience. The true desert Arabs, the bedouins, are criticized by the Qur'an; their Islam is seen as suspect. (See, for example, 49:14.)
18. 34:34-35.
19. 89:17-20; Arberry.
20. 93:6-8; Arberry.

are turned to hollow bones," they asked, "shall we be restored to life?"[21] They knew full well what happened to dead bodies, and their question was purely rhetorical. They were already certain of the answer. "There is no other life but this; nor shall we ever be raised to life again."[22] "There is this life and no other. We live and die; nothing but Time destroys us."[23] "When we and our fathers are turned to dust, shall we be raised to life? We were promised this once before, and so were our fathers. It is but a fable of the ancients."[24]

The Qur'an, however, insists upon the literal reality of physical resurrection, which it frequently compares to the resuscitation of fields after a rain.[25] It also points out that God, who was able to create the universe in the first place, and whose creative power gives rise to our physical bodies, will certainly be able to recreate our bodies after their dissolution in death. That, it says, is a relatively small thing.[26] And, finally, the Qur'an points to the motive of the unbelievers in denying the resurrection of the dead. Numerous skeptics today say that belief in life after death is a childish notion, tailor-made for those who fear death. But for many, especially for many in premodern times who believed firmly that any God who existed must be a God of judgment, it was often *disbelief* in life after death that was comforting. "Eat, drink, and be merry," the Book of Mormon quotes such people as saying, "for tomorrow we die; and it shall be well with us."[27] The Qur'an, however, will not allow unbelievers to rest secure in their disbelief. It quotes their familiar rhetorical question and then directs Muhammad how to answer: "'What!

---

21. 79:10-11; compare 13:5; 17:49-52; 19:66; 23:35-37; 34:7; 44:35-36; 50:3; 56:47-48; 64:7.
22. 6:29.
23. 45:24.
24. 27:67-68; compare 23:82-83.
25. 75:3-4; 7:57; 22:5-8; 30:50; 35:9; 41:39; 43:10-13; 50:6-11.
26. 36:77-79; 46:33. See also the discussion of these arguments in Daniel C. Peterson, "Does the Qur'an Teach Creation *Ex Nihilo?*" in *By Study and Also By Faith: Essays in Honor of Hugh W. Nibley*, edited by John M. Lundquist and Stephen D. Ricks, 2 vols. (Salt Lake City and Provo: Deseret Book and the Foundation for Ancient Research and Mormon Studies, 1990), 1:584-610.
27. 2 Nephi 28:7. The next verse seems to refer to those who do believe in life after death, but do not believe that God will truly judge them for their sins.

When we are dead and turned to dust and bones, shall we be raised to life, we and our forefathers?' Say: 'Yes. And you shall be held in shame.'"[28]

For this belief and others, the doubters made fun of the faithful.[29] Whenever possible, they would deliberately interrupt the recitation of the Qur'an. Always they would laugh at it as just "old fairy tales."[30] Muhammad was accused of magic. Sometimes he was said to be demon-possessed or merely a crazy poet.[31]

It is evident from the historical record that such treatment bothered Muhammad deeply. "We know too well that what they say grieves you," the Qur'an tells him. "Other Messengers have been denied before you. But they patiently bore with disbelief and persecution."[32] Other Messengers had been mocked.[33] Muhammad was not to think himself unique if the unbelievers treated him without respect. "If they deny you, remember that before them the peoples of Noah, Abraham and Lot, the tribes of Thamoud and Aad, and the dwellers of Midian had denied their Messengers: Moses himself was charged with imposture."[34] "If they reject you, know that other Messengers have been rejected before you, although they worked miracles and brought down psalms and the light-giving Scriptures."[35]

To the unbelievers, though, Muhammad was just an ordinary man, someone who ate food like anybody else and who walked through the streets of Mecca just like anybody else.[36] This charge the Qur'an was quite willing to admit. "Muhammad is no more than a Messenger; other Messengers have passed away before him."[37] The Prophet was commanded to say to those who questioned him,

---

28. 37:16-18.
29. 83:29-32.
30. 41:26; 6:25; 26:137; 68:15.
31. 10:2; 34:43; 37:15; 46:7; 51:52-53; 54:2; 74:24-25; 68:51; 37:36.
32. 6:33-34; compare 35:4, 25. God, as the Qur'an quotes him, always speaks in the royal "we."
33. 13:32; compare 6:10; 15:11.
34. 22:42-44.
35. 3:184.
36. 21:3; 23:33-34; 25:7.
37. 3:144.

"I am but a mortal like yourselves."[38] "The Messengers We sent before you were no more than men whom We inspired. Let them ask the People of the Book if they do not know this. The bodies We gave them could not dispense with food, nor were they immortal."[39]

The unbelievers demanded to know why the Qur'an hadn't been sent to one of the leading men of the region, instead of to an insignificant nobody.[40] Some insisted that Muhammad must have had a human helper, someone more competent, more learned than he.[41] And the Qur'an admits that he was unlearned, that he had never read the scriptures of earlier prophets.[42] This was in fact one of the evidences of his calling. "This Qur'an," the book itself says, "could not have been composed by any but God."[43] In fact, it is beyond even the reach of human imitation. "If men and *jinn* combined to write the like of this Qur'an, they would surely fail to compose one like it."[44] But this did not stop some from trying. And, since it did not, Muhammad was given advice on how to deal with such presumption. "If they say: 'It is your own invention,' say: 'Compose one chapter like it.'"[45] (A certain al-Nadr ibn al-Harith took up the task, but his inability to imitate the Qur'an left him utterly abashed.)

---

38. 18:110.
39. 21:7-8.
40. 43:31.
41. 16:103. Compare the charge made by anti-Mormons, especially in the nineteenth century, that someone else—usually Parley P. Pratt, Sidney Rigdon, Solomon Spalding, or some combination of the three—was the actual author of the Book of Mormon. Joseph Smith, they reasoned, was incapable of having written so complex a volume. And as for the obvious alternative, that it was inspired by God, well, *that* possibility was simply not acceptable.
42. 29:48. It is probably in this sense that we are to understand references to Muhammad as "the unlettered Prophet" (7:157, 158). Muslims today almost universally argue that the Prophet was wholly illiterate. However, in view of his career as a successful caravan merchant, I find this unlikely. Writing was well known among the Meccan merchant class, and Muhammad probably knew at least enough to keep commercial accounts. This would still not detract from the remarkable literary quality of the Qur'an, though. Even in my opinion, it cannot be attributed to scholarship or literary experience on Muhammad's part.
43. 10:37.
44. 17:88.
45. 10:38; compare 6:93; 11:13; 28:49; 52:33-34.

This challenge is reminiscent of the one issued by the Lord in our own dispensation, at Hiram, Ohio:

> And now I, the Lord, give unto you a testimony of the truth of these commandments which are lying before you. Your eyes have been upon my servant Joseph Smith, Jun., and his language you have known, and his imperfections you have known; and you have sought in your hearts knowledge that you might express beyond his language; this you also know. Now, seek ye out of the Book of Commandments, even the least that is among them, and appoint him that is the most wise among you; or, if there be any among you that shall make one like unto it, then ye are justified in saying that ye do not know that they are true; but if ye cannot make one like unto it, ye are under condemnation if ye do not bear record that they are true.[46]

William E. McLellin, a new convert to the Church who was rather proud of his education, took up the challenge but failed miserably. The parallel is striking. Even non-Latter-day Saint orientalists have noticed it, and some have gone so far as to label al-Nadr ibn al-Harith "the McLellin of Islam."

The unbelievers were always seeking signs as evidence of Muhammad's prophetic calling, but he steadfastly refused to perform such miracles.[47] Indeed, he never claimed that he could. The Qur'an was his only miracle, he said. And, in fact, the individual verses of the Qur'an are called "signs" [*ayaat*] in Arabic, just as in the gospel of John the miracles of Jesus are called "signs."[48] Even if some spectacular sign were given to the unbelievers, the Qur'an pointed out, it would not convert them; they would simply find some excuse to explain it away.[49] In a comment which could as well be applied to the Book of Mormon and the golden plates, the Qur'an quotes God as observing, "If we sent down to you a Book

---

46. Doctrine and Covenants 67:4-8.
47. See 17:90-93, for instance.
48. The honorific title "Ayatollah," used among Iranian Shiite Muslims, means "sign [*aya*] of God [Allah]."
49. 15:14-15. This is quite true to life. Think of the response of the unbelieving Nephites and Lamanites in Helaman 16:15-16.

inscribed on real parchment and the unbelievers touched it with their own hands, they would still say: 'This is nothing but plain magic.'"[50]

Paganism Condemned

Another common theme beginning in the earliest chapters of the Qur'an is a denunciation of paganism, the worshiping of pagan gods. This theme drew enthusiastic praise from Parley P. Pratt:

> Mahometanism included the doctrine that there was one God—that He was great, even the creator of all things, and that the people by right should worship Him... On this account, on the simple subject of the Deity and His worship, if nothing more, I should rather incline, of the two, after all my early traditions, education, and prejudices, to the side of Mahomet, for on this point he is on the side of truth, and the Christian world on the side of idolatry and heathenism.[51]

The false gods of the pagan Arabs, says the Qur'an, can create nothing, but are themselves created. They cannot help their worshipers because they are unable to help themselves. They have neither feet nor hands nor eyes nor ears and so can neither move nor perceive.[52] (Notice the interesting fact that gods without human shape are seen as helpless and ineffectual.) "Those whom you invoke besides God could never create a single fly though they combined to do this. And if a fly carried away a speck of dust from them they could never retrieve it. Powerless is the suppliant, and powerless he whom he supplicates."[53] Polytheism, the Qur'an says, is merely something invented by uninspired men, without authorization or revelation from God. Especially ironic is the fact that, according to the pagan Arabs, the divine beings are goddesses! "Is He to have daughters and you sons?"[54] "They give daughters to God (glory be to Him!), but they themselves would have what they desire. When the birth of a girl is

---

50. 6:7.
51. *Journal of Discourses* 3:38.
52. 7:191-97.
53. 22:73.
54. 53:19-23.

announced to one of them, his face grows dark and he is filled with inward gloom. Because of the bad news he hides himself from men: should he keep her with disgrace or bury her under the dust?"[55]

This last passage points to one other part of the early Qur'anic message. Although it can hardly be called a true "theme" of the book, it is worthy of mention here: Among the pre-Islamic Arabs, female infanticide was a common practice. This means that parents commonly took their newborn infants, upon discovering that they were girls, and buried them alive. (Obviously, this practice was not universal, or there would soon have been no pre-Islamic Arabs.) The reasons for such a practice are fairly obvious. Raising children was an expensive and demanding undertaking, and especially so in an Arabia where life was often still quite uncertain and marginal. And after all the effort expended in raising a daughter, what was the outcome? She joined somebody else's tribe or clan at just the point she was becoming useful. Better, this attitude said, to raise boys. The irony noted by the Qur'an in connection with the alleged goddess-daughters of Allah is that, of course, while the pre-Islamic Arabs were themselves not at all happy to have daughters, they were perfectly willing to ascribe them to God.

The Qur'an put an end to the practice of female infanticide in Arabia. Among other things, it said the day of judgment will be a day on which "the infant girl, buried alive, is asked for what crime she was slain."[56] Obviously, it is implied, her answer will not help her parents at that day. But the Qur'an does not leave the implication to be puzzled out by its audience. It states the principle clearly: "You shall not kill your children for fear of want. We will provide for them and for you."[57] It is important, I think, that we in the West remember this reform instituted and enforced by the authority of the Qur'an. For those who like to view Muhammad and Islam as hostile to women, this ending of female infanticide ought to be weighed in the balance.

---

55. 16:57-59.
56. 81:8-9.
57. 17:31; compare 6:151. This passage has implications, too, for the Muslim view of abortion, which has historically been quite negative.

Muhammad's Reception among the Arabs

In these early days of his prophetic ministry in Mecca, Muhammad reaped much ridicule but few converts. (Among those who did convert, however, were some of the greatest names in later Islamic history, names such as Ali, Umar, Uthman, and Abu Bakr. We shall meet them all again.) His call to worship the one God, Allah, and to abandon the worship of the false gods of paganism, fell mostly on deaf ears—the more so since, as we have seen, Mecca derived considerable income from the idolatrous worship at its shrine.

The elite of the town felt themselves threatened. In this regard, they were rather like the silversmiths of Ephesus whose income seemed to be menaced by the preaching of Paul and the other Christians.[58] In other words, "priestcraft," as the Book of Mormon calls it, was at stake here. Eventually, they determined to take some sort of action against the Prophet and against those who followed him. Of the two, however, it was considerably easier to get at the Prophet's followers. Many of them were slaves or of the lower classes. Thus they had no powerful clan to protect them by means of threatened blood feuds. (The insulting words of the unbelievers to Noah, quoted in the Qur'an, are probably not unlike those to Muhammad: "We regard you as a mortal like ourselves. Nor can we find any among your followers but men of hasty judgement, the lowliest of our tribe. We see no virtue in you: indeed we know that you are lying.")[59] And for people without tribal protection, as we have seen, there was no government in Arabia to step in on their behalf.

The Qur'an warned the Muslims that believers are not exempt from testing and from affliction, and indeed they were not. "Did you suppose that you would go to Paradise untouched by the suffering which was endured by those before you? Affliction and adversity befell them; and so battered were they that each Messenger, and those who shared his faith, cried out: 'When will the help of God come?'"[60]

---

58. For that amusing story, see Acts 19:23-41.
59. 11:27; compare 26:111.
60. 2:214; compare 2:155-57; 29:2-3.

But Muhammad did not wait for God to help. While he undoubtedly trusted in God, he also took action on his own, as any responsible religious leader should. He began casting around for a place where his fledgling community of believers might be safe. He sent one group to Ethiopia, for instance, but that did not prove to be a good long-term solution.

Then the answer walked right up to him. Several days' journey north of Mecca lay an agricultural oasis by the name of Yathrib. Yathrib was not really a town, but a collection of huts occupied by several different tribes, tribes that did not get along with one another. Life in the settlement was one conflict after another. It was often violent, always unpleasant and prone to disruption. In 620, a group of pilgrims from Yathrib came to Mecca. In the course of their visit, they interrupted their religious observances to make an important offer to Muhammad. They had, they said, heard of his intelligence and his integrity, and they also knew of his interest in getting himself and his people out of Mecca. Would he, they asked, please come to Yathrib? There, he could serve as an arbitrator between the conflicting factions of the oasis. Standing as he did outside any of the tribes, he would be able to stand apart from the disputes and to judge fairly.

Muhammad accepted the invitation on the condition that the people of Yathrib would recognize him as the Messenger of God. The delegation accepted his requirement. They were pagans and certainly did not fully realize the import of what they were committing to. It was one of the most important agreements in the history of mankind.

In 622, the Prophet and his followers emigrated from Mecca to Yathrib. This emigration, or *hijra*, as it is called in Arabic, now serves to mark the beginning of the Islamic calendar. Notice that the calendar does not start with the Prophet's birth, or with the beginning of the Qur'anic revelation, but with the emigration to Yathrib. Why? Because Muhammad went from being merely a prophet, a voice crying in the wilderness, to being the leader of a fairly sizeable community by the standards of seventh-century Arabia. He thus became a political figure, as well as a prophet.

As the nature of Muhammad's responsibilities changed, so did the nature of the revelations he received. The *suras* received in Mecca had been short, with short verses and strong rhymes. They had been obscure, apocalyptic, oracular. In Yathrib, they became more concerned with legal or legislative matters, with the issues that arise in governing a community. Their form changed, too. They tended to be less poetic, more prosaic. The revelations or chapters were longer, and the individual verses within them were also longer. One verse from the second chapter of the Qur'an will demonstrate quite clearly the way Medinan revelations—as they are called, for reasons which will appear in a moment—differ from Meccan revelations. It will be noted that this represents simply one verse. (Compare it with, say, the entire hundredth chapter, cited above, which contains fully eleven verses within its brief compass.)

> Believers, when you contract a debt for a fixed period, put it in writing. Let a scribe write it down for you with fairness; no scribe should refuse to write as God has taught him. Therefore let him write; and let the debtor dictate, fearing God his Lord and not diminishing the sum he owes. If the debtor be a feeble-minded or ignorant person, or one who cannot dictate, let his guardian dictate for him in fairness. Call in two male witnesses from among you, but if two men cannot be found, then one man and two women whom you judge fit to act as witnesses; so that if either of them commit an error, the other will remember. Witnesses must not refuse to give evidence if called upon to do so. So do not fail to put your debts in writing, be they small or big, together with the date of payment. This is more just in the sight of God; it ensures accuracy in testifying and is the best way to remove all doubt. But if the transaction in hand be a bargain concluded on the spot, it is no offence for you if you do not commit it to writing. See that witnesses are present when you barter with one another, and let no harm be done to either scribe or witness. If you harm them you shall commit a transgression. Have fear of God, who teaches you; He has knowledge of all things. (2:282)

It would be wrong, however, to suggest that the old power and beauty had gone out of the Qur'an by the Medinan period. Passages like the so-called "Light Verse," which some modern commentators believe refers to the lighted altar of a seventh-century Christian church, conclusively demonstrate that this was not so:

God is the Light of the heavens and the earth;
the likeness of His Light is as a niche
wherein is a lamp
(the lamp in a glass,
the glass as it were a glittering star)
kindled from a Blessed Tree,
an olive that is neither of the East nor of the West
whose oil well-nigh would shine, even if no fire touched it;
Light upon Light;
(God guides to His Light whom He will.)[61]

Nevertheless, Muhammad's transformation from prophet to prophet-statesman had profound consequences for the nature of the religion that was developing—Islam. This is because the nature of his example to the Muslims changed along with his change of role. Christians who want an ideal model to follow naturally look to Jesus of Nazareth as the person who most perfectly embodies their faith. But Jesus never held any political office or exercised any state power, and this fact allows Christians to concentrate on personal salvation and holiness without fearing that a failure to be politically involved jeopardizes their salvation. Muhammad, on the other hand, presided for the last ten years of his life over a community and attempted to enact Islam into law and political practice. A Muslim who seeks the ideal model for his faith naturally turns to Muhammad as the man who best understood and embodied it—and Muhammad was a statesman. Therefore, a pious Muslim cannot be indifferent to politics.

This is one of the reasons that Islam has the political tinge to it that so infuriates (or at least puzzles) Westerners. We should not, however, be so puzzled. During the seventh century, nobody anywhere, in Mecca or in Constantinople or in Rome, had a very firm notion of or commitment to the separation of church and

---

61. 24:35; Arberry.

state. We should not be surprised, then, that Islam does not. And, in a religion whose source of authority is firmly in the past, there is little chance of evolving beyond seventh-century positions on the subject.

And what of Yathrib? Why do we not hear of that important town today? In fact, we do. After the arrival of the Prophet, the old name of the town gradually fell into disuse. Instead, it began to be known as Madinat al-Nabi, "the city of the Prophet," or, simply, as al-Madina, "the City." And today Medina (as it is generally spelled in English) has come to be regarded as, after Mecca itself, the most holy city of Islam. (Jerusalem, most frequently known in Arabic as al-Quds, "the holy," is the third.)

In Medina, the Muslims became a kind of superclan, a tribe held together not by ties of kinship but by a common faith. And they began to act in a manner consistent with accepted behavior in early Arabia. They sent out raiding parties and clashed with Quraysh—an unthinkable thing for most of them under old Arabian ideas, since most of them were of Quraysh. But Quraysh had expelled and abused them, and they had declared their loyalty to the new tribe of Islam.

Eventually, Muhammad and his followers scored a major victory over the Quraysh of Mecca and won the privilege to make the pilgrimage to the Ka'ba there. The city fathers, it now became clear, need never have worried. For the victorious Muslims proceeded to "Islamicize" the Ka'ba. Under the direction of their Prophet, they incorporated its rites and rituals, in a purified form, into the new religion—the legend of Abraham and Ishmael certainly helped here—and those rites and rituals were now on their way to an importance that the early Meccan pagans could scarcely have foreseen. Since then, Mecca has gone from being a pilgrimage center for the Arabian peninsula, to being the center of the earth for nearly a billion Muslims the world over.

In Medina, as Muhammad's faith began to spread throughout the Arabian peninsula, Islam began to distinguish itself from the two earlier religions. This was partly because adherents of those religions refused to recognize Muhammad as a legitimate prophet within their traditions. According to the Qur'an, the Jews objected to the notion that God could call anybody he chose, not feeling himself restricted to one of *them*.[62] "When it is said to them: 'Believe in what God has revealed,' they reply: 'We believe in what was revealed to *us*.'" But the Qur'an then points out, much as Jesus did in similar circumstances, that they had *killed* the prophets who came to them in the past.[63]

But it was not only the Jews who rejected the claims of the new prophet. The Qur'an describes both Jews and Christians as claiming that they are the only ones who will enter paradise. To this, the Qur'an responds that whoever "surrenders" (*aslama*) to God and does works of righteousness will be rewarded and need not fear.[64] Indeed, the Qur'an claims to go back beyond Judaism and Christianity, to a time before either one had come into being, to the more basic faith that underlies both.[65] "They say: 'Accept the Jewish or the Christian faith and you shall be rightly guided.' Say: 'By no means! We believe in the faith of Abraham, the upright one. He was no idolater.' Say: 'We believe in God and that which is revealed to us; in what was revealed to Abraham, Ishmael, Isaac, Jacob, and the tribes; to Moses and Jesus and the other prophets by their Lord. We make no distinction amongst any of them, and to God we have surrendered ourselves [*muslimun*].'"[66] The Christians and Jews, according to the Qur'an, have distorted that original revelation, that pure submission (*islam*), and now they quarrel with one another over issues that neither one of them really understands. "The Jews say the Christians are misguided, and the Christians say it is the Jews who are misguided. Yet they both read the Scriptures. And the pagans say the same of both."[67] This is almost precisely the comment made by Joseph Smith about the warring sects of his day:

---

62. 2:90.
63. 2:91; italics in Dawood's translation.
64. 2:111-12.
65. Much as the apostle Paul seems to do in Galatians 3. In doing this, clearly, Muhammad could draw on the awareness of Abraham and Ishmael that was, as we have seen, already present among the Arabians.
66. 2:135-36; compare 3:84.
67. 2:133.

They "understood the same passages of scripture so differently as to destroy all confidence in settling the question by an appeal to the Bible."[68] And in each case, the solution was not to tinker with what the sects of the day taught, but to restore the truth in its ancient purity, to go back to a time before it was corrupted.

For all that it criticizes the unbelievers of Arabia, though, the Qur'an does not spare Muhammad either. He was never allowed to forget that he too was human. At one point, for example, despite all the Qur'an's denunciations of the wealthy, Muhammad seems to have shown too much deference to a rich man. He had violated one of the cardinal tenets of true Islam, the equality of all men before God and before his Prophet:

> He [Muhammad] frowned and turned his back when the blind man came towards him. How could you [Muhammad] tell? He might have sought to purify himself. He might have been forewarned, and might have profited from Our warning. But to the wealthy man you were all attention: although the fault would not be yours if he remained uncleansed. Yet you gave no heed to him that came to you with zeal and awe.[69]

Muhammad was not to yield to such temptations, and he was not to give in to the unbelievers, no matter how much their mocking troubled him, no matter how much more comfortable he could have been if he had made just a few small concessions. No, his responsibility was too great to allow him to make the small adjustments that seem to make life tolerable for most of the world's less-than-saintly human beings: "If you succumb to their desires after all the knowledge you have been given, none shall save or protect you from God."[70]

The Death of Muhammad

By the year 632, Muhammad had subdued all of the Arabian peninsula. The revelation of Islam was complete. "This day I have perfected

---

68. Joseph Smith—History 1:12.
69. 80:1-10. Abrupt and often puzzling shifts in person (as here, from "he" to "you") are typical of Qur'anic style. Similar shifts appear in other Semitic writings, such as the biblical Psalms.
70. 13:37.

your religion for you and completed My favour to you," says God, in what many believe to be the last verse of the Qur'an to be revealed. "I have chosen Islam to be your faith."[71] The tribes were now united, and the question arose, where could they plunder? They could not attack one another any more than members of a tribe were allowed to raid and pillage their fellow tribesmen. In fact, Muslims now regarded themselves precisely *as* a tribe. An expedition was therefore planned against the Ghassanids, a small Byzantine vassal state of Arabic background.

But in that same year, after a brief illness and before the planned expedition could be carried out, Muhammad died. This was unquestionably a shattering experience for the vast majority of Muslims. Muhammad was the Prophet of God; they had known no other. He had given Arabia a government for the first time in its recorded history. He had established their religion and welded both Muslims and Arabs into a people. A story will perhaps illustrate the awful impact the Prophet's passing had upon the community of the believers.

When the news reached him that Muhammad was gone, Umar, a strong man who would later rule over the entire Islamic empire, seems to have grown virtually hysterical. He stood among the people and cried out that Muhammad was not dead, that he had merely gone to the Lord for a brief time. After forty days, he declared, the Prophet would return and would punish those who had falsely proclaimed his death. When Abu Bakr, an older man who would soon emerge as Muhammad's first successor, heard the commotion, he entered into the room where the body of the Prophet lay. He uncovered Muhammad's face and kissed him, saying, "You are dearer [to me] than my father and mother. You have tasted the death which God had decreed: a second death will never overtake you." Then he covered the Prophet's face again and went out. Umar was still manically denying Muhammad's death outside of the mosque. "Gently, Umar. Be quiet," Abu Bakr whispered to him. But Umar continued to cry out. Finally, standing up and

71. 5:3.

addressing the bystanders, Abu Bakr said, "O men, if anyone worships Muhammad, Muhammad is dead. If anyone worships God, God is alive and cannot die." Then he recited the words of the Qur'an:

> Muhammad is naught but a Messenger; Messengers have passed away before him. Why, if he should die or is slain, will you turn about on your heels? If any man should turn about on his heels, he will not harm God in any way; and God will recompense the thankful.[72]

The effect on the old Muslim hero's audience was immediate and profound. Even Umar later recalled, "When I heard Abu Bakr recite these words I was dumbfounded so that my legs would not bear me and I fell to the ground knowing that the apostle was indeed dead."[73]

What Are We to Make of Muhammad?

Evaluations of Muhammad have varied wildly. Skeptical Western writers for years regarded him as a fraud. (Indeed, many liked to link him with Joseph Smith in that regard. To associate the two was to damn both.)[74] The great fourteenth-century Christian poet Dante placed him in one of the deepest reaches of hell.[75] For Muslims, on

---

72. 3:138.

73. The story is told in Ibn Hisham's biography of Muhammad. I have borrowed some of the language of my paraphrase from A. Guillaume's English translation of that biography, *The Life of Muhammad* (Karachi: Oxford University Press, 1967). Incidentally, critics of the Book of Mormon have often ridiculed the tendency of characters in the Nephite record to "fall to the ground" when under intense emotion or great religious excitement. Some have seen in such incidents echoes of nineteenth-century frontier revivalism. But similar behavior is abundantly recorded in the medieval Arab world—which, it must be remembered, is closely related to the world out of which the Book of Mormon claims to have come.

74. I am currently preparing an article on this subject.

75. At Canto XXVIII, lines 22-48 of his *Inferno*. Ali is also there. The two are ranked among the sowers of scandal and schism. This is understandable—if utterly unfair—in the case of Ali, but is hard to make much sense of in the case of Muhammad unless, as has been suggested, Dante shared the common medieval Western view that Muhammad was an apostate Christian (perhaps even a cardinal whose papal ambitions had been thwarted).

the other hand, he is the incomparable Messenger of God, "the seal of the prophets." His place in Islamic piety is astonishingly high, although Muslims strictly avoid worship of him and are offended at any suggestion that they do.[76] (This is similar to what Latter-day Saints feel when it is claimed that they worship Joseph Smith.)

I learned this lesson on my mission in Switzerland. During my time there, at least, it was rather rare for us to actually be invited into someone's apartment while tracting. So my companion and I were delighted one evening when a Pakistani banker came to the door and said, "Mormons! I have always wanted to know something of your religion. Please come in!" I well recall thinking to myself what a lucky fellow this guy was, to have chanced upon perhaps the most knowledgeable missionary in Switzerland on the subject of Islam. He must have been living right. I was just the person to teach him. What actually happened was a swift illustration of the folly of relying upon one's own wisdom in attempting to teach the gospel. (It was also a sharp reminder that I knew very little about Islam, actually. I had not yet begun my real study of the subject. And today I am less confident than I was then about how I would approach Muslims.) Within about two minutes of our entrance into the man's apartment, we were politely but firmly asked to leave. The reason? In a clear instance of lack of inspiration, I had chosen as my starting gambit, my point of entry, something that I thought would furnish common ground upon which we could talk. I brought up the idea of Joseph Smith, a postbiblical prophet. The Pakistani banker looked unexpectedly glum. "You mean," he asked, "a prophet after Muhammad?" "Yes!" I replied, beaming with enthusiasm. A short pause. "I'm sorry," he responded. "I would love to talk with you more, but I cannot allow discussion of a prophet after Muhammad to be conducted in my apartment. Please do not be offended." And out we went.

I learned from this that it is going to be a difficult matter to speak with Muslims about the gospel without offending them and

---

76. Annemarie Schimmel's book, *And Muhammad Is His Messenger: The Veneration of the Prophet in Islamic Piety* (Chapel Hill: The University of North Carolina Press, 1985), gives a good overview of this subject for those who might be interested.

without contradicting some of their deepest beliefs. I also learned that our task of someday taking the gospel to the Muslims—and we cannot conceal that we desire to do so, although we are careful to observe the law and although we try carefully to respect the religious sensitivities of others—will be greatly eased to the extent we can say good things about Muhammad, the founder of Islam.

Fortunately, we *can* say good things without cynicism or pretense. From its earliest years, leaders of The Church of Jesus Christ of Latter-day Saints have had good things to say about Muhammad. This is one of the things that I am most proud of in the gospel. Let me explain. For many people today, even for religious people, the concept of a "prophet" has so lost its meaning that they are willing to apply the title to any person they regard as good and as having good ideas or standing up for a good cause. Thus, Martin Luther King and Mahatma Gandhi and Leo Tolstoy have all been called prophets. But this, it is clear from a Latter-day Saint viewpoint, is to lessen the concept of "prophet." Not, I hasten to add, because of anything particularly wrong with these or similar people to whom the title is often applied, but because they lack the one characteristic that distinguishes prophets from other people, even from good and great ones—revelation from God, the capacity to speak authoritatively in the name of our Heavenly Father.[77]

There is another group of people in our Western society that, unlike the liberals I have just sketched, takes a very high view of prophecy. I am thinking, for example, of certain conservative Protestants. The trouble is that, where the first group was too inclusive, and was willing to call almost any good person a prophet, this group is too restrictive. They are quite willing to ascribe the origins of all world religions to the devil, and are even willing to consign all their adherents to hell. (Mormons are often assigned to the same place by the same people.) For these conservative believers, there is

---

77. Of course, God is the source of all truth, so it is perhaps a little harder to separate prophets from truth-speaking non-prophets than might at first glance appear. To the extent that even Caiaphas spoke the divinely-inspired truth, I suppose he was temporarily a kind of prophet. The principles enunciated in Doctrine and Covenants 91 seem to me to have wide application.

no truth outside of their own particular denomination or brand of religion.

I am delighted that Mormonism is in the middle. The gospel of Jesus Christ makes no apology for its claim that it is the truth and that The Church of Jesus Christ of Latter-day Saints contains all the truths needed to save us. Yet it does not take a bigoted and narrow view of truth. We are willing to accept true insights wherever we find them. "The first and fundamental principle of our holy religion," the Prophet Joseph Smith taught, "is, that we believe that we have a right to embrace all, and every item of truth, without limitation or without being circumscribed or prohibited by the creeds or superstitious notions of men."[78] President John Taylor was equally enthusiastic. "If there is any truth in heaven, earth, or hell," he declared, "I want to embrace it, I care not what shape it comes in to me, who brings it, or who believes in it, whether it is popular or unpopular. Truth, eternal truth, I wish to float in and enjoy."[79] "We believe in all truth," President Joseph F. Smith agreed,

> no matter to what subject it may refer. No sect or religious denomination in the world possesses a single principle of truth that we do not accept or that we will reject. We are willing to receive all truth, from whatever source it may come; for truth will stand, truth will endure.[80]

So, the impatient reader is asking by now, just what *are* we to think of Muhammad? Was he a genuine prophet, or was he not? My answer to that is a clear and resolute "I don't know." Or perhaps a decisive "Yes and no." Parley P. Pratt, who was enthusiastic in his praise of Muhammad and Islam, observed that the blessings of the priesthood were not intended to flow through the line of Ishmael, but rather through that of Isaac.

> And God said, Sarah thy wife shall bear thee a son indeed; and thou shalt call his name Isaac: and I will establish my covenant

---

78. *Times and Seasons* (February 1840), 54.
79. *Journal of Discourses* 1:155.
80. Joseph F. Smith, *Gospel Doctrine*, 5th ed. (Salt Lake City: Deseret Book, 1939), 1.

> with him for an everlasting covenant, and with his seed after him. And as for Ishmael, I have heard thee: Behold, I have blessed him, and will make him fruitful, and will multiply him exceedingly; twelve princes shall he beget, and I will make him a great nation. But my covenant will I establish with Isaac.[81]

Elder Pratt seems to have believed, therefore, that Muhammad was not, in the fullest sense of the word, a prophet of the living God.[82] Nevertheless, he felt, as I do, that Muhammad was absolutely sincere, and that he appears to have been an inspired instrument in the hands of God. This seems also to have been the position taken by the First Presidency, in a statement issued on 15 February 1978. That statement reads, in part, as follows:

> The great religious leaders of the world such as Mohammed, Confucius, and the Reformers, as well as philosophers including Socrates, Plato, and others, received a portion of God's light. Moral truths were given to them by God to enlighten whole nations and to bring a higher level of understanding to individuals.[83]

This is my view as well. (I'm always pleased when the First Presidency agrees with me.) If we can say that Martin Luther was inspired—and we do—I certainly believe that we can make the same statement about Muhammad. Whether we can consider him a full prophet is more doubtful. In the next chapter, I shall present clear reason to believe that, if the text of the Qur'an as we now have it actually goes back to Muhammad, which is likely, he was mistaken on certain issues too central to the gospel as it has been revealed to the Latter-day Saints for us to be able to endorse or accept him as a prophet in the fullest sense. But I would be quite willing to be shown otherwise.

The Succession to Muhammad

Muhammad was dead. Now came the question of succession. The founder of Islam left no clear instructions on this question. Some

---

81. Genesis 17:19-21. The twelve princes are listed at Genesis 25:13-16.
82. *Journal of Discourses* 3:40.
83. A more complete text of this statement is printed as the frontispiece to Spencer J. Palmer, *The Expanding Church* (Salt Lake City: Deseret Book, 1978).

felt that he had designated Ali, his cousin and son-in-law and one of the earliest male converts to Islam, to be his successor, but most in the community, including many whose loyalty to the Prophet cannot plausibly be denied, seem to have known of no such thing.

By the time of his passing, the Prophet had come to control the entire Arabian landmass. Virtually every tribe and individual in the peninsula had pledged obedience to him. Many of the Arabian tribes, however, understood their submission agreements as applying only to Muhammad personally. Now that he was gone, they would certainly feel no allegiance to his successors. They could be expected to go their own way. They would recognize no obligation to do otherwise. (They had, it will be recalled, no notion of government. Their loyalty was to a person; of a continuing institution apart from individuals they had no concept.) Therefore, in all the chaos surrounding the Prophet's unexpected death, certain clear thinkers understood that some action had to be taken quickly before the whole structure of a kind of Arabian state unravelled. Umar, the sources say, grabbed Abu Bakr, the elderly and highly respected Muslim whom we have already met, and took him to a place where a meeting on the succession question was underway. (The Prophet was not yet buried, and Ali was busy attending to the details of the funeral.)

At that meeting, perhaps before many of those present had a very clear idea of what was going on, Abu Bakr was acclaimed the leader of the community. All there solemnly pledged their loyalty to him. Then others in the community did so as well.

Some, though, did not. Ali, the Prophet's cousin and son-in-law who had distinguished himself by heroic deeds on behalf of the faith in earlier military conflicts, felt that it was his right as kinsman to Muhammad to succeed him in the rule of the community.[84] (No man could succeed Muhammad in his prophetic capacity.

---

84. Several nineteenth-century Orientalists saw a similarity between the Shiites and the Reorganized Church of Jesus Christ of Latter Day Saints. Both groups expected the succession to the founding prophet to remain in the prophet's family. But the Shiites have the more radical theology in Islam, whereas the Reorganized Church is far closer to mainstream Protestantism than are the Mormons and is now abandoning the notion of family succession..

Muhammad, virtually all of his followers are agreed, was the last of the prophets.) A number of pious Muslims supported Ali's claim. As the years and generations passed, this group came to be known in Arabic as the *shi'at 'Ali*, "the faction of Ali." This is the origin of the group that we know in English today as the "Shiites."[85] The dispute between them and their opponents, who gradually assumed the name of "Sunnis," deepened and grew sharper.[86] Where once the dispute had been political, it came to include differences over theology and law. The political disagreement festered. The Shiites grew more and more embittered as their leaders were harassed and kept from power. (This is one of the reasons, I suspect, that Shiite rule can be so harsh when they finally do come to power.) There is among them a deep sense of grievance, of having been usurped, abused. This tradition or traditional position is kept alive, even nourished, by rituals designed to do just that. The most spectacular and significant instance of these recalls the killing of Husayn, the Prophet's grandson, at a place in Iraq called Karbala, and the massacre of much of his family. This horrible event occurred on the tenth day of the Muslim month Muharram, in the year 680 A.D.[87] Shiites around the world still commemorate it annually. Indeed, in something very similar to the passion plays of medieval Europe, they actually reenact it, flagellating themselves, chanting lamentations, working themselves to a high pitch of emotion and excitement. This is the holy time of Ashura, or "the tenth."

Abu Bakr was the first man to bear the title of "caliph," to serve as the political successor of the Prophet.[88] He lived for only two more years beyond the death of Muhammad, but it was during his rule that a series of small campaigns known as the "Wars of the Ridda" reestablished the control of the new Islamic "state" over the Arabian peninsula. Just before his death in 634 A.D., Abu Bakr nominated Umar as his successor.

---

85. Pronounced, of course, "*Shee*-ites."
86. The singular, "Sunni," should be pronounced roughly "*Soon*-nee."
87. 10 October 680 A.D.
88. The word "caliph" is usually pronounced "*kay*-liff" in English, although the Arabic is "kha*lee*fa." It means something like "stand-in," or "deputy" (to the Prophet).

Under Umar's leadership, the wars that had first been directed against "rebellious" Arabian tribes went on. But now, with the entire Arabian peninsula pacified and back under Muslim control, the military and raiding energies of the Arabs had to be directed outward. Oddly enough, the Arab empire does not seem to have been planned. It simply happened. (Although perhaps no event in human history is really so simple as that. This one, the rise of an Arab empire, seems quite clearly to have fulfilled the words of the angel to Hagar, exiled in the desert and resigned to the death of her son Ishmael: "Arise, lift up the lad, and hold him in thine hand; for I will make him a great nation.")[89] One weak state after another fell to the Arabs, who must have been as amazed at their good fortune as we are today in reading about it. Even the Byzantines and the Persians, exhausted by their long war with one another, were no match for the upstarts from the desert.

Arab armies conquered Syria easily (635–636), including Palestine and Jerusalem itself. (The Arabs appear to have been welcomed by the local Jewish population there. After the conquest, the reasoning seems to have gone, things could only get better for the Jews. And they did. Tiberias, the Galilean town where the so-called Jerusalem Talmud was completed, remained a center for Jewish study of the Bible and for the study of the Hebrew language for generations beyond the Arab conquest.) By 637, Arab forces occupied lower Iraq, and by 641 they had taken all of the Tigris and Euphrates river valleys. The Persian empire, where the Jews again welcomed the Arab liberators, also came under attack. By the 650s, it had ceased to exist. The Byzantines took heavy losses as well. In 642, Egypt, which had been the breadbasket of the Roman empire since the days of the first Caesars, fell to the Arabs. (The invaders were assisted by local Christians, furious at the treatment their denomination was receiving from the imperial governors sent from Constantinople.) Garrison towns were established throughout the conquered territories, including such famous places as Basra, Kufa, and Fustat, which would eventually become the great city of Cairo.

---

89. Genesis 21:18. Compare Genesis 17:20, already quoted.

These were astonishing conquests, rapid and seemingly without end, and it was not only the ancient Christians who saw them as fortunate (indeed, perhaps even as God-ordained). Parley P. Pratt was enthused about them as well. "Now," he said,

> if we take Mahometanism during those dark ages, and the corruptions that are so universally prevalent over the earth, and the idolatrous systems of religion, falsely called Christianity, and weigh them in a balance; with all my education in favor of Christian nations and Christian powers, and Christian institutions, so called, with all my prejudices of early youth, and habits of thought and reading, my rational faculties would compel me to admit that the Mahometan history and Mahometan doctrine was a standard raised against the most corrupt and abominable idolatry that ever perverted our earth, found in the creeds and worship of Christians, falsely so named.[90]

Umar was assassinated in 644 A.D. and was succeeded by a gentle if weak old man named Uthman.[91] He was assassinated, in turn, in 656 A.D., and finally it was Ali's turn to assume the caliphate. It seemed for a while that the dreams of the Shiites had come true, or at least that they were about to do so. But conditions were terribly unstable, and Ali himself fell at the hands of an assassin in

---

90. *Journal of Discourses* 3:40. Elder Pratt is probably a bit too enthusiastic. His comment on the following page *certainly* is: "So far as that one point is concerned, of worshipping the one true God under the name of Mahometanism, together with many moral precepts, and in war acting only on the defensive, I think they have exceeded in righteousness and truthfulness of religion, the idolatrous and corrupt church that has borne the name of Christianity." I suspect that Elder Pratt was acting on the basis of something like the old Arabic proverb, "The enemy of my enemy is my friend." Protestant despisers of the Latter-day Saints in his day loved to compare Mormonism to allegedly pagan and sensual (i.e. polygamous) Islam. They also liked to compare the two "false prophets," Muhammad and Joseph Smith. In response, certain Latter-day Saints seem to have felt that, if their "Christian" enemies hated Muhammad and Islam, well then, neither Muhammad nor Islam could be all that bad. They were right, of course, that Muhammad and Islam are not altogether evil, which was a fairly revolutionary thought for nineteenth-century Americans. But they went too far. The Muslim doctrine of God is far different from that held by the Latter-day Saints. And Arab Muslim armies—particularly after the death of the Prophet—often fought offensively as well as defensively.

91. Pronounced roughly "Oth-*maan*."

661 A.D. The Shiites look back to the days of Ali as their golden age. But the Sunnis, too, look back to roughly this period as the time when sincere, believing Muslims ruled over a vast empire. For them, the period from 632 to 661 A.D., the time of Abu Bakr, Umar, Uthman, and Ali, is the age of the four "rightly guided caliphs." It was followed by a period of relative darkness. Each faction of Islam, both Sunni and Shiite, began to dream of a return to the heady days of the seventh century, when a prophet walked the earth and when his successors conquered much of the known world and reached a pinnacle of wealth that the Arabs had never before known. But that time still has not returned.

Dominion over the Arab empire now came into the hands of a family known as the Umayyads, descendants of the very leaders of Quraysh who had opposed Muhammad during the Prophet's lifetime. Now it was not only the Shiites who felt alienated from power, but the pious Sunnis as well. The Shiites felt that alienation more intensely, no doubt, because, as a group deeply resentful of the ruling authorities, they came in for special attention from the government. And their leaders, the descendants of Muhammad and Ali, were an especially visible set of rivals to the throne whom the Umayyads kept special watch on and occasionally murdered.

History, however, is not the main focus here, so we must let many of the details pass. Now, it is necessary to look more closely at the nature of the new religion, Islam.

The words of the Qur'an do much more than merely guide, comfort, and instruct the world's Muslims. As here, on the Dome of the Rock, they are an important element of architectural decoration.

Islam and the Qur'an

Muslims believe that the Qur'an as they have it today is an actual transcript from a heavenly volume known as the "Preserved Tablet," or the "Mother of the Book."[1] They believe that Muhammad did not write it and that it contains no admixture of his own personality or individual idiosyncrasies. He was merely the pipeline, as it were, the conduit through whom God's revelation came. Given such an understanding, we are not surprised to learn that, for virtually all Muslims, the Qur'an is considered flawless. It is the actual, literal word of God. There can be no possibility of error in it.[2] It contains the whole and absolute truth about God and about what mankind must do to be saved.

Holding this high view of their scripture, Muslims see even the physical book itself as holy, for it holds the word of God. (One of my copies of the Qur'an, which I had bound in leather while I was

---

1. 43:1-3; 85:22; 3:7; 13:39; 43:4. The idea of a celestial record, containing information on both past and future, is a very ancient Near Eastern notion and is probably reflected in the book that Lehi saw (1 Nephi 1:8-15) as well as in the books seen by John the Revelator in his visions (Revelation 5:1-4: 20:12; compare Malachi 3:16). The ninety-seventh *sura* of the Qur'an declares that the book was revealed on the "Night of Qadr," which resembles ancient (Babylonian) ideas of a night on which the gods came down to the lowest heaven and disclosed their will and the events of the coming year to specially selected listeners. Later Muslim theologians, believing that God is unchanging and that his speech must therefore be similarly eternal and unchanging, argued that the Qur'an is uncreated and co-existent with God himself.

2. 39:28.

living in Cairo, bears on its spine the Arabic inscription, "Let none touch it but the pure.") Many Muslims are horrified, therefore, when they see a Latter-day Saint sit down in a classroom and place the Bible or the Book of Mormon on the floor under his chair. If Mormons really took their scriptures to be what they claim them to be, these observers reason, they would not treat them with such disrespect.

The Qur'an is Muhammad's miracle, the major proof of his prophethood. Its creation was utterly beyond his human ability. For devout Muslims, the sacred book is pure beauty. It is art—although not only art, and certainly not "art for art's sake." Quotations from it are engraved on plates, carved into the walls of buildings, lovingly inscribed on parchment in elaborate and beautiful calligraphy. Muslims love to hear the Qur'an chanted, and it moves them deeply. Qur'anic recitation begins and ends the broadcast day on Arabic television and radio and forms a major element of Muslim funerals. There are complex rules for such recitation, and those whose mastery of the rules and whose native talent makes them exceptional reciters actually become popular "stars" in Islamic society. But the Qur'an is also ritual. It is the substance of prayer, and its verses are recited by ordinary people at every important moment of their lives.

This Muslim emphasis on the words and style of the Arabic Qur'an was vividly illustrated for me once on a trip to Cyprus. That island, of course, is divided between Christian Greeks and Muslim Turks. I found myself, one day, driving with others in the Turkish part of the island. It occurred to me that I ought to buy a Turkish translation of the Qur'an while I was there and use it to try to improve my understanding of that language. So I went into a small village bookstore that seemed likely and, after a while, emerged with what I thought was a Turkish Qur'an. I climbed into the car and, as we drove away, began to leaf through the book. I was amazed at how much I could understand. Although it was in Roman letters (the alphabet that modern Turkish uses) it contained an astonishing number of Arabic words. In fact, once I got used to seeing them in my own alphabet, I realized that every single word in the book was

Arabic! What on earth? I thought. For a few seconds, I was a bit upset. I had asked for a Turkish Qur'an, but had ended up only with a bizarre version of the familiar Arabic original. Then I realized that this was actually something quite important. This was the Arabic Qur'an put into letters that a Turkish Muslim could read to enable him to recite the Qur'an in its original language with something like the accurate sounds. He probably wouldn't understand much of it, because if he knew Arabic he would be able to read it in the Arabic alphabet. (We would never produce such a volume in Mormonism. Can you imagine a Chinese transliteration of the Book of Mormon? Not a *translation*, mind you, but simply a rendering of the English sounds into Chinese characters so that uncomprehending members of the Church in Taiwan and Hong Kong could sound out English phrases like "I, Nephi, having been born of goodly parents"? It's inconceivable.)

Muslims are virtually unanimous in insisting that the Qur'an cannot be translated. One devout English convert to Islam, a man with the improbable name of Mohammed Marmaduke Pickthall, put it this way in the foreword to his translation of the Muslims' holy book:

> The Koran cannot be translated. That is the belief of old-fashioned Sheykhs and the view of the present writer. The Book is here rendered almost literally and every effort has been made to choose befitting language. But the result is not the Glorious Koran, that inimitable symphony, the very sounds of which move men to tears and ecstasy. It is only an attempt to present the meaning of the Koran—and peradventure something of the charm—in English. It can never take the place of the Koran in Arabic, nor was it meant to do so.[3]

It was on the basis of such reasoning that Pickthall chose to call his translation, not "The Koran," but *The Meaning of the Glorious*

---

3. Mohammed Marmaduke Pickthall, translator, *The Meaning of the Glorious Koran* (New York: New American Library, n.d.), vii. Some of my own observations on the literary quality of the Qur'an appear in my "Editor's Introduction: By What Measure Shall We Mete?" in *Review of Books on the Book of Mormon* 2 (1990): vii-xxvi.

Koran. Other translators, such as the illustrious A. J. Arberry, have shown similar modesty in denying that what they have produced in English is actually the Qur'an. (Arberry's version is *The Koran Interpreted*.) Instead, what they have given us, they say, is merely the basic meaning of the text. The intoxicating magic of the book's language, its "poetry," its powerful emotional impact, cannot be conveyed across the language frontier. In the Muslim view, there is saving value in reciting the actual words of God, spoken to Muhammad. And those words were in Arabic, not in English or Turkish or any other language. That is why a Turkish Muslim might value the book I found as a way of entering into the language of God himself, where meaning is only a fraction of the divine power.

But there is a deeper theological reason for the claim that the Qur'an cannot truly be translated, that what results from the process of translation is something related to the Qur'an but cannot properly be said to be identical with it. I have said that Muslims believe the Qur'an to be the word of God. We hear such a phrase—"the word of God"—and think we know what it means. But Muslims take the phrase more literally than even the most conservative Protestant does. Many Protestants will say that the Bible is the inerrant word of God. But they do not mean to deny by that claim that the personality of Paul is visible in his letters, or that Isaiah and Ezekiel can be distinguished. God, they will say, inspired Matthew to write his gospel, but did not obliterate his personality in the process. So it is not surprising, in their view, to discover that Matthew takes a different approach, and manifests a different style and personality, than does, say, the gospel of John. This, however, is not the Muslim view of the Qur'an. There is, according to Muslims, no trace of Muhammad's personality or environment in the scripture that was revealed through him. He was the transmitter, nothing more.

This explains one of the reasons why the Qur'an cannot be considered equivalent to the Bible or the Book of Mormon. It is not a contemporary history of the ministry of Muhammad, it contains no biography of Muhammad, and nowhere in the book does

Muhammad speak. This is very different from the Book of Mormon and the Bible, in which inspired prophets chronicle the events of their days, pointing out the lessons that we should learn. Direct revelations are included in both volumes, of course, but they jostle with histories, poems, sermons, proverbs, and numerous other literary forms. In the Qur'an, by contrast, there is only the imperious voice of God. I myself prefer to compare the Qur'an—if I must compare it to anything in our own more familiar experience—to the Doctrine and Covenants. Like the sections of the Doctrine and Covenants, the 114 *suras* of the Qur'an are arranged in roughly chronological order. (With a twist, however. The Qur'anic revelations are placed in reverse order, so that, excepting the opening chapter, the earliest of them are at the back of the book.)[4]

I shall now proceed to examine some of the teachings of the Qur'an in detail.

Dispensations

The Qur'an clearly and repeatedly teaches a dispensational view of the earth's religious history, in which there have been repeated revelations of God's truth and repeated human apostasies from that truth that required it to be restored again. There was a time, it says, when men followed a single religion. But then discord arose.[5] God tried to remedy this situation. Every nation has had a messenger from God who warned it of its sins and attempted to teach it the truth.[6] "Your Lord will not destroy a nation without just cause and due warning."[7] Thus, the ancient ruins that dot the Near East are regarded by the Qur'an as symbols of the justice of God and as warnings against neglecting the message of his prophets:

> How many a city We have destroyed that flourished in insolent ease! Those are their dwelling-places, undwelt in after them,

---

[4] Length seems to have been the real organizing principle in the case of the Qur'an. The later revelations are longer than the earlier ones, and the chapters are arranged in order of decreasing length.

[5] 10:19.

[6] 10:47; compare 16:36; 17:13–14; 26:208–9; 35:24.

[7] 6:131.

> except a little; Ourselves are the inheritors. Yet thy Lord never destroyed the cities until He sent in their mother-city a Messenger, to recite Our signs unto them; and We never destroyed the cities, save that their inhabitants were evildoers.[8]

"Every age has its scripture," the Qur'an informs Muhammad.[9] "We have sent forth other Messengers before you; of some you have already heard, of others We have told you nothing."[10] Specifically listed with the Qur'an itself among the revelations of God to mankind are the Torah and the gospel.[11]

The Torah was "a guide and a mercy" to mankind when it was revealed.[12] It continues to have religious value even today:

> There is guidance, and there is light, in the Torah which We have revealed. By it the prophets who surrendered themselves [*aslamu*] to God judged the Jews, and so did the rabbis and the divines; they gave judgement according to God's scriptures which had been committed to their keeping and to which they themselves were witnesses.[13]

Yet the Jews themselves, in the view of the Qur'an, have proven unworthy of the blessing that was entrusted to them. "Those to whom the burden of the Torah was entrusted and yet refused to bear it are like a donkey laden with books" that he does not understand.[14] The Jews broke the covenant of Sinai, denied God's revelations, and killed His prophets unjustly.[15] Because they broke their covenant, God cursed them and hardened their hearts. "They have perverted the words of the Scriptures and forgotten much of what they were enjoined."[16]

---

8. 28:58-59 (Arberry); compare 30:9; 35:44; 40:21-22, 82-83; 54:51.
9. 13:38.
10. 40:78.
11. 9:111.
12. 46:12.
13. 5:44.
14. 62:5.
15. 3:187; 4:155; 5:12-13.
16. 5:13. Compare 2 Nephi 10:3-6 and many other passages in the Book of Mormon and the New Testament. The supposed "anti-Semitism" of the Qur'an is much like that of Jesus in the gospels.

> After those prophets We sent forth Jesus, the son of Mary, confirming the Torah already revealed, and gave him the gospel, in which there is guidance and light, corroborating that which was revealed before it in the Torah, a guide and an admonition to the righteous.[17]

Jesus came as a messenger to confirm that which had gone before, according to the Qur'an, and to restore to the earth the pure truth that had been lost through sin and rebellion. However, the long-term prospects for his own dispensation were known to be poor, since he also foretold the coming of a messenger whose name would be Ahmad and who would serve as the final restorer of the truth.[18] In fact, Muslims claim, Muhammad—for that is the more common name of Ahmad, built off of the same three-letter Arabic root (*hmd*, connected with the idea of "praise")—was foretold in both the Torah and the gospel.[19]

And, again according to the Qur'an, Christianity did not long remain pure. Monasticism, for instance, was a human invention for which God revealed no authority.[20] "With those who said they were Christians We made a covenant also, but they too have forgotten much of what they were enjoined."[21] Nevertheless, it can be argued that the Qur'an shows a clear preference for Christians over Jews, or, at least, for Christianity over Judaism.[22] The Qur'an expresses admiration for Christianity at several places. God's light is found, it says, in Christian churches,

> in temples God has allowed to be raised up,
> and His Name to be commemorated therein;
> therein glorifying Him, in the mornings and the evenings,
> are men whom neither commerce nor trafficking
> diverts from the remembrance of God
> and to perform the prayer, and to pay the alms.[23]

17. 5:46.
18. 61:6.
19. 7:157.
20. 57:27.
21. 5:14.
22. 5:82-85. This is slightly surprising, since it can be argued that Islam is actually closer theologically to Judaism than to Christianity.
23. 24:36-37.

Still, it was necessary and foreseen that a final messenger would have to be sent to bring the truth to the earth one final time before the consummation of all things. And it was fitting that, as the *hanifs* had begged, this final messenger was sent to a people who had never yet had the privilege of entertaining a messenger of God. Muhammad, as depicted in the Qur'an, is a messenger sent forth "among the gentiles."[24] Yet the Qur'an points out that each messenger that God has sent has spoken only in the language of his own people, so that he might make his message plain to them. The similarity of this principle to the teachings of Joseph Smith is manifest. One might paraphrase it and say without distortion that "these commandments...were given unto [God's] servants in their weakness, after the manner of their language, that they might come to understanding."[25]

> We have sent you forth as a blessing from your Lord to forewarn a nation to whom no Messenger has been sent before, so that they may take heed and may not say, when evil befalls them on account of their misdeeds: "Lord, had You sent us a Messenger, we should have obeyed Your revelations and believed in them."[26]

Muhammad's calling, as had been the case with earlier messengers from God, was simply to warn; he was not responsible for the people's response.[27] This was the same principle that had motivated Paul's farewell speech to the elders of the church at Ephesus centuries before:

> And now, behold, I know that ye all, among whom I have gone preaching the kingdom of God, shall see my face no more. Wherefore I take you to record this day, that I am pure from the blood of all men. For I have not shunned to declare unto you all the counsel of God.[28]

---

24. 62:2. This is Dawood's rendition. The phrase could also be interpreted to mean that Muhammad was sent forth "among the unlettered," or "among the common people." I like Dawood's translation on this point because it discloses a parallel with Joseph Smith.
25. 14:4. Compare Doctrine and Covenants 1:24.
26. 28:47.
27. 88:21-22, etc.
28. Acts 20:25-27.

It was also a principle revealed to Moroni, and it was the subject of Hyrum Smith's reflections just before he met martyrdom with his brother at the hands of a vicious mob.

> And it came to pass that I prayed unto the Lord that he would give unto the Gentiles grace, that they might have charity. And it came to pass that the Lord said unto me: If they have not charity it mattereth not unto thee, thou hast been faithful; wherefore thy garments shall be made clean… And now I [Moroni] bid farewell unto the Gentiles; yea, and also unto my brethren whom I love, until we shall meet before the judgment-seat of Christ, where all men shall know that my garments are not spotted with your blood.[29]

Muhammad was directed to announce to the people of Arabia that "Truth has come. Falsehood has vanished and shall return no more."[30] This was the last dispensation. There would never be another complete apostasy, and no complete restoration would ever be required again. Muhammad, thus, was the "seal of the prophets."[31]

Yet the Qur'an does not bring any new truths. It does not claim to do so. It is merely a restoration of those truths that had been revealed from the beginning. It carries forward what was written in the books of Abraham and Moses, confirming the earlier scriptures and particularly the Torah and the gospel.[32] "Nothing is said to you," Muhammad is told, "that has not been said to other Messengers before you."[33] In fact, the Qur'an addresses the heirs of the former prophets, the Jews and Christians of Muhammad's day, directly: "People of the Book! Our Messenger has come to reveal to you Our will after an interval during which there were no Messengers, lest you should say: 'No one has come to give us good news or

---

29. Doctrine and Covenants 135:5. Perhaps the most eloquent statement of this principle is to be found at Ezekiel 33:1–9, 11.
30. 34:49. Dawood's translation here is a bit loose, perhaps, but I like it.
31. 33:40.
32. 2:91; 3:3; 4:47; 5:48; 6:92; 10:37; 12:111, 35:31; 46:12, 30. For the books of Abraham and Moses, see 87:18–19.
33. 41:43.

to warn us.' Now a prophet has come to give you good news and to warn you."[34]

When the Christians and the Jews rejected Muhammad's prophethood, the Qur'an announced that it was a restoration of the faith of Abraham, who was an "excellent example" for the believers.[35] "Follow the religion of Abraham!" it told them.[36] Thus, the religion of Islam is seen to be the true religion of God, the religion revealed to Abraham before human invention and rebelliousness gave rise to the historical deviations known as Judaism and Christianity. "Abraham was neither Jew nor Christian. He was an upright man [*hanif*], one who had surrendered himself [*muslim*] to God. He was no idolater."[37] Why should Muhammad or his followers give up the pure truth that had come to them from heaven in exchange for muddy and impure traditions of men that only vaguely and distantly recall their divine origin?

> Who but a foolish man would renounce the faith of Abraham? We chose him in this world, and in the world to come he shall dwell among the righteous. When his Lord said to him: 'Submit [*aslim*],' he answered: "I have submitted [*aslamtu*] to the Lord of the Creation."[38]

Abraham had, says the Qur'an, prayed for the coming of Muhammad.[39] Thus, the Qur'an gives Muhammad a place in the long and distinguished line of Semitic prophets.

> We have revealed Our will to you as We revealed it to Noah and to the prophets who came after him, as We revealed it to Abraham, Ishmael, Isaac, Jacob, and the tribes; to Jesus, Job, Jonah, Aaron, Solomon and David, to whom We gave the Psalms. Of some Messengers We have already told you (how God spoke directly to Moses); but there are others of whom We have not yet

---

34. 5:19.
35. 60:4; compare 3:95.
36. 3:95.
37. 3:67. The last phrase of this quotation may possibly be a veiled criticism of the Christians of the day, with their Trinity and their icons.
38. 2:130-31.
39. 2:129.

> spoken: Messengers who brought good news to mankind and admonished them, so that they might have no plea against God after their coming.[40]

Muhammad may be the last of the prophets, in Muslim belief, but he was certainly not the first. Thus, fragments of God's truth remain scattered about the world, owing to the earlier ministries of divinely-sent messengers. Judaism and Christianity are included in this view. Because, although they are encrusted with heresies and innovations, Judaism and Christianity are essentially divine, adherents of the two faiths are given a divine assurance of salvation if only they will remain faithful to the fundamental truths of their religions:

> There are among the People of the Book some upright men who all night long recite the revelations of God and worship Him; who believe in God and the Last Day; who enjoin justice and forbid evil and vie with each other in good works. These are righteous men; whatever good they do, its reward shall not be denied them. God knows the righteous.[41]

Believers—Jews, Christians, and Sabaeans, whoever believes in God and the Last Day and does what is right—shall be rewarded by their Lord, says the Qur'an. They have nothing to fear or to regret.[42]

The Last Day

As we saw in the last chapter, one of the major themes of the Qur'an is the Day of Judgment, when the Lord will come with his angels.[43] On that day, which will be announced by a trumpet, there will be a new heaven and a new earth. In terms that are similar to those of the Bible, the Qur'an says that great earthquakes will accompany that terrible day. Even the mountains, the most solid thing in the physical world to ancient peoples, will be in motion, which will

---

40. 4:163-65.
41. 3:113-15.
42. 2:62; compare 2:112; 5:69; 22:17.
43. 89:22. The very notion that the Lord can "come," that he can change location, is just one of many ideas in the Qur'an that point to an originally anthropomorphic view of God—a view that attributed bodily form to him—within Islam.

contribute to a general sense of unease, even seasickness, among the people. The sky will split open, heaven will be "stripped off," rolled up like a parchment scroll. The sun will cease to shine, the stars will be scattered and fall down upon the earth. The oceans will boil over. The graves will be opened up, with the earth bringing forth its burdens—the hidden sins, the lost stories, the dead. Men will vainly seek to flee from God's wrath.[44]

The unbeliever will cry out, "O would that I were dust!"[45] Nevertheless, there will be no escaping from the just and accurate accounting of God. For one thing, men will be witnesses against themselves.[46] "We shall be brought to stand before God," Amulek taught, "knowing even as we know now, and have a bright recollection of all our guilt."[47] The Qur'an agrees, declaring that, at that great Day of Judgment, "a soul shall know its works; the former and the latter."[48] Even the earth will testify at the trial.[49] Most fatal for the sinner is that God and his angels have been watching over us. Although men deny the Final Judgment, the Qur'an informs them, "there are over you watchers noble, writers who know whatever you do."[50] God cannot be deceived because He is nearer to each individual human being than that person's own jugular vein.[51] "Your Lord," says the Qur'an, "has knowledge of what they hide in their bosoms and what they say aloud. There is no secret in heaven or earth but is recorded in His glorious book."[52]

> We are the witnesses of all your thoughts and all your prayers and all your actions. Not an atom's weight in earth or heaven escapes your Lord, nor is there any object smaller or greater, but is recorded in a glorious book.[53]

---

44. 14:48; 21:104; 39:68; 75:7-15; 81:1-14; 82:1-4; 99:1-2; 100:9-11.
45. 78:40; 4:42. Compare Revelation 6:15-17.
46. 75:14; compare 17:13-14.
47. Alma 11:43.
48. 82:5; compare 89:23.
49. 99:4-5. For a parallel notion of the earth as a conscious, articulate creature, aware of the sins of humankind, see Moses 7:48-49.
50. 82:9-12 (Arberry).
51. 50:16; compare 56:85; 58:7.
52. 27:74-75; compare 18:49.
53. 10:61; compare 17:13-14; 45:28-29; 54:52-53.

> The records of men's deeds will be opened up.[54]

> Upon that day men shall issue in scatterings to see their works,
> and whoso has done an atom's weight of good shall see it,
> and whoso has done an atom's weight of evil shall see it.[55]

"Woe on that day to the disbelievers!" the Qur'an declares. "When they are bidden to kneel down, they do not kneel."[56] But at the last day, every knee shall bow and every tongue confess its sins. "All who dwell in the heavens and on earth shall prostrate themselves before God, some willingly and some by force."[57] "You shall see all the nations on their knees."[58]

The souls of men and women will be judged on the basis of their works.[59] God will not wrong anybody; if wrong is done by anybody, it will be done by oneself. "He that commits sin, commits it against his own soul."[60] Repentance is possible, but the Qur'an does not approve of death-bed repentance, delayed until sin has been savored to its last drop.[61] If their works have been evil and they have not repented, the souls of human beings will receive a terrible punishment. "On that day you shall see the guilty bound with chains, their garments blackened with pitch, and their heads covered with flames."[62] The sinner on that day would gladly sacrifice his children, his wife, his brother, his kinsmen who have given him shelter, even all the people of the earth—if only this might deliver him. But it will not.[63]

Nevertheless, there is divine grace in Islam, which God will bestow upon those who have sought to know Him and to carry out

---

54. 81:10.
55. 99:6–8 (Arberry); compare 21:47.
56. 77:47–48.
57. 13:15.
58. 45:28.
59. 14:51.
60. 4:111; compare 10:44; 11:101; 16:33; 29:40; 43:76. Also, compare the Book of Mormon's Ether 10:11, where we find the striking description of Morianton as a king who "did do justice unto the people, but not unto himself."
61. 4:17–18; 8:38.
62. 14:49–50.
63. 10:54; 70:11–18.

His will. "God will do away with their foulest deeds and reward them according to their noblest actions."[64] How will individual people be notified of the fate that will be theirs? According to the Qur'an, each soul will be handed his or her "book," containing an accurate record of the deeds done in the flesh. If the book is placed in the soul's right hand, it may know that it will enjoy eternal bliss in paradise. If, however, the book is placed in the left hand, it will be a sure sign that, in the just verdict of God, that particular soul's deeds merit damnation.[65]

The Qur'an does not predict a specific time for the Day of Judgment. "They question you about the Hour of Doom," it tells Muhammad. "When will it come? How are you to know? Your Lord alone knows when it will come. Your duty is but to warn those that fear it."[66] The fact that mankind has been supplied no specific time and does not know the Lord's timetable cannot justify the common assumption that the dreaded hour will not come. Nor, for that matter, should people complacently assume that it is far away: "They think the Day of Judgement is far off: but We see it near at hand."[67]

> Your hearts are taken up with worldly gain from the cradle to the grave. But you shall know. You shall before long come to know. Indeed, if you knew the truth with certainty, you would see the fire of Hell: you would see it with your very eyes. Then, on that day, you shall be questioned about comfort.[68]

Hell

The ultimate destination of the damned is described in the Qur'an with highly picturesque language. Hell is a place of raging and roaring fire, of towering columns of destroying flame, and of scorching winds that drive pitch-black smoke across a blighted landscape. The souls of the unrighteous are prevented from escaping by fetters

64. 39:35.
65. 69:18-29.
66. 79:42-45 (Arberry); compare 7:187; 67:25-26.
67. 70:6-7.
68. This is the entire text of the 102nd chapter of the Qur'an and a good example of the conciseness of the chapters revealed at Mecca.

(hammered out of the very wealth that they lusted after on earth) that bind them to their place of punishment. Still subject to hunger and thirst, they are offered only food that chokes—including a horrific fruit that is said to look like devils' heads—and a drink as hot as molten brass. "Yet you shall drink it as the thirsty camel drinks."[69] The unrighteous rich are singled out for special mention.

> Proclaim a woeful punishment to those that hoard up gold and silver and do not spend it in God's cause. The day will surely come when their treasures shall be heated in the fire of Hell, and their foreheads, sides, and backs branded with them. Their tormentors will say to them: "These are the riches which you hoarded. Taste then the punishment which is your due."[70]

However, it is not only the miserly who have reason to fear. None of the unrighteous will have an easy or pleasant time in the Qur'anic hell. The situation of the sinful soul will be desperate there, yet there is no hope. Of the sinner, the Qur'an says that "death comes upon him from every side, yet he cannot die."[71] (One thinks of the inscription over the gate of hell in Dante's *Inferno*, written in early fourteenth-century Italy: "Abandon all hope, ye who enter here.")[72] "Those that deny Our revelations We will burn in Hell-fire," God is quoted as saying. "No sooner will their skins be consumed than We shall give them other skins, so that they may truly taste Our scourge."[73]

Paradise

Even more detailed than the Qur'an's portrayal of hell is its depiction of paradise. It is a picture that has inspired much derision among Westerners—most of it quite ignorant and beside the point.

---

69. Representative passages concerning Hell include 3:180; 14:16-17; 18:29; 25:12; 37:62-74; 38:55-59; 44:43-50; 56:41-56; 73:12-13; 104:4-9.
70. 9:34-35.
71. 14:17.
72. Dante, *Inferno*, Canto III, line 9: *Lasciate ogne speranza, voi ch'entrate.*
73. 4:56. The Christian Dante assigns a similar punishment to thieves, at Canto XXIV, lines 97-105, of his *Inferno*. Compare the fate of the sowers of schism and discord—among whom Dante unfairly places Muhammad—at Canto XXVIII.

The Qur'anic paradise is a garden, a place of darkest green, filled with palms and pomegranates and running streams. A shady region "as vast as heaven and earth," it suffers from neither scorching heat nor biting cold. It is a very different place from the hell sketched above.

The saved are radiant. They recline on couches, clothed in garments of fine green silk and rich brocade, with bracelets of silver and gold on their arms. Luscious fruit hangs in clusters above and about them, and beneath them rich carpets are spread. Their lofty mansions provide them a view of the sufferings of the damned in hell, far below them. No idle talk is heard in paradise, but rather reflections upon the goodness of God and upon their lives and the lives of the damned in mortality. Meanwhile, their attendants, young boys whose beauty resembles that of scattered pearls, scurry about with vessels of silver and gold and goblets of crystal, serving to the righteous pure drink from a paradisiacal fountain, a pure wine that neither intoxicates nor gives a hangover.[74]

No aspect of the Qur'anic paradise has brought more leering comment than the so-called *houris*.[75] According to the Qur'an, these are maidens of bashful glance, dark-eyed and full-breasted. Their beauty resembles that of rubies and corals. Untouched by men, pure, cloistered in the pavilions of paradise where they remain "chaste like hidden pearls" or like "the sheltered eggs of ostriches," they await the arrival of the blessed to the mansions prepared for them.[76] Are they fully human? Where do they come from? Are they righteous, believing women from the earth? The Qur'an does not say. But one of the great gifts bestowed by paradise upon the righteous is that God will marry them to these dark-eyed *houris*.[77]

This aspect of the Qur'anic paradise has, as I say, received much mockery in the West, and such criticism has often put educated

---

[74] Representative texts on the Qur'anic paradise include 2:25; 3:15, 133-36; 4:57; 13:35; 18:31; 19:62; 22:23; 29:58; 37:40-61; 43:70-73; 44:51-57; 52:17-28; 55:46-77; 56:15-38; 57:21; 76:5-6, 11-22; 77:41-44; 78:31-36; 83:22-28; 88:8-16; 98:7-8.

[75] The singular, *houri*, is pronounced something like "*hoo*-ree."

[76] On them, see 2:25; 3:15; 4:57; 37:48-49; 38:52; 55:56, 58, 70, 72, 74; 56:22-23, 35-38; 78:33.

[77] 2:25; 3:15; 4:57; 44:54; 52:20.

Muslims on the defensive. Today and almost since the rise of Islam, there have been claims that these very tangible and material blessings are meant metaphorically. The point, according to many defenders of the Qur'an, is to illustrate even to simple believers that paradise contains "whatever the souls desire, and the eyes delight in."[78] The metaphor should not, they insist, be taken as literal fact. Moreover, all these material symbols of the joy awaiting the righteous fail to convey adequately what bliss is really there. "No mortal knows," the Qur'an declares, "what bliss is in store for [the righteous] as a reward for their labours."[79] The real blessing of paradise, say the nonliteralists, is the blessing next to which all the trees and streams and nonintoxicating wines and *houris* dwindle into insignificance. In that place "the righteous shall dwell in gardens where rivers flow, honourably seated in the presence of a Mighty King."[80] Being in the presence of God himself is the crown of all paradisiacal blessings. But one cannot leave the Qur'an's very literal-sounding and graphic description of paradise without noting that Syriac Christian writings of a few centuries earlier contain almost precisely identical elements.

Righteous Behavior

It is on the basis of his or her faith and good works, the Qur'an explains, that the fate of the individual soul is determined.[81] We are assured that life and death were created in order to test us: "We try you with evil and good for a testing, then unto Us you shall be returned."[82] This test is fairly and carefully constructed, and every man and woman has the capacity to pass it. No soul is asked to do

---

78. 43:71.

79. 32:17. Compare the similar claim made by the Apostle Paul at 1 Corinthians 2:9. Paul's own words show up in later Islamic tradition as a statement made by the Prophet Muhammad.

80. 54:54-55. Even here, the plain meaning of the Qur'anic text suggests the possibility of literally being in the presence of a God who has spatial location. Actually, though, the Qur'an contains verses which can easily be used against an anthropomorphic view of deity. For example, it says, "Nothing can be compared with Him." (42:11.) The real question is how such verses are to be received.

81. 2:82, 277; 5:9; 7:42; 11:23; 14:23, 22:23; 29:7, 9; 30:15; 31:8; 40:40; 41:8; 47:2; 103:3.

82. 21:35 (Arberry); compare 18:7; 67:2.

more than it is able to do, none is burdened with more than it can bear.[83]

> Then he whose deeds weigh heavy in the Balance
> shall inherit a pleasing life,
> but he whose deeds weigh light in the Balance
> shall plunge in the womb of the Pit.[84]

But this is all generality. What specific kinds of behavior are required in order to reside in paradise rather than hell? Many in the West think that the religion of Islam praises as virtuous behavior a wide range of acts which we would consider bizarre and, at worst, positively evil. Some who really should know better have declared, for instance, that Islam praises the murder of Christians or advocates the mistreatment of women. This is simply not the case.

Elder George A. Smith said of Muhammad that "there was nothing in his religion to license iniquity or corruption; he preached the moral doctrines which the Savior taught; viz., to do as they would be done by; and not to do violence to any man, nor to render evil for evil; and to worship one God."[85] Elder Parley P. Pratt agreed:

> Though Mahometan institutions are corrupt enough, and need reforming by the gospel, I am inclined to think, upon the whole, leaving out the corruptions of men in high places among them, that they have better morals and better institutions than many Christian nations; and in many localities there have been high standards of morals.[86]

True, the sacred book of Islam does sanction cutting off the hands of thieves and teaches that those who die while fighting for God are saved in paradise.[87] But the behavior commended by the

---

83. 2:286; 7:42; 23:62. Compare the assurances given at 1 Corinthians 10:13; Phillipians 4:13; 1 Nephi 3:7.
84. 101:6-9 (Arberry); compare 7:8-9; 21:47; 23:102-3.
85. *Journal of Discourses* 3:31.
86. *Journal of Discourses* 3:41.
87. 5:38; 47:4-6.

Qur'an is the basic morality also taught by the Bible. For example: Men and women should show kindness to their parents.[88] They should be modest in dress, humble, pious, sincere, and steadfast in prayer.[89] They should keep any promises they make and should never bear false witness. "Speak for justice," the Qur'an advises, "even if it affects your own kinsmen."[90] Hypocrisy and hypocrites are criticized throughout the Qur'an.[91] Drinking and gambling are prohibited.[92] The Qur'an's proscription of usury, the lending of money at interest, has given rise to an entire Islamic banking industry which attempts to function profitably on the basis of principles quite different from those underlying financial institutions in the West.[93]

Muslims should be just, but should soften that justice with kindness and with generosity to the needy and the dispossessed and, above all, to their kinfolk. The Qur'an commends such actions as

> The freeing of a slave,
> or giving food upon a day of hunger
> to an orphan near of kin
> or a needy man in misery.[94]

Certainly, people should not commit adultery, nor murder, but should restrain their appetites and passions. (According to the Qur'an the unrighteous have made their appetites into gods.)[95] Fasting is a specific instance of how the human soul could learn to control the appetites of its physical body. Fortitude and patience in adversity and trial are highly esteemed virtues in the Qur'an, essentially as they were in pre-Islamic Arabia. "Do not swear," the Qur'an

88. 6:151; 17:23-24; 29:8; 31:14; 46:15. Representative general texts on Qur'anic morality and ethics include 2:1-5; 3:133-136; 6:151; 9:112; 13:19-24; 16:90-91; 17:32-33; 23:1-11, 57-61; 25:63-76; 27:62; 31:18-19; 33:35; 52:15-19; 70:22-35.
89. 24:30-31.
90. 6:152.
91. 61:2-3.
92. 2:219; 5:90-91.
93. See 2:275-76; 3:130.
94. 90:13-18 (Arberry).
95. 25:42.

advises believers. "Honourable obedience is sufficient."[96] Crowning these practical virtues are what might be called theological virtues: The truly righteous will hold to a monotheistic belief in God, the Last Day, the angels, and the scriptures and the prophets. They will worship no other god but the one true God and will believe in and fear the just judgment of God at the end of time.

In some respects, the detailed rules of the Qur'an seem reminiscent of the laws of Judaism. For example, carrion, blood, and the flesh of swine are forbidden to Muslims by the Qur'an, as is the flesh of strangled, beaten, or gored animals and the meat of animals killed by predators or by a fall. This prohibition extends as well to flesh dedicated to other gods and to meat that has been sacrificed to idols.[97] Believers are told by the Qur'an to eat only of meat that has been consecrated in the name of God.[98] The fact that these dietary rules are similar to those of the Jews was not unknown to the Muslims, for the Qur'an itself links the two, saying only that Jewish rules are stricter because the Jews were unrighteous and were therefore punished by God with a more rigid dietary code.[99] But it is not only in matters of food that Islam seems to echo Jewish regulations. In another note reminiscent of Old Testament legislation, the Qur'an lays out forbidden degrees of kinship in marriage.[100]

The sins that are likely to characterize the wealthy in a commercial society come in for particular attention. For instance, believers are told to give just weight and full measure in their market and trade exchanges.[101] The Qur'an shows special solicitude for the treatment of orphans. Its admonitions resemble the principle in the epistle of James, that "pure religion and undefiled before God and the Father is this, to visit the fatherless and widows in their affliction, and to keep himself unspotted from the world."[102]

---

96. 24:53. Compare the words of Jesus at Matthew 5:33-37.
97. 2:173; 5:3; 6:145. Compare the counsel given by the apostles at Acts 15:19-20, 28-29.
98. 6:118, 121.
99. 5:5; 6:146.
100. 4:23.
101. 17:35; 55:9; 83:1-3.
102. James 1:27.

> As for the orphan, do not oppress him, and as for the beggar, scold him not.[103]

> Have you thought of him that denies the Last Judgement? It is he who turns away the orphan and does not urge others to feed the poor.[104]

The damned in hell, says the Qur'an, will be asked why they are there, and they will reply: "We never prayed or fed the hungry."[105] But kindness to the poor is not enough by itself, either. Wastefulness and extravagant living are condemned.[106]

Knowing its audience, the Qur'an once again slips into the merchant language of Mecca in order to make its point: If you make a good loan to God, it says, he will multiply it for you. Righteous living, in other words, is a good bargain; it shows sound business sense.[107] Those who "prefer the present life over the world to come"[108] are simply foolish. They are shortsighted. After all, it is the life to come that is the real life—not this one.[109] God says in the Qur'an that human existence here upon this earth is "as water that We send down out of heaven, and the plants of the earth mingle with it; and in the morning it is straw the winds scatter."[110] It passes away and cannot give lasting satisfaction.

> And as for the unbelievers,
> their works are as a mirage in a spacious plain
> which the man athirst supposes to be water,
> till, when he comes to it, he finds it is nothing.[111]

Treatment of Women

In terms of their prospects for going to either heaven or hell, men

---

103. 93:9-10; compare 2:177; 4:2-3, 9-10; 6:152; 17:34; 90:15. On the notion of not "scolding" beggars, compare the words of King Benjamin at Mosiah 4:16-22.
104. 107:1-3.
105. 74:43-44.
106. At, for instance, 7:31; 17:26-27; 25:67.
107. 64:17; 57:11, 18.
108. 14:3.
109. 29:64.
110. 18:45 (Arberry); compare 57:20.
111. 24:39 (Arberry). Compare 2 Nephi 27:3; Jeremiah 2:13.

and women are equal in Islam. "All human beings are equal," the Prophet Muhammad taught, "equal as the teeth of a comb. There is no superiority of a white over a black nor of any male over the female." "Men as well as women," declares the Qur'an, "shall be rewarded for their labours."[112] "The believers who do good works, whether men or women, shall enter the gardens of paradise."[113] (It must be noted, however, that there does not seem to be a male equivalent to the paradisiacal *houris*.)

But, it may be objected, whatever its claims with regard to the life to come, Islam plainly discriminates against women in this life. Indeed, one of the most frequently heard complaints against Islam concerns the treatment of women. But one issue needs to be addressed up front. "Islam," as such, does not "treat" women in any way, good or bad. Islam is merely a body of beliefs and practices; it is individual Muslims who behave in good or bad ways. And, just as in the West, there are good and bad Muslims, kind and unkind, fair and unfair. Evil treatment of women such as has been featured in several recent films and best-selling books often seems to have more to do with the pathological character of certain personalities than with the core values of Islam itself. (In one popular movie, for instance, an abusive Muslim husband is shown repeatedly striking his American wife in the face. No doubt many in the audience saw this as just one more indication of the evils of Islam. But hitting one's wife in the face is expressly forbidden by Islamic law.) What is more, cultures inclined to the oppression of women have often twisted and abused Islam—and not only Islam—to justify such behavior, but Islam should not be blamed for this. And certainly Latter-day Saints will understand that the values encouraged or tolerated by one's society and culture are not always those at the heart of one's religion.

As a matter of fact, Islam often treats men and women equally in this world. For instance, adulterers and adulteresses are each given 100 lashes.[114] There is no double standard. Furthermore, the

---

112. 4:32.
113. 4:124.
114. 24:2.

Qur'an makes it difficult to accuse a married woman of adultery—which was a common way of getting rid of a spouse. Those who make false accusations of adultery, or even those who cannot produce four witnesses in order to confirm a charge of adultery, get 80 lashes.[115] We should not forget the context in which the Qur'an came to be: In pre-Islamic Arabia, female infanticide was common. Men could have an unlimited number of wives and could divorce them for any reason whatsoever or for no reason at all. Inheritance always went to adult males, even if the closest surviving relative was a female. Muhammad and the Qur'an abolished female infanticide, permitted women to inherit, required that men pay a dowry to their wives that could not be taken away even by divorce. Men were required to sign prenuptial and marriage contracts which guaranteed certain rights and conditions to their wives. Women were given the right to initiate divorce, and to have final approval on any marriage partner selected by their parents. Widows were granted the right to remarry and were, in fact, encouraged to do so. Muhammad's high opinion of women is reflected in a famous saying ascribed to him: "Paradise," he is reported to have said, "lies at the feet of mothers."

However, we cannot avoid the fact that Islam does make distinctions between men and women. The Qur'an makes one point rather bluntly: "Good women are obedient," it declares.[116] Such language is hardly fashionable in the late twentieth century.[117] And there is more. "Women shall with justice have rights similar to those exercised against them, although men have a status above women."[118] Under Islamic rules of inheritance, males inherit twice as much as females do.[119] This apparent inequity is justified, Muslims say, because men need extra income in order to support their families, an obligation that women do not have: "Men have authority

115. 24:4-9.
116. 4:34. It is, perhaps, worth noting that, as I write, the prime ministers of both Turkey and Pakistan are Muslim women.
117. Compare Ephesians 5:22-24.
118. 2:228.
119. Qur'anic inheritance rules are laid out at 4:11-12.

over women because God has made the one superior to the other, and because they [men] spend their wealth to maintain them."[120]

One practice notably denounced in most of the Christian West as an obvious injustice against women is the practice of polygamy (or, more precisely, of polygyny). Although it is probably dying out in most of the Muslim world, the Qur'an does explicitly permit as many as four wives: "You may marry other women who seem good to you: two, three, or four of them. But if you fear that you cannot maintain equality among them, marry one only."[121] It is this last phrase that has led many contemporary Muslims to think that God desired the believers to discontinue the practice. He was not explicit about prohibiting polygamy because He wanted to be gentle to the people and not ask of them something that they were not yet in a position to fulfill. But the Qur'an later observes that "try as you may, you cannot treat all your wives impartially."[122]

Another issue that should be mentioned is that of veiling. Many outside the Muslim world see this as an obvious instance of Muslim oppression of women. But the Qur'an really has very little to say about veils. Mostly, it speaks of female modesty, in terms not so different from those that Latter-day Saints might employ. And not a few Muslim women respond to the claim that they are oppressed by the veil with the insistence that, in fact, they feel precisely the opposite: Modestly dressed and veiled, they say, they are free from the offensive leers and comments of crude males passing by. They are no longer mere sexual objects in a world dominated by and for men.

We should always be careful, it seems to me, not to evaluate other cultures by the (usually uninspired) standard of our own; things may look very different to our neighbors than they appear to us. Western critics of Islam say that Muslim women suffer from rules imposed upon them by males. Most Muslim women believe, rather, that those rules have been given to them by God, and they often resent efforts made to "liberate" them because they do not

120. 4:34.
121. 4:3.
122. 4:129.

want to be liberated from their religion. In this regard, perhaps Latter-day Saints can understand them a bit better than most.

The Five Pillars of Islam

President Spencer W. Kimball used to talk of the thirteen Articles of Faith, encouraging members of the Church to memorize them so that they would have in their minds a simple and orderly outline of some of the basic teachings of the restored gospel. There is nothing in Islam that is precisely comparable to the Articles of Faith. But there exists a list of five essential Islamic practices—the so-called "Five Pillars of Islam"—that can serve for us something of the same purpose. If we know and understand the Five Pillars, we know and understand a fair portion of Islam itself. These five items are (1) the *shahada*, or "profession of faith"; (2) prayer; (3) almsgiving; (4) fasting, especially during the month of Ramadan; and (5) pilgrimage to Mecca. A sixth concept, *jihad*, never found quite the universal acceptance as a "pillar" that it required to formally enter the list. Nonetheless, it remains highly important, and following brief discussions of each of the Five Pillars, I shall have a few words to say about it as well.

The *Shahada*

The *shahada*, or "profession of faith," is a verbal formula that is perhaps familiar to some readers of this book already. In English translation, it goes roughly as follows: "I testify that there is no god but God, and that Muhammad is the messenger of God."[123] This statement is the key to membership in the Islamic community. If a person utters it sincerely, and with real intent, that person becomes a Muslim. No ordinance of baptism is required, no bishop's interview, no ritual of any kind. There is no Islamic priesthood to perform any of these functions.

Some Muslim scholars have argued, with good reason, that the *shahada* contains all the essence of Islam within its brief compass.

---

123. The word *shahada*, which is pronounced "sheh-*hah*-da," literally means "testimony." The Church publishes an Arabic pamphlet entitled "Shahadat Yusuf Smith." (Perhaps readers might surmise the translation of the title.)

They like to break it into its two component parts. When the believer says, "I testify that there is no god [*ilah*, 'a god'] but God [Allah, '*the* God']," he affirms his belief in a timeless monotheism. In the second portion of the statement, when he declares that "Muhammad is the messenger of God," he identifies his commitment to a particular community of monotheistic believers from among the several that have existed in the various dispensations of earth's history and commits himself to the particular historical and legal details of that community's life. Since they recognize Jews and Christians as "People of the Book," Muslim jurists allow those two groups their own versions of the *shahada*. A Jew can validly say, "I testify that there is no god but God and that Moses is the messenger of God." A Christian can validly make the same testimony with regard to Jesus.

Prayer

There are essentially two kinds of prayer in Islam. The one with which we in the West are most familiar is, paradoxically, the one most foreign to us. This is the formal prayer known as *salat*.[124] Five times daily—at sunrise, midday, afternoon, evening, and night—pious Muslims prostrate themselves before God, bowing low and touching foreheads to the ground a fixed number of times. A complex set of gestures and motions accompanies the recitation of certain phrases during these prayers, which actually resemble some sort of liturgical worship more than they do the kinds of prayers that Latter-day Saints generally offer. The other kind of prayer is far more spontaneous and lacks the prescribed recitations and motions. It can be offered anywhere and at any time and is quite similar to private Christian prayer.

The liturgical prayers, too, can be performed anywhere, and there is little shyness among Muslims about offering them in public. Male Muslims should, whenever possible, perform the Friday noon prayer in a formal Islamic place of worship known as a "mosque."[125] (Female Muslims may also attend the mosque but are

---

124. The emphasis is on the second syllable: "sa-*lat*."
125. The English word is a corruption of the Arabic *masjid*, meaning "a place of prostration."

not obliged to do so.) In the mosque, worshipers line up in rows behind a man bearing the title of *imam*.[126] Closely following his actions as he prays, they move in impressive unison. They are praying toward Mecca, the holy city of Islam. The direction of that city is marked on the wall by a recessed niche known as a *mihrab*, which is inevitably the most elaborately decorated spot in the mosque. (It is a common misconception among Westerners, by the way, that Muslims pray toward the east. This may derive from the fact that the West is in the west. Thus, any Muslims that we are likely to encounter will tend to pray toward the east. In fact, Muslims pray toward Mecca. Therefore, the direction of their prayer will vary depending upon where they are and the direction of Mecca. If they are south of Mecca, they will pray to the north. Indonesian Muslims pray roughly toward the west.) It is necessary to make ablutions—that is, to wash oneself until one is ritually clean—before prayer, and virtually every mosque will have a fountain for this purpose. Sometimes these ablution fountains are architectural landmarks in their own right; in many modern mosques, on the other hand, they are simple water spigots. If no water is available, sand may be used in its stead.[127]

Remarkably, although the duty of prayer is often mentioned in the Qur'an, that book never specifically mentions a duty of praying formally five times daily. One legend says that Muhammad received the commandment of five daily prayers during his miraculous ascension into heaven from the temple mount at Jerusalem. Originally, so the story goes, the Lord imposed a duty of fifty prayers daily on Muhammad and the Muslims. Then, when Muhammad was descending from the presence of God, he encountered Moses. The Prophet told him of the requirement for fifty prayers a day. Moses was horrified. "Go back to the Lord," he told Muhammad, "and ask for a lower number. Verily, your people will never be able to bear fifty prayers a day. I tried during my lifetime with the children of

---

126. From the Arabic preposition *amama*, meaning "in front of," the word is pronounced "i-*mam*," with the emphasis on the second syllable. In Sunni Islam, the imam is simply a prayer leader in a mosque. Among the Shiites, the term has come to signify the true leader of all Islam—a descendant of Ali—or his stand-in.

127. 4:43; 5:6.

Israel, but they couldn't manage it." So Muhammad went back up to the presence of God and got a reduction to ten prayers a day. This still was too much for Moses, though, and he sent Muhammad back up to gain yet a greater reduction. Finally, Muhammad got the number down to five. "Oh no!" Moses said. "I tried the children of Israel with just five, and they still couldn't handle it. Go back!" This time, Muhammad refused. "I've asked until I'm ashamed," he is supposed to have said, "and I'm too embarrassed to ask again."[128]

Almsgiving

The Qur'an's oft-stated concern for widows, orphans, and the poor is taken very seriously by many Muslims. Islamic governments generally collect a tax, known as *zakaat*, to be distributed among the poor, which is set at two-and-one-half percent of one's annual savings after personal and business expenditures. Additionally, private Muslims are likely to give at least small amounts of money to beggars as they walk down the street. I have learned a great deal by going around Cairo with Near Eastern friends who unhesitatingly place coins in the outstretched hands of poor people on the sidewalks, at the doors of mosques, and in the commuter trains. They are (and I have asked them about this) quite unconcerned with the question of whether the objects of their charity really merit such generosity. The answer to that question, they say, is known only to God. Their duty is to give. It isn't enough simply to have warm feelings toward the poor. (We are speaking here, I should point out, of personal charity. Institutional giving certainly needs to establish criteria by which to distinguish those who deserve assistance from those who, for whatever reason, do not.)

Fasting

Each lunar year, Muslims fast during the entire month of Ramadan—from the rising of the sun until its setting. "Eat and drink," the Qur'an directs, "until you can tell a white thread from a

---

128. The popular tales of Muhammad's heavenly journey are interesting for many reasons—not the least of which is their patently anthropomorphic character. (One goes toward God, and leaves him, and talks to him as if he were a man seated on a throne.)

black one in the light of the coming dawn. Then resume the fast till nightfall."[129] It will be recalled that it was during the month of Ramadan that the Qur'an was revealed to Muhammad. The fast during this month is, at least in part, a commemoration of that most central of all Islamic events, and very pious Muslims frequently make it a practice to read or recite the entire Qur'an during the fast. Ramadan must also be thought of in connection with earlier Jewish and Christian fasting practices. The Qur'an says of it that it was decreed for Muslims as it had been for those who went before.[130] Although the majority of Muslims observe the fast of Ramadan, some are more serious than others. In some cities, people fast during the day and then party all night—thus reducing industrial and office productivity to almost nil during the month. Driving along the banks of the Nile during Ramadan, I have observed hundreds of Muslims waiting on their picnic blankets, knives and forks in hand, peering eagerly at the western horizon for the setting of the sun. (While they are so occupied, it is wonderfully easy to cruise the deserted streets of Cairo and enjoy the empty movie theaters.)

Certain people are exempted from the rigors of the fast, such as those who are ill or pregnant or on a journey. God, the Qur'an points out, is not unreasonable. (One might recall here the exceptions for ablution before prayer when travelling.)

The *Hajj*

It is incumbent upon every Muslim who can afford to do so to make the pilgrimage to "the Ancient House" (the Ka'ba) at Mecca at least once in his or her life.[131] Those who cannot afford to do so or are otherwise unable are exempt from the requirement.

> Make the pilgrimage and visit the Sacred House for His sake. If you cannot, send such offerings as you can afford... Make the pilgrimage in the appointed months. He that intends to perform it in those months must abstain from sexual intercourse,

129. See 2:183-87 for general information on the fast of Ramadan.
130. 22:33.
131. 22:33.

> obscene language, and acrimonious disputes while on pilgrimage... Provide [for] yourselves well: the best provision is piety.[132]

What this means, in practice, is that for a few days each year the population of Mecca swells by tens and hundreds of thousands. Muslims from around the world gather and dress in white to perform the complex multi-day rituals of the *hajj*. In premodern times, this was a remarkable opportunity for Muslims from Morocco to meet and share ideas with Muslims from Indonesia and Kenya. Many a coup was planned there, as well. It is a time of great international solidarity, when Muslims are reminded of the worldwide character of their faith and of the strength of their numbers. (In this regard, it somewhat resembles the annual general conference of the Latter-day Saints.)

Some of the rituals seem to be of astronomical origin. Others commemorate historical events such as the travails of Hagar and Ishmael in the desert. Unfortunately, for many years non-Muslims have been legally prohibited from entering either Mecca or Medina—on pain of death. Nevertheless, the rituals are not secret, and photography is allowed, so non-Muslim scholars in the West actually know a great deal about the *hajj* although we ourselves cannot observe it.[133]

Jihad

The sixth of the five pillars of Islam never quite made it into the authoritative lists, although there were a number of prestigious thinkers who argued that it ought to be included. The word *jihad* is often translated as "holy war," but its meaning is really broader than this.[134] Its primary definition is "battle," "struggle," or "striving." Muhammad is said to have taught that "holy war," of a literal, military kind, was merely the "lesser *jihad*"; the "greater *jihad*," by

---

132. 2:196-97.

133. The intrepid nineteenth-century explorer Sir Richard Francis Burton managed to sneak into Mecca and Medina and to make the pilgrimage. He published a two-volume *Personal Narrative of a Pilgrimage to al-Madinah & Meccah* which is still available in paperback reprint from Dover Books.

134. Pronounced "jee-*had*."

contrast, was warfare or striving against the evil inclinations within one's own soul. Traditionally, Islam has distinguished four distinct kinds of *jihad*: The *jihad* of the tongue is speaking about one's faith, or what we would call doing missionary work. The *jihad* of the hand is putting one's faith into action by good works. The *jihad* of the heart means to make one's faith real as a genuine spiritual force in one's daily life and motivations. Finally, the *jihad* of the sword means to defend one's faith when it comes under attack, which can include verbal apologetics as well as physical self-defense. Some modernizing Muslims argue, I think rather plausibly, that *jihad* in today's world can be any practical action (not mere meditation) aimed at building up Islam and the Muslims. It emphasizes making one's religion real in one's life and in one's society. Thus, for instance, it might involve working to strengthen a Muslim nation's industrial base or education system. In this sense, *jihad* would not be so very different from the Latter-day Saint notion of "building up the kingdom of God," which can include such very this-worldly activities as colonizing, digging irrigation canals, sprucing up a yard or a barn, or working in a welfare cannery.

Nevertheless, "holy war" is what most Westerners who have heard the term will think of in connection with it, and the subject is important enough that it merits some attention on our part. First of all, *jihad* is primarily seen by Muslims as defensive. Although the Qur'an generally advises that we requite evil with good, it does authorize defensive warfare.[135]

> Fight for the sake of God those that fight against you, but do not attack them first.[136]

> Permission to take up arms is hereby given to those who are attacked, because they have been wronged.[137]

Islam has a very realistic view of the issues involved here, a view that does not easily lend itself to the support of pacifism.

---

135. 23:96.
136. 2:190.
137. 22:39.

> Had God not defended some men by the might of others, the monasteries and churches, the synagogues and mosques in which His praise is daily celebrated, would have been utterly destroyed.[138]

The Qur'an does, as common rumor claims, promise paradise to those who fall in *jihad*.

> Do not say that those who were slain in the cause of God are dead; they are alive, although you are not aware of them.[139]

> You must not think that those who were slain in the cause of God are dead, They are alive, and well provided for by their Lord; pleased with His gifts and...rejoicing in God's grace and bounty.[140]

But it should not be concluded from this that Islam is uniquely violent, nor that it favors forced conversions. The latter are, in fact, expressly forbidden by the Qur'an, which teaches that "there shall be no compulsion in religion."[141] Obviously, in a history that covers nearly a millennium and a half, ranging from Soviet Central Asia to Central Africa and from Morocco to Indonesia and beyond, there will be exceptions, but it can be confidently said that Islam's record of religious toleration is considerably better than that of Christianity. Parley Pratt made this case to his audience in 1855:

> History abundantly shows the followers of Mahomet did not take the sword, either to enforce their religion or to defend themselves, until compelled to do so by the persecutions of their enemies, and then it was the only alternative that presented itself, to take up the sword and put down idolatry, and establish the worship of the one God; or, on the other hand, be crushed and cease to be, on account of the idolatrous nations around them; they seemed to act on the defensive, although it might legally be considered aggression.[142]

---

138. 22:40.
139. 2:154.
140. 3:169-71.
141. 2:256.

Islamic law forbids aggression. *Jihad* can only be defensive and may not include the deliberate killing of noncombatants or the torture of prisoners. Even the unnecessary destruction of crops, animals, and homes is banned. I think it can easily be seen, therefore, that many of the things done in the name of Islam have no more to do with the religion preached by Muhammad than certain acts of terrorism in Ireland have to do with Roman Catholic doctrine or the teachings of Jesus.

Similarities

Some readers will already have noticed a number of similarities between the Qur'an and the standard works of The Church of Jesus Christ of Latter-day Saints. And, indeed, there are many. The present section will attempt to point some of them out. In this regard, perhaps the most obvious feature of the Qur'an is the fact that it contains many of the same stories and refers to many of the same historical figures that are familiar to the West from the pages of the Bible.

The Qur'an speaks, for instance, about the fall of Lucifer and the temptation and fall of Adam and Eve.[143] It is familiar with the story of Adam's naming of the animals and the conflict between Cain and Abel.[144] The story of Noah appears more than once.[145] Job is mentioned, as is a figure called Idris, who is universally identified by Muslim commentators with Enoch.[146] Even Jonah is mentioned.[147]

Told often, and in considerable detail, are the stories of Abraham and his nephew Lot, including the miraculous annunciation of Isaac, Abraham's near-sacrifice of his son, and the destruction of Sodom and Gomorrah.[148] The story of Abraham's youthful renunciation of his idolatrous family and people is favored and referred

142. *Journal of Discourses* 3:38.
143. 2:30-39; 7:11-25; 15:26-44; 17:61-65; 20:115-23; 38:71-85.
144. 2:31-33; 5:27-31.
145. As at 10:71-73; 11:25-49.
146. 21:83-84; 19:56-57, with perhaps a hint of his translation. "Idris" is pronounced with a hissing "s," as "Ih-*drees*."
147. 37:139-49; 68:48-50.
148. 11:69-83; 17:50-77; 27:54-58; 29:28-35; 37:99-111, 113-38; 51:24-37; 54:33-40.

to numerous times throughout the Qur'an.[149] The Qur'anic retelling of the story, however, contains a number of interesting details which either do not occur in the Bible or are not emphasized at all. Abraham appears in the Qur'an as a watcher of the skies, much as he does in the third chapter of the book of Abraham. And the prayer for wisdom and righteousness that the Qur'anic Abraham offers seems to parallel his quest as recorded in Abraham 1:2. Some details are even amusing, as in the following dialogue between the patriarch and an unidentified royal idol worshiper:

> Have you not heard of him who argued with Abraham about his Lord because He had bestowed upon him the Kingdom?
>
> Abraham said: "My Lord is He who has power to give life and to cause death."
>
> "I, too," replied the other, "have power to give life and to cause death."
>
> "God brings up the sun from the east," said Abraham. "Bring it up yourself from the west."[150]

A personal favorite of mine, however, is a story to which the Qur'an merely alludes, without telling it all in detail. (This is the usual approach of the Qur'an, which frequently refers to stories that it presumes its audience will be already familiar with. The somewhat elliptical quality of the Qu'ran is the main reason that many Western readers find it so off-putting.) This is the story of Abraham and the idols of his father, with which some Latter-day Saint readers will already be familiar, from the book called Jasher:

Attempting to demonstrate to his father Terah the futility of worshiping idols, Abraham one day went into his father's shrine with a hatchet and hacked all of the gods—except for their chief—to pieces. Then, before leaving the room, he placed the hatchet in the hands of the still-intact chief god. His father, hearing the noise of violent chopping in his private sanctuary, ran and met Abraham at the door. Pushing past his son, Terah went into the shrine. There he found all the idols fallen down and broken, while the chief idol still stood

149. For instance, at 6:74-79; 19:41-50; 21:51-72; 26:70-102; 37:83-98.
150. 2:258.

with the hatchet in its hand. He was furious. Knowing his son's attitude toward idolatry, and having seen his son emerging from the shrine, he naturally demanded to know of Abraham what he had done to the gods of his father. But Abraham denied having anything to do with the destruction of the idols. "No," he said, "it was the chief god who did it, out of jealousy when the other, subordinate gods had tried to beat him to the meat offering." Terah roared with anger. "You are lying!" he told his son. "These gods are just wood and stone. I made them myself." How could they possibly have done anything like what Abraham had described? "Ah," said Abraham, "but that is precisely the point! They are merely wood and stone, which can neither hear nor speak nor act. So why pray to them?"[151]

I have already spoken about the common assumption that the Qur'an identifies the son of Abraham who was nearly sacrificed upon Mount Moriah as Ishmael, rather than the Bible account's Isaac. We have seen, though, that the Qur'an nowhere names the son who came so near to human sacrifice. In fact, the Qur'an has a great respect for Isaac. Of Abraham, the God of the Qur'an says, "We gave him Isaac and Jacob and bestowed on his descendants prophethood and the Scriptures."[152] Clearly, this passage teaches the continuation of the prophetic gift in the Jewish line, through Jacob or Israel. Ishmael appears in the Qur'an and is treated with immense respect as a chosen servant of God and a messenger, but Isaac is described as a prophet.[153]

The entire twelfth chapter of the Qur'an is devoted to a beautiful retelling of the story of Joseph of Egypt. It is the only chapter of the Qur'an that is entirely occupied by a single story.

The story of Moses is one of the more commonly repeated in the Qur'an.[154] Saul, David, and Solomon are also mentioned.[155]

---

151. This story is told at Jasher 11:16-51. See *The Book of Jasher* (Thousand Oaks, CA: Artisan Sales, 1990), 25-27. This translation of the Book of Jasher first appeared in 1840. It was reprinted, at Salt Lake City, in 1887.
152. 29:27; compare 4:54.
153. 19:54-55; 37:112.
154. See, for example, 2:40-71, 246-48; 5:20-26; 7:103-75; 10:75-93; 19:51-53; 20:10-98; 26:10-69; 27:7-14; 28:3-46, 76-82; 40:23-53; 43:46-56; 79:15-26.
155. 2:249-53; 27:15-44; 34:12-14; 38:21-26.

The Qur'an knows the biblical stories of David and Goliath, as well as the parable Nathan tells to David in 2 Samuel 11-12. King David is a great revelator in the Qur'an. "To David We gave the Psalms."[156] Moreover, Solomon appears in the Qur'an not only as a great king of Israel but also as a magician, just as he does in post-biblical Jewish lore. And at one point the Qur'an seems to make Solomon the star of a story which the Bible connects with Gideon instead.[157]

It is not only the stories of the Old Testament or Hebrew Bible that seem to find their counterparts in the Qur'an; the New Testament has Qur'anic parallels as well. A similar parable to that of the ten virgins occurs.[158] The miraculous birth of John the Baptist is alluded to at several points.[159] So, too, is the story of Mary, including Gabriel's annunciation to her of the advent of the Savior and the virgin birth of Jesus.[160] Certain Western scholars have seen a reminiscence of the institution of the eucharist or sacrament and the miracle of loaves and fishes.[161]

Many of the similarities are verbal. There are passages in the Qur'an that are virtually identical to passages in the Bible.[162] Thus, when the Qur'an talks about the ruins of past civilizations, destroyed for their disobedience to God and to the prophets he had sent to them, it comments that "your Lord would not have ruined those cities without just cause, had their inhabitants been righteous men."[163] It rejects the notion that God prefers one people over another because of their lineage or ancestry. "The noblest of you in God's sight," it says, "is he who fears Him most."[164] This is reminiscent of the justification given by the Book of Mormon for the expulsion of the Canaanites by the children of Israel:

---

156. 4:163; 17:55.
157. Compare 2:249 with Judges 7:2-7.
158. 57:12-15; compare Matthew 25:1-13.
159. 3:38-41; 19:2-15; 21:89-90.
160. 3:35-37, 42-51; 19:16-34.
161. 5:112-15.
162. It might be of interest to compare the 55th chapter of the Qur'an with Psalm 136. However, such a comparison is beyond the scope of the present book.
163. 11:117.
164. 49:13.

> And now, do ye suppose that the children of this land, who were in the land of promise, who were driven out by our fathers, do ye suppose that they were righteous? Behold, I say unto you, Nay. Do ye suppose that our fathers would have been more choice than they if they had been righteous? I say unto you, Nay. Behold, the Lord esteemeth all flesh in one; he that is righteous is favored of God. But behold, this people had rejected every word of God, and they were ripe in iniquity.[165]

The Qur'an's view of human hardheartedness is very close to that found in the Latter-day Saint scriptures. "When misfortune befalls a man, he prays to Us standing, sitting, and lying down. But as soon as We relieve his affliction he pursues his former ways, as though he never prayed for Our help."[166] This could serve as a summary of Nephite history, but its applicability is not only to past dispensations. "In the day of their peace," said the Lord about the persecuted Saints in 1833 Missouri, "they esteemed lightly my counsel; but, in the day of their trouble, of necessity they feel after me."[167] This leads occasionally to a highly negative view of human nature, which contrasts us unfavorably with inanimate nature: "If We had sent down this Qur'an upon a mountain, thou wouldst have seen it humbled, split asunder out of the fear of God."[168] The prophet Mormon seems to have held a similar opinion: "O how great is the nothingness of the children of men; yea, even they are less than the dust of the earth. For behold, the dust of the earth moveth hither and thither, to the dividing asunder, at the command of our great and everlasting God. Yea, behold at his voice do the hills and the mountains tremble and quake."[169] Nevertheless, despite their persistent rebellion against the will of God, the wicked seem to be quite serene in both the Qur'an and the Book of Mormon. "They declare: 'The Fire will never touch us—except for a few days.'"[170]

---

165. 1 Nephi 17:33-35.
166. 10:12; compare 30:33-34; 39:8.
167. Doctrine and Covenants 101:8.
168. 59:21 (Arberry).
169. Helaman 12:7-9.
170. 2:80; compare 3:24.

"And there shall also be many which shall say: Eat, drink, and be merry; nevertheless, fear God—he will justify in committing a little sin; yea, lie a little, take the advantage of one because of his words, dig a pit for thy neighbor; there is no harm in this; and do all these things, for tomorrow we die; and if it so be that we are guilty, God will beat us with a few stripes, and at last we shall be saved in the kingdom of God."[171]

Like the Bible, the Qur'an distinguishes between rocky soil and the deep soil in a garden, as a parable for the distinction between believers and unbelievers.[172] But the believers comprehend the parables of God, while unbelievers do not understand what they mean.[173] Part of the problem is that unbelievers hold family and kin dearer than true religion. The Qur'an advises against this, just as Jesus does.[174] But if believers choose to serve God first, he will intervene on their behalf. "If God be for us," asks the apostle Paul, "who can be against us?" "If God helps you," declares the Qur'an, "none can overcome you. If He abandons you, who then can help you?"[175] "Keep your covenant," Allah says, "and I will be true to Mine."[176] This is similar to what God told Joseph Smith: "I, the Lord, am bound when ye do what I say; but when ye do not what I say, ye have no promise."[177]

There are some parallels that are still closer. "Those that cry lies to Our signs," declares the Qur'an, "and wax proud against them—the gates of heaven shall not be opened to them, nor shall they enter Paradise until the camel passes through the eye of the needle."[178] Of the unrighteous, who refuse to listen to the prophets, the Qur'an says, "They have hearts, but understand not with them; they have eyes, but perceive not with them; they have ears, but they hear not with them."[179] Only once does the Qur'an actually quote the Bible: "We wrote in the Psalms after the Torah had

171. 2 Nephi 28:8.
172. 2:264-65. Compare Matthew 13:3-9, 18-23; Mark 4:3-9, 14-20; Luke 8:5-8, 11-15.
173. 2:26. Compare Matthew 13:10-17; Mark 4:11-12; Luke 8:10.
174. 9:23-24. Compare Matthew 10:34-37.
175. Romans 8:31. Qur'an 3:160.
176. 2:40.
177. Doctrine and Covenants 82:10.

been given: 'The righteous among My servants shall inherit the earth.'"[180]

Sometimes the similarities are more conceptual. Thus, for example, the Qur'an believes that the earth was created in six days.[181] It is also known that a day with the Lord is equivalent to a thousand years of our time.[182] According to both the Qur'an and Alma the Younger, the heavenly bodies follow assigned courses as a sign for men and women upon the earth.[183] The Qur'an condemns those who pray, who make a show of piety, but do not give alms to the poor.[184] So does the Book of Mormon:

> If ye turn away the needy, and the naked, and visit not the sick and afflicted, and impart of your substance, if ye have, to those who stand in need—I say unto you, if ye do not any of these things, behold, your prayer is vain, and availeth you nothing.[185]

Similarly, the Qur'an apparently recognizes the futility of trying to limit the words of God merely to what can be contained in one book. At a certain point, Muhammad is commanded to say: "If the sea were ink for the Words of my Lord, the sea would be spent before the Words of my Lord are spent, though We brought replenishment the like of it." At another place, we read that "if all the trees in the earth were pens, and the sea, with seven more seas to replenish it, were ink, the writing of God's words could never be finished."[186]

---

178. 7:40. Here, the implication is that it is truly impossible for such people to enter paradise. At Matthew 19:23-26, Jesus presents a seemingly impossible condition but, nonetheless, tells his disciples: "With men this is impossible; but with God all things are possible." It could be argued that this difference indicates a real difference between Islam, a religion which tends to emphasize justice, and Christianity, which tends to emphasize God's grace. This issue should not be pressed too far, however, since there is grace in Islam, and, clearly, justice in Christianity.

179. 7:179. Compare Jeremiah 5:21; Matthew 13:13-14; Mark 8:17-18; Romans 11:8.

180. 21:21:105 (Arberry); compare Psalms 25:13; 37:11; 37:29; Matthew 5:3.

181. 10:3; 32:4; 57:4.

182. 22:47; 32:5.

183. 55:5; Alma 30:44. Compare Doctrine and Covenants 88:42-47.

184. 107:4-7.

185. Alma 34:28.

186. 18:109 (Arberry); 31:27.

Similar statements from the standard works of the Latter-day Saints provide a powerful argument for continuing revelation:

> My works are without end, and also my words, for they never cease... [T]here is no end to my works, neither to my words.[187]

> And there are also many other things which Jesus did, the which, if they should be written every one, I suppose that even the world itself could not contain the books that should be written.[188]

Some parallels are intriguing from a particularly Latter-day Saint viewpoint. The Qur'an seems, for example, to hint at the continuation of family relationships after death. "Enter Paradise," it says, "you and your wives, walking with joy!"[189] And of "those who believe and whose posterity follows them in faith," the God of the Qur'an says, "we shall join their posterity to them" in paradise.[190] (Remember, these phrases represent only a few scattered passages. Muslims do not, historically, seem to have taken them seriously. Certainly no reader should get the impression that Islam teaches anything like celestial or eternal marriage. But the passages may suggest the vestiges, at least, of true revelation, if only dimly remembered.) Perhaps even more intriguing, and certainly better represented throughout the Qur'an and throughout classical Islamic tradition, is the concept of different degrees of blessedness among the saved in paradise. Specifically the Qur'an speaks of three groups of people after death and the judgment—those of the left hand (the wicked), those of the right hand (the righteous), and, most exalted, those "brought near" unto God.[191] (The latter group must be people of quite extraordinary righteousness to be so distinguished.)

Differences

So far, I have emphasized the similarities between Islam and Christianity. Specifically, I have concentrated on resemblances between

---

187. Moses 1:4, 38.
188. John 21:25.
189. 43:70.
190. 52:21 (my translation); compare 13:23; 40:8.
191. 56:7-12.

Islam and the restored gospel. This has been deliberate. I have tried to correct the misperception held by many people that Islam is a totally foreign religion, even a form of paganism. Such opinions are far from the truth. Islam is a child of Abraham, a half-sister to Christianity and Judaism. It is true that there has been a long historical antagonism between Islam and Christendom, and it is also true that no such hostility exists between Christianity and Buddhism, or Christianity and Hinduism. This is not a refutation of the close relationship that exists between Islam and other Abrahamic religions. The historical rivalry between the Dar al-Islam ("the abode of Islam") and Christendom is actually a *result* of their close relationship: Domestic hostilities, or civil wars, are often far worse than conflicts between strangers. Islam and Christianity are so similar that the differences between them loom large by contrast. (Buddhism and Hinduism, on the other hand, are so different from Christianity that they have virtually no common ground upon which to have a conflict.) Furthermore, there is the historical fact that Christianity and Islam have often faced off over shared borders. Such squabbling over territory has never been a factor in Christian relations with the religions of India. It must be remembered that Islam is a monotheistic religion closely related to Christianity. It is this point that Elder Parley P. Pratt attempted to make in 1855:

> I am aware it is not without a great deal of prejudice that we, as Europeans, and Americans, and Christians in religion and in our education, so called, have looked upon the history of Mahomet, or even the name; and even now we may think that Mahometanism, compared with Christianity as it exists in the world, is a kind of heathenism, or something dreadful, and the other we look upon as something very pretty, only a little crippled; and for my part, I hardly know which to call the idolatrous side of the question, unless we consider Mahometanism Christianity, in one sense, and that which has been called Christianity, heathenism.[192]

It is entirely incorrect to regard Islam as paganism, when it is actually a religion closely akin to our own. There is, however, an

---

[192] *Journal of Discourses* 3:38.

equal and opposite error, which I also wish to correct. Perhaps Elder Pratt himself fell into it. I remember, some years ago, a conversation with a Latter-day Saint friend who had visited the Near East on several occasions. We were talking about Islam and about the long-term prospects for spreading the gospel in the Arab world. He was much more optimistic than I. To my astonishment, this intelligent man told me that he felt that Muslims were virtually Mormons already and that all we needed to do was to clarify a few truths that they had gotten confused and perhaps to add a few doctrinal touches. Now, I'm all for a sympathetic understanding of the religions of other people. I do like to emphasize areas of common understanding. (I hope this book itself is evidence of that.) But to suggest, as my friend did, that, because of their abstinence from alcohol and their belief in strong family ties, Muslims are nearly Mormons is to misconceive both the nature of Islam and, I firmly believe, of Mormonism. There is more to the restored gospel, far more, than merely the Word of Wisdom and Family Home Evenings.

So, having labored at some length to establish similarities between the teachings of the Qur'an and the teachings of the Latter-day Saint scriptures, I must now mention some of the ways in which they diverge. And it must be said that Islam has further diverged from the teachings of the Qur'an, and from what we as Latter-day Saints regard as the truth, in the years since the passing of Muhammad. (Almost all Muslim thinkers would passionately reject this claim. Indeed, they have vehemently rejected it at academic conferences where it has been advanced. It remains my opinion, though, and is a carefully considered and well-documented view.)

I have hinted in this chapter of some of the differences between the Qur'anic version of biblical stories and the earlier Hebrew accounts. It will be recalled that, according to the Qur'an, Abraham and Ishmael came down to west central Arabia and there founded the Meccan Ka'ba, asking that they might be given a posterity that "submits" to God (i.e., is "Muslim").[193] This incident is totally

[193] 2:125-29; 14:35-37.

unknown to the Old Testament, but it serves to give ancient Arabia—which had previously seemed an utter blank spot in the record of God's dealings with humankind—a role in the divine scheme of world history, a role that extends back even beyond the coming of the Prophet Muhammad. (Some non-Latter-day Saint scholars have argued that the Book of Mormon served the same purpose for the Americas.) As I have noted, it is intriguing that the Qur'an rarely argues for this visit by Abraham and Ishmael, but simply refers to it as a story already well known to both believers and nonbelievers alike in early Arabia.

Far more important is the different view of Jesus taken by the Qur'an. It is not merely the stories about Jesus' boyhood that are different. Tales about his speaking in the cradle and about his making a bird out of clay and then breathing life into it and watching it fly away are well known from the so-called "infancy gospels" that circulated in early Christianity.[194] No, the distinction between Islam and Christianity concerning the place of Jesus is much wider and much more significant than any issue raised by such stories.

First, Islam denies that Jesus died upon the cross. The Jews are quoted in the Qur'an as saying, "'We slew the Messiah, Jesus Son of Mary, the Messenger of God'—yet they did not slay him, neither crucified him, only a likeness of that was shown to them… And they slew him not of a certainty—no indeed; God raised him up to Him."[195] A similar position, claiming that Jesus did not actually suffer under Pontius Pilate but only seemed to do so, is associated with Christian history by a heresy known as "docetism." (The name of the movement comes from the Greek verb *dokeo*, meaning "to seem.") The Christian theological tendency that went under that title argued that Jesus, as God, was too exalted a being to suffer pain and that the real Christ, therefore, must have been removed from the scene before the actual suffering began. Other Christians rejected it as a heresy because there cannot be an atonement if there was no death. But where Christians would regard such an implication as

194. 3:46; 5:110; 19:29-33; 3:49; 5:110.
195. 4:157-58 (Arberry).

fatal for the docetist view, Muslims would not be troubled at all. Indeed, the Qur'an denies the possibility of intercession by one soul for another.[196]

Islam has consistently denied the divinity of Christ. "If the Lord of Mercy had a son," Muhammad is commanded to say, "I would be the first to worship him."[197] But this the Qur'an explicitly and repeatedly denies. "How should He have a son when He had no consort?" it asks.[198] But this commonsensical question—the same that was often asked by the late Elder LeGrand Richards of the Council of the Twelve—is used not to establish the possibility that God the Father has a wife, but the impossibility of his being a father. "He (exalted be the glory of our Lord!) has taken no wife, nor has He begotten any children."[199] Probably the strongest statement of this principle occurs toward the end of the Qur'an—which means, most likely, that it came as one of the earliest chapters:

> Say: "He is God, One,
> God, the Everlasting Refuge,
> who has not begotten, and has not been begotten,
> and equal to Him is not any one."[200]

The language of the Qur'an is often quite vigorous on this subject. There can be no doubt about its opinion of the importance of the issue.

> And they say, 'The All-merciful
> has taken unto Himself a son.'
> You have indeed advanced something hideous!
> The heavens are well-nigh rent of it
> and the earth split asunder, and
> the mountains well-nigh fall down crashing
> for that they have attributed to the All-merciful a son; and it
> behooves not the All-merciful to take a son.

---

196. 2:48; 17:15; 21:28; 35:18; 39:7, 44; 53:38-39.
197. 43:81.
198. 6:101.
199. 72:3.
200. This is the entire text of *sura* 177 of the Qur'an.

> None is there in the heavens and earth
> but he comes to the All-merciful
> as a servant.[201]

The Qur'an does not deny the concept of the Virgin Birth; in fact, it speaks emphatically of "Mary,...who preserved her chastity and into whose womb We breathed of Our spirit."[202] But this does not make Jesus the son of God, according to Islamic views. Rather, it simply makes Jesus the only human being in history born to only one parent; to use technical language, he represents a case of parthenogenesis. Jesus has a special place in Islamic thought and in Islamic expectations for the last days. But he is definitely not, according to Islamic doctrine, the Son of God. Indeed, the Qur'an represents him as denying this himself:

> Then God will say: "Jesus, son of Mary, did you ever say to mankind: 'Worship me and my mother as gods beside God?'"
>
> "Glory to You," he will answer, "how could I say that to which I have no right? If I had ever said so, You would surely have known it. You know what is in my mind, but I cannot tell what is in Yours. You alone know what is hidden. I spoke to them of nothing except what You bade me. I said: 'Serve God, my Lord and your Lord.'"[203]

Islam is an absolutely rigid, pure monotheism. "To God alone is true worship due," declares the Qur'an.[204] In this regard, it resembles Judaism rather more than Christianity. There is no God-man in Islam, no divine Son. A chasm separates man from God. Even the doctrine of the Trinity, with its claim that three persons are really one God, has never satisfied Muslim critics:

> People of the Book, do not transgress the bounds of your religion. Speak nothing but the truth about God. The Messiah, Jesus the son of Mary, was no more than God's Messenger and His Word

---

201. 19:88-93 (Arberry); compare 2:116; 10:68-69; 17:111; 18:4-5; 19:35; 21:26-29; 23:91; 25:2; 39:4; 43:59.
202. 66:12.
203. 5:116-17.
204. 39:3.

> which He conveyed to Mary: a spirit from Him. So believe in God and His Messengers and do not say: 'Three.' Forbear, and it shall be better for you. God is but one God. God forbid that He should have a son! ... The Messiah does not disdain to be a servant of God, nor do the angels who are nearest to Him.[205]

From a Latter-day Saint point of view, the Qur'an is crucially wrong on this important matter. Yet I have to confess that I have always found an amusing implication here. Many enemies of The Church of Jesus Christ of Latter-day Saints like to denounce us as polytheistic and therefore as non-Christian. They think that they escape the charge of polytheism themselves by simply declaring that the Father and the Son and the Holy Spirit are somehow, incomprehensibly, one. But the Muslims, whose mathematical abilities are historically well developed (as we shall see, they invented algebra), are not taken in by this. They have frequently denounced mainstream Christianity as polytheism. But it is not only Christians who are under the accusation of worshiping more than the one God. Even Jewish monotheism is suspect in the Qur'an.[206]

The irony is compounded by the historical fact that some early Latter-day Saints saw themselves as monotheistic allies of the Muslims, confronting a Christianity corrupted by saint-worship and the veneration of relics. (After all, they correctly reasoned, Latter-day Saints worship only one God. As much as Latter-day Saint scriptures and leaders may talk of "the Gods," our worship is strictly limited to the Father. Therefore, we cannot plausibly be considered polytheists—a label we reject vehemently.) This is the thinking that undergirds some of Parley P. Pratt's more militant declarations:

> Mahometanism included the doctrine that there was one God—that He was great, even the creator of all things, and that the

---

205. 4:171-72. Note that the Qur'an seems to call Jesus God's "Word" here, much as does the first chapter of the gospel of John. Thus, even though it rejects Christ's divinity, the Qur'an retains an extraordinarily high and reverent view of him.

206. 9:30-31. Most Western scholars would say that the denunciation of Jewish polytheism here rests upon a misunderstanding, but it is possible that at least some of the Jews of Arabia held false doctrines. Certainly the Qur'an's rebuke does not seem to apply to Judaism as we know it, either today or historically.

> people by right should worship Him... On this account, on the simple subject of the Deity and His worship, if nothing more, I should rather incline, of the two, after all my early traditions, education, and prejudices, to the side of Mahomet, for on this point he is on the side of truth, and the Christian world on the side of idolatry and heathenism.[207]
>
> Now, if we take Mahometanism during those dark ages, and the corruptions that are so universally prevalent over the earth, and the idolatrous systems of religion, falsely called Christianity, and weigh them in a balance; with all my education in favor of Christian nations and Christian powers, and Christian institutions, so called, with all my prejudices of early youth, and habits of thought and reading, my rational faculties would compel me to admit that the Mahometan history and Mahometan doctrine was a standard raised against the most corrupt and abominable idolatry that ever perverted our earth, found in the creeds and worship of Christians, falsely so named.[208]
>
> So far as that one point is concerned, of worshipping the one true God under the name of Mahometanism, together with many moral precepts, and in war acting only on the defensive, I think they have exceeded in righteousness and truthfulness of religion, the idolatrous and corrupt church that has borne the name of Christianity.[209]

So seriously does the Qur'an take this issue that it falls into what appears to be an inconsistency. It generally speaks with favor of both Christians and Jews. They are the "People of the Book," and it tells them that they have little to worry about if only they will live up to the remnants of revelation still in their custody. But the Qur'an labels trinitarian Christians "unbelievers" at one point and threatens them with an unpleasant fate if they do not repent of their grave theological error:

---

207. *Journal of Discourses* 3:38.
208. *Journal of Discourses* 3:40.
209. *Journal of Discourses* 3:41. As noted above, Elder Pratt was probably guilty of some exaggerated rhetoric here.

> Unbelievers are those that say: 'God is the Messiah, the son of Mary.' For the Messiah himself said: 'Children of Israel, serve God, my Lord and your Lord.' He that worships other gods besides God shall be forbidden Paradise and shall be cast into the fire of Hell... Unbelievers are those who say: 'God is one of three.' There is but one God. If they do not desist from so saying, those of them that disbelieve shall be sternly punished... The Messiah, the son of Mary, was no more than a Messenger: other Messengers passed away before him. His mother was a saintly woman. They both ate earthly food.[210]

Islam insists on an absolute gulf, an unbridgeable chasm, between God and everything else in the universe. There is no kinship between Creator and creature, any more than there was a genetic relationship between Thomas Edison and the lightbulb.[211] In Islam, Jesus, too, is a creature.[212] Educated Muslims will probably understand what we Christians mean when we speak of "the brotherhood of man under the Fatherhood of God," and they may even have sympathy for the sentiment. But their theology cannot permit them to accept such a statement literally.

Another point that can perhaps be clarified here is the proper name of the religion of Muhammad and his place within the religion. If Islam refuses to recognize the divine Sonship of Jesus, it also rejects even the barest hint that Muhammad was more than human. Many contemporary Muslims are offended when their religion is called "Muhammadanism." Not only is that long word somewhat awkward to say, but, they point out, it implies that Muhammad plays the same role within their religion that Christ plays within Christianity. Nothing, however, could be further from the truth. Muhammad does not atone for our sins, he is not divine, and he receives no worship. Rather, they say, the true name of their

210. 5:72-73, 75; compare 5:17.
211. In popular Islam, especially among the uneducated, there is a flourishing practice of venerating "saints," holy men and women who have passed on to the presence of God. I suspect that the unapproachability of the Islamic God, his sheer distance, is an important factor in this.
212. Like all other prophets. The Qur'an is quite clear on this: As in the case of Adam, God simply said "Be!" and Jesus came into existence. See 3:47, 59; 19:35.

religion is the name it has always borne, Islam.[213] And believers in their religion are to be called "Muslims," not "Muhammadans."[214] ("Muslim" bears the same relation to "Islam" that "Christian" bears to "Christianity," or "Mormon" to "Mormonism." The first is a term for the believer; the second refers to the doctrine or movement itself.)[215] The Arabic word *islam* means "submission." It derives from the same Semitic root (*s-l-m*) that gives us the words for "peace" in Hebrew (*shalom*) and in Arabic (*salaam*). The model of *islam* is the prophet Abraham, for it is not submission to just anybody or anything that is meant by the term as the Qur'an uses it, but specifically submission to the sovereign will of God. One who so yields himself or herself to the divine will is a "submitter," or, in Arabic, a *muslim*—from the same root, *s-l-m*. Thus, in a sense, to call believers in the message of Muhammad "Muslims" is very much like calling believers in the prophetic mission of Joseph Smith "Saints." Each term is as much an expression of hope as a statement of present reality.

This focus upon submission to the inscrutable will of God as the characteristic mark of true religion points to Islam's emphasis upon the omnipotence of God. It is an emphasis that is absolutely fundamental to the religion. It underlies Muslim rejection of the doctrine of the atonement of Christ and flavors daily life and speech throughout the Islamic world. To elaborate, God forgives whomever He chooses to forgive, and denies forgiveness to anybody he wants, for any reason he chooses. God is an absolute sovereign. There is no law to which he is subject, nobody to whom he must give an account. All creatures, all planets, all people, all prophets (including Jesus of Nazareth), all natural laws and moral principles are, in the Islamic view, equally powerless before the Lord of the universe.[216]

---

213. Pronounced with the hissing "s" of "this" rather than with the "z" sound of "these," and with the emphasis on the second syllable, "Iss-*laam*."

214. Pronounced somewhere in between "*muss*-lim" and "*moose*-lim."

215. I often hear people in the West refer to the Arabs as "Islams." This would be like referring to Latter-day Saints as "Mormonisms."

216. The situation is not unlike the equality of all peoples before the Abbasid caliph, to which I shall refer in the next chapter. I would argue that the resemblance between Islamic theology and the reality of the Islamic empire in which it developed is probably not mere coincidence.

Muslims would strenuously reject the view, often heard in Mormon circles, that the atoning sacrifice of Christ was necessary in order to satisfy the demands of cosmic law, and that it was only then that God could extend forgiveness without upsetting the universal balance of things. (This view is prominent in the Book of Mormon. "What," asked Alma the Younger of his son Corianton, "do ye suppose that mercy can rob justice? I say unto you, Nay; not one whit. If so, God would cease to be God.")[217] They would want to know who would depose God, why he would "cease to be God." Actions are right, in the standard Muslim view, because God says they are; he does not say they are right because of some celestial standard, independent of him and, in a sense, prior to him that tells him to do so. Thus, as a chemistry professor at the University of Cairo once told me, "God doesn't need to sacrifice somebody in order to buy himself out of the need to punish us."[218]

God's all-powerful Lordship is an ever-present reality in the daily life of Muslims. The Qur'an directs its people to say "If God wills" whenever they announce their intention to do something. "Do not say, regarding anything, 'I am going to do that tomorrow,' but only, 'If God wills.'"[219] It is not surprising, thus, that *in sha'a Allah* ("if God wills") is one of the most commonly heard phrases in the Arabic language. But many Westerners tend to take it as a mere verbal formula, a cultural habit with little or no thought behind it. Sometimes they think of it as an excuse, offered in advance, for not fulfilling a promise. (The employee says, "I'll do this right away, *in sha'a Allah.*" God, it will be explained, just hadn't willed that the task be completed so soon.) The phrase can become quite an irritant for time-ridden Westerners trying to transact business in a culture that is clearly less concerned about deadlines and rushing

217. Alma 42:25.

218. In these terms, Christian belief does seem a bit strange. Paul was right. The doctrine of "Christ crucified" does appear "unto the Jews a stumbling-block, and unto the Greeks foolishness." (1 Corinthians 1:23.) We can hardly be surprised that a modern Muslim, heir to a Semitic religion mingled with Greek philosophical thought patterns, would find it difficult to accept.

219 68:17-33; 18:23-24.

219. James 4:13-16.

about. But it is taken very seriously by devout followers of Islam. I was once rebuked when I told a Muslim friend that I would meet him at a certain place at noon the next day. He waited silently, clearly expecting me to say something else. When I said nothing, he told me politely but firmly to say "If God wills." "How do you know that you will meet me tomorrow?" he asked. "How do you even know that you'll still be alive? You could have a heart attack. A car could run over you. Your apartment building could collapse on your head." (Both of these last two possibilities are real concerns in a place like Cairo.) "It is sheer irreligious arrogance," he told me, "to believe that you are in charge of your own soul and to leave God out of the picture. If God does not will it," he said, "you will most definitely not meet me tomorrow at noon!" I must admit, I was chastened.

The Islamic emphasis on the supremacy of God's will can certainly lead to a kind of fatalism, to a resigned apathy which doesn't try to improve conditions or to find solutions or to fight diseases or to take care of our health. Things as they are, this view suggests, are the things God has ordained; it would be futile and even blasphemous to seek to change them! I do think that many Muslims tend to overemphasize God's power and their powerlessness in just that way. Still, there are clear biblical grounds for similar belief:

> Go to now, ye that say, Today or tomorrow we will go into such a city, and continue there a year, and buy and sell, and get gain: Whereas ye know not what shall be on the morrow. For what is your life? It is even a vapour, that appeareth for a little time, and then vanisheth away. For that ye ought to say, If the Lord will, we shall live, and do this, or that. But now ye rejoice in your boastings: all such rejoicing is evil.[220]

If Islamic culture perhaps overstresses God's determination of all things, we in the modern West probably fail to recognize it enough. Overconfidently, we sometimes imagine that all of the problems that have confronted humankind through the centuries

---

220. James 4:13-16.

have now begun to yield before our technology, our money, and our rational planning. Yet we are not, in the final analysis, really the masters of our fates and the captains of our souls. Our most advanced medical machinery cannot prolong our lives indefinitely, a snowstorm can bring our biggest cities to a standstill, a slight rocking of the earth can level them to the ground. A little more humility before nature and nature's God would not be amiss. In this respect, as in others, I think we can learn from our Muslim brothers and sisters.

The vast ninth-century mosque of Ibu Tulun, in Cairo, tells much of the power and glory of the Arab empire. The minaret or prayer tower in the background probably borrows its design from ancient Mesopotamian ziggurauts like the tower of Babel.

Classical Arabic Civilization

The late Marshall G. S. Hodgson, one of the greatest Western students of Islam in our century, developed an outline of Islamic history that I find very helpful.[1] In it, he distinguishes seven different periods. Let me summarize them here.

First, Hodgson states, there was the "Pre-Islamic Period." It isn't hard to understand what this is about, since it simply refers to the years from earliest time up to about 570 A.D., when the Prophet Muhammad was born. The next interval, which he calls the "Formative Period," extends from Muhammad's birth up to 692 A.D.[2] Among other things, this is the time in which the most important document of Islam, the Qur'an, was revealed and recorded, and the time in which the Prophet himself and his first four successors (the "rightly guided caliphs") established powerful examples of what it means to live as a Muslim. We have already discussed important items from the Formative Period. Hodgson labels the next distinct phase of Islamic history the "High Caliphal Period." It shall be discussed in more detail below, but briefly, it was during this period that the Arab or Islamic empire attained its greatest power and prosperity. Things fell apart by 945 A.D., and the Muslims entered what Hodgson terms the "Middle Periods" of their history, lasting

1. In his staggeringly brilliant three-volume work *The Venture of Islam: Conscience and History in a World Civilization* (Chicago: The University of Chicago Press, 1974).

2. Hodgson has his reasons for choosing precisely this year as his cut-off date for the Formative Period, but they are beyond the scope of this book.

until 1500. (Hodgson divides this era in two. He distinguishes the "Early Middle Period" from the "Later Middle Period.") When gunpowder and other modern technologies made it possible for certain innovative states to swallow up those around them, the Muslims entered a period of partial recentralization. This Hodgson terms the age of the "Gunpowder Empires." Finally, at the beginning of the nineteenth century, Western imperialism entered the Islamic world—first in the person of Napoleon. With this, the Muslims entered the Modern Period.

The High Caliphal Period

By the end of the seventh century, although institutions continued to be formed, the basic structures of Islamic practice were pretty much in place. The Arabs who had poured out of the Arabian peninsula and launched their astonishing series of conquests had left the old local bureaucracies in control of day-to-day governance. The conquerors were uninterested in such lowly matters and probably had no competence anyway, since, as we have seen, the Arabian peninsula really had no traditions of government in any recognizable sense. Thus, native Christians in one part of the new empire and Mazdaeans or Zoroastrians in the other continued to administer daily affairs in languages like Aramaic and Persian, just as they had in the years before the conquest.

Finally, in the late seventh century, Arabic was made the language of administration. This had notable consequences. Fluency in Arabic now became the passport to social advancement and prestige. People who wanted to get ahead in the new order had to learn it. This was relatively easy for speakers of Aramaic to do, since, as a Semitic language like Hebrew, it was closely related to Arabic. (It was similar to a speaker of Spanish having to learn Portuguese.) It is probably for this reason that Aramaic essentially died out. It was simply absorbed into the dominant language. Persian, on the other hand, is a language utterly unrelated to Arabic.[3] This made the speech of the conquerors perhaps more difficult for native Persian-speakers to learn, but it also led to a clear distinction between the native language and the learned second language that prevented

Persian from assimilating to Arabic and simply disappearing. Thus, while Persian disappeared for a number of centuries from public or official use, it continued to be spoken at home. This is shown clearly by its reappearance in literary form around the year 1000 A.D. (Since then, of course, it has had a continuous history. Today, Persian is the language of the Islamic Republic of Iran.)

Islamic Law

Making Arabic the language of administration in the empire was part of a larger and very important process by which the Middle East became both Arab and, overwhelmingly, Muslim. The first Arab conquerors had been content to let the old bureaucracies from the Persian and Byzantine states continue to run things. But now, some Muslim thinkers wondered if there was not a specifically Islamic way of doing things and whether they ought to be following it. Naturally, when first they wanted to find Islamic solutions to the challenges posed to them by their radically changed circumstances, they looked to the Qur'an for guidance. The Qur'an is an impressive book that covers a wide range of issues. But it is of a finite length, and it was not systematized or complete or specific enough to answer every question that arose as the Arab or Islamic empire expanded. Questions of maritime law, for instance, that had never occupied center stage among desert Arabs now pressed for resolution. How was a Muslim to handle issues on which the Qur'an offered little or no guidance? There was no continuing revelation within Islam, no living prophet, and there was no pope with the authority to settle disputes.

Faced with this problem, the Muslims fell back upon an old Arab notion, the idea of *sunna* ("tradition," "custom," "usage"). Pre-Islamic Arabia had, in many ways, been remarkably conservative. Guidance was sought in the past, according to the custom of the

---

[3] I will refer throughout this book to Persian, rather than speaking of the language by its own native title, "Farsi." It has become fashionable in some circles to talk of "Farsi" when speaking English, and some will be puzzled by my refusal to do so. But there is a simple reason for it: We do not usually talk in English about "Deutsch" or "Français" or "Español." I see no point in making an exception for Persian.

community, as to how various questions had been coped with by ancestors. Information from the past was handed down from one generation to another by oral tradition.

Muslim Arab thinkers adopted the old, pre-Islamic way of discerning good from bad, wise from unwise. For them, *sunna* came to mean the established practice of the original Islamic community, particularly as it could be discerned in the lives and actions of the Prophet and his companions. Just as God's book, the Qur'an, had been revealed in the past, so too, for the vast majority of Muslim thinkers, the ideal Islamic life had been lived in the past and was available for study. It had been lived by the Messenger of God himself. If he didn't understand Islam, who did? If he hadn't lived it fully and well, who ever had? Secondarily, that ideal Muslim life had been lived by those who had been privileged to know and observe the Prophet personally. Muhammad, the Qur'an taught, is a good example for the believers, a pattern for their conduct.[4] And his example is not limited to purely religious matters. Rather, somewhat like the prophets of the Latter-day Saints, Muhammad's counsel and example were authoritative for all areas of human life, whether secular or sacred. "It is not for true believers—men or women—to take their choice in their affairs if God and His Messenger decree otherwise."[5] The Prophet spoke for God upon the earth. "Those who swear fealty to thee swear fealty in truth to God." "He that obeys the Messenger obeys God Himself."[6]

The opposite of *sunna*, first in pre-Islamic Arabia and ultimately within Islam itself, was *bid'a* ("innovation"), which eventually came to mean "heresy." Thus, the Islamic community became a conservative one in which "heresy" was divergence from the established practice of the community. (It might be seen why one sect of Islam claimed for itself the title of "Sunni." They were calling themselves orthodox—and, not by accident, implying that those who disagreed with them were heretics.)

---

4. 33:21.
5. 33:36.
6. 4:80; compare 48:10. It isn't difficult to find parallels to these ideas in the scriptures of the Latter-day Saints. See, for example, Matthew 10:40; Doctrine and Covenants 1:38; 68:4; 84:36-37; 89.

Again in keeping with the practice of Arabs before Islam, information about the Prophet's customary behavior, his *sunna*, was passed down in the form of *hadith*, or, as they are commonly called in English, "traditions."[7] These were generally short narrations—anecdotes, really—originally told by one of the "companions" or associates of the Prophet and passed down by a chain of scholars, or at least by a series of pious Muslims, who served as transmitters.

A typical example of the *hadith* comes from the standard, almost canonical, collection of al-Bukhari.[8] "It was told us," records al-Bukhari,

> by Abdullah ibn Yusuf who said, it was told us by al-Layth, who had it from Yazid, who had it from Abu al-Khayr, who had it from Uqba ibn Amir, who said, "Someone sent the Prophet a silk gown and he wore it during the prayers, but on withdrawing he pulled it off violently with a gesture of disgust and said 'This is unfitting for Godfearing men.'"[9]

It was on material like this that later generations of Muslim thinkers would exercise their skills of analysis. What did the anecdote mean? Was the Prophet saying that silk gowns were too ostentatious, too foreign to the simplicity that ought to characterize a man of God? Was it the silk fabric of the garment to which the Prophet had objected? Or was it, rather, the cut of the garment? Muhammad wore the gown during prayer; only afterward did he take it off. Did he receive some sort of divine guidance while he was praying? When, and how, did he decide that the garment was inappropriate? Are elegant clothes appropriate for prayer and worship, but not for a Muslim's everyday life? Those who studied the *hadith* reports about the Prophet and his companions often subjected the traditions to minute analysis.

---

7. The Arabic word *hadith* is pronounced "hah-*deeth*." Strictly speaking, it is singular. I will follow common English usage, however, and regard it as both singular and plural, depending on the context.

8. Pronounced "Boo-*kar*-ee."

9. This *hadith* is cited, in fragmentary form, by H. A. R. Gibb, in his *Mohammedanism* (London: Oxford University Press, 1970), 51-52. I have modified it slightly.

Actually, what I have been saying is an oversimplification. It was only gradually that the chain of transmitters, known in Arabic as an *isnad*, became a required part of a *hadith* report. For approximately the first century after the death of the Prophet, no special care was taken in the transmission of traditions about him. Perhaps the Muslims could not imagine anybody willing to lie or to forge in the name of religion. If so, they were naive, for the period saw thousands of forged traditions emerge, supporting this or that religious or political faction against its rivals. There were, in fact, powerful reasons to want various religious and political and judicial questions to be resolved in one's own interest, and some unscrupulous people were quite willing to put words into the Prophet's mouth to make sure that such would be the case.[10]

Serious students saw the need for some control, some method of sorting out the *hadith* reports and separating the authentic from the spurious and self-interested. They required each narrator to state his source, preferably back to the time of the Prophet. Gradually, a science of *hadith* criticism emerged in the second and third centuries after Muhammad. This criticism was undertaken especially by those concerned with law, who had an obvious interest in making certain that the legal precedents upon which they based their decisions were accurately reported.

The first need was for biographies of the people who showed up prominently in the various traditions and in the lists of those who transmitted them. Thus, there is a rich body of biographical works on the Prophet himself, on his companions, and on each generation thereafter. Beyond sheer interest in the lives of important people, there was generally a very practical goal in this study, and that goal was to check the trustworthiness of each transmitter. Looking back at the sample *hadith* quoted above, scholars of the subject would want to know whether Abdullah ibn Yusuf and al-Layth actually lived at the proper time and place. Could they really have met? If it could be demonstrated that Abdullah spent his entire life in Spain,

---

10. Many Latter-day Saint historians accepted Mark Hoffman's forgeries for similar reasons. It had never entered their minds that anyone would want to create fraudulent Mormon historical texts.

while al-Layth never left Iraq, that would be sufficient reason to reject the report. Or perhaps Abu al-Khayr, the transmitter who supposedly heard the report from a man named Uqba ibn Amir, was born after Uqba's death, or was only eighteen months old when Uqba passed away. In either case, obviously, Abu al-Khayr could hardly have heard and passed on a report from Uqba, and the tradition would, again, have to be ruled out as a probable fraud. (Such things were occasionally discovered in *isnads* that, on the surface, looked perfectly plausible.) Was Yazid a reliable transmitter? Did he have a reputation as an honest man? Did he have any particular reason for passing on a tradition that condemned the wearing of silk? (Was he, perhaps, a cotton merchant?) In the consideration of many *hadith* reports, the question of the transmitters' religious commitments had to be taken into account. Were they heretics? Were they Shiites? Did they have a particular theological axe to grind?

Over the course of many years, students of the traditions about Muhammad and his companions worked out a complex and sophisticated system for testing and classifying *hadith*. Some *hadith* reports were ranked as *sahih*, or "sound," which is to say that all of the links in their *isnads*, their chains of transmission, were good ones going back directly to the purported source of the tradition, who was usually the Prophet himself.[11] A slightly less reliable group of traditions were determined to be *hasan*, "good." These "good" traditions had a weak link in their chain of transmission—someone whose integrity was questionable or whose contact with another transmitter was subject to doubt—but they were nevertheless acceptable if they were really needed because there was some outside corroboration that led scholars to think they were most likely true. Finally, and acceptable for very little, were those *hadith* reports that were judged to be *da'if*, or "weak."[12] They would be used only when a judge or a theologian was desperate and would not be convincing to many.

A mastery of the thousands of *hadith* circulating in the Islamic world was what constituted *ilm*, or "knowledge," and those who

---

11. The Arabic word *sahih* is pronounced "sa-*heeh*"—with the final "h" being sounded as if it began a syllable.
12. *Da'if* is pronounced "da-*eef*."

had such knowledge were the "knowers" (*ulama*) *par excellence.*[13] Eventually, the *ulama* came to be a kind of rabbi class, the nearest thing that Islam has to a clergy. Authority did not proceed from ordination or priesthood, but from knowledge of the law.

Finally, after the process of seeking out and sifting *hadith* reports for many decades, the time came for gathering the ones that had been adjudged to be reliable into accessible works of reference. The need was especially pressing in the law courts of the empire. It is to this that we owe the great collections of "sound" *hadith* which have taken on almost scriptural status in Sunni Islam. Foremost among these are two multivolume works, each entitled *al-Sahih*, compiled by al-Bukhari (d. 870) and Muslim (d. 875). As these and other manuals of *hadith* won acceptance, it was a knowledge of them—extending to memorization—that came to constitute real *ilm* and would win an aspiring young scholar a place among the *ulama*.

Al-Bukhari's *Sahih*, which holds undisputed pride of place among Sunnis, is worth describing here in a bit of detail. It is composed of ninety-seven books divided into a total of 3,450 chapters. Each book is devoted to a general subject, such as prayer, fasting, alms, testimony, buying and selling, marriage, and the like. About 2,762 separate *hadith* reports occur in Bukhari's volumes, but they are often repeated under different headings, for a total of approximately 7,300. As the name of his vast work indicates, it is composed only of *hadith* reports that were judged by Bukhari and his associates to be *sahih*, or "sound." These were the best he could find. Muslim tradition says that these "sound" reports were culled from the best 200,000 *hadith* Bukhari had encountered in the course of a lifetime spent crisscrossing the Arab empire in quest of anecdotal material about the Prophet and his companions. The obviously spurious or biased reports he had not even taken into account. These facts give some idea of the magnitude of the problem of forgery faced by Muslim scholars and jurists in those early centuries.

---

13. This word, which is spelled in a wide variety of ways by Western scholars, is pronounced roughly "oo-la-*maa*."

Western scholars, in their turn, have been quick to criticize the classical Islamic method of testing *hadith* by their chains of transmitters, or *isnads*. They have pointed out, no doubt correctly, that anybody clever enough to forge the substance of a plausible *hadith* report could also, if he knew it would come under scrutiny, forge a perfectly plausible chain of transmitters for his report. In fact, as biographical dictionaries began to appear, he would have at his disposal a highly useful set of reference works to help him do so. Such criticism is well aimed, it seems, but there can be little doubt that Muslim *isnad*-criticism did manage to exclude the most blatantly propagandistic forgeries of the first and second centuries after the Prophet. And we must also be grateful for the impetus given by these investigations of *hadith* and *hadith*-transmitters to the study of history, which grew up as a side—or sub—discipline to them.

The greatest contribution to the study of *hadith*, however, was the creation of the vast, complex, and sophisticated body of Islamic law known as the *shariah*.[14] The *ulama* began an attempt early to codify Islamic law, to systematize it on the basis of the Qur'an and the *sunna*. Several basic principles governed their work. The first and perhaps most important was that, if clear commands existed in the Qur'an or in authenticated *hadith*, those were to be accepted without human speculation or modification. (This is actually less rigid than it sounds, though, since the human mind had to determine how widely a given rule applies and precisely what it means. This called for the minute study of Arabic grammar and of the meanings of words, including metaphors, and allowed for some differences of opinion and emphasis.) If, on the other hand, a situation was not covered in either the Qur'an or the *hadith*, most jurists would permit the use of "analogy" (*qiyas*), by which an old principle could be applied to a new situation.[15] For instance, if the Prophet had forbidden the marriage of a Muslim girl to a pagan Arab on the grounds that he worshiped many gods, a later Muslim

14. Pronounced "sha-*ree*-ah."
15. Pronounced "kee-*yas*."

judge might rule against the marriage of a Muslim girl to a Hindu, reasoning by analogy from the first case.

Of course, there was always the danger that an irresponsible, ignorant or incompetent judge might misapply a Qur'anic rule or see an analogy where in fact none existed. So a new principle, "consensus" (*ijma*), came into play. This principle represented an effective insurance against the whims and odd ideas of isolated individuals. But when we talk about the "consensus" of the community, we are not talking about a democratic process in which peasants and shopkeepers carried an equal vote with the learned. Only certain opinions were allowed to carry weight regarding matters of technical law. In practice, the *ulama* came to represent the entire Muslim community, and "consensus" eventually came to mean the agreement of the scholars. Someone discovered a convenient *hadith* report that gave strong support to this principle of "consensus" and in fact raised it to the level of practical infallibility: "My community will never agree on error," the Prophet was quoted as saying.

More needs to be said on this notion of the infallibility of the scholarly consensus, since it is one of the strengths of Islam. It is hard for many in the West to understand Islam because it does not appear to function in ways familiar to us. There is, for instance, no Islamic "church" or "priesthood." There is no pope or president who stands clearly at the head of the entire Islamic community. There is, simply, a vast number of *ulama*, men who have received the same training, read the same books, who think in the same way, and whose consensus on most matters is remarkably uniform from Morocco to the former Soviet Central Asia and from Nigeria to Indonesia. We sometimes wonder how a certain Muslim thinker gains authority within the community and is able to make his opinions count more than the opinions of others. It is certainly not because he holds a certain office. There are no living prophets or apostles, and certainly no popes and cardinals, in Islam. There is not even an authoritative committee on doctrine or theology or practice that all Muslims are obliged to accept. The situation is actually much like that in rabbinic Judaism. Certain rabbis or scholars, men like Hillel and Akiva and Maimonides, have carried authority down through the years not because of their offices, but because of their insights and their brilliance and the force of their personalities. Recognition has simply grown up among generations of Jews that this particular rabbi X, rather than those others who lived at the same time, is an authority worth taking into account. Very much the same process occurs in Islam.

I say that this formlessness, this diffuseness of authority, this absence of a tightly organized "church," has been a strength for Islam. Why? Because the consensus of the *ulama* is, in many ways, comparable to a mighty river. It is very difficult to turn and almost impossible to dam. No one man, and probably no group of men, can hijack Islam as a whole and easily turn it to private purposes or reformulate it according to private whims. On the other hand, this striking uniformity and diffuseness of the Islamic community makes it very hard for anyone to reform or change Islam. In The Church of Jesus Christ of Latter-day Saints, a revelation to the president can change a policy overnight that has been in place since the beginnings of Mormonism. (The 1978 revelation regarding priesthood is a case in point. Men of African ancestry began to be ordained within the week.) The pope has a somewhat similar power within the Roman Catholic faith. But no such person or institution exists in Islam. And, since the source of the authority held by the *ulama* is their knowledge of the past, it is the past that tends to control Islam. To lightly cast it off is to give up the source of authority, the link to God that Muslims believe they have in the life and teachings of Muhammad.

Islamic law is seen not as a product of human intelligence, nor as something that can be adapted to changing social needs and ideals. Rather, it is direct from God. In theory, it is immutable. As I have pointed out, there have been various ways in which Muslim jurists have been able to adapt the *shariah* to changing circumstances. But there is no doubt that this adaptation is quite difficult and can only operate under considerable restriction. Westerners sometimes accuse conservative Muslims of wanting to "turn the clock back." The charge is often actually true, and many Muslims would cheerfully admit it. They are in fact attempting to go back to the pristine Islam of the seventh century. For Sunnis, it is a return to the days of the "rightly guided caliphs"—Abu Bakr, Umar, Uthman, and Ali—that is wanted. (For the Shiites, it is only Ali who counts.)

There was another potential source of rulings within Islamic law. That principle is known as *ijtihad*, and means something like "independent reasoning" or "private judgment." (The word *ijtihad* comes from an Arabic three-consonant root, *jhd*, with the basic sense of "striving." It is closely related to the word *jihad*, which, as we have seen, is often rendered in English as "holy war.") Of course, it wasn't just anybody whose "private judgment" could be validly applied to legal matters. It had to be someone thoroughly versed in the Qur'an, in the body of *hadith* traditions, and in legal precedent. Qualified judges were to use their own independent reasoning when no clear rule could be found in either the Qur'an or the *hadith* and when a clear consensus on the question did not exist among their colleagues. Obviously, this allowed for a certain amount of freedom on the part of early Muslim judges. But, gradually, as *ijma* was reached on more and more issues, the "door of *ijtihad*" (as Islamic writers call it) was shut.

Today, that door seems firmly closed. Thus, the sources of Islamic *shariah* law are, beginning at the most authoritative: (1) the Qur'an, (2) accepted *hadith* reports, (3) reasoning by analogy (*qiyas*), (4) consensus (*ijma*), and (5) personal judicial judgment (*ijtihad*). However, since it is the consensus of the learned community that infallibly separates valid interpretations of the Qur'an and *sunna* from invalid ones, and that distinguishes analogies that work from those that do not, *ijma* assumes, in practice, a dominant role in the elaboration of Islamic law.

This is important because Islamic law covers a far wider range of actions than anything we know of as law in our own experience. After centuries of analysis and refinement, Muslim legal thinkers worked out a system in which all possible human acts were placed into one or another of five classes. Some were "obligatory." These actions must be done by every person. (Prayer might serve as a good example.) Others were merely "desirable." It would be good to perform these acts, but a person would not be punished if he or she did not do so. While becoming a scholar of Islamic law is a good thing, for instance, a peasant will not be punished because he is not such a scholar. Nor, among educated people, will a doctor or an engineer be condemned simply because he or she has chosen a different but respectable career path. A third category comprises acts to which the law is "indifferent." Whether a man or woman performs one or another of these acts is of no concern to Islam. (Should Mahmud work as an accountant, or should he seek to be a doctor? The law doesn't care.) There are also actions that the law considers "objectionable." People who act in such ways will not be punished, but it would be better if they avoided such actions. (Slurping one's soup is not a moral offense, and will not land anybody in hell, but it is still not exactly admirable behavior.) Finally, there are actions like adultery and murder that are simply "prohibited." This fifth category of actions consists of things that all people should avoid and for which, if they do not, they will be punished.

Only two of these five categories of action fall within the scope of enforceable law, either in the West or the Middle East.[16] Our own legal system speaks of things that are obligatory (paying taxes, for instance) and of things that are prohibited (such as murder), but it is generally silent when it comes to mere recommendations and certainly has nothing to say about matters of indifference. The *shariah*, however, speaks explicitly about all these things and thus includes much more than our Western law. It makes no real distinction between legal matters as we understand them and things that we would tend to think of as purely religious. Its provisions cover religious duties—what Muslims call "acts of worship," such as ablution, prayer, and pilgrimage—but also embrace criminal law and rules of inheritance. It is a remarkable construction, and even where I disagree, I must confess that I admire the *shariah*'s vastness and intricacy, its comprehensive effort to show, in all aspects of life, what is involved in being a true Muslim. We might therefore think of it as a "grand ideal," a portrait of the ideal human life and the ideal human

16. Adultery no longer seems to fall under this category in Western law—although it once did, and although it seems to be a clear case of breach of contract at the very least.

society. And even though such ideals have certainly not been reached in Islam any more than they have been achieved in the West, it can be safely said that the *shariah* permeates all social life in Islamic countries even today and affects all aspects of their cultures.

But there is a problem. The *shariah* has never been fully implemented anywhere. Islamic legal theorists developed an approach to the law that does not recognize an intermediary or intercessor between God and man—contrary to some of the claims that were being made for the ever more powerful caliph—and allowed for neither priests nor ritual acts performed by one person on behalf of another. The rulers of the state soon discovered that this was not to their taste. They did not want to be bound by the detailed rules of Islamic law, which placed both caliphal government and ordinary citizen on an equal plane before the justice of God. So they ignored it. More precisely, they allowed Islamic law to govern in areas of life which they deemed beneath their notice. Thus, a dual system of courts was established. Islamic law was permitted to regulate marriages and divorces and estate questions, as well as certain commercial transactions, but it could not interfere with the ruler's right to be arbitrary and self-seeking in his relationships with those beneath him. The caliphal courts, designed to handle questions in which the ruler took more urgent interest, were more likely to reach whatever verdict the government desired. Customary law and sheer whimsy were the only controls placed on the rulers of Islamic nations for most of the premodern era.

Later, the West began to penetrate into Muslim lands. Thereafter, it was to the Western code of legal rules—either the Napoleonic code or English common law—that the rising nation-states of the Near East often looked for guidance in constructing their own constitutions and legislation. They did not look to the *shariah*. From their point of view they had good reason. Islamic law was delivered to a prophet by God. In principle, it could not be modified or even adapted to modern circumstances. Nobody had the authority to do so. The situation was very similar to that in Judaism and the Hebrew Bible, where God himself is the lawgiver and no room is left over for human legislators.

Unlike the famous Babylonian Hammurabi, no Israelite king ever formulated a law-code.[17] Moses was a prophet, not a king. And Moses was not viewed as a sovereign law-giver, but rather as a transmitter of the will of God. Thus, from its very beginnings, Jewish law like Islamic law made no distinction between religious and secular, sacred and profane. All aspects of life were thought of as one. And, just as in the Islamic *shariah*, no difference was drawn between civil and criminal law on the one hand and moral law on the other. More important for my intent and purpose here, the law was regarded by both Jews and Muslims as something divinely delivered rather than humanly evolved. Thus, Islamic rulers who wanted a legal system that they could tinker with, whether for their own benefit or for the actual benefit of their people, avoided the *shariah*.

Today, the split personality of Middle Eastern law is under attack. Not only among Muslims but among Israeli Jews there are those who demand that their ancient God-revealed law codes be enforced by the coercive arm of the state. The issue has led to agitation in Pakistan and Egypt and other Muslim nations, and even to a civil war in the Sudan. In Israel, it is a matter of constant debate in parliament and in the newspapers, and has even played a role in disputes about the building of Brigham Young University's Jerusalem Center for Near Eastern Studies.

The Spread of Islam

The Arab expansion continued in the early years of the High Caliphal Period. Muslim soldiers moved up the valley of the Oxus River into Central Asia, and continued their march across North Africa into Morocco, where they conquered and converted the tribal Berbers. Thus, the entire northern coast of the African continent, once a stronghold of Christianity and the home of Tertullian and of St. Augustine, fell under Muslim control. In the year 711, Berber Muslim forces crossed the Straits of Gibraltar and conquered much of what we know today as Spain and Portugal. Arabic-speaking

---

17. Hammurabi actually claimed to have received his famous 282 laws from the god Shamash.

Muslims would rule the Iberian peninsula until 1492—a nearly eight-century stay that had a profound impact on literature and language and culture, there and in Latin America. (The splashing fountains in the central courtyards of Spanish colonial buildings, cool and green behind thick walls, are right out of the Arab world.)

It must be stressed, however, that these were Arab conquests, not Islamic conquests. As noted, the Qur'an prohibits forced conversions. But the Umayyads[18] did not even *encourage* conversions. To understand this, it must be remembered that the Umayyads were the descendants of Muhammad's old enemies, who had opposed him virtually throughout his ministry. Finally, when they saw no alternative, they converted to Islam. But their lifestyle always gave plenty of reason for suspecting that their conversion was only skin-deep. The empire at times seemed to be merely an unusually large family business, with hereditary succession of Umayyads at the top. They apparently regarded Islam as a religion for the Arab ruling class. But even so, their attitude toward the religion was somewhat free. Many of the caliphs of the Umayyad dynasty have lived on in Islamic tradition as symbols of debauchery. They became notorious for drunkenness.[19] While the subject peoples at first continued in whatever Hellenistic or Sassanian cultural patterns that they had inherited, perhaps looking up only briefly to notice a change of rulers, the Umayyads too tried to maintain the old ways. In this case those old ways were the ways of the desert.

However, there was something artificial about this nostalgia for the simple past. It was inconceivable that the rulers of much of the known world could go on living in the manner of their old desert-dwelling tribal ancestors. And it is not even certain that they really wanted to. Near Jericho, the ruins of the hunting palace belonging to the Umayyad caliph Hisham are still to be found. They certainly suggest something a bit more lavish than a bedouin tent. One is

18. Pronounced "oo-*my*-yad."

19. This picture is perhaps not wholly fair. After all, most of the historians upon whom we rely for information about the Umayyads wrote under the later Abbasid dynasty, which overthrew the Umayyads and had every interest in promoting a negative image of them.

reminded of Marie Antoinette playing at being a peasant girl, surrounded by an elaborate mock village on the grounds of the palace of Versailles. Or, perhaps, of the Hearst family "roughing it" in circus-size tents, camping on the beach at San Simeon accompanied by dozens of servants.

Change was inevitable. The subject peoples began, slowly, to convert to Islam. There were good reasons for this, of course. Being Muslim was the key to social advancement. Even more tangibly, converts escaped the *dhimmi* taxes imposed by Islam upon non-Muslims in order to support the military and other institutions from which non-Muslims were exempt. (Such escape was permitted only after considerable Umayyad resistance. Far from forcing conversions, the Umayyads demonstrated by their resistance that they were actually more concerned about money, about fiscal revenues, than they were about the souls of their subjects.)

The old distinctions between Arabs and non-Arabs began to break down. In a sense, the Umayyads, with their old Arab notions, were being left behind by history. A new generation of Arabs was growing up in the provinces, a generation that had never seen Arabia. The new Arabs gradually ceased to be occupying troops. They sent down roots into the soil of Iraq or Egypt or Syria or North Africa and became a ruling class with local interests. They began to resemble the old landlords of the eastern Mediterranean and Iranian culture areas and began to function like the old local aristocracies.

There was movement from the other side as well. Attracted by the concentration of wealth in the Arab garrison camps, local merchants and craftsmen moved out to them, learned Arabic, and converted to Islam. (This explains how the military camps of Basra and Kufa, in Iraq, and Fustat in Egypt eventually grew into actual cities.)[20] A whole Islamic society was developing in which those who spoke Arabic (especially if they were Muslims) were privileged politically, economically, intellectually, and socially. The old notion of Islam as a religion for the Arabs survived for a considerable time, however, and resulted in a practice which is of some interest from a

20. Grossly oversimplifying, Fustat became today's Cairo.

Latter-day Saint perspective: In order for a Persian or a native Syrian to be accepted as a Muslim, it was not enough simply to convert to Islam. In the Umayyad period, he or she also had to be affiliated with one of the old Arab tribes. Converts thus became *mawali* ("clients") of Arab tribes and were, in effect, adopted into them. This was a practice which had existed in pre-Islamic Arabia, by which a person would be given fictional descent from the same founder of the tribe (who was sometimes himself fictional) to whom all the other members traced their genealogy. Eventually, the distinction between the person's fictional genealogy and his real one would be forgotten, and he would be considered a full member of the tribe.

With the conversion of Christians from Aramaic and Greek and Coptic backgrounds, with the entry into Islam of large numbers of Persians, and with the conquest of areas where Indian culture prevailed, the Arabs gained access to the unimaginable richness of world civilizations stretching from the Atlantic to the Himalayas. A great new world civilization was being formed, a distinctive one that drew upon virtually all of its predecessors but refined them through a comprehensive new religious worldview. The leaders of the empire eventually proved themselves voracious consumers of world culture. They devoured everything they could get. They set up professional translation bureaus that systematically gathered scientific, medical, and philosophical texts from around the world (especially from Greek) and rendered them into Arabic. It was a time of great prosperity, of commercial expansion, and cultural blossoming.

But the Umayyads, with backward ideas, had to leave. They had offended vast numbers of their subjects and they had ruthlessly put down various rebels against their rule. They killed the Shiite leader Husayn ibn Ali ibn Muhammad and butchered most of his family. Their reluctance to treat their non-Arab subjects as equals—even when those subjects had converted to Islam—irritated vast numbers of people across the empire. Pious Muslims, those most concerned with the implications of Islam, also found much left to be desired in Umayyad rule. They feared that their fellow believers were enjoying the fruits of the Arab conquests with perhaps a little too much enthusiasm and were not really serious about Islam. Furthermore, they insisted, it was Islam that was to be the basis of society, not mere Arabness. (After all, they pointed out, it had been only a few years since "Arabness" meant paganism and female infanticide.)

The alienation of these pious Muslims was crucial for the direction in which Islam was to develop. It is from this period that Islamic law and tradition began to develop virtually in oppositional mode, as mentioned previously.

The Abbasids

In the middle of the eighth century, a revolt commenced in far-off Khurasan, in the area of what is today Afghanistan or eastern Iran. This was an area occupied largely by non-Arabs, who resented their second-class status within the empire. The revolutionaries also appealed to the Shiites by claiming that they were acting on behalf of an unnamed member of the Prophet's family. Pious Muslims flocked to the black banners of the rebels, hoping for an overthrow of the hated Umayyads and their worldly ways. (The unnamed relative of Muhammad was the Prophet's uncle Abbas, who had accepted Islam only at the last moment, when it became clear who was going to win. This was an omen for those who had eyes to see it.)

In the year 750 A.D., the Umayyads were overthrown and replaced by a new dynasty called the Abbasids.[21] The capital was moved from Damascus, in Syria, eastward to Iraq, to be closer to the Abbasid power base. Soon thereafter, the Abbasids actually founded a new city, Baghdad, to be their capital. It rapidly became the unrivalled cultural and economic center of the empire and one of the great cities of human history. For those who had supported the Abbasid revolt out of idealism, however, the triumph proved a hollow one. Nearly everybody was disappointed with the results, but the disappointment was especially bitter for the Shiites and for the pious. The situation was no better than under the Umayyads. The Abbasids made no great effort to live or to rule by Islam.

---

21. The name of the dynasty is pronounced "Ab-*bas*-id."

Instead, they based their power solidly on sheer military force. (This was demonstrated in one of their first acts after coming to power, which was to massacre every member of the Umayyad family that they could find.)[22] Their reliance on coercion continued to be symbolized in the Abbasid court itself: The royal executioner routinely stood directly behind the caliph's throne, a stark reminder to any who came seeking an audience with the ruler of just what kind of power he had. (As Samuel Johnson observed of hangmen, the sight of the executioner concentrates a person's mind wonderfully.) He serves perhaps as a fitting symbol of the summary "justice" that the caliphal courts were likely to hand out in criminal and political matters.

With the dependence of the Abbasids on eastern or Persian support, and with physical movement in the direction of Iran, it is not surprising that the Abbasid caliph, surrounded by pomp, came eventually to be a model Sassanid-style king, very much in the style of the old Persian absolute monarchy. He was a benevolent despot, generally, but a despot nonetheless. And he was a far cry from the old Arab *shaykh*, or the early caliphs. Equality and egalitarian ideals were implicit in Islam, as well as in the Arab tradition, and these were completely ignored by the Abbasid caliph. But he did meet some of the demands of those who, in opposition to the Umayyads, had supported the Abbasid revolution. Taxes, for instance, were made considerably more fair. And there was no more delegating them out to rapacious "tax-farmers" who, like the publicans during New Testament times, kept any money they extorted from the population beyond the revenue quota they turned over to the government. Furthermore, strong central authority could defend the weak against oppression. The new regime made no distinction between *mawali* (new) Muslims and old Arab Muslims. In clear distinction to their predecessors, who had run the empire to benefit themselves and their followers in Syria, no province was preferred by the Abbasids over another province. Absolute monarchy, by its very

---

22. One Umayyad prince, known to history as Abd al-Rahman I, managed to escape and to perpetuate Umayyad rule in the distant province of Andalusia (essentially Spain). His exciting story is an adventure movie just waiting to be made.

nature, aids in breaking down distinctions, and this was certainly true of the Abbasids. The caliph was far above all his subjects, who were all equally nothing before him. All alike were subject to the caliph's absolute power.

The more pious Muslims continued to find themselves in opposition to the regime, usually silently but occasionally (and briefly) in the open. Prominent among these were the intellectuals or thinkers who came to be known collectively as *ulama*. It will be recalled that the Arabic word *ulama* means "learned (ones)" and that the main focus of their learning was Islamic law (*shariah*) and jurisprudence. But they were devoted, as well, to Arabic grammar (for better understanding of the precise meaning of the Qur'an, especially now that so many nonnative speakers of the language were embracing Islam) and to certain kinds of history.

The emphasis of the *ulama* on history and law set the tone of Islam from that time forward. Islam has been, like Judaism, a religion that emphasizes *orthopraxis*, right behavior, more than it concentrates on orthodoxy, or right belief. Like Judaism, it has been far less interested in theological speculation than is mainstream Christianity. In this respect, it seems to me that Islam and Judaism have remained true to what we might loosely call their "Semitic character." Christianity, on the other hand, has departed from that character to a certain degree. In his classic Hibbert lectures of 1888, the Oxford scholar Edwin Hatch argued, with reference to the history of the early Church, that "the change in the centre of gravity from conduct to belief is coincident with the transference of Christianity from a Semitic to a Greek soil."[23]

> It is impossible for any one, whether he be a student of history or no, to fail to notice a difference of both form and content between the Sermon on the Mount and the Nicene Creed. The Sermon on the Mount is the promulgation of a new law of conduct; it assumes beliefs rather than formulates them; the theological conceptions which underlie it belong to the ethical rather

23. Hatch, *The Influence of Greek Ideas on Christianity* (New York: Harper and Row, 1957), 2.

> than the speculative side of theology; metaphysics are wholly absent. The Nicene Creed is a statement partly of historical facts and partly of dogmatic inferences; the metaphysical terms which it contains would probably have been unintelligible to the first disciples; ethics have no place in it. The one belongs to a world of Syrian peasants, the other to a world of Greek philosophers. The contrast is patent...[T]he question why an ethical sermon stood in the forefront of the teaching of Jesus Christ, and a metaphysical creed in the forefront of the Christianity of the fourth century, is a problem which claims investigation.[24]

But the emphasis of the *ulama* on law and on behavior came, in the eyes of some highly committed Muslims, to seem a mere concentration on the externals, on the letter and not the spirit of Islam. They yearned for a more personal and warm relationship with God than plain obedience to a law code could possibly supply. Among these pious Muslims were the Sufis, the Islamic mystics, who were more concerned with contemplative or introspective spirituality. (Their name comes from the simple woolen clothing they preferred.)[25] The Sufis prevented Islam from becoming a cold religion of heartless external observance, and they gave to the Muslims and to the world in general some of the finest religious literature produced anywhere.

The worldly culture of the court and the "polite classes," by contrast, proceeded without much real reference to the *ulama*. The courtiers and the administrators of the empire gave honor to the *ulama*—often, no doubt, sincerely—but generally followed lifestyles of which the *ulama* did not approve. Etiquette, conversation, clothing, fine arts, literature, poetry, music, these were the concerns of the political and social elite. Manuals were actually published, for the benefit of the courtiers and the scribes, that listed in concise form the basic information that a cultivated man ought to know. (It was a kind of intellectual "Dress for Success" technique, with scraps of literature, history, geography and biology—especially of the

---

24. Hatch, *The Influence of Greek Ideas on Christianity*, 1.
25. The Arabic word *suf* means "wool." It is pronounced "soof," and the individual mystic is a "*soo*-fee."

"Believe It or Not" variety. The emphasis was on anecdotes and curiosities, to enable the would-be social climber to sparkle in polite conversation.)

The high point of the Abbasid caliphate and of the empire over which the caliph presided probably came during the splendid and luxurious reign of Harun al-Rashid.[26] Ruling from the great city of Baghdad around the year 800 A.D., Harun was a contemporary of Charlemagne. But his empire was incomparably more magnificent than Charlemagne's, excelling it as far as Baghdad excelled Aachen, Charlemagne's capital. Harun was a great patron of culture. Poets, musicians, jurists, historians, scientists, architects, creative minds and hands of all types found support from him. His reign is recalled so fondly in Arab tradition that he even finds a prominent place in the tales of the *Thousand and One Nights*. In those stories, he is depicted wandering around Baghdad in disguise, with his prime minister at his side, to see what his city and its residents were really up to. He gets into many adventures, and has many a narrow escape, but emerges from it all as a kindly and good-natured man, sincerely interested in the welfare of his subjects. (However, these stories of the disguised and wandering ruler seem to have been directly inspired by an eleventh-century Egyptian ruler, al-Hakim bi Amr Allah of the Fatimid dynasty, rather than by the historical Harun al-Rashid. Harun's name somehow became attached to the figure, and the scene of the action was somehow transferred from Cairo to Baghdad.) It was a time of peace and great prosperity; a check could be written in Egypt and drawn on a bank in Iraq (which may be more difficult today than it was then.) The government's policy was what we might today call *laissez faire* or the free market. This may have been one of the secrets of the era's wealth. The purpose of the state was little more than to maintain law courts, to defend the frontiers, and to preserve the citizens' security in the streets and on the roads of the empire. Government inspectors saw to it that weights and measures were honest and that the coinage was sound; otherwise,

---

26. Pronounced "Hah-*roon* ar-Ra-*sheed*," the name or title of this ruler is Arabic for "Aaron the Rightly-Guided."

commerce was free and, on the whole, unregulated. The wealthy members of society, including the caliph, gave generously to charities in their capacities as private people.

By the time that the ninth century was well underway, however, the caliph's office had grown much weaker. There were several reasons for this. First, the caliphs had begun to rely upon imported soldiery. The old military fire had gone out of the Arabians—those who had actually come from the Arabian peninsula, or whose ancestors had done so. They were rich, comfortable, and had little enthusiasm for toilsome and risky adventures. How, after all, could they possibly be more comfortable than they already were? Why look for more? And there was a good chance that military service might cost them more than mere comfort.

So the caliphs began to import young barbarian slaves, mostly Turks from central Asia, who had never known the soft life. But these soldiers, barbarians though they might be, were not at all stupid. They soon realized, much like the Roman Praetorian guard centuries before them, that, if they were in total control of the ruler's safety, they could also control the ruler himself. And if they controlled him, they knew, they would profit immensely. Indeed, after 860 A.D. they actually named the caliph, preferring to choose weak men whom they could control in their own interests. Needless to say, both the institution of the caliphate and the empire itself suffered. To make things worse, the center of the empire was growing weak, while the extremities were strong.

A kind of political centrifugal force began to pull the empire apart. Strong military governors in outlying areas became *de facto* independent, while still formally declaring their loyalty to Baghdad. They had long since lost their enthusiasm for sending the tax revenues of their provinces to Baghdad; they wanted the money to stay at home, to do good—or to do mischief—in their own lands. They were far away, communications were poor, and it would have been difficult for the caliph to impose his will on them at the best of times, when the caliphate was robust. But it was not robust. And when a provincial governor, like Ibn Tulun in Egypt, wrote to the caliph asking that his son be recognized as his successor, there was little the caliph could do. He knew, of course, that approving father-son succession was tantamount to blessing the rise of a new and more or less independent dynasty, but he also knew that, if he said "no," he would be ignored and there would be a dynasty anyway. So both sides decided to maintain the myth of loyalty to Baghdad. The new dynasty received a certain kind of legitimacy from the transaction, while the caliph managed to save face and to receive, if everything went well, some token tax revenues from the provinces. But these were not enough, and the caliph's finances deteriorated even further. To complicate things, the vastly important irrigation canals of Mesopotamia had begun to silt up and to deteriorate, and the central authorities lacked the funds to repair them. Finally, it became clear that Baghdad was, for all intents and purposes, bankrupt.

What the West Owes the East

In the meantime, an immensely rich civilization—rich in every way—had been created. A bare bones description of this vast realm and of the marvelous art and architecture, literature, music, philosophy, and science that it produced would far exceed the space available in this book. It seems to me, however, that a good method of giving at least an impression of the riches of Arabic civilization (to say nothing of the broader Islamic civilization to which it belongs) is to suggest some of the debts that we in the West owe it.

There is another reason for making the attempt. We tend to overlook our debt, even to suppress it. (The West has often been at war with the Arabs and has been reluctant to admit that it owes a great deal to the "infidel" enemy.) Our unwillingness to acknowledge our indebtedness, or to express any gratitude, is something that irritates many Arabs considerably. Yet the extent of our debt to them is surprisingly large. Recognizing it will help to drive out the completely false image many Westerners have of the Arabs as a bunch of camel herders who have somehow, rather like the Beverly Hillbillies, come into a vast sum of undeserved money. It will also help to clarify why some Arabs think of us as arrogant newcomers.

I start with my own favorite field.

Philosophy

The very word used by the Arabs for "philosophy," *falsafa*, demonstrates that the subject grew out of Greek *philosophia* (literally "the love of wisdom"). As the Arabs came to know it, philosophy was based on Greek texts. They adopted Greek philosophy—the legacies of Socrates, Plato, Aristotle, and Plotinus. They expanded it, commented upon it, refined it, and then, when their own creative light went out, passed it on to the West.

The process by which this happened is interesting. The rulers of the Byzantine Empire, based in Constantinople, saw themselves not only as a worldly government, but as the representatives of God on the earth. There was no real separation of church and state. (Had not Constantine, the founder of the city he so modestly named after himself, presided at the council of Nicea? Even though he was not yet even baptized? So who could deny the right of the emperor to rule in religious matters?) The elegant word for this is "caesaropapism," which indicates a state of affairs in which the ruler is simultaneously caesar or emperor and pope. It is also a state of affairs in which religious disagreement is tantamount to treason. The drawback, from the ruler's perspective, is that religious dissent could actually *become* treason. After all, if the government viewed it as treason, why shouldn't it really become such? Tourists today are still shown the gate in the old Babylon fortress, south of Cairo, where a Coptic Christian managed to sneak down and open the gates to the besieging Muslim army. He evidently felt, as did many of his fellow Copts, that Arab Muslim rule could not possibly be worse than the intolerant rule of the Byzantines and might even be better. He was probably right.

The Nestorian Christians were a persecuted minority whose ancestors had lost one of the innumerable nitpicking theological disputes that constantly divided the apostate church. They could see that conditions were rapidly becoming intolerable under the Byzantines, who were determined to have not only political unity but religious uniformity in their domain. So those Nestorians who could moved to the east, often right into the domain of the Persian king, who could not tell one Christian sect from another and was disposed to leave them alone. Thus, when the Arabs inherited much of the Middle East, they also came into possession of a sizeable and, eventually, highly useful Nestorian minority.

In the ninth century, translation from Greek into Arabic developed rapidly. Since possibly the middle of the eighth century, there had been periodic translations, but the ninth century saw the establishment of a systematic, organized effort. The caliph al-Ma'mun, son of Harun al-Rashid, founded a translation bureau called the *Dar al-Hikma* ("House of Wisdom"), which was presided over by a Nestorian Christian named Hunayn ibn Ishaq.[27] (Hunayn's son eventually succeeded him in the leadership of the institution.) The Nestorians were useful because they had a foot in both cultures. At the time of the Arab conquests, their native language was Syriac, a dialect of Aramaic. As we have seen, this made it easier for them to understand Arabic. But they were also oriented toward the West, the original homeland of their doctrine, and their most important writings were in Greek. Nestorian intellectuals, therefore, had typically mastered Greek, Syriac, and Arabic, and were perfectly equipped to serve as human bridges over whom the culture of the ancient classical world could enter into the new Arab empire.

However, it was not only Nestorian Christians who worked in the House of Wisdom. The bureau of translation was truly ecumenical and was staffed by Christians, Muslims, and Jews. Such collaboration between the various religious groups continued and was in fact of the greatest importance for the whole enterprise. Thus, for instance, the foremost student of al-Farabi (d. 950 A.D.), one of the greatest of the Arab philosophers, was a Christian. And Moses Maimonides (Arabic, Musa ibn Maymun; d. 1204), the greatest rabbi and Jewish philosopher of the Middle Ages, served as a court physician in Cairo, where he read and pondered the works of earlier Arab Muslim thinkers and wrote his philosophical books in Arabic.[28]

---

27. Al-Ma'mun's name is pronounced "Ma'*moon*." The common name "Ishaq" is the Arabic equivalent of "Isaac" and is pronounced "*Iss*-hak."

28. To be precise, Maimonides wrote in the Arabic language but used the Hebrew alphabet. This is just one of many instances from the ancient and medieval periods of using the script of one language to write in another language. It is something that has been ridiculed in the Book of Mormon, whose writers evidently used a form of Egyptian script to write in Hebrew. But it was not unusual.

Later, when Arabic philosophy—for reasons that will not be elaborated upon—lost its own creative spark, it helped to kindle a philosophical flame in western Europe. In this process, the Jews of Spain played a role very much like that played by the Nestorian Christians in the East. Like the Nestorians, the Jews had a foot in both worlds. Their own language was Hebrew, which was close enough to Arabic that they had no problem mastering that language. Yet they were also familiar with Latin. Consequently they served as the middlemen, the transmitters of Arabic philosophical texts to the West.

And it was a rich body of texts that was transmitted. Besides al-Farabi, there was the great Ibn Sina (d. 1037), who became famous in the West under the name "Avicenna," a Latin distortion of a Hebrew corruption of his original Arabic name. There was also Ibn Rushd, who, through a process similar to that of Avicenna, became Averroës in the West.[29] He was the author of the most famous commentaries on Aristotle to come out of the Middle Ages. It is an impressive tribute to these men that Dante, in his brilliant *Divine Comedy*, placed them in the highest circle of hell. (That was the best he could do for them, given the religious beliefs of the day.) According to that long and famous poem, while Dante is being given a tour of hell in Canto IV of the *Inferno*, Virgil, the classical Roman poet who was his guide, points out many of the more famous inhabitants. In the first circle, the mildest place in the infernal realm, were many of the great heroes of the past, whose major sin was that they had not been able to receive Christianity. Among these unfortunates, obviously deeply admired by Dante, were such heroic figures of classical history and literature as Hector, Aeneas, and Caesar. But he also included among them philosophers, such as Socrates, Plato, Cicero, Seneca, and "the master of the men who know," Aristotle. Great pagan scientists, like "Euclid the geometer," Ptolemy, Hippocrates, and Galen, make their appearance. But there too, in the best part of Dante's *Inferno*, despite all the enmity that divided their civilization from his, were Avicenna

---

29. Usually pronounced "A-*ver*-o-*eez*."

and "Averroës, of the Great Commentary." These great individuals were in hell only because they lacked the ordinance of baptism. (It is one of the greatest features of the true gospel that such injustice is banished by the ordinances of the temple.) Virgil, Dante's guide through hell, explained the situation to him.

> The kindly master said: "Do you not ask
> who are these spirits whom you see before you?
> I'd have you know, before you go ahead,
> they did not sin; and yet, though they have merits,
> that's not enough, because they lacked baptism,
> the portal of the faith...
> and of such spirits I myself am one.
> For these defects, and for no other evil,
> we now are lost and punished just with this:
> we have no hope and yet we live in longing."[30]

Thomas Aquinas (d. 1274), the "Angelic Doctor," was, until perhaps the last few years, the official theologian of the Roman Catholic Church. He was influenced by the Arab philosophers, especially by Averroës and Avicenna, and placed the latter on a par with Plato. They attracted even the attention of kings: In 1473, King Louis XII of France decreed that Aristotle had to be taught with the commentaries of Averroës. As late as the sixteenth century, the Arab philosophers were required reading (in Latin translation) in the great European universities of Bologna, Padua, Paris, and Oxford.

Mathematics

Arab Muslims had very practical reasons for their interest in mathematics. The calculation of the precise direction of the *qibla* (the direction of prayer to Mecca), something that was required for the proper orientation of mosques, relied upon rather sophisticated mathematical operations. So did the calculation of the exact date of the holy fasting month of Ramadan. (Being a lunar month, Ramadan moves through the seasons. Sometimes it occurs in winter, sometimes summer, sometimes fall or spring.)

---

30. Dante, *Inferno*, Canto IV, lines 31-42, in the translation of Allen Mandelbaum.

The exact reckoning of inheritance according to detailed Qur'anic rules needed attention. And the *hajj*, the pilgrimage to Mecca, had tens or even hundreds of thousands of Muslims converging upon the holy cities of Arabia from all corners of the globe, by land and by sea. This was an operation that required navigational skills of the highest order.

However, unlike the ancient Egyptians before them, the Arabs did not limit their mathematical investigations to merely practical matters. Their work went far beyond utilitarian purposes. They made significant contributions, for example, to trigonometry and spherical geometry. It was an Arab, al-Khwarizmi (d. 850), who invented the technique of using letters and other non-numerical symbols to represent numerical values that we know as "algebra." In fact, the very term "algebra" comes from the title of one of al-Khwarizmi's books. He used the word *al-jabr* to mean "joining," that is, "joining" mathematical quantities together; it originally pertained to "joining" or "setting" broken bones. Al-Khwarizmi's name itself shows up in Western mathematics, in a distorted form, as the term "algorithm," which denotes a system of rules or a process for calculations. (Algorithms have become especially important in our age of electronic calculators and computers.)

It was also from al-Khwarizmi that the West learned of Arabic numerals. However, the transfer took a while to occur, since his work had to wait three centuries before being translated by an Englishman named Abelard of Bath. And it was only after considerable objection that Arabic numerals were finally adopted by Europe in the thirteenth century. Europeans found the Arabs' notion of "zero" especially amusing. It was, they said, "a meaningless nothing." Why have a symbol for nothing at all? But eventually even Europeans began to recognize that these numerals, and the idea of the place system that accompanied them, had certain advantages over Roman numerals. (Try, just as an experiment, to do long division or multiplication with "MDCCCXLVIII" and "CDXIV" instead of "1848" and "414"! You will soon see why the Europeans eventually gave up their resistance.) Today, our words "cipher" and "decipher" and even "zero" itself come from the Arabic term for "emptiness" or "nothingness," *sifr*.

Gradually, as the West noticed the riches that were available in Arabic scientific and mathematical writings, the pace of translation picked up. "From the second half of the eighth to the end of the eleventh century," writes the great historian of science George Sarton, "Arabic was the scientific, the progressive language of mankind...When the West was sufficiently mature to feel the need of deeper knowledge, it turned its attention first of all, not to Greek sources, but to the Arabic ones."[31] A "College of Translators," established at Toledo in the high Middle Ages and functioning very much along the lines of the earlier House of Wisdom at Baghdad, was instrumental in transmitting Arab science to the West. This fact left its own mark upon Western mathematics, as a simple illustration will show:

We commonly use the letter "*x*" to represent an unknown quantity. Originally, this was merely the practice in algebra and mathematics, but it eventually entered into everyday life, where we speak of things like "Brand X." How did we come to choose the letter "*x*" for this? Why not some other letter? Well, as you might have begun to suspect, this habit comes in a roundabout way from Arabic. Older Spanish and Portuguese spelling used to use the letter "*x*" to represent what we in English know as the "*sh*" sound. It so happens that the word for "thing" or "something" in Arabic is "*shay.*" Thus, when the Spanish and Portuguese translators who transmitted Arabic mathematics to the West wanted an easy-to-write symbol that stood for an unknown quantity, they simply took the first letter of the Arabic word "something."

Now is the time to mention the immense influence of Arabic on the Spanish language itself. As I have said, there was an important Arab presence in Spain and Portugal for nearly 800 years, from 711 A.D. to the year 1492. It is not surprising, in view of this long contact between the Arabs and the Iberian peninsula, that many place names on the peninsula are clearly derived from Arabic. When we say that something is "as solid as the rock of Gibraltar," we are speaking at least some fractured Arabic, for the name "Gibraltar" is a distorted memory of the Arabic phrase *jabal al-Tariq*, meaning "al-Tariq's

---

31. George Sarton, *Introduction to the History of Science.*

mountain." Many of those place names were actually carried into the New World by the conquistadors. One common element that appears frequently is the Arabic word *wadi* ("valley"). In the corrupt form of *Guad-*, it appears as a part of numerous place names both in Europe and in the Americas. The beautiful Mexican city of Guadalajara comes immediately to mind, but it is merely one example among many. In Spain itself, there is Guadalquivir—from the Arabic phrase *al-wadi al-kabir* ("the big valley").[32] Other Spanish words also come directly from Arabic, such as *alcalde* ("mayor"), which remembers the old office of *al-qadi*, "the (religious) judge."[33]

Such influence through Spanish is yet another way that the Arabs have had impact on the West, and particularly on the American West and Southwest where many of the readers of this book no doubt live. I myself graduated from a school in the Alhambra High School District in southern California, not realizing at the time that the Alhambra was a famous Arab palace in the south of Spain. (*Al-Qasr al-Hamra* means "The Red Castle.") The adjacent town was actually called Alhambra, and one of the town's streets, "Almansor," was named after a great Arab ruler of Spain known as al-Mansur.[34]

Medicine

In medicine, the Western debt to the Arabs is every bit as great as in the fields already mentioned. The great Montpelier medical school in France, for instance, was founded by Arab doctors fleeing from Spain during the *Reconquista*. Up to the end of the sixteenth century, the medical curriculum of European universities was based upon Avicenna's great textbook *al-Qanun* ("The Canon").

A brief listing of Arab innovations in the medical and biological sciences should serve to illustrate how creative they were in this area. Al-Razi, a leading philosopher and physician of the ninth and tenth centuries, was the first doctor to diagnose and correctly

---

32. Pronounced "al-*wah*-dee al-kuh-*beer*."

33. Some have thought that the Spanish *usted* might come from the Arabic *ustadh*, an honorific form of address meaning "master" (or, in contemporary Arabic, "professor"). This is probably not true.

34. Pronounced "al-Man-*soor*."

describe smallpox. Furthermore, he and Avicenna invented a therapeutic technique that they called *al-ilaj al-nafsani*, or "the spiritual cure." It involved leading the patient back to forgotten memories as a step toward his or her recovery and can easily be considered a ninth century forerunner to psychoanalysis. By the tenth century, an Arab named al-Majusi had a rudimentary idea of the capillary system. At the same time, a prolific writer named al-Mas'udi was speculating about the evolution of more complex animals from simpler ones. Was he a precursor of Darwin? Already in early medieval Baghdad, there were hospitals devoted to such specialties as ophthalmology, teaching and training new physicians, and caring for the insane. (And these early mental asylums were a far cry from the barbarous and inhuman places that came along much later in Europe, places like London's St. Mary of Bethlehem hospital for lunatics, from which our word "bedlam" comes.) Ibn Khatib, a scholar and physician of fourteenth century Grenada, was the first known person to recognize the fact of contagion.

During the Crusades, Frankish (Western) and Muslim doctors often worked side by side. The Muslims were appalled by what they saw. For a leg or an arm wound, the Europeans would cut the appendage off with an axe. Not surprisingly, the usual outcome of such "treatment" was either the patient's instantaneous death or a lingering and painful demise from gangrene. Less drastic treatments, but no more effective in aiding recovery, included shaving the patient's head, exorcism of the evil spirit that was causing his fever or his infection, or the incision of a cross in the afflicted part of his body to let the sickness, or injury-demon, out. It is small wonder that the Crusader states tended to adopt Arab ways. Once they got a feel for their new Near Eastern environment, and realized how far advanced were the Muslims by whom they were surrounded, they were eager to learn. They wanted, after all, to live quality lives. Indeed, they simply wanted to live.

Other Science

"In the sciences," writes the German scholar Enno Littmann, "namely in medicine, mathematics, and the natural sciences, the

Arabs (or, at least, the people who had adopted the Arabic language) were the master teachers [*die Lehrmeister*] of medieval Europe.[35] We have already seen some evidence that this was true with regard to medicine and mathematics. I shall now present some materials on the other sciences, in which the debt is just as plain.

I have mentioned the Arab interest in navigation. Given the vastness of the Islamic world, next to which western Europe seems absurdly small, it was natural that their competence in navigation and geography would be high. They travelled extensively. Ibn Battuta, who lived during the fourteenth century, will serve as a spectacular example of this.[36] He was twenty years junior to Marco Polo and covered far more territory than that famous Italian ever did. It has been estimated that Ibn Battuta travelled seventy-five thousand miles, in an era lacking automobiles, jet aircraft, trains, or even steamships. His travels began, as did those of many others, with the pilgrimage to Mecca and Medina. But he went far beyond that. Leaving his native Morocco he visited not only all of the Arab countries, but also Turkey, Bulgaria, southern Russia, Iran, and what was known until recently as Soviet Central Asia. He lived several years in India and then served as an ambassador to China. Later, after returning to Morocco and finding it a bit dull, he travelled to Iberia (Spain and Portugal), and to Mali and Niger in black, sub-Saharan Africa. He even visited the famous and remote city of Timbuktu. Ibn Battuta left behind him valuable memoirs that are increasingly treasured by historians as accurate depictions of the many exotic places he saw, places that are now irrecoverably gone or changed by modern technology and Westernization.

The Arabs were using compasses for navigation by the ninth or tenth century, considerably earlier than the Europeans. But their capacities went far beyond practical navigation. Roger II, the Norman ruler of Sicily, didn't ask Western geographers to come to his capital of Palermo when he wanted to commision a great book on world geography. He summoned an Arab, instead. And the resulting book,

---

35. Enno Littmann, *Morgenländische Wörter im Deutschen* (Tübingen: Verlag von J. C. B. Mohr, 1924), 74.
36. The name is pronounced "Ibn Bah-*too*-tah."

al-Idrisi's *Kitab al-Rujari* ("Roger's Book"), is widely regarded as the best description of the world known to us from medieval times. It was an Arab by the name of Ahmad ibn Majid who navigated Vasco da Gama's boat during da Gama's famous and important circumnavigation of Africa. Later on, when Christopher Columbus was looking for the earth's other pole—the one that Arab geographical theory predicted would lie opposite India or Mecca—he took along a Spanish Jew. Why? I suspect it was because Spanish Jews—remember their role as middlemen, or go-betweens, who helped to transmit Arab learning to the West?—were in the best position of anyone in Spain to understand and apply Arab geographical and navigational learning. (The last Arab Muslims in Spain were expelled from that country in 1492.) Much of our knowledge of Africa before the great explorations of the nineteenth century (including the names of African animals like the "gazelle" and the "giraffe") came from the Arabs, as well. Leo Africanus, the great sixteenth-century authority on that vast and difficult continent, was actually an Arab by the name of Hasan al-Wazzan.

Few readers are surprised, probably, to learn that the name "Sahara" is Arabic (it means "deserts"), but the extent of our debt to the Arabs in the field of navigation and geography is shown by such Arabic terms as "nadir," "zenith," and "azimuth," which still form an important part of those disciplines in our own language. Even weather terms like "monsoon" (*mawsim*, "season") and "scirocco"—probably more familiar as the name of an automobile than in its original meaning of "the east wind" (*sharqi*)—come to us from the Arabs.[37] (The same Arabic term for "eastern," *sharqi*, is the source for the name by which the Crusaders called their Muslim opponents in the Middle Ages: "Saracens.")[38]

---

[37]. It has even been argued that our word "typhoon" comes from Arabic *tufan* ("flood," "inundation," "deluge"), but I think this must be rejected.

[38]. I'm tempted to suggest, for the benefit of fellow fans of J. R. R. Tolkien's trilogy, *The Lord of the Rings*, that the undignified nickname given at the end of the story to the fallen wizard Saruman—"Sharkey"—may also be related to the Arabic *sharqi*, "Easterner." After all, throughout the trilogy "the West" is good and the "the East" is bad. Tolkien was a medievalist, and his good friend C. S. Lewis indisputably borrowed the Turkish word *arslan*, "lion," as the name of the hero of his *Chronicles of Narnia*. Other commentators have claimed that "Sharkey" derives from the Orkish *sharku*, "old man." Both theories may be right.

In the physical sciences, the Arab Ibn Haytham came to an essentially modern view of the nature of human vision in the tenth century by rejecting the incorrect views of Euclid and Ptolemy. (The question of how external objects come to form images within our minds is a very difficult one. The solution is not at all obvious.) Ibn Haytham's work on the principles of optics also led him to a theory of what makes rainbows. In the thirteenth century, a scientist by the name of Kamal al-Din concluded, correctly, that the speed of light, although great, cannot be infinite. (We know this now, but, again, it is hardly obvious.) Our term "alchemy" furnishes an important clue to the connection of that discipline, and of chemistry in general, with the Arabs. The term *al-kimiya* is the Arab word for both "alchemy" and "chemistry." (The "*al-*" prefix is simply the article "the." We have borrowed it in Arabic-English words like "alfalfa" and "albatross" and "alcatraz.")[39] As Arabic chemical treatises began to enter Western languages, so, too, did items of Arabic chemical vocabulary such as "alembic," "alkali," "benzene," "camphor," "elixir," "talc," and "talcum."[40] Ironically, the word "alcohol" also comes to us from the Arabs—most of whom, as Muslims, do not drink "alcoholic" beverages. In Arabic the word *al-kohl* ("the powder") refers to a substance known in English as "antimony" or even, borrowing the Arabic term directly, as "kohl"; it is commonly used by Arab women as a cosmetic, to darken their eyelids.

The Arabs were also adept at engineering. In hydraulics, the Abbasid dynasty was already thinking of constructing a Suez canal, connecting the Mediterranean Sea with the Red Sea. Unfortunately, they had to give up the idea. It was only finally completed, to the huge benefit of the region, in the nineteenth century. (Giuseppi Verdi's famous Egyptian opera *Aïda* was composed to commemorate the great event.) The waterwheel, invented by the Arabs, was brought to Europe by the Crusaders and played an important role in Western economic development. One of the most famous creations of Arab

---

39. In terms of their origin, "albatross" and "alcatraz" are the same word. Both go back to the Arabic *al-qadus*, meaning "waterwheel bucket," "scoop," or "waterbearer."

40. Some have suggested an Arabic etymology for the word "lava," but this appears doubtful.

technical expertise was a mechanical tree with silver and gold birds that dazzled ambassadors of the Byzantine emperor Constantine VII, who were visiting the court of al-Muqtadir at Baghdad in 917 A.D.

A representative figure for general Arab science in the medieval period might be al-Biruni (d. 1048), whom the famous Western historian of science George Sarton calls "one of the greatest [scientists] of all times...His critical spirit, toleration, love of truth, and intellectual courage were almost without parallel in medieval times."[41] Very few in the West have heard of him, but he was perhaps the first person to make an accurate determination of latitude and longitude. He discussed the possible rotation of the earth on its axis six centuries before Galileo did. And, an example of his wide-ranging interests, he studied Sanskrit and composed a very accurate and objective *History of India*.

Astronomy and Calendrics

The very size and extent of the Islamic world was a great help in astronomical research. Observations from widely separated points were written up in Arabic, the great scientific language of the day, and could be compared by scientists living thousands of miles apart. Muslims, Christians, and even Chinese astronomers were collaborating at the great observatory of Maragheh, in northwestern Iran, by medieval times.

Our debt to Arab astronomy is shown in the large number of Arabic star names that have entered our own astronomical lore. A few examples should be enough to make the point. The name of the star Aldebaran, for instance, means "the one behind," and comes from the fact that, in the Arab view, it was situated behind the constellation known to us as the Pleiades. Vega, the fifth brightest star in the night sky, bears a distorted Arabic name, which may be a little bit easier to understand if we recall that the letter "*v*" in Latin, the language of medieval Western science, is pronounced like the English "*w*": classical Arab astronomy knew Vega as *al-waqi*, "the

---

41. George Sarton, *Introduction to the History of Science*, 2 vols. (Washington: Carnegie Institution of Washington, 1927), 1:707.

faller." The constellation of the "Twins," known to us as Gemini, is called *al-jawza* by the Arabs. Betelgeuse, the oddly named star that has shown up recently in an astonishingly bizarre Hollywood movie, is one of the stars at the top of Gemini. The Arabs called it *bat al-jawza*, meaning "shoulder of the twins." The star Deneb forms the tail of the constellation Cygnus, or the "Swan." Its name in Arabic means "tail." The name of Altair, the twelfth brightest star visible from earth, is Arabic for "the flier." Fomalhaut, another strangely-named star that is the eighteenth brightest in the sky, is part of the constellation known as Pisces, or the "Fish"; its Arabic name means "mouth of the fish." Algol, which we now know to be actually two stars, revolving around each other, fluctuates in brightness approximately every three days as the brighter of the two stars is eclipsed by the dimmer one. This strange variation in brightness, easily visible to the naked eye, may have been a reason that led the Arabs to call it "the demon." (Our word "ghoul" comes from the same source; in early Arabian lore, a *ghul* was a desert demon who appeared in varying shapes.) Rigel, the seventh brightest star in the sky, is one of the feet of the constellation known to us as Orion the Hunter; in Arabic, *rijl* means "foot."[42]

A field closely related to astronomy is calendrics, the making of calendars. It is not easy, since the earth is unfortunately uncooperative and does not revolve around the sun in precisely 365 days—to say nothing of other complications. Here, a major figure is Omar Khayyam, who is best known in the West as the author of the famous *Rubaiyat*, translated into English by Edward Fitzgerald. But Omar Khayyam is not particularly well known in his native Iran as a poet. Instead, he is regarded as a great mathematician and astronomer. And justly so. His calendar loses only one day in 5000 years, whereas the Gregorian calendar that we currently use in the West loses one day in 3500 years.

---

42. Some students of the Book of Abraham, including the present author, have suggested that the great star Kolob, referred to in Abraham 3, may be linked in some way with the visible star Sirius. Sirius is, by a considerable distance, the brightest star in the night sky. It has been widely known since ancient times as the "Dog Star." The word for "dog" in Arabic is *kalb*.

Our English word "almanac" has a colorful derivation. Today it can refer to an annual publication on sports or theater or almost any subject, but its original English usage—as in *Poor Richard's Almanack*, published by Benjamin Franklin—was for an annual publication that included a calendar with times of sunrise and sunset, astronomical data, and other miscellaneous information. The presence of the "*al-*" is a hint that "almanac" might be connected with the Arabs, and, in fact, it is. The Arabic root *n-w-kh* is related to kneeling. A noun derived from this root, *munaakh*, originally meant a "halting place," "a place where camels kneel down." Soon, it came to mean a "place of residence." Then it began to refer to the quality of that place and especially to its weather. Thus, today, the word *munaakh* or *manaakh* can mean, simply, "weather" or "climate." And it is from this, the idea of kneeling camels, that we have today's almanacs.

Literature

Did Arabic literature have any impact upon the literature of the West? Few people in the West would suspect that it did. Yet the answer is almost certainly yes.

It has been argued, for instance, that a book written in twelfth century Spain by a friend of Averroës may have served as the inspiration for Daniel Defoe's famous novel Robinson Crusoe. The Arabic book is a short philosophical allegory entitled *Hayy ibn Yaqzan* ("Alive, Son of the Awake"), about a boy who was raised by a doe on a desert island far away from human company. Written by a Spanish Arab named Ibn Tufayl, it tells how he learned, on his own and without the help of human teachers or books, first to cope with his environment and to survive, and then to understand the universe in a scientific way. More importantly, it explains how, without the aid of revelation, and with only the simple use of his own powerful mind, the boy, as he matured into a man, came to understand the nature and existence of God. This marvelous little narrative was first translated into English by Simon Pococke, just prior to the time Defoe wrote his story.

It has also been argued that the medieval troubadors, those wandering minstrels who sang of pure, unapproachable love throughout the courts of medieval Europe, borrowed their themes and many of their poetic techniques from the *ghazal* poems of the Umayyad period, transmitted through Muslim Spain. (It will be recalled that an Umayyad prince, Abd al-Rahman I, managed to maintain an Umayyad state in Spain even after the Abbasids overthrew and massacred his family in other parts of the Islamic empire.) These love poems shared the theme of the beautiful girl who must be virtuously admired from afar. Dante uses the same technique in his *Divine Comedy*, where his guide through paradise is the virtuous Beatrice, whom he had met when he was nine and whom he had continued to love even after her premature death. (His own wife is scarcely mentioned in his works.) And speaking of Dante, one of the most serious arguments for Islamic influence on the West has been made in connection with his *Divine Comedy*. Scholars like the great Spanish Islamicist Miguel Asín Palacios have argued that his tour of heaven and hell relies on Arab Muslim models.[43]

Arabic influence shows up in sometimes surprising places in Western drama, opera, and musical theater. For instance, the Arabic word *babgha'* or *babagha'*, meaning "parrot," entered the German language as *Papagei*. That is why, in Mozart's opera *The Magic Flute*, we now have the two prominent humorous characters who dress in bird feathers and are named "Papageno" and "Papagena." To choose another example, Shakespeare's *Othello* illustrates the sympathetic treatment that could occasionally be received by a Muslim figure in Western literature. Othello, the good and heroic Moor, is the victim of prejudice and, eventually, of a scheming lieutenant. On a more popular level, some may be interested to know that the title of the popular musical *Kismet* comes from the Arabic *qisma(t)*, meaning "portion," "share," or "fate."

One book that did not have influence in the West, but should have, is the great *Muqaddima* of Ibn Khaldun. It served as the introduction (*muqaddima*) to his history of the world, and it is from this role that the title is derived. But it is now universally thought to be

43. Miguel Asín Palacios, *La Escatólogia musulmana en la Divina comedia* (Madrid: Estanislao Maestre, 1919).

far more valuable even than the important set of historical volumes that it serves to introduce. In his "Introduction," Ibn Khaldun lays out what he regards as the laws of history, based on his extensive reading and his wide experience as a diplomat, judge, and government official in north Africa and Egypt. Among other things, he sees a historical pattern of rise and decline that is very similar to the one sketched by the Book of Mormon. The illustrious modern historian Arnold Toynbee was not reserved in his praise of Ibn Khaldun's work. As he repeatedly stated, he considered it perhaps the greatest work of its kind ever produced.

The Arts

Arabic influence is clearly visible in the arts and crafts of the West. Many materials associated with Western clothing were originally of Arab design. Thus, *damask*, a silk or linen with a design visible from either side, is named after the great Syrian city of Damascus. *Muslin*, a thin cotton cloth, comes to us from Mosul, an important town in Iraq. Sicilian silk weaving, for which that island is famous, is modelled on the Arab silk industry and in fact dates from the days when the Arabs ruled Sicily. "Mohair" and "cotton" and "kaftan" are all originally Arabic terms. "Satin" comes to us from the Arabic name for the great medieval Chinese seaport of Tzu-t'ing, where the fabric was first manufactured; it is eloquent evidence of the vast extent of Arab merchant trading. The term *fustian*, which today (for some odd reason) generally means "pompous language," or "bombast," originally identified a thick, twilled cotton cloth with a short nap that was usually dyed dark and dull. The word seems to come from Fustat, the name of the Arab military encampment founded in Egypt right after the conquest of that cotton-producing country. Another odd transformation was undergone by the word *baldachin*. It originally referred to a rich embroidered cloth of silk and gold, a brocade. Then it came to refer to a canopy, originally to one made of that particular cloth or brocade. Eventually, though, it seems to have come to refer to canopies in general. It is for this reason that we now have Bernini's early seventeenth-century *baldacchino*, the centerpiece of the most important church in Catholic Christendom, St. Peter's

Basilica at Rome. This huge baroque canopy, standing under the main dome and covering the high altar of the Pope's own church, was intended to mark the tomb of St. Peter. Nearly a hundred feet high, it is made not of brocade, but of bronze. But whatever transformations in meaning the word may have undergone, it is clear that it derives from *Baldac*, a medieval corruption of "Baghdad."

Other Western crafts have received important contributions from the Arabs. Dutch blue china, or delftware, for instance, seems to have been invented by the Arabs rather than by the Dutch, who merely borrowed the technique. And Damascus and Toledo blades, carryovers from the old weapons manufacturers of Muslim Spain, tell their own story of Arab influence, as does Moroccan leather.

But the fine arts also receive their share of Arab influence. Sometimes this is very striking, as in Fra Lippo Lippi's Italian Renaissance painting of "The Coronation of the Virgin," in which the angels surrounding the Madonna hold transparent ribbons inscribed with Arab words in praise of Allah. This is not so surprising because, ironically, many of the church vestments used in the Roman Catholic liturgy during the period were of Arab manufacture. This is apparent in certain paintings of Giotto and Fra Angelico.

The word "arabesque" tells us all we need to know about its inspiration or origin. The Italian *campanile*, the bell tower that is so characteristic of Italian churches, seems to have been inspired by the Islamic minaret, or prayer tower. And it is only a short jump from the marvelous *campanile* at the Piazza di San Marco, in Venice, to the look-alike Sather Tower on the campus of the University of California at Berkeley. And from there, it is no great distance to other bell towers on university campuses across the United States, including the carillon tower at Brigham Young University. Arab influence on certain buildings is undeniable. For example, the medallions of the Christian saints in the Norman Palatine Chapel in Palermo, Sicily, bear inscriptions in Kufic Arabic script.

A Word Sampler

Finally, I offer a grab bag of words on various subjects, to illustrate the wide range of things in everyday life which we either owe to the

Arabs absolutely or for which we have borrowed words from the Arabic language.

I start with something very near and dear to most of us—food. The names of many of our most common foods—"artichoke" and "lemon," for instance—come from Arabic.[44] It was the Arabs who introduced *isbanakh* (spinach) into Spain, and from there it spread throughout the rest of Europe and, to the disgust of generations of children, North America. Our word "orange" comes from the Arabic *naranj*, which meant specifically "bitter orange." (The initial "*n*" still shows up in the Spanish word for "orange," *naranja*.)[45] Our word "apricot" derives from the Arabic *al-barquq* (which, oddly, means "plum" in the modern language). The tropical fruit known to us as "tamarind" was, to the Arabs, an "Indian date" (*tamr hindi*); the evergreen shrub "tamarisk" comes to us from basically the same source.

The word "marzipan" has a long and rather strange history. Today, it is the name of a perfectly disgusting paste of ground almonds, egg whites, and sugar that some people pretend to like. This was not always so, however. Originally, the very old and very rare Arabic word *mawthaban* referred to a king who sat still and did

---

44. Here, and elsewhere in this chapter, I have relied heavily upon the researches of other scholars for my notes on word origins. For those who are interested in pursuing the subject further, I shall mention my primary sources. Most important among them is Enno Littmann's *Morgenländische Wörter im Deutschen*. However, I have also made heavy use of Eric Partridge's *Origins: A Short Etymological Dictionary of Modern English* (New York: Greenwich House, 1983). To a far lesser degree, I have used *Etymologie: Herkunftswörterbuch der deutschen Sprache*, vol. 7 in the series *Der Grosse Duden*, edited by Günther Drosdowski, et al. (Mannheim: Bibliographisches Institut, 1963). As a last resort, I have employed speculation. Naturally, I have checked my conclusions against a wide range of modern and classical dictionaries of the Arabic language. I do not, incidentally, claim that Arabic is the *ultimate* source of every word discussed here. Sometimes Arabic itself borrowed the word from another language (e.g. from Greek, Persian, or Sanskrit). But I do maintain, in every instance, that Arabic is the direct or indirect source of the word as we now have it in English.

45. It was the Portuguese who brought sweet oranges from South China soon after 1500. That is why the Arabs call such oranges *burtuqal*. The Germans, who first encountered the fruit when it arrived at the northern ports of Amsterdam and Hamburg sometimes around 1700, still often call if *Apfelsine*, or "apple from China." ("Sina" is an old German form of the name "China"; in English, we use a related word in phrases like "Sino-Soviet relations" and "Sino-American trade.")

not go out on military expeditions. (A *withab* was a throne.) In the course of time, however, the term entered Latin as *matapanus*, the name of a coin issued by the republic of Venice with an image of a seated Christ on one side. Next, the term came to mean a dry measure—perhaps the amount of grain that could be purchased with one *matapanus* coin. In the next step, the word referred to a small box, usually rather elegant, that was used to hold a certain type of candy.[46] Finally, in the last phase of the word's evolution, it came to mean the candy in the box itself.

The words "sherbet," "syrup," and "sorbet" all come from the common Arabic verb *shariba*, "to drink." (And this gets into an area where a committed member of the Church fears to tread. But for the sake of completeness, let us press forward.) The Arabic word *qahwa* originally meant a kind of wine; now, however, it has come to mean "coffee," and it has given us both that word and such derivatives of it as "café" and "cafeteria." Another term for the same drink, as well as for ice creams bearing the appropriate flavor, is "mocha," which comes from the port town of al-Mukha, at the southern end of the Red Sea in what is today Yemen. Many years ago, al-Mukha was the most important town in the coffee trade. (And, incidentally, where would many coffee drinkers be without *sukkar* to sweeten it?) Finally, in this category, I bring up "arrack," or "arrak," a word that will be unfamiliar to many practicing Latter-day Saints: "Arrack" is a strong, colorless liquor made of raisins or sometimes of dates. (It becomes milky white when, as is commonly done, it is diluted with water.) Perhaps the drink would be less tempting to its users if they knew that, in Arabic, *araq* means "sweat."

Changing gears, it is worth noting that many terms connected with warfare have entered our Western languages from the Arabs. (Perhaps this says something of the state of war that has existed between Islam and Christendom through much of their shared history.) Some of these words have amusing histories in themselves. Our navy rank of "admiral," for instance, seems to have arisen out of a misunderstanding of the original Arabic word. The most

46. Or *alleged* candy, depending on your point of view.

likely explanation is that "admiral" derives from the Arabic title *amir al-bahr*, "commander of the sea." Westerners, so the theory goes, heard this as *amiral bahr*, or, as they interpreted it, "Admiral Bahr." Actually, of course, *bahr* is not somebody's name, but merely means "sea," and *amir al-* means "commander [of] the."

Other borrowings were more straightforward. The Arabic *ghazw* ("raid") entered English via Italian as "razzia." Our word "magazine," which first meant "warehouse" or "storehouse" (of weapons or cartridges, as in a "powder magazine"), only began to mean a "storehouse" of information or of entertainment—that is, a periodical publication—in the 1700s. It comes from the Arabic word *makhzan* ("storehouse"). Another word for much the same thing, "arsenal," meaning a place where weapons and ammunition are either manufactured or stored, is a corruption of the Arabic *dar al-sina* or *dar as-sina* ("house of manufacturing"). The weapons in such a place are likely to be of different "calibers." This word, like its relatives "caliper," "calibrate," and "calibration," comes to us from the Arabic *qalib*, meaning "form," "mold," or "model." Those who enter into an arsenal or a powder magazine do so, incidentally, at their own "risk." (Arabic *rizq* signifies the things bestowed upon us by God—usually for our good, but possibly for ill.)

Two other words borrowed from Arabic deserve mention here, perhaps. The first is "assassin." Unfortunately, few readers will be surprised to learn that this word comes to the West from Arabic, but the history of the term is interesting nonetheless. The original "Assassins" were an order of religious revolutionaries, a sect of Shiite Muslims, who were founded toward the end of the eleventh century and who made a great impression on the minds (and sometimes the bodies) of the Crusaders. The legend of the Assassins claims, almost certainly without basis in fact, that they would work themselves up to perform terrible deeds of political murder by using what we today know as marijuana or *hashish* (as the Arabic term itself has entered the English language). That is supposedly why they came to be called the *hashishin*.[47] When the Crusaders returned to Europe,

[47] The pronunciation for these two words is "ha-*sheesh*" and "ha-sheesh-*een*."

they brought with them horrifying tales of these fearsome political "assassins," and the word has remained sadly useful in our vocabulary ever since.

The second word has to do with a more cheerful subject (except for those of us who are routinely humiliated at the game)—namely, chess. Chess is a very old form of entertainment, with roots deep in the military tactics of the Near East. (It is nothing more than a war game, which is obvious when you think about it.) Since it was royalty who were most concerned with matters of war in ancient times, we are not surprised to learn that the very word "chess" comes from the Persian term *shah*, or "king." (You'll have to trust me on this one; the process by which *shah* became "chess" is too long and too complex to detail here.) The relationship is less heavily disguised in the related English word "checkers," which is also related—isn't this fun?—to the British "Exchequer," or royal treasury. And the German name for chess, *Schach*, makes the connection absolutely clear. Once we have this royal connection in mind, it is no longer difficult to understand the chess term "checkmate," which otherwise makes no sense at all in English. It is nothing other than the Persian-Arabic phrase *shah mat* ("the king is dead"), which also shows up in the Russian name for "chess," *shakhmaty*.

The idea behind the notion of "checkmate" is worth pursuing. Players of chess will remember that nothing else really matters in the game except neutralizing your opponent's king. Even if the other player still has his queen and all his other pieces, he loses the game if his king is taken out. This was a very common idea in antiquity; chess merely reflects premodern military thinking. A clear historical illustration can be found in a book called the *Anabasis*, a classic piece of autobiography written by the ancient Greek writer Xenophon. Xenophon was part of a force of Greek mercenary soldiers who set out for Persia to help put a particular member of that nation's royal family on the throne in place of his brother. When the battle began, things were going well until their leader, inflamed by the victory that was soon to be his, went too far ahead of his bodyguards and was killed. Immediately, his armies, poised on the brink of triumph, melted away and fled. The war was over. The "king" was dead. Checkmate.

Why do I find this of particular interest? Because a similar idea seems to occur in the Book of Mormon. When Teancum managed, at great personal risk, to sneak into the tent of Amalickiah and drive a javelin through that evil man's heart, "the Lamanites... were affrighted; and they abandoned their design in marching into the land northward, and retreated with all their army into the city of Mulek, and sought protection in their fortifications."[48] Later, Teancum died in a successful attempt to do the same thing to Ammoron, Amalickiah's equally wicked brother and successor.[49] Why would Teancum be willing to undergo so great a risk merely to get the king? Because when the king is dead, the game is effectively over. That this authentically ancient idea pervades the Book of Mormon is shown by the way the book uses the term "destroy." The Jaredites were utterly "destroyed," and yet it is clear that many survived. What is actually meant is that their leadership was eliminated, not necessarily that every last man, woman, and child of them was killed.[50] Thus, as in so many ways, the Book of Mormon seems to reveal its connections with the Near East. (Chess as evidence of the gospel!)

But we return to our investigation of words that the West has borrowed from Arabic. Several common items of Western furniture bear Arab names. The "mattress" that we sleep on, for example, was at first merely a *matrah*, a place where something is "thrown down." (I suppose, then, that it is perfectly appropriate for us to "throw" ourselves on our beds.) And our "sofa," a long, upholstered seat with raised arms at each end, is simply a softer, more comfortable

---

48. See Alma 51:33–52:2.

49. Alma 62:35–39.

50. For good discussions of this matter as it relates to the Book of Mormon, see Hugh Nibley, *Lehi in the Deseret/The World of the Jaredites/There Were Jaredites*, Volume 5 in the Collected Works of Hugh Nibley, edited by John W. Welch, et al. (Salt Lake City and Provo: Deseret Book and the Foundation for Ancient Research and Mormon Studies, 1988), 237–54; John L. Sorenson, *An Ancient American Setting for the Book of Mormon* (Salt Lake City and Provo: Deseret Book and the Foundation for Ancient Research and Mormon Studies, 1985), 119–20.

version of a *suffa*, a stone molding or ledge. An "Ottoman," on the other hand, a long, upholstered seat that has neither back nor arms, recalls the name of the third caliph, Uthman. Actually, though, it refers to another individual of the same name. Uthman, or "Osman," was also the name of the founder of the great Ottoman Turkish Empire, of whom we shall speak in a later chapter, and it was the Ottomans who favored the low "Ottoman" seat in their government offices. French and Italian diplomats in Istanbul liked it, too, and brought it back to Europe with them.

The type of seat known as a "divan" comes from the same source as the "Ottoman," and, in fact, the two seats are rather similar. "Divan" derives originally from the Arabic word *diwan* ("registry," "government office"), and it is related to another word that travelers to continental Europe will recognize: Upon entering France or Belgium or French Switzerland, tourists are required to pass by the customs officials at the border or in the airport. "Customs," in French, is *douane*. (Amusingly, the Arabs, having given Europe one of its names for "customs," in their turn borrowed a European word for the same institution. Sounding a little like something one of J.R.R. Tolkien's orcs or goblins might say, the ugly word *gumruk*, "customs," comes from the old Latin *commercium*—in which the letter *c* is pronounced like our *k*.) Another governmental term that comes to us from the Arabs, one for which we are probably not entirely grateful, is "tariff," from the Arabic *ta'rif* ("notification").

Finally, a grab bag of word derivations: Once in a while, a particularly splendid personage, or one who wishes to be thought of as someone particularly splendid, is called a "nabob." (Spiro Agnew, in a more negative vein, once referred to "the nittering nabobs of nihilism.") The word "nabob" comes from the Arabic *naib* (*nuwwab* in the plural), meaning a governor of a province. (Governors used to be thought of as splendid.)

In music, "tambourine" comes to us from Arabic, as does the name of that most Western-seeming, most apparently Renaissance European of all instruments, the "lute." Our word "cable" somehow managed to substitute a *c* for the *h* of Arabic *habl* ("rope"), but still can't hide its origin in the Near East. "Fanfare," a word we use to describe a showy or ceremonial sounding of trumpets, generally used to introduce some important person or event, apparently derives from Arabic. So, too, does our word "carousel," which once meant a kind of knightly jousting tournament and only later came to refer to the common carnival ride for children on sculpted horses. Whenever we buy a "ream" of paper, we use a distorted Arabic word. The Arabs "bundle" or "wrap" (*razama*) things in paper and buy paper by the *rizma*. Whenever we are stuck in "traffic," we may wish that the word still meant what its apparent Arabic original: *tafriq* means "division," "dispersion."

One friend of mine even argues that our farewell "So long!" derives from the Arabic *salaam* ("peace"), which is used in much the same way. After all, he points out, "So long!" doesn't make much sense, does it? If we used it as a greeting, maybe we could interpret it as a shortened form of "It's been so long since we've seen each other!" or some such thing, just as "Good day!" is a shortened form of "Have a good day!" But we never use "So long!" to say "Hello," only to say "Good-bye." So he contends that "So long!" was brought back from the Near East by returning Crusaders and then turned into a fairly nonsensical phrase by Europeans who couldn't understand it but at least wanted it made up of words that they knew.[51]

Whether or not my friend is right in his guess about "So long!" and *salaam*, the word *salaam* itself is probably worth a line or two. Many readers will recognize that it is very similar to the Hebrew word *shalom*, which also means "peace." And, of course, the two words are closely related, just as the Arabic and Hebrew languages themselves are closely related. But there is something more that can be said. The slightly formal greeting *salaam alaykum* ("Peace [be] upon you!") is still a commonly repeated phrase in Arabic, as is its

---

51. This sort of thing happens all the time. One of T. S. Eliot's *Four Quartets* is a poem entitled "The Dry Salvages." The Dry Salvages are a rock formation off the northeast coast of Cape Ann, Massachusetts, whose original name was probably *les trois sauvages*—French for "the three savages." The English-speaking locals, who could not understand *les trois sauvages*, changed it to similar-sounding English words, even though the change really didn't help the meaning.

Hebrew equivalent, *shalom aleichem*. My knowing this has altered the way I read Luke's account of the resurrected Savior's appearance to the apostles: "And as they thus spake, Jesus himself stood in the midst of them, and saith unto them, Peace be unto you."[52] I have heard good sermons on the theme of peace based on this very passage. They read a deep and useful meaning into it. But I can't help but wonder if it wasn't simply the Savior's formal way of greeting the eleven apostles—more dignified than "Hello," but serving essentially the same purpose.

The End of the High Caliphal Period

I have tried, by this rather lengthy digression into word origins and word borrowings, to give some idea of the variety and richness of Islamic civilization at its peak. It was a remarkable human achievement. Yet, like other human creations, the great Abbasid Arab empire was fated to perish.

In 945, a clan of rather barbaric Shiite converts from mountainous areas south of the Caspian Sea conquered all of the central Islamic lands, including the Abbasid capital city of Baghdad. They placed the caliph under virtual house arrest, but did not depose him. Why not? Why, when a group of Shiites actually came to power, did they not immediately get rid of the Sunni usurper and install their own leader as the ruler of the empire? There are several reasons. The first and most important is that, sometime late in the ninth century, the main line of Shiite imams had died out. At least, that is what skeptical Westerners think. Believing Shiites argue that the last imam left behind an infant child, who was immediately taken into hiding so that hostile government authorities could not kill him. They have waited for many centuries for the return of their "Hidden Imam," as he is called. Today's Shiite leaders of Iran view themselves merely as stand-ins for their absent master, trying to do what he would do were he here.

The other reason that this group of barbarians from the Caspian Sea, known as the Buyids, did not immediately install a Shiite

52. Luke 24:36.

theocracy is probably that they would have felt obliged to obey it. And, frankly, since they were in charge they had very little interest in obeying anyone. So they kept the powerless Sunni caliph captive, a symbol of their legitimacy in what amounted virtually to a large-scale game of Capture the Flag. Actual power belonged to the Buyid amir, or "commander." In reality, though, the Abbasid caliphate was dead. The High Caliphal Period was over, and the so-called "Shiite Century" had begun.

In the early tenth century, another Shiite sect known as the Fatimids had set up a state in the area of modern Tunisia, in northern Africa. But they were not content with a comfortable state on the fringes of the Arab world. Their goal was to rule all Muslims. For a few years, it looked as if they might actually do it. In 969 A.D., they conquered Egypt and founded a city named Cairo. From there, they would menace other Islamic states for many years. As the Abbasid empire continued to fragment, other Shiites seized whatever they could get. The Hamdanids set up an independent state in the cities of Mosul and Aleppo in northern Syria. Even Yemen was ruled by Shiites.

The sixth-century church of Hagia Sophia ("Holy Wisdom") in Constantinople, was the glory of the Byzantine empire. But the Ottoman Turks conquered the city in the fifteenth century, and renamed it Istanbul. (Hagia Sophia gained four minarets, and became a mosque.) In the next century, the Ottoman Turks conquered their Arab fellow Muslims, and continued to rule over them until our own century.

Decline and Response

The Early Middle Period, from 945 to 1258

The so-called "Shiite Century" that followed the close of the High Caliphal period actually lasted for a little more than a hundred years, from 945 to 1055 A.D. But the complete takeover of the Islamic world by Shiites, hoped for by some and feared by others, never materialized. In fact, with the exception of the Fatimid empire, based in Egypt, the Shiite states grew continuously smaller and smaller as ambitious military commanders broke away and tried to go it alone. In the eastern part of the Islamic world, the old Persian landed class resurfaced after several centuries of near-invisibility. These people, whose public language was Arabic, had been speaking Persian at home and felt more comfortable with it. Now that they again held political power, they felt themselves free to prefer their mother tongue publicly. If they were going to hire poets to glorify themselves and the life of their courts, they wanted poetry they could understand. So, in large areas, Persian was resurrected as a literary language. Now, however, it was written in Arabic script and enriched with thousands of loan-words from Arabic. Hence, it is called new Persian, or neo-Persian, to distinguish it from the ancient language of Darius and Cyrus. This is essentially the Persian language as it is spoken today in Iran. The most striking illustration of this resurgent Iranian nationalism, perhaps, is Firdawsi's eleventh-century *Shah-Nameh*, the "Book of Kings." Drawing on both history and mythology, the *Shah-Nameh* is a versified retelling of the struggle between Iran, the land of light, and its eternal enemy, "Turan." It is generally regarded by Persian-speakers even today as their national epic. It has also, perhaps, established the manner in which many Iranians continue to view the outside world.

The era of Shiite dominance was on the wane. The dynasties that had seized various parts of the Islamic world decayed and fell apart. Finally, between 1055 and 1092, hordes of Turks, sweeping down out of Central Asia, conquered the central Islamic lands. (The Ghaznavid Turkish dynasty already controlled the Afghan mountains and a substantial portion of northern India.) These Turks had been converted to Islam by Sunni missionaries, and, consequently, the Sunni state that they set up—known to history as the Great Saljuk empire—sounded the death knell to Shiite hopes in much of the Near East. (The Fatimids of Egypt held out until 1171.) For thirty-five years, the Great Saljuk empire was ruled by three extraordinarily competent kings, one after the other.[1] But then the process of political disintegration began again. It seemed as though the very air of the period would not tolerate political unity, and the Sunni Saljuk state could no more hold out against it than the Shiites before.

At the same time, in distant Spain, the surviving Umayyad caliphate, which had endured for so long after the Abbasid overthrow of the Umayyads in every other part of the empire, also collapsed. Muslim Spain, lovingly known to the Arabs as Andalusia, became a collection of warring city states, led by men known as "the party kings" (Arabic *muluk at-tawaa'if*; Spanish *reyes taifas*). They gained this title not because they liked a good time—although the historical record indicates that many of them did—but because they were always involved in political intrigue and alliances against one another.

Meanwhile, as the Near East shattered into pieces, the Christian West was growing aggressive. On 26 November 1095, Pope

---

1. The second of these was named Alp Arslan. As I already mentioned, for the benefit of readers of C. S. Lewis's *Chronicles of Narnia*, *Arslan* is the Turkish word for "lion."

Urban II convinced the princes and nobles of Catholic Christendom to join in a crusade of liberation against the Muslims who ruled the Holy Land. "Deus lo volt!" he cried. "God wills it!" Restless knights and landless aristocrats signed up enthusiastically for the new campaign, urged on by a zeal for holy war, a desire to make the pilgrimage to Jerusalem, and by a burning ambition to carve out kingdoms for themselves in a new land. After a long and dangerous journey and after many fierce battles, the Crusaders arrived at the holy city of Jerusalem and laid siege to it in the summer of 1099. On the 15th of July, after a five-week siege, they breached the city's final defenses and poured in. Every Muslim man, woman, and child in the city was put to the sword. Corpses and blood were literally knee-high on the temple mount, where Arabs hiding in the mosque of al-Aqsa had received promises of mercy from the Europeans. The Jews of the city crowded into their chief synagogue, where they were burned alive. When nobody was left to kill, the Crusader princes rode solemnly to the Church of the Holy Sepulchre to give thanks to God for their glorious victory. Jerusalem had been restored to Christian rule.

The Crusaders enjoyed some success in the Near East, most of it temporary, but the interesting fact about them for my purposes here is that the states they founded behaved in precisely the same manner as did other small states of the Early Middle Period. They could not unite together. They made alliances with one another, and sometimes with Muslims against each other. And the Muslim states often sought alliances with the Crusader states against one another. As seems clear to us now, if the Near East had been united, the Crusades would have achieved little or no success. It was the division of the Muslims, the political vacuum created by the disintegration of the Abbasid empire, that invited the Crusaders in and permitted them to stay. (Many modern Arabs see Israel as simply the last of the Crusader states, as yet another invasion from the West, and they point out with some bitterness that, once again, it is the divisions among the Arabs that have permitted such a foreign presence to survive.) But the assimilation of the Crusaders to the pattern of Middle Period states in the Near East was not limited to their military and diplomatic behavior. When they arrived in the region, the Crusaders came into contact with a civilization that was far more advanced than that of Europe; thus, it is not surprising that they began to dress like Arabs, that they learned to speak Arabic, and that they absorbed much from their Muslim neighbors. In some ways, they behaved very much the way the Arabs had themselves, five centuries earlier. And when the various Crusaders and knightly orders returned to Europe, they brought with them some of the things that they had learned during their sojourn in the Arab world. (Among these were spices. Think how dull English food must have been when there were no spices at all!)

Overall, it can be said that the characteristic of the Middle Periods of Islamic history is political disintegration. Constantly shifting political boundaries made for instability and unceasing conflict. And the distinguishing mark of what Hodgson calls the Early Middle Period is, with the obvious exception of far-off Spain, Turkish domination. The Arabs had lost control of their own political destiny—something that would last for centuries and that has continued to rankle them well into our own time. A new ruling class had emerged, separated from the mass of the people and even from the learned classes by a different culture and different language. Many of the rulers of the Middle Period never really learned to speak Arabic—much less to write it. The power of the *amir* ("commander," "prince") rested on something similar to medieval European feudalism.[2] Unlike the European system, however, the *amir* seldom, if ever, lived on his own land. Instead, he lived in the capital and siphoned off the revenues of the rural areas to the city. The *amir* was often totally separated from local life, not only ethnically and linguistically, but even geographically. He gained legitimacy not from popular consent, but from "recognition" by the caliph who, rather like today's queen of England, often had very little choice but to grant it.

Despite this political disintegration—or even, as I would argue, because of it—it is possible to consider the Early Middle Period the high point of Islamic civilization. The military commanders and

2. Arabic *amir* (often spelled emir) is pronounced "a-*meer*."

princes of the small states competed one with another to attract the best poets and architects, knowing that the elegance of their courts and the quality of their architecture offered an important way to their glory and fame. And this competition did, indeed, call forth an astonishingly high quality of work. Furthermore, apart from the role of patron, the rulers of these small states concentrated on military and diplomatic matters, leaving most people throughout the Islamic world free to do and act as they pleased, so long as there was no threat to the ruler's political control.[3] An international society established itself across the Islamic world precisely because the political sphere and political institutions were reduced to a minimum. This *laissez faire* attitude led, predictably enough, to commercial expansion, great prosperity, and to trade in the most varied luxury goods, which passed unimpeded from China to Morocco. Art and architecture flourished. The majority of the population was Muslim by now, and Islam was central to all activities. This was a period of great scientists and poets. If the Early Middle Period saw the rebirth of Persian literature, elegant Arabic also reached new heights. It was an era of famous philosophers like Avicenna and Averroës.

How was the Islamic world able to maintain so much unity in the midst of political chaos and breakdown? Perhaps the crucial factor was the existence of the international class that we have called the *ulama*. These religious authorities, whom I have compared to Jewish rabbis, received the same education wherever they were. They read the same books, cited the same authorities, spoke the same language. Thus, they were able to stand above regional

---

3. Jeanne Kirkpatrick's distinction between "authoritarian" and "totalitarian" states is useful here: "Totalitarian" states—such as those of the Communists, the German Nazis, and the Italian Fascists—make a claim on every aspect of individual and social life. Art, literature, music, religion, the economy, all fields of human activity are subject to state interference. (The Church cannot function in such environments, until they at least begin to loosen up.) In "authoritarian" states, on the other hand, the ruler is inclined to let people do what they want, so long as they do not menace his rule. This is, by and large, the way things have shaped up in places like Singapore, Korea, Taiwan, and many Latin American states (where the Church, on the whole, functions quite well). The states of the Early Middle Period clearly fit into the "authoritarian" category.

peculiarities, to transcend local politics. A Muslim religious judge could work equally well in Morocco or India or Egypt. Some, like the great historian and social theorist Ibn Khaldun, actually did. The long period during which the *ulama* had worked out their legal theories now paid off. The Islamic institutions that had been developed to function in opposition to the state now worked perfectly well in virtual independence of it and without regard to the constantly shifting political situation that characterized the Middle Periods.

The illustrious Saladin (Salaah ad-Deen), famous in the West as the chivalrous opponent of Richard the Lionhearted, mercifully put an end to the long-sick Fatimid dynasty in the latter half of the twelfth century.[4] The last Shiite threat was gone. (It had actually died years before. Saladin merely signed the death certificate.) He eventually managed to drive the Crusaders out of Jerusalem as well and put an end to that Crusader state. A word about Saladin is timely here: He is widely regarded as a great Arab hero, and with good reason. (Even Dante Alighieri, devout medieval Christian that he was, put Saladin in the very highest circle of his *Inferno* among those virtuous heroes such as Hector, Aeneas, and Caesar whose only sin was that they had never received baptism.)[5] In recent years, some Arabs tried to portray Saddam Hussein as the new Saladin. But there is no comparison. Beside the moral gulf that separates the two, there is yet another highly ironic difference: Although he spoke Arabic, Saladin was not ethnically an Arab, but a Kurd. Were he alive today, it is true that Saladin might well be ruling Baghdad. Not, however, in the role of Saddam Hussein, the butcher of Kurdish civilians. Instead, he would have been their avenger.

Saladin established a dynasty in Egypt and Syria, but it never quite measured up to the qualities of its founder. I am more interested in what followed. Like earlier rulers in the Islamic Near East, Saladin brought in fresh warriors from central Asia to serve in his army. These slave soldiers were known as *mamluks*.[6] The word

4. Arabic Salah al-Din, pronounced *Salaah ad-Deen* (with a strong "h").

5. Dante, *Inferno*, Canto IV, line 129.

6. The word is pronounced "*mam*-luke." Indeed, it is sometimes spelled that way ("mamluke"), particularly in older English books and articles.

mamluk means "owned," and it is a common term used in Arabic to describe slaves. Saladin's successors followed him in this practice of importing *mamluks*. But when the dynasty began to run out of steam, something unusual and highly interesting took place. The slave soldiers took charge. Thus arose what is often, and quite misleadingly, called the *Mamluk* dynasty of Egypt.

To explain, the rulers of Egypt and their leading associates bought central Asian *mamluks* to serve in their own personal armies. When these owners died, the *mamluks* were considered free. (To fully understand the situation, we need to get out of our minds any pictures of slavery as it existed in the American South. We are not talking here of plantations and the like. Even when they were still slaves, the *mamluks* were highly trained in their business of war and often lived extremely well. It was simply that they owed obedience to their master.) They owed no particular allegiance to the children of their owner, unless for some reason—perhaps by reason of affection for their late master—they chose to do so. And that was rare. They would then begin to buy their own *mamluks*, if they had not already done so. When the dynasty founded by Saladin dissolved, the *mamluks* of the last sultan took control in their own behalf.

But the regime that they founded should not, properly speaking, be called a dynasty. Only rarely was a father succeeded by his son. A *mamluk*'s children were not themselves *mamluks*. More importantly, perhaps, it was considered that the children of a *mamluk*, who had grown up in the relatively posh conditions of Egypt rather than in the tough warrior-producing steppes of central Asia as their father had, were too soft to be real warriors. Thus, there was no succession within the *mamluk* system. Whenever a *mamluk* sultan of Egypt died, there would be a struggle among the other *mamluks* to see who would succeed him. Eventually, one would triumph over the others, and the regime would go on.

Although an extreme example, the *mamluk* system serves to illustrate several important facets of Islamic society, some of them characteristic not only of the Middle Periods but also of the Near

East today. The *mamluk* system created a ruling elite whose foreignness was astonishing even by the standards of the period. Not only was that elite racially distinct and linguistically separate, but it remained so because fresh blood was constantly brought in from central Asia to replenish it. Men who were born on Egyptian soil to Egyptian mothers, were raised along the Nile, and were fluent in Egyptian Arabic were barred from rule. Both *amirs* and the *ulama* of the Middle Periods rose by personal ability and prestige to whatever status they attained. Islamic law recognizes no inherited distinctions of rank. Everything is by contract. Under the *mamluks* and in the Middle Periods generally, this created real problems in the matter of political succession. (Remember that the tribes of Arabia thought when Muhammad died that they no longer owed any loyalty to the Muslim regime in Medina. Their agreement was only with the Prophet personally.) Even a ruler's designation of his son or somebody else as his successor might or might not be honored; his followers did not feel obliged to obey him after his death.

This question of succession has been a difficult one around the world. We tend to take it for granted in the United States, but I remember the reaction of the Egyptians when Ronald Reagan defeated Jimmy Carter for the American presidency. First of all, it was amazing to many Egyptians that Carter had lost the election in the first place. He was wildly popular in Egypt because of his role in working out the Camp David peace accord between Egypt and Israel, and they could not imagine that many Americans were not just as delirious about him as they were. I recall once seeing "God bless Jimmy Kartar!" spray-painted on a building in Cairo, and I often saw young Cairenes walking around in T-shirts bearing a picture of Carter and Sadat. (It was something I never saw in the United States. Another striking fact was that nobody in Egypt ever wore a picture of Israeli prime minister Menachem Begin, nor, so far as I know, did any spray-painted graffiti invoke God's blessing upon *him*.) Secondly, in the Near East as in Latin America, the incumbent president generally wins elections by 98.7 percent of the vote. It was difficult for Egyptians to imagine that a sitting president, in full control of both the military and the police, could lose an election. But what really astonished some of the Egyptians I spoke to was that, when the day came around, Jimmy Carter voluntarily walked out of the White House and yielded up the most powerful political office on the face of the earth to Ronald Reagan. Carter offered no resistance, and no tanks had to ring the presidential mansion. This astonished them. The question of succession has, for the most part, not yet been solved in the Near East.

In time, the Turkish overlords of the Arab world lost their grip on power. In 1220, the Mongols poured out of the steppes of central Asia and began the process of substantially destroying the central lands of Islam. The irrigation canals of the Iranian plateau, on which the rulers of Persia had lavished attention and money for centuries, were severely damaged if not utterly destroyed. The area received a blow from which it never fully recovered. These Mongol invaders were great horsemen, highly mobile, who had perfected the art of shooting arrows from horseback at great speeds. Needless to say, this was extremely effective in combat. But I have long thought that the real secret of their success came from their attitude to water. Medieval sources report that the Mongols considered water so sacred that they refused to soil it by bathing in it. Instead, they anointed themselves in horse butter. Now, imagine. After, say, thirty years of horse butter anointings, the typical Mongol of the thirteenth century must have been a fairly potent individual. (All a Mongol army had to do was to get upwind of a town. The place was almost certain to surrender.)

In 1258, the Mongol armies overwhelmed and obliterated Baghdad. Out of respect for the high office of the caliph, however, they did not subject him to the kind of death they had imposed on tens of thousands of others. Instead, they wrapped him up in a Persian carpet and trampled him to death with their horses. Thus perished the greatest Muslim city of the High Caliphal period. It has never really recovered, and the prospects of recovery seem dim under its current owners.

Finally, in 1260, the Mamluks of Egypt stopped the Mongol military advance at a place called Ayn Jalut, in Palestine.[7] This must have been an immense shock to the Mongols. No army or city had ever successfully resisted them before. It required a group of central Asian warriors much like themselves to resist them now. Yet, although the Mamluks never receive any credit for this victory in most world history textbooks, their heroism and effectiveness in putting a stop to the Mongols has to be ranked as one of the crucial battles in human history. The invaders had advanced all the way from China, and there is no telling how far they might have gone had a group of unappreciated Muslims not stopped them in Palestine.

The Late Middle Period, from 1258 to 1500

As is to be expected, Hodgson's "Late Middle Period" of Islamic history is marked by Mongol dominance. The problem of political fragmentation was still there, as was the problem of the military elite controlling a population whose language and culture they never fully grasped. But the identity of the foreign ruling class had changed. The Turks who dominated the Early Middle Period were now replaced in many areas by Mongols.

Like the Crusaders before them, the Mongols were intruders who encountered a vastly superior civilization. Soon, they were smitten by it—that is, with the portion that they themselves had not smitten—and began to take on Islamic ways. Indeed, the Mongols who settled in the Islamic world actually converted to the religion of Muhammad. Like the other regimes of the Middle Periods, the Mongols richly patronized the arts. (Hodgson calls these "military-patronage states.") The maidens looking out from the miniature paintings of this new era have pale, round faces, with almond eyes—the Mongol ideal of beauty. But, in keeping with the spirit or the demon of the age, the new conquerors could not maintain unity. Several Mongol empires resulted, including the White Horde, the Golden Horde, the Il-Khanid empire, and the Chaghatay empire. But these were, for the most part, in the Persian area of Islam which lay to the East. Thus, they are somewhat beyond the scope of the present book, which is focused on the Arabs as children and heirs of Abraham. We will return to the Arab world.

---

7. Pronounced "Ayn Jah-*loot*," this phrase means "Goliath's Spring."

In Egypt and Syria, the stock of the Mamluks was definitely on the rise. The desolation of Baghdad in 1258 left Cairo the greatest of Muslim cities. It had been founded only in 969, by the Fatimids, and so was a comparatively new city by Near Eastern standards. (It was built near the old seventh-century Arab military garrison town of Fustat, which was built near an even older Christian settlement. And the capital of the Old Kingdom pharaohs, Memphis, with its great pyramids across the Nile, was not far away. Cairo itself, though, was new.) But the city rose to its new status. A new group of Mamluks, loosely called "Circassians," from a region in the Caucasus mountains, were passionate builders and patrons of art. The years after 1200 A.D. saw Cairo's greatest blossoming as a Mamluk city, overflowing with great wealth and lovely architecture.

For all its elegance and appeal, there were factors that would make Circassian blossoming a brief and transitory thing. In the middle of the 14th century, the Black Death swept through the Near East, killing hundreds of thousands, leaving many cities and towns at a fraction of their former populations. Still, the lavish building programs of the Circassian Mamluks continued. Each sultan attempted to outshine his predecessor in the glory of the mosques he built and in the magnificence of the mausoleum he constructed to be his own final resting place. (Something in the air of Egypt seems to encourage the building of spectacular tombs.) Members of the ruling elite vied with one another in their patronage of architecture. Such efforts required large sums of money, but the economic base of the country was now weaker than before. So the Egyptian regime turned to taxes and to tariffs on trade, desperate for new revenue. But their demands grew so high that European merchants began to seek cheaper ways to do business, ways that would not require them to cross Mamluk domains. When, in 1498, Vasco da Gama found the sea route to India, the Egyptian economy took yet another blow.

As the Arabs declined, however, new Islamic powers were on the rise. Prominent among these was the Ottoman Turkish Empire. In 1453, the Ottoman sultan Mehmet II conquered the city of Constantinople, the capital of the Byzantine Empire. Importantly, he used gunpowder and artillery to do so—an omen of things to come. The Turks renamed Constantinople "Istanbul," and it became the most prosperous city in Europe. For, although we don't often think of Istanbul in this way, it was at least partially in Europe. Most of the sprawling Ottoman capital was in Asia, but a section of it lay across the straits of the Bosporus in what was, technically, Europe. Some writers have called Istanbul a very special place because it straddles two continents. But the line dividing Europe from Asia is purely artificial, appearing only on a map; there is no black line running down the middle of the Bosporus.

Still, the conquest of Constantinople merely completed what had obviously been underway for a long time. The Byzantine Empire, which deserves far more credit from the West than it ever receives for serving as a bulwark against Arab expansion, had been shrinking steadily for years. By the time of Mehmet II, it was little more than a city-state—though a city-state with immense walls and an immensely impressive past. But those who had seen the handwriting on the wall and who could do so had been fleeing for years, knowing a sinking ship when they saw one. And they had been fleeing, for the most part, to the West. With them, they brought Greek manuscripts and a knowledge of the Greek language which was still the everyday language of the Byzantines. This new influx of Greek learning had a great deal to do with the European Renaissance. It opened Western eyes to the long-lost glories of Hellenistic civilization and expanded horizons beyond the rather cramped world of late Latin scholasticism.

But even as Islam seemed to be advancing in the East by taking the long-coveted city of the Byzantine emperors, it was losing ground in the West. There, in Spain and Portugal, Islamic civilization had been under attack and on the retreat for many years. In 1492, the last Muslim ruler was finally driven out of the Iberian peninsula, and one of the finest chapters in the cultural history of Islam came to a close.[8] Along with certain other events, 1492 was a

8. A. J. Arberry's chapter, "Lyrical Interlude," in his *Aspects of Islamic Civilization*, 256-78, uses Spanish Arabic poetry to paint a pleasant picture of life in Andalusia.

rather good year for Ferdinand and Isabella of Spain. Whether the expulsion of the Arabs from Europe was a good thing for the Europeans is an entirely different question.

The Period of the Gunpowder Empires, from 1500 to 1800

As might be guessed from Hodgson's title for this period, the important fact about the time was gunpowder. This new technology, borrowed from the West (and, ultimately, from China), allowed the existence of greater states and thus permitted greater centralization of power. Putting it less abstractly, the states that adopted the new military technology gobbled up the states that did not. What marks the period, then, is a partial recovery from the political fragmentation that was the special characteristic of the Middle Periods. But if that seems like a healthy development for the Muslims, it should be remembered that the period also saw the beginning of the spectacular rise of the West and its expansion in every direction. Muslim rulers were not aware of it yet, but their states were headed for turmoil.

Three notable Islamic empires flourished during the "Gunpowder Period." These were the Mogul or Mughal Empire in India, the Safavid Empire in Persia, and the Ottoman Empire in the remainder of the Islamic world. I shall have something to say about each one of these.

As their name indicates, the Mughal or Mogul dynasty derived from Mongol stock, converted to the religion of Islam. They ruled most of India and Afghanistan during the 1500s and 1600s. The most glorious of their sultans was the great city-builder and patron of the arts Akbar the Great, who reigned from 1556 to 1605 and was thus a contemporary of Queen Elizabeth of England. But the best known fact about the Mughals in the West is unquestionably the building of the beautiful Taj Mahal, one of the world's finest pieces of architecture, during the reign of Shah Jahan (1627–1658).

Early in the 1700s, the empire began to break up. Nevertheless, the Mughals continued to rule a small kingdom centered in the city of Delhi until the British conquest of India in the nineteenth century. It is worth stopping for a moment to consider the remarkable fact that the British were able to complete so stunning an achievement, to reflect that we are tempted simply to say "the British conquest of India" without being properly astonished at the improbability of it. Yet it is amazing to realize that the small island nation of Great Britain was able to conquer the entire Indian subcontinent, thousands of miles away, and to hold it for a long period of time. That they were able to do so is yet another example of the fact that disunity invites conquest. If the Indians had been united, and the Mughal Empire intact, the British could never have dreamed of controlling that vast nation.

The Safavis, a Turkish tribe, gained control over areas of Iran in the late 1400s and early 1500s. But the official beginning of the Safavid Empire must be placed in the year 1501, when the tribe's leader, Ismail Safavi, was crowned shah, or king. It is the Safavids who made Iran a Shiite nation and linked Shiism with the Persians in a firm bond that has never been challenged in the intervening centuries. The greatest ruler of the dynasty was Shah Abbas, who reigned between 1587 and 1629 and was thus himself a younger contemporary of Elizabeth I. He and his successors strongly supported architecture and the other arts, and—something that is considerably more rare—showed remarkable good taste in doing so. The blue and gold mosques of Iran, the Persian miniature paintings that were used to illustrate books of the period, and the magnificent carpets produced by the country's craftsmen all testify to the remarkable legacy of civilization given to the world by Iran. In 1598, Shah Abbas made the city of Isfahan his capital and devoted himself to planning parks and mosques and large public squares. It rapidly became known as one of the world's most beautiful cities. But beauty does not abide forever. In 1722, little more than a century after Shah Abbas, fierce Afghan armies invaded Iran and conquered the city, putting an end to the Safavid dynasty.

Fascinating as they are, though, neither the Safavids nor the Mughals ruled over Arab peoples. It is the Ottoman Empire that most particularly concerns us, since it was the Ottomans who came to rule over the Arabs, and since it is the Arabs who are the special concern of this book. The Ottoman Empire lasted for a long time. It began somewhere around the year 1300, and at least limped on until 1922. In the 1500s and 1600s, it was far and away the most powerful empire in the world; at its height it held not only Anatolia (modern Turkey) but also southwest Asia (Syria, Palestine, part of Iraq, the Arabian peninsula), southeast Europe (including Greece and the Balkans), Egypt, and much of North Africa. The walls of the present-day Old City of Jerusalem were built by its Turkish imperial masters.

The Ottomans were originally nomadic Turkic tribes from Central Asia enlisted, as many Turks had been, to help fight the "infidel" Byzantines. They converted to Sunni Islam, as Turks generally did, and indeed became truly fearsome border warriors. But they soon realized that they could also fight on their own behalf. Why not carve out their own state? Their founder and first sultan was a man named Osman.[9] He inaugurated a series of successful rulers that, for sheer consistency, has little parallel anywhere in world history. One of the first notable achievements of the Ottomans was the conquest of the city of Bursa in Anatolia (Asia Minor, or contemporary Turkey) in the year 1326. Bursa would serve as their capital until the conquest of Constantinople in the sixteenth century, and they adorned it with notable and distinctive buildings. Ottoman expansion was made at the expense of the Byzantines in Anatolia. This is not surprising, of course. It was their duty and their reason for being brought to the region in the first place. Their efforts culminated in the seizing of Constantinople in 1453 with the collapse of the Byzantine Empire. From this point on, there was no Byzantine Empire left to fight, so the holy warriors of the Ottoman Empire turned their cannons and their muskets to the East, against their fellow Muslims.

But before we speak of the significant Ottoman impact on the Arab world, another of their opponents merits brief mention if only because he is famous in the West. It is a peculiar fame. Very few Westerners have any idea who this person really was, and many

---

9. This is the Turkish form of the Arabic name Uthman—the same as that of the third of the "rightly-guided caliphs" who succeeded the Prophet Muhammad—and it is from a distortion of his name that we derive the name of the empire itself, "Ottoman."

would not even recognize his title. He seems almost to have been a particular obsession of Mehmet II, the Conqueror, the man who had succeeded in taking Constantinople after centuries of Muslim daydreaming and failed attempts. Mehmet was never able to put an end to this man, who tormented him for years and finally died peacefully in bed. The man's name was Vlad Tepish. He lived in a region known as Transylvania, or modern Romania. Vlad was also known as Vlad Dracul, "Vlad the Impaler," because he had the endearing habit of impaling captured enemies on stakes. The legend of "Dracula"—or that portion of it that was not invented in Hollywood (and a large part of the vampire legend was, in fact, devised by Hollywood screenwriters)—seems to be derived from this cruel man.

For a long time after 1453, most Ottoman opponents were Muslim. (Certainly there were more Muslims than vampires.) In 1516, Syria fell to a successor of Mehmet II, a sultan known somewhat menacingly as Selim the Grim. The next year, 1517, saw the conquest of Egypt and the end of the Mamluks. One is almost inclined to pity them. They were, in a sense, prisoners of their own virtues. Their horseback heroism, so effective against the thirteenth-century Mongols, was pathetically (although perhaps nobly) out of date. When they defended Cairo against Selim's armies, they took no cannons. They disdained artillery and firearms as beneath the dignity of a knight. And they were cut to shreds, as was anybody else who, for whatever reasons, failed to keep up with the times. Dignity and chivalry, as the armored knights of Europe also discovered, could not stand up to a peasant with a gun.

The Ottomans had yet another military asset that served them well. That was the so-called Jannisary Corps. (The name is from the Turkish *yeni cheri*, meaning "new troops.") These were soldiers very much on the old *mamluk* model, but instead of being conscripted from central Asia, the jannisaries were taken from the Christian villages of Anatolia and the Balkans. They converted to Islam and like the *mamluks* were personally loyal to the person of the sultan himself, who was their owner. As in the case of the *mamluks*, their children were not allowed to become jannisaries, being considered too soft. Interestingly, although no doubt some of the Christian villagers were horrified when they saw the sultan's recruiters approaching, the evidence suggests that many pushed their able-bodied young sons forward, hoping that they would be chosen, knowing that this was a path to advancement that would never be duplicated in the farmyard routine of the home village. The jannisaries enjoyed exalted status in the empire. They earned enormous rewards and were the elite Ottoman military corps, rather like today's Rangers or Green Berets. They were one of the major reasons for the success of the Ottoman expansion.

The high point of the empire's history is probably to be identified with Suleiman I—whose reign, from 1520 to 1566, overlapped that of England's Henry VIII and the first part of the reign of Queen Elizabeth I. He is appropriately known as Suleiman the Magnificent. Suleiman conquered Hungary, northern Africa, and the Red Sea coast all the way down to Yemen. This left him in possession of the holy cities of Mecca and Medina, giving him immense prestige throughout the Islamic world as the protector of the most sacred shrines of his faith.

Prestige, of course, does not pay the bills or put food on the table. The economy of the Ottoman Empire was largely agrarian. Most Ottoman subjects were farmers. While most Westerners picture the Near East as one large desert, it is actually not. (Many parts of it are high and semiarid, but not desert. They are much like Utah, in fact, which also enjoys an undeserved reputation as nothing but desert.) The fertile areas of Egypt, Syria, and the region around the Black Sea produced large quantities of grain. Trade was also important, of course, and the Ottoman Empire fully exploited its location linking Asia and Europe. (Perhaps bicontinental Istanbul is not such a bad symbol, after all.) Chinese porcelains and European woolens, Persian silks, and spices from Asia were to be found in the covered bazaars of the empire, traveling back and forth across it. But the Ottomans were not only consumers and traders of other people's crafts and arts, they were makers of their own. They were especially well known for their monumental architecture (which, unfortunately, could neither be transported nor traded), as well as for their carpet weaving (Ottoman rugs) and their beautiful tiles.

This vast and industrious empire was presided over by an all-powerful sultan. (Appropriately enough, the title "sultan" comes from an Arabic word meaning "power.") Fortunately for the Ottomans, they enjoyed ten successive sultans of astonishingly high competence (to name a few: Selim the Grim, Mehmet the Conqueror, and Suleiman the Magnificent). Each sultan had numerous wives and concubines and, therefore, numerous sons. Following his death, the sultan would be succeeded by his eldest son, the eldest son of a favorite wife, or simply by a favorite son previously designated. As can easily be imagined, this kind of situation led to constant and often brutal scheming. And those conspiracies were made worse by another Ottoman custom. The successful candidate for the sultanate often killed his rivals or, if feeling especially kind, confined them to the *harim*, the women's quarters of the palace.[10] This raised the stakes considerably. To lose in the rivalry for the sultanate was to suffer lifetime house arrest or risk death. The Ottomans gave us the phrase "harem intrigue."

Eventually, the reigning sultan sat so insecurely on his throne that even likely heirs to it were locked up in the *harim*. No longer could they be trusted with governorships or important military commands. There was the immediate danger that they would use those positions of power to hasten the retirement of the ruler and take his position. So, instead of coming to the throne after years of activity and learning in the far-flung regions of the empire, a new sultan would arise out of the women's quarters of the palace. More likely than not, he was unacquainted with affairs of state, having been kept purposely out of touch with the real world. He was unqualified for rule and, not infrequently, demented.

The Ottoman Empire gradually, but steadily, declined over its last 300 years. Eventually, lingering well past the time when most people would have expected it to collapse, it became known as "the sick man of Europe." Perhaps it was continuing on the sheer momentum given to it by its competent early leaders. Nevertheless,

---

10. This Arabic word, pronounced "ha-*reem*," is, as noted earlier, connected with the idea of forbiddenness and is often spelled "harem" in English.

corruption, bloated bureaucracy, inflation, and a string of weak sultans as incompetent as their predecessors had been competent took their toll. As at the time of the Abbasid Empire's decline, more states began to gain independence, and there was nothing more the sultan could do.

In 1571, the combined naval forces of Venice, Spain, and the Italian papal states nearly destroyed the Ottoman navy at the Battle of Lepanto. But, like an unexpectedly resilient boxer who is knocked down but manages to get back up, it rebounded. Indeed, the empire continued to pose a military threat to Europe for many more years. In 1683, desperate Austrian and Polish troops turned back an Ottoman siege of Vienna. This marked the end of Ottoman expansion.

But the Ottomans left their mark on the Near East in general and on the Arab world in particular. Ottoman mosques, for example, with their distinctively tall, pencil-shaped minarets, dot the horizon of the region (though, unfortunately, many of these have been deliberately destroyed during the recent troubles in the Balkans). But the most profound Ottoman impact was probably upon the government and social organization of the Near East. The various religious groups of the empire had been organized and represented under the millet system (from the Arabic word *milla*, meaning "religious community" or "denomination"). Under this system, each religious group, including Muslims, was represented before the government by its leader. People tended, naturally, to identify themselves as much by their religious affiliation—Druze, Shiite, Sunni, Maronite Christian, Jewish—as by their place of residence. This tendency helped to retard the growth of nationalism in the region. A man was not Lebanese, but Shiite. A woman in Baghdad might well view herself as a Sunni Muslim rather than Iraqi. Thus, nationalism came late to the Near East, and many of the countries in the region today can be considered nations only by courtesy. They grew out of British and French map exercises rather than from the consciousness of the people. In Iraq, in Lebanon, and in the former Yugoslavia, we are now reaping what those shortsighted diplomats unwittingly sowed.

The Modern Period, from 1800 to the Present

In 1798, Napoleon Bonaparte, the ruler of France, occupied Egypt. This was a crucial event, symbolically and realistically. For this reason, Marshall Hodgson chose it as the event that marked the "Modern Period" of Islamic history. (For convenience's sake, he rounded the number off to 1800.) Why was this event so important? A Western nation had managed to take control of one of the central and largest of Islamic states. Cairo, the greatest Arab city, was under the control of foreigners. Foreigners, of course, had been ruling Egypt for some time. Indeed, they had been ruling since the Persian conquest of Pharaonic Egypt in the sixth century before Christ. Persians, Macedonians (the Ptolemies, who included Cleopatra), Romans, Byzantines, Arabs, Kurds, Turks, Circassians, Ottomans, even Albanians—the rulers had come and gone, but no real Egyptian ruled Egypt for 2500 years until the 1952 revolution, which eventually put Gamal Abdel Nasser, Anwar al-Sadat, and Hosni Mubarrak in power. It was not Napoleon's foreign nationality, nor his inability to speak Arabic, that marked his occupation of Egypt as something new and different. The surprising fact about the French takeover was not that another foreign elite had replaced the preceding one, but that this new foreign elite was Christian.

And the French were soon replaced by the British, but that hardly mattered. The British were still Christians. Furthermore, before long, many of the other Islamic nations had fallen to Western control, if not to outright Western governance. India was the brightest jewel in Queen Victoria's crown. Of all her titles, including the title of "Defender of the Faith" that she had inherited from her predecessor, Henry VIII, it is said that she most enjoyed "Empress of India." Iran, though nominally independent, took orders from the British and Russian ambassadors. The French and Spanish quarrelled over Morocco, while the French ruled Algeria. Not to be left out, the Italians conquered Libya.

This was politically humiliating. But it was also troubling in another very important way, a way that goes far beyond mere politics. A hypothetical analogy may help bring home something of the emotional impact that the modern age has had upon many Muslims.

As Latter-day Saints, we are used to hearing of new milestones reached by the Church. Missionaries enter new nations, spectacular new temples are dedicated, stakes are divided, hundreds of thousands of converts enter the faith each year. We have come to expect this. And we expect it not merely because it has happened so regularly in the past, but also because, according to our theology, this is exactly the way it's supposed to happen. We are living in the dispensation of the fulness of times. The gospel has been restored for the last time. It is the stone cut out of the mountain without hands, a stone that will come ultimately to fill the whole earth.[11]

With few changes, the last lines could easily have been a description of Islam's view of itself. Muhammad, Muslims affirm, is the last of God's messengers, "the seal of the prophets." Islam is the last revealed religion. Islam is superior to other religions and is destined to triumph. And, indeed, if one looks even briefly at Islamic history, it is clear that Islam did triumph for many years. Within a century of the death of the Prophet, Muslim soldiers had fought their way from the Arabian peninsula across the vast expanse of North Africa and up through Spain into France. They had eliminated one of the two great Mediterranean empires of the era, the Persian, and had taken away some of the richest provinces of the Byzantines. Egypt, the breadbasket of the ancient Roman Empire, was theirs.

This was the province that the Roman emperor had kept under his own personal command. Other provinces might be left to the theoretical control of the Senate, in keeping with the long-standing myth that the emperor was merely First Citizen of Rome. But not Egypt. It was too important. Its two annual crops, and the endless streams of grain boats crossing and recrossing the Mediterranean between Alexandria and Rome, were essential to the "bread and circuses" that the emperor had offered to the urban masses of his capital city, and by which he kept them satisfied and quiet.

Arabs controlled Iraq, the ancient land of the Tigris and Euphrates. They owned the ancient city of Damascus. The scientific,

---

11. Daniel 2:34-35.

medical, philosophical schools of Syria and Mesopotamia were theirs. This was not a transient situation. The civilization that grew out of the Arab conquests and the spread of Islam was, for several centuries, the undisputed leader of the world in virtually every field of intellectual activity. We have seen that Arabic was the language of science and mathematics, and of philosophy. Into it poured the riches of literature and thought of India and Greece and ancient Persia as well as the unleashed creativity of the Muslims themselves. In a like manner, vast trade networks linked China to Morocco, and central Asia to both coasts of Africa. The wealth of the bazaars of Isfahan, Cairo, Damascus, Baghdad, Istanbul, and Casablanca was staggering.

By contrast, the history of the West can seem backward and provincial during the same period. As pointed out, what we often mean by the history of the West, or even by world history, is really the history of part of a peninsula extending westward from the Eurasian landmass. I remember when the realization of how big the Islamic world was, and how constricted the world of Europe seemed, first hit me with real force. I was sitting in a graduate seminar in Cairo, listening to a masterful lecturer discuss the Safavid, Ottoman, and Mughal Empires. India, Morocco, Iran, central Asia—all were interwoven in the vast fabric. Suddenly, the history of Europe, with its little wars between English counties and its struggles over which warlord should control a portion of western France, seemed small and petty. In fact, they reminded me of one of the "rumbles" between the Sharks and the Jets in *West Side Story.*

I do not mean to be snide; the art and history of the West are rich and fascinating. I myself am a passionate lover of Europe. But our neglect of the East cannot be justified. We Westerners have often spoken of "the unchanging East," but this has been merely to conceal our ignorance of the many and tumultuous changes that have constantly affected the region throughout its history. It may help us, and humble us, to know that the Arabs often had this same attitude about *us* during their prime. One very famous Arab historian, writing near the end of the fourteenth century, surveyed developments in science and the arts around the world. He talked about the Chinese and the Indians and, of course, the Arabs and the Persians. He had much to say of their civilizations. Then he came to Northern Europe. "Who knows what's going on up there?" he said in effect. "And who cares?" Europe was backwater, a nowhere. Nothing of any interest had every happened in those dense forests and cold murky villages, and, most likely, nothing ever would.

Thus, it came as a shock when the West suddenly took the lead, in politics, science, technology, and in wealth. And, to make matters worse, the Islamic world almost simultaneously discovered itself to be in clear, evident, and well-advanced decline. Furthermore, it wasn't only in relative terms that the Islamic world had deteriorated, although this was manifestly a large part of it. The West's sudden surge forward is a fact historians still do not fully understand. Was it the rise of free markets? The influx of wealth from the Americas? The Protestant work ethic? No one really knows. Whatever the explanation may be, the flowering of Islam had also declined in absolute terms. It was not the creative society it had once been. Little great literature was being produced. Few, if any, new commentaries were appearing on the Qur'an. Instead, there were commentaries on earlier commentaries. There were dictionaries and compilations, but the originality was gone. Worse, perhaps, is that the Islamic world had closed upon itself. Where, in earlier centuries, it had eagerly, almost greedily, consumed and assimilated as much Greek medicine, science, and philosophy as it could get, and where once it had imported Sanskrit and Persian literature as well as astronomy, it now seemed unable to absorb new ideas. Indeed, it often rejected new ideas in a defensive obsession with the past. There had always been a tension between custom (*sunna*) and innovation (*bid'a*) within Islam and Islamic culture. Such tension was probably even healthy. But now, it seemed, the past had gained the upper hand.

As Muslims began to realize the extent of Western technical and material superiority, they were often appalled. Islam was no longer at the cutting edge, no longer triumphant. Islam, it seemed, was losing ground. The impact was as if not at merely one general conference but at one after another after another, the announcement were to be made from the pulpit of the Tabernacle that we had actually lost members during the preceding year. That our missionary force had dropped, and our stakes were being disbanded. That we were having to sell chapels and maybe even our temples.

How would Latter-day Saints respond to such a disquieting situation? Some, perhaps many, would wonder if the Church were really true. They would wonder why the expectations they had about its future progress were so clearly unfulfilled. But I have no doubt that many would ask themselves what they and the other members of the Church had done wrong. How had we failed the Lord? What could we do to get back on track? More fasting? Deeper, more sincere prayer? A more careful obedience to the Lord's commandments? Have we been too much taken with the fashions and values of the world?

Precisely this kind of soul-searching is currently happening among many Muslims around the world. It has been for some time. *Why Did the Muslims Become Backward While Others Progressed?* was the title of one book published in 1939.[12] Their answer tends to be much the same response that a Mormon would give. Indeed, at least one Latter-day Saint had already given that answer for them, years earlier. Elder George A. Smith, reflecting in 1855 on the history of the Muslims, concluded that "just as long as they abode in the teachings which Mahomet gave them, and walked in strict accordance with them, they were united, and prospered; but when they ceased to do this, they lost their power and influence, to a very great extent."[13] We should not be surprised if Muslims themselves come to the same conclusion. It is, I am convinced, this anxiety over what has gone wrong, and this concern to make it right, that plays a major role in the current resurgence of Islam and in what has come to be called "Islamic fundamentalism."

The hatred of the West that is so prominent a feature of Islamic fundamentalist movements comes, possibly, from insecurity. It is interesting and highly significant that there seems to be no similar

---

12. By Shakib Arslan.
13. *Journal of Discourses* 3:34-35.

hatred of atheistic communism. Even while the Soviet Union was butchering Muslims in Afghanistan, it was American embassies that were destroyed by angry mobs in places like Pakistan. Even mere rumors of American activities allegedly against Islam were enough to bring out tens of thousands of angry protesters, while the brutally real activities of the Soviets brought very little response.

This may come from the love/hate relationship that many Muslims, and other nations, feel towards the United States. Very few people who traveled to the Soviet Union found it alluring. The big gray buildings of Moscow, the vast and empty streets, the pervasive gloom, did not draw, they did not tempt. But the lifestyle of the West is tempting. It is seductive. And the people of the Near East are subjected to it constantly. They are reminded of it everywhere. They see it in the movies and on television. (The only time that I ever watched the TV series *Dallas* was on Cairo television. It was presented every night and was for me a somewhat pleasant bit of Americana.) The Arabs see images of it in their newspapers and magazines. Very likely, they have relatives or friends who live in Europe or North America or who have visited there. Perhaps they have studied at a Western university themselves.

They know much more about the West than we know about them—even if much of what they know isn't true.[14] The image projected of the West is not always a good one. It is rich but shallow, dazzling but corrupt. And we cannot always blame others for this. Much of the time, it is the West itself that creates this image. To sit in a vast Cairo movie palace—like the old theaters in the United States—and to watch an American film amidst a sea of Egyptians is to become acutely aware of that image. It is rather like bringing an investigator or a nonmember friend to a sacrament meeting. You become painfully aware of all the strange people in your ward, of all their odd turns of speech, and of the strange themes that sometimes emerge in gospel doctrine class. (The main speaker is likely to take as his major subject—as one in fact did, in my experience—

14. An Iranian friend of mine, returning to Tehran to visit her family, was amused by the things that people there "knew" about life in the United States. "Aren't you embarrassed," her niece asked her, "to walk around the streets naked all the time?"

the resurrection of insects.) Censored though they often are, these films portray a glitzy world of staggering amorality. I think that much of the disrespectful treatment that many American women claim to receive in Arab countries when walking down the street can be laid at the doorstep of American movie producers, who have told the world everything that it thinks it needs to know about American women. What is more—and worse—is that the image is not altogether false. Many of the criticisms that Muslims make of the West find their echoes in April and October from the pulpit of the Salt Lake Tabernacle.

The West's image is one that many Muslims find simultaneously attractive and repulsive. They feel themselves being seduced, and they hate it—and themselves—for that fact. Thus, they lash out in anger at something that threatens them and their traditional way of life by reason of its very attractiveness. Occasionally, the French culture minister will likewise assail the United States, furious that his own countrymen often seem to prefer American movies and television shows and fast foods and commercial products to their French equivalents. (One wit has called this sort of thing Coca-Colonization.) This is a much less violent reaction—but still very like the one that we often encounter among Muslims.

However, in the interest of historical accuracy I must say that the Islamic fundamentalist response to the dominance of the West is not the only response that the Islamic world has made. And it is only comparatively recently that it has become the most obvious one.

In the early days of the Modern Period, it was thought that things simply needed to be adjusted somewhat. Islamic peoples and nations had been world leaders in the past, and they would be so again, if only a few changes could be made. The Ottoman sultan, for example, began to bring in military advisers from the West—especially from Prussia—to make some changes in the organization of military technology. What he did not reckon with, however, was the fact that Western technology and techniques were really inseparable from Western ideas. Like the leaders of mainland China today, he sought engineering and technological prowess, but ended up getting notions of democracy and human rights as well. (And this was, at least partially, from *Prussians*! It just goes to show how bad things were in the Ottoman empire.) He did not like this but found it virtually impossible to stop.

The coming of the printing press, which arrived relatively late in the Near East, helped to spread these new ideas, and it looked for a time as if the Arab world and other nations of Islamic background would go through the same evolution that the nations of Europe and North America had gone through. There would be resistance, but ultimately something like parliamentary democracy or a constitutional republic would emerge. After all, Islam is not by nature opposed to such ideas. The history of the "rightly-guided caliphs" contains plenty of mention of such things as advisory assemblies and the like.

It would have been wonderful if such an outcome had evolved. But it did not, and part of the blame, at least, must be placed upon the nations of western Europe. The freshly organized political parties of the Near East, armed with their newspapers, promised a new prosperity and flourishing for the Near East if only democratic ideals and notions of human rights could be adopted. The region simply had to catch up with what had made Europe great. They also promised that, when they had shown that they too were capable of enlightened rule and stability under law, they would be able to persuade the French and the English and the other colonial powers to leave. But the colonial powers did not leave. They overstayed their welcome.

Indeed, the French, in particular, stiffened their efforts to obliterate local patriotism. I said above that it hardly mattered whether the French or the English remained in Egypt. But this was not entirely true. The French tended to be far rougher in colonization. The British basically wanted to maintain the Suez Canal as a pathway to India, but French colonists, with their so-called "civilizing mission," actually sought to make Algeria part of France. They banned the teaching of Arabic in schools, making the absurd claim that it was too primitive a language to meet the demands of modern life and technology.

The refusal of the British and of the French to leave their colonies in a timely fashion badly discredited the liberal political parties that had promised their departure. People lost patience with those parties and with the notions of parliamentary democracy and republicanism that were associated with them and with Western models. After all, they reasoned, those ideas certainly did not make the Western nations treat them any better. They had made a conscientious effort to adopt such ideas, while the West persisted in its haughty disdain.

However, there was a new ideology on the horizon, one that claimed to be anti-imperialist, opposed to colonialism. It was embodied in a vast country of seemingly immense power, a country that had promised to use that power to oppose colonialism. Furthermore, this new ideology claimed to know the magical formula that would eliminate the gap between the haves and the have-nots. This was Marxism, and its appeal to the Arab world would only be heightened when the West emerged as the chief backer of Israel, which the Arabs saw as just another colonial state, another Crusader kingdom, occupying their land. Not, of course, that atheistic Marxism could ever fully appeal to the vast majority of Muslims. But it had an appeal for many, and it was a handy ally in the view of many others.

Marxism, or some form or other of what was often called "Arab socialism," became the newly fashionable ideology. The 1952 revolt of the Egyptian Free Officers put Gamal Abdel Nasser in power, and he inaugurated a period of Egyptian socialism that, not unpredictably, virtually destroyed the Egyptian economy. He meant well. He was fascinated by Lenin-style Five Year Plans and the glories of central economic planning by the government. He really seems to have believed Soviet propaganda concerning Marxist economic triumphs. So Egypt today is littered with unneeded industrial plants operating at twenty percent of capacity and cursed with an agricultural economy, once the breadbasket of the Roman empire, that cannot even feed its own citizens.

I once lived across the street from the large American school that is located in a southern suburb of Cairo. During one period, a new building was under construction. What was noteworthy and very irritating about this was that deliveries of sand and gravel to the construction site seemed always to occur between the hours of two and four in the morning. We were constantly being awakened by the sound of dump trucks unloading materials at the most awful hours of the night. Finally, I found someone who could explain this. The government, he said, had rigid controls on building materials, and these were black-market deliveries. A higher price was paid in order to avoid the multiyear wait for materials that could sometimes delay construction of a building. Marvelous! I thought. Astonishing! Only socialist economic planning could create a shortage of sand and gravel in Egypt. We should perhaps be gentle on Arab socialists, though. Many of them genuinely sought the welfare of their people. They simply chose the wrong instrument. It is only in the last few years that the entire world, apparently including the former Soviet Union, has been obliged to admit what many have known for decades—namely, that Marxist economic planning has been an unmixed disaster.

What is more, the notion that communism is anti-imperialistic has now been shown to be a delusion. Indeed, the Soviet Union, which broke up as I was writing the first edition of this book, may have been the last of the great multiethnic empires. (A Sovietologist friend of mine—what, by the way, do we call Sovietologists nowadays?—once asked in mock puzzlement why people were making fun of Ronald Reagan for calling the Soviet Union an "evil empire." "It's indisputably evil," he pointed out, "and it's undeniably an empire. So why not call it what it is?") Russians, Ukrainians, Uighur Turks, Georgians, and Armenians struggled mightily to get out from under the thumb of a government for which, it is now clear, they never felt much affection. Residents of the Near East—and especially pious Muslims—could hardly be expected to love the Soviet regime more than its own people did. As Nasser invited the Soviets into Egypt, they grew more and more demanding, and less and less respectful of the local population. They were an imperial power, and they, at least, knew it. They acted accordingly. (I have been told of this by many a Cairo taxi driver and shopkeeper, people who remember those days with some bitterness.)

Needless to say, Marxism could not deliver on its promises, nor give dissatisfied and humiliated residents of the Near East the dignity that they craved.What other answer was available? The Islamic answer was there. It had always been there, but now its rivals were discredited. "Why," devout Muslim thinkers asked, "should the Muslims turn to the West for clues on how to be successful?" They hadn't needed Western assistance in the early days, when they conquered the Mediterranean world. They hadn't needed the West when they invented algebra. This search for a solution in the West was misguided and unnecessary, they argued. And, these thinkers pointed out, Marxism was every bit as Western as was liberal democracy and market capitalism.

Why turn to the West when the Near East had everything that was necessary? Islamic law was every bit as sophisticated as anything that the West had to offer. Islamic doctrine presented an entire comprehensive view, not only of how one ought to live as an individual but also of how society ought to be constituted. And so we have seen an outpouring in recent years of works on Islamic economics, the Islamic view of international relations, critiques of mechanistic Western science, and fierce denunciations of Western materialism. Islam, in the hands of many thinkers, has gone on the offensive. One Iranian author, the late Jalal Al-i Ahmad, wrote a best-selling book entitled, in Persian, *Gharbzadagi*, literally "West-Sickness," which has appeared in English translation under the clever title of *Occidentosis*.[15] Westernness, in the view of such Muslim thinkers, is a disease. It is something to be thrown off, as one would throw off a fever or, perhaps more to the point, an infection.

In recent years, there has been a widespread sense among Muslims that Islam might indeed be on the rebound. The Islamic Republic of Iran, for instance, seems to many of the faithful, not

15. Jalal Al-i Ahmad, *Occidentosis: A Plague from the West*, translated by R. Campbell (Berkeley: Mizan Press, 1984).

only to Iranians, to have stood up to the West. This appears to many a breath of fresh air. Whatever the moral qualifications of the Iranian regime—and even many of its admirers will admit to serious doubts about those—there is something in this that many in the Arab world and elsewhere in the Near East find undeniably attractive. It is much the same thing that created so much support for Saddam Hussein during the recent crisis in the Persian Gulf. He was standing up to the West—an Arab, looking the presidents of France and the United States and the British prime minister right in the eye as an equal! (To paraphrase a famous remark made about another head of state, and to do so in a manner that will be acceptable to Latter-day Saint readers, the Arabs might have said something like this about Saddam Hussein: "He may be a @#$&#, but he's *our* @#$&#." And, in fact, many of them did say essentially this to me during the crisis and the war.) Given the managed press which is the only source of news for many of these people, it is not surprising, therefore, that they were proud of how long the war lasted, attributing it to Saddam's courage rather than to Western restraint.

One problem, however, is that it is very difficult for any Muslim, even the most devout, to escape the influence of the West. He may rail against it, and consign it and all its offspring to hell, but he will probably do so over a loudspeaker manufactured on the basis of Western technology. The Ayatollah Khomeini, first exiled in Iraq and then in France, communicated with his followers within Iran by means of sermons recorded on cassette tapes. When he returned to Tehran, he flew in on a Boeing 747 jetliner and then rode in triumph through the crowds in a Chevrolet. Such facts as these never allow the Muslim to forget the fact of Western dominance.

This seemingly one-sided relationship hurts Muslim pride. Many educated Arabs are wounded by the realization of how uninformed the West is about them. They follow the West almost with obsessiveness, but the West, and especially the United States, has often been abysmally ignorant of them. Muslims feel that the West has persistently denied its debt to the civilization created by their ancestors. They are proud of their contributions to mathematics and medicine and other disciplines, yet they see no evidence that people in the West know about these contributions or care. They feel unappreciated, especially in view of the great debt they know they owe to the West in modern times. Our ignorance, they rightly note, has practical consequences. We have tended to favor the Israelis over the Palestinians simply because we knew nothing about the Palestinians. We didn't care about the wrongs and injustices that they had suffered because we had never heard of them. There is no Arabic equivalent to the novel or the movie *Exodus*. If most of us can't find the United States on a map, and most of our high school students thought Mikhail Gorbachev was a ballet dancer, it isn't very likely that we'll be able to find Qatar or Bahrayn, or to identify the emir of Kuwait. The terrorism and sabre-rattling that have so often characterized relations with the West, the cruel taking and keeping of hostages, are often simply ways of getting our attention. By grabbing an American off the streets of Beirut, an immature college graduate with an identity crisis and no decent job prospects can attract the gaze of the president of the United States. It is much the same reason that leads nonentities to shoot celebrities. (John Hinckley so badly wanted the actress Jodi Foster to notice him, that he shot President Ronald Reagan.)

But this understandable desire to get the attention of the West is frequently joined with an unwillingness on the part of Near Easterners to take responsibility for the flaws of their own native area. The fact of Western dominance is exaggerated to the point of hallucination. It overwhelms them, much as the absolute sovereignty of God has swallowed up human will in Islamic theology. Many Arabs and other Muslims that I have known seem genuinely to believe that all of the problems in the region are the doing of Western imperialists. (I recall an outbreak of anthrax in southern Iran, some years ago, that the Iranian government blamed upon CIA parachutists dropping in and injecting the cattle.) There is no sense that anybody in the region has the ability to do anything about the region's problems, which are seen as depending wholly upon the superpowers and especially upon the United States. And this, of course, is a formula for stagnation. The hard truth is that the fate of a people is generally in its own hands. Character, as the saying goes, generally *is* destiny. To deny this basic truth means that nobody will lift a finger to do anything, since to do so would be futile. But the first step that must be taken toward regional recovery is the awakening of a sense that the fate of the region is in the hands of the people of that region, very much as the first step in recovery from alcoholism is the recognition that one is, in fact, an alcoholic and that the problem is one's own.

I have tried elsewhere to argue against this view that all the problems of the region are the result of superpower meddling, by pointing out that the area must have been flawed to have invited outside intervention in the first place. India, of course, is a case where this is absolutely clear: As I have pointed out, it was only India's internal weaknesses that allowed the British to move in and take over the subcontinent.

A contrary example is Switzerland during the Second World War. The Swiss were surrounded, by Nazi Germany on the north, occupied Austria on the east, Vichy France on the west, and fascist Italy in the south. The Nazis wanted to seize Switzerland, a Germanic country, and add it to the Third Reich. But they did not. Why? Largely because Switzerland, for all its variety and its ethnic and linguistic divisions, was united. And that unity made the price just too high—higher, anyway, than Hitler and his associates were willing to pay. It is this kind of unity that the Arabs and the Muslims generally lacked during the time of European colonialism and the period of the Crusades, and that they still lack today. (The recent Gulf War demonstrated this with depressing clarity.)

The struggle that today's Muslims have with the massive fact of the West is well illustrated in contemporary Arabic and other Near Eastern literatures. Several issues constantly appear: How is Western scientific rationalism to be balanced against faith? This is the old issue, faced also in the West itself, of reason versus revelation, of faith versus science. And how are traditional ways to be balanced against innovations? What about dress? What about economic progress? How far should it be allowed to damage the real values of the people? Their uncertainty is well illustrated in the title of a book published in 1964 by the well-known Arab thinker Muhammad Qutb: *Are We Still Muslims?* it asked.[16]

Do any of these struggles sound familiar? I have argued that we in the West have much to learn in observing these issues and how they are dealt with by Muslims because these are our issues as well. The advantage is that they are more clearly drawn, more starkly apparent, in the Near East. When we are making compromises, we are often not even aware that we are doing so because both our religion and our science, our religious values and the secular values that often threaten them, are clothed in the same language. Things are clearer, in some ways, for the Muslim. The ideas that threaten his traditional values often come clothed in a foreign accent. Ours come in clothes like our own, speaking in a familiar tongue.

I do not want to give the impression that Islam is faltering across the board. This would be completely, and even dramatically, untrue. Several million Muslims now live in North America, making Islam a larger religion in our own society than several of the religious denominations that we still call "mainstream." And Islam is spreading rapidly here. It is also growing spectacularly in Africa. There, I suspect, it may serve the same role that it served for the *hanifs* in early Arabia: It allows people to choose a religion that is not politically involved with any perceived oppressor. To choose Christianity or even secular consumerism is to align oneself with the West. To choose communism is to align oneself with what was once considered the other superpower. But Islam is a religion that, for some reason, comes free of the taint of imperialism or aggression. Why this should be so is not precisely clear. After all, the early Arab conquests, though not unusual by ancient standards, were clearly imperialistic by today's standard. And although Islam's record on racial matters is considerably better than Christianity's, Arab Muslims were centrally involved in the African slave trade until very recent times.[17] Nevertheless, many blacks in the United States—athletes like Muhammad Ali (Cassius Clay) and Kareem Abdul Jabbar (Lew Alcindor)—have opted

---

16. His brother, Sayyid Qutb, is even more famous.

17. See, on this question, Bernard Lewis's *Race and Slavery in the Middle East: An Historical Inquiry* (New York: Oxford University Press, 1990).

to reject their "slave-names" and the "slave religion" that went with them, Christianity, and to adopt Islam and Arabic names instead.

Lamin Sanneh, then of Harvard Divinity School, visited Brigham Young University some years ago for a conference on religion in Africa. Prof. Sanneh, a West African Christian who had received an Islamic education, had much to say about the relations between Islam and Christianity in Africa.[18] One of his insights in particular stood out, and I have continued to reflect upon it ever since: Christians, he observed, go out of their way to translate the Bible into every language they can. And when they take its message, they make every effort to strip the nonessentials. "You do not need to wear Western clothing to be a Christian," they point out. "Nor do you need to adopt a Western lifestyle or favor Western politics." They try to fit Christianity into the local culture with the least possible disruption, hoping to minimize the obstacles that will always be there to hinder people from accepting Christ. And these efforts have been very successful. Christianity is growing quite rapidly in parts of Africa, for instance. But Muslims' efforts to spread their religion have tended to be quite different. If you want to read the Islamic scripture, they point out, you should preferably do it in Arabic. You should pray in Arabic. You should probably adopt an Arabic name. Perhaps, in some areas, you should even begin to dress like an Arab. Islam, in other words, makes little or no effort to fit into the local culture. And Islam is growing more rapidly in Africa than Christianity.

The Rise of Zionism

Meanwhile, as Arabs and Muslims faltered and desperately sought a reason why, a new humiliation was brewing. A new movement was beginning to gain force among the world's scattered Jews. This was Zionism, a movement designed to realize the long-standing Jewish dream of a return to the Holy Land. It arose during the very

---

18. A version of Prof. Sanneh's presentation has been published as Lamin Sanneh, "Translatability in Islam and in Christianity in Africa: A Thematic Approach," in *Religion in Africa: Experience and Expression*, edited by Thomas D. Blakely, Walter E. A. van Beek, and Dennis L. Thomson (London: James Currey, and Portsmouth, New Hampshire: Heinemann, 1994), 23-45.

period when a liberal European-style nationalism, with dreams of parliaments and self-determination, was finally beginning to grow on Arab soil. The two nationalistic movements were bound to clash.

Ever since their dispersion from Palestine early in the Christian era, Jews had yearned for their lost homeland. Prayers for a return to the Land were often on their lips. The great twelfth-century Spanish Jewish poet and philosopher Yahuda Halevi expressed the sadness of exile eloquently when he wrote, "My heart is in the East, but I am at the furthest West." Yet for many centuries, nothing happened. And with every passing year, any realistic observer would have concluded that the restoration of a significant Jewish presence in the Holy Land was growing more and more improbable. Many Jews, apparently drawing that very conclusion, in fact began to sink their roots deeply down into the soil of the countries in which their families had lived for generations. When, for instance, the king of Prussia summoned all his subjects to unite in fighting Napoleon, the Jews were as enthusiastic as anybody in their response. "Oh, what a heavenly feeling to possess a fatherland!" a patriotic Jewish manifesto cried out. "Oh what a rapturous idea to call a spot, a place, a nook one's own upon this lovely earth."[19] The old anti-Jewish persecutions and regulations seemed to be a thing of the past. Tired of living as perpetual exiles, the Jews of Europe understandably wanted—for perhaps the first time in nearly two thousand years—to feel really at home. Was the dream of Zion dying?

In 1876, Elder John Taylor recalled a conversation he had had with the prominent French Jewish financier Baron Rothschild. When the Baron asked him what the Jews could do to reestablish themselves as a nation in the Holy Land, Elder Taylor replied,

> You can do nothing unless God directs. You as a people are tied hand and foot, and have been for generations, and you can't move a peg unless God strikes off your fetters. When he says the word the things spoken of by the prophets will be fulfilled.

---

19. Walter Laqueur, *A History of Zionism* (New York: Schocken Books, 1989), 3. Laqueur's is the standard work on the subject.

> Then, the measuring line will go forth again in Jerusalem, then your Messiah will come, and all those things spoken of by the prophets will be fulfilled.[20]

Within a few years, it had become clear that the Lord had, indeed, begun to act in this matter. After nearly two thousand years of dispersion, it was time for the Jews to begin the return to the land of their fathers. But God moves in mysterious ways, and the manner in which the Jews were encouraged to return was not, perhaps, a way that any human mind could have foreseen or would have designed. It was a series of *pogroms*—organized persecutions, and even systematic massacres, of Russian Jews—that spurred the first significant wave of Jewish immigration from Europe to Palestine. Thus, the initial impetus for the rise of the Zionist movement came less from desire for Palestine than from discomfort in Europe.

In 1882, young Jews calling themselves "Lovers of Zion" began actively to promote immigration to Palestine among their people. This was the beginning of what came to be known as "practical Zionism," which advocated building Jewish settlements in Palestine. (It was "practical" in the sense that it pushed for real action to implement the dream Jews had been dreaming for nearly two millennia.) Jews returning to Palestine in the late 1800s and early 1900s began the heavy work of draining swamps, digging wells, replanting forests, and reclaiming arid land for cultivation through the establishment of irrigation systems. Farm settlements, following various patterns of cooperative organization, began to appear throughout Palestine. These were an important part of Zionist colonization, since many of the Zionists were influenced by the socialist ideals and theories that were widespread among "progressive" European thinkers at the time.

"Political Zionism," which went beyond merely calling for Jewish settlement in Palestine and sought the establishment of a Jewish state, was largely the creation of an Austrian journalist by the name of Theodor Herzl. He had been a reporter at the notorious 1894 trial of Alfred Dreyfus, in which Dreyfus, a French army officer of Jewish

---

20. *Journal of Discourses* 18:200.

background, was falsely convicted of treason. Dreyfus's Jewishness had been a central factor in the case. (The great novelist Émile Zola wrote an open letter, *J'accuse*—"I accuse"—in 1898 that helped to win Captain Dreyfus a new trial and, eventually, acquittal.) Herzl, a nonreligious Jew himself, was shocked to the core. If anti-Semitism, prejudice against the Jews, could become so powerful in a modern, enlightened country like France, it seemed to him that things could only be worse elsewhere. The hope of many Jews to fit in, to assimilate and be accepted as Frenchmen and Germans and Englishmen just like anyone else, now appeared to Herzl to be an illusion. If, after nearly two thousand years of Christianity, it had not yet happened, there was good reason to believe that it never would.

The only possible solution, in Herzl's view, was for Jews to create an independent Jewish state, in which they would not need to depend on the passing goodwill of Christians. He decided to devote the rest of his life to that cause. It was Herzl, essentially, who put the international Zionist movement in motion. He worked tirelessly, appealing to Jewish leaders and the rulers of many nations, writing, speaking, and traveling indefatigably. An important milestone occurred when the First Zionist Congress was held in Basel, Switzerland, in 1897. The movement that would culminate in the establishment of the state of Israel was well underway.

Not all Jews were enthusiastic about Herzl's ideas; some, in fact, are still not. Certain Jews, perhaps still hoping to be accepted and assimilated into the countries of their birth, denied that Judaism was an ethnic or national category. Such a claim, they said, just made the situation worse. If Jews themselves were claiming that they were not really Germans, or not true Frenchmen, but had primary loyalty to another, foreign nation, how could they possibly complain when German and French anti-Semites accused them of precisely that? Others rejected political Zionism on the belief that only God could or should restore the Jews to their ancient homeland.

Despite numerous dissenting voices, the political Zionist movement nonetheless began to gain momentum during the First World War, in which Great Britain defeated the Ottoman Empire and freed much of the Arab world, including Palestine, from Turkish domination. Latter-day Saints, too, tended to look upon the fall of Jerusalem into the hands of the British as "one of the steps in the foretold gathering of the Jews in the latter days, and as the beginning of the fulfillment of ancient and modern prophecy."[21] They were undoubtedly correct to do so. In 1917, the British government issued the so-called "Balfour Declaration," which pledged support for a Jewish national homeland in Palestine. And when, in 1920, the British began to carry out the League of Nations mandate that gave them authority to administer Palestine, they acted on the basis of that Balfour Declaration. This came in direct fulfillment of a prophecy given by Orson Hyde in 1842:

> It was by political power and influence that the Jewish nation was broken down, and her subjects dispersed abroad; and I will here hazard the opinion, that by political power and influence they will be gathered and built up; and further, that England is destined in the wisdom and economy of heaven to stretch forth the arm of political power, and advance in the front ranks of this glorious enterprize.[22]

In many respects, the Balfour Declaration can be compared with the decree issued by the great Persian ruler Cyrus, in 536 B.C., which permitted a remnant of the Jews to return from Babylon and to rebuild Jerusalem. Nevertheless, however much it may have been part of the divine plan, British intervention on behalf of the Jews brought an angry and often violent response from the Arab residents in Palestine. And, in many ways, it must be admitted that the Arab response was thoroughly understandable. For the situation of Palestine in the twentieth century after Christ was not comparable in all respects with the situation in the sixth century before his birth. Some differences can be briefly alluded to here:

The Babylonian captivity, for all its trauma, lasted only half a century or thereabouts. There were undoubtedly people living in

---

21. See "Editor's Table: The Fall of Jerusalem" in *Improvement Era* 21, 259-61. The quotation occurs on p. 261, where the editor says that "the Saints are glad to behold the signs of the coming day."

22. Orson Hyde, in *The Latter-day Saints' Millennial Star* (11 March 1842), 168-69.

Palestine who still remembered the Jews before them being carried off into captivity, just as there were almost certainly exiles living in Babylon at the time of Cyrus's decree who still recalled their homes in Judea. The modern *diaspora*, on the other hand, was nearly two thousand years old. Other people had settled in Palestine and had sent down deep roots in that land. It was, they felt, their land. They could certainly argue—and did—that whatever legal claim the Jews might once have had on the land had long since lapsed. Furthermore, the land of Palestine had never really been entirely swept clean. There were people there whose families almost certainly go back to the time before the dispersion of the Jews, whose roots were deeper still. It is highly probable that some among these actually *were* Jews, even if they had long forgotten the fact. How could the land not belong to those who had possessed it for two millennia?[23] Those in Palestine who still professed to be Jews were distinctly in the minority well into the twentieth century.

Cyrus was exercising his right, as ruler of the Persian Empire, to transfer people to any part of the empire that he chose or to allow them to move themselves. Palestine was an undisputed part of his empire. In the twentieth century, however, Palestine was not part of the British Empire. It had, it is true, been part of the Ottoman Empire. But the Arabs had fought alongside the British, against the Ottoman Turks, to win independence for themselves and their lands. Their sense of nationalism was riding high. They did not understand it to be the right of the British or of anybody else to grant their land to anyone, however altruistic the act might be. (It is easy, as we all know, to be generous with somebody else's money.)

---

23. Many Americans today probably feel much the same way about Indian and Mexican claims to parts of the United States. Even if these claims have some validity—as in many instances they undoubtedly do—it is widely felt that simply too much water has gone under the bridge. Too much time has elapsed. To give Los Angeles back to Mexico, or to give Arizona back to the Indians, evicting the non-Mexican or non-Indian populations of these places, would be to perpetrate yet another huge injustice. After a certain lapse of time, old injustices must often be allowed to continue. Or, frankly, they must be forgotten. To choose an example from the very period in which the Jewish dispersion began, we would consider it odd if the French or the English began to file damage claims against Italy based on injuries suffered under Roman occupation.

And as people of the twentieth century, they were less inclined, perhaps, than ancient people were to admit that a ruler, any ruler, has a right to transfer populations around and to grant and bestow whole countries without the consent of their inhabitants.

There were serious clashes between Arabs and Jewish settlers throughout the 1920s and 1930s, until the point in 1939 when, hoping to gain Arab support against the Axis powers in World War II, the British began to restrict Jewish immigration to the Holy Land. This, in turn, brought an angry and often violent response from the Jews of Palestine. Fed up with the situation, Great Britain submitted the problem to the United Nations after the close of the war, and, on 29 November 1947, that international organization decided to relieve the British of responsibility for Palestine and to approve partition of the area into two states; one for the Jews and the other for the Palestinian Arabs.

The Zionists accepted the United Nations plan, although they did so with some reluctance, since it failed to grant them control over many of the areas of Palestine that were most important to them and to Jewish history. Their reasoning, clearly, was that it was better to get half a loaf of bread than to get no loaf at all. With the two-thousand-year-old dream of a Jewish state so nearly within reach, they seized the opportunity that the U.N. plan offered them. The Arabs, on the other hand, rejected the partition plan. They considered all of Palestine to be theirs and could not see why they should agree to demands from outsiders that they give up part of their land. Even today, some Palestinians like to point to the indisputable fact that it was partly European horror and revulsion at what had been done to the Jews by the Nazis in the 1930s and 1940s that finally led the United Nations to set up a Jewish homeland in the Middle East. "If the West felt so guilty," these Arabs ask, "why didn't it create a Jewish state in *Bavaria*? After all, it was the Germans who carried out the Holocaust, not the Arabs." The Arab nations around Palestine began to prepare for military intervention to thwart the partition plan.

Modern-day Arabs are still searching for a leader who will help them regain their ancient pride and glory.

Today

The Middle East is a mess. That is perhaps the most obvious fact about the area. It is possibly the worst-governed region on the globe. Or perhaps it just seems to be because we give the area so much attention. We do so because the place is so important to us, and not merely because of its oil reserves. It is the source of much of our own culture. Many of our most sacred values come from a barren peninsula known as the Sinai. The region exercises a huge influence on our imaginations. Hardly a schoolchild is unaware of the pyramids or the Sphinx. Bible readers who may know nothing of ancient history in general know of Babylon and Nebuchadnezzar, of the Philistines and the Canaanites. More importantly, they know of Israel, and the place names of a small territory called Palestine linger in our minds: Galilee, Sodom and Gomorrah, Jerusalem, the River Jordan.

The continent of Africa, too, suffers from incompetent and evil rulers, but we in the West seldom notice it. For most of us, Africa is not so central to our belief system or to our own identities. Furthermore, with spectacular recent exceptions like Rwanda and Somalia, Africans generally do not intrude upon our consciousness. They suffer, relative to us, in silence. Their agonies rarely make the front pages of our newspapers. But disputes in the Middle East are likely to spill over into terrorist attacks in Asia or to bring down airliners over Scotland. Why this should be so deserves our attention.

Politics in the Middle East can be seen as a combination of three entirely different traditions, interacting somewhat uneasily.[1] The first of these traditions can be loosely described as the politics of the tribe. This is probably the oldest form of politics in the region and perhaps the oldest anywhere. And it is the form of politics to which, when things get rough, the Arab situation tends to revert. The modern national boundaries of the Middle East are often artificial, and the governments that rule the nations of the region, although they may appear to the superficial eye to be modern and to have all the institutional trappings of an up-to-date regime (presidents, prime ministers, parliaments, and the like), are frequently every bit as inauthentic. In tribal politics, the individual's loyalty is given first and foremost to his kinship group, his clan, or to his religious denomination. The object of his loyalties may or may not be a literal tribe as in Arabia before Islam, but it will often behave as if it were. (We have seen this reflected in the Ottoman Empire's *millet* system.) Relations between the tribes are characterized by suspicion, rivalry, and terrible vengeance for wrongs suffered or perceived. It is only by taking such vengeance, by intimidating and discouraging potential enemies, that one can be reasonably certain of safety in the future. There is, as there was in pre-Islamic Arabia, no higher authority to appeal to, no police force to protect. Thus, we have an Alawite religious minority dominating Syria to its own benefit. In Iraq, a kind of mafia from the village of Tikrit rules the country at the time of

---

1. My formulation of these three traditions rests heavily upon Thomas L. Friedman, *From Beirut to Jerusalem* (New York: Farrar Straus Giroux, 1989), 87-101, although I have long thought along these general lines and have, I hope, given the subject my own twist. (The brilliant Arab historian and social theorist Ibn Khaldun had, after all, developed the idea of tribal "solidarity" [*asabiyya*] as a force in history already by the end of the fourteenth century.) Still, I have learned a great deal from Friedman's extraordinarily insightful book, as is demonstrated throughout this chapter. Other books that have taught me much include Gilles Kepel, *The Revenge of God: The Resurgence of Islam, Christianity and Judaism in the Modern World*, translated by Alan Braley (University Park: Pennsylvania State, 1994); Emmanuel Sivan, *Radical Islam: Medieval Theology and Modern Politics* (New Haven: Yale, 1985); Barry Rubin, *Revolution until Victory? The Politics and History of the PLO* (Cambridge: Harvard, 1994). Ziad Abu-Amr, *Islamic Fundamentalism in the West Bank and Gaza: Muslim Brotherhood and Islamic Jihad* (Bloomington and Indianapolis: Indiana, 1994), is a useful guide into the confusing world of Palestinian Islamic militancy.

this writing. It persecutes the Kurds of the north and, being itself Sunni Muslim (at least in name), persecutes the Shiite majority that resides mainly in the country's south. The classic illustration of this tribal politics is to be found in Lebanon, which will be discussed below, but it is certainly not foreign to Israel, where a tribe of Palestinian Arabs is locked in a struggle with a tribe of Israeli Jews. Today, just as in the Middle Periods, the ruling elite in the Near East is often religiously or otherwise foreign to the populace. There is a gulf between the ruler and the ruled.

The second political tradition characteristic of the Middle East is authoritarianism. This means that a single ruler or an elite group (often a "tribe," in the sense just mentioned) has virtually unlimited political power concentrated in its hands, without being bound by either a constitution or by the will of the people over whom he or it rules. After all, given the tradition of tribalism mentioned above, there is often little in common between the ruler and the people. The people endure the ruler. They put up with him but frequently feel little affection for him. In this regard, Islamic fatalism has probably often been a help. The government is simply something that the ordinary member of society must tolerate. God's will is inscrutable.[2] And the elite's rule is based simply on the power to coerce. Like tribalism, this is an old tradition. (Remember the Abbasids and their executioner.) The story is told that, when the Fatimids conquered Egypt in the tenth century, claiming a right to rule based on their alleged descent from the Prophet through Fatima, the wife of Ali, a delegation of Egyptian religious dignitaries mustered the courage to go up to the Fatimid imam and demand proof of his descent. His answer was swift. "This," he said, brandishing his sword, "is the proof of my genealogy." The delegation appears to have been convinced.

Where the ruler has been able to achieve some legitimacy, where his claims of genealogy or religious authority have been accepted by the populace at large, where the people consent to his rule (as in the Jordan of King Hussein and in Saudi Arabia and the Gulf states), it has been possible to mute the claims of the sword. In societies that

2. Compare Paul, on "the powers that be," in Romans 13:1.

hold together fairly well by nature, such as Egypt, it has also been possible to hide the fact that government claims rest on the fact of force, even though the sword is always there. (Of course, even in countries like the United States, where the government enjoys virtually the full consent of its people, power still rests upon the fact that, ultimately, the state can compel you to pay taxes and to obey its laws. Secession is not permitted, for individuals or for states.) It is in societies which do not work, where there is a natural tendency to fragment, that the authoritarianism which is so characteristic of Arabic rule (and has been since the High Caliphal period) turns particularly brutal. Insecure rulers, particularly those unbound by any sense of ethics, tend to avail themselves of any available instrument to maintain their power. Today, those instruments are not merely the sword or the executioner's axe; they include chemical weapons and jet fighter-bombers. Thus, places like Syria, Iraq, and Lebanon have witnessed scenes of the most incredible brutality.

The newcomer among the three political traditions that we are discussing here is the idea of the modern nation-state. It is a foreign idea, brought to the Middle East in the early twentieth century by British and French and, to a lesser degree, Italian colonialists. This was a new concept to the Middle East, but it must be said that, although it seems natural to us in the West today, it is not so very old even in the West. As we have seen in our discussion of the Ottoman *millet* system, and in the discussion of "tribalism," people in the Middle East have historically tended to give their loyalty to their religious affiliation, or to their kinship group or village or neighborhood (which was often pretty much the same thing). The ruler was distant and quite possibly foreign or of a different religious persuasion. One tolerated him, one obeyed him, but one was not necessarily loyal to him in any especially enthusiastic way.

When the French and the British found themselves in mandatory control of the Middle East after World War I, however, and following the breakup of the Ottoman Empire, they determined to restructure the Middle East in the only fashion that, by then, made any sense to them. They got out their maps and, based on what seems amazingly limited knowledge and understanding of the area, divided it into nation-states. The ethnic, linguistic, and religious realities of the region were by and large ignored, and the diplomatic and economic interests of the imperial powers were allowed to dictate how the region should be restructured. Modern Syria, Iraq, Jordan, Palestine, Lebanon, and the oil states of the Persian Gulf all owe their borders to this rather artificial and arbitrary process, undertaken not by the local populations but by interventionist Europeans claiming to act on their behalf. Neither the concept of a nation-state nor the various individual nation-states of the region grew naturally out of the soil of the Middle East; both concept and application were imposed from outside. (To this extent, Saddam Hussein's accusation that the border between Kuwait and Iraq was artificial, and imposed by Western imperialists, is true.) Governments or states were established, from which a sense of nationhood was supposed to grow—a process directly counter to the usual one, in which governments grow out of a sense of nationhood. In some cases, this actually seems to have worked, at least to a degree. In others, notably Iraq and Lebanon, it has not.

The institutional details of government were often imposed from the outside as well. Political parties and national anthems, cabinets, parliaments, and constitutions—all of these are foreign notions of which, for the most part, the form but not the substance has taken root in the Middle East. Today, many of these institutions are a charade. The parliamentarians are playacting, their only real function being to rubber-stamp the decisions of a dictator. (The most extreme illustration of this is the astonishing Colonel Qaddafi of Libya, who insists with a straight face that he holds absolutely no office in the government of his country, which, he says, is actually run by direct democracy.)

Perhaps the most effective way to give an overview of the Arab world today is to survey a few selected Arab states, to investigate specific cases.

Egypt

Having said that many Arab and Near Eastern states are artificial creations with no roots in reality, I commence my survey with the most obvious counterexample. Egypt is a notable exception to the general truth that the nations of the contemporary Middle East were invented with map and pencil. Egypt has existed in much its present area since the earliest days of human history. This is so because it has an obvious natural shape. It is actually far smaller than it appears on maps because its population is crowded along the banks of the Nile River. Other than a few oases, the rest of the country is uninhabitable sandy desert, which has always served to protect Egypt from the ambitions of those around her.

The Egyptian identity is fairly secure. When Anwar Sadat and his countrymen were kicked out of many Arab organizations after his peace agreement with Israel, they immediately began to note that their ancestors had been building pyramids while the ancestors of "the Arabs" were eating lizards. They didn't care, they said, if "the Arabs" didn't like them. They were not "Arabs," they were Egyptians! This ability to fall back on a well-established older national identity has spared them some of the problems that today afflict a number of other, less psychologically fortunate Arab states.

It has not, however, spared them a difficult history. As I have pointed out already, from the fall of the pharaonic state just after Lehi's day until very recent times, Egypt was ruled by foreigners. The 1952 army coup that eventually put Gamal Abdel Nasser in power brought an end to rule by non-Egyptians but did little or nothing to end the nation's problems, which included poverty and a rapidly rising population. Instead of dealing with those problems, Nasser chose to focus on the fight against Israel, combatting Western influence (which made him an ally of the Soviet Union), and building a socialist state (with what results I have already stated).

His most important mission, though, as he saw it, was the restoration of Arab unity. Ever since the break-up of the Arab empire centuries before, various leaders and regimes had sought to restore it. Now, under the influence of nationalism—which was itself a Western notion—Nasser sought to reestablish not an Islamic empire based upon religion, but a vast and unified Arab state based upon a shared history and a common language. In 1958, Egypt and Syria merged as a first step toward the broader goal and became the

"United Arab Republic." Shortly thereafter, Yemen, too, joined. Nasser's popularity throughout the Arab world was vast. He was the savior who would restore their lost unity and rebuild their lost pride.

Even when the union with Syria and Yemen collapsed after only a few years, Nasser's prestige was immense. When he suddenly died in 1970, his funeral attracted many hundred thousand emotional mourners to the streets of Cairo. Although his wars against Israel had been failures, and although his grand socialist economic plans had brought his country to the brink of bankruptcy, the name of Nasser continues to be a powerful one. His picture is still frequently displayed in Egypt. And when his successor, Anwar al-Sadat, opted to leave behind the ruinous struggle with Israel and to concentrate, not on the almost impossible dream of unifying the Arabs, but on improving his nation's economy through a more free-market approach, other Arab leaders began to scramble for Nasser's mantle as unifier of the Arabs. Muammar Qaddafi of Libya explicitly likens himself to Nasser, and Saddam Hussein of Iraq clearly wants the role as well.[3] (Saddam seems willing to try to unify the Arabs by force if he can't do so by persuasion.)

Syria and Iraq

British troops took Mesopotamia away from the Ottoman Turks during the First World War (1914-1918), and in 1920 they received a mandate from the League of Nations to administer the area. Losing little time, they helped the locals to set up a government in 1921, under the name of "Iraq," and brought in a new ruler to serve as monarch under the title of Faisal I. (This was the same Faisal whose troops the British officer known as "Lawrence of Arabia" had fought in league with against the Turks during the war.) But Faisal and his government were allowed precious little freedom to govern

---

3. An amusing note on Qaddafi's name: The Arabic root *q-dh-f*, from which his name comes, means "to throw" or "to hurl" something. A bomb, for example. (This is the very illustration used by the leading Arabic-English dictionary.) And Saddam's self-adopted name comes from the root *s-d-m*, meaning "to collide, to clash, to bang something, to run into something." What's in a name?

their new nation as they saw fit; Great Britain reserved for itself authority over Iraq's economic, military, and foreign affairs. In 1932, the League of Nations finally ended the British mandate over Iraq and admitted the newly independent state to membership.

In 1958, though, a group of army officers, led by General Abdul Karim Qasim, overthrew the monarchy, wiping out the royal family and declaring Iraq a republic. It was hardly that, though. The new government ruled by decree. It reversed Iraq's traditional pro-Western stance and turned to the Communist world for economic and military assistance. (This was about the time that Nasser in Egypt was doing much the same thing.) General Qasim's government was corrupt and treated the people harshly. Among other things, he dispatched the army against Kurdish separatists in the north in 1961.

In 1963, another military coup assassinated General Qasim. The new revolutionary regime, led by officers who belonged to a political party known as the Ba'th, promised justice and reform. There was rejoicing in the streets and among Iraqi exiles abroad. Badr Shakir al-Sayyab's poem "An Ode to Revolutionary Iraq," written while he was undergoing medical treatment in London, is dramatic testimony to the high hopes that the new leaders of the country aroused in the hearts of many.

> The agents of Qasim open fire upon the spring,
> But all the illicit wealth they have amassed
> Will melt like ice, to be again water,
> Gushing along streams and brooks,
> Bringing back the luster of life to the dry branches,
> Restoring, without loss, all stolen from them in Qasim's winter.
> O Iraq!
> O Iraq! I can almost glimpse, across the raging seas,
> At every turn, in every street and road and alley,
> Beyond the ports and highways,
> Smiling faces that say: "The Tatars have fled,
> God has returned to the mosques with the break of day,
> A day on which the sun shall never set!"
> O Hafsa! Smile, for your mouth is a flower of the plain,

You are avenged on the traitors at the hands of my people in revolt.
The enemy of the people is cast down to the lowest hell...
The doctor hurried to my side.
Was it that he had found a cure for the disease in my body?
The doctor hurried to my side and said:
"What is this news from Iraq?
The army has rebelled, Qasim is dead!"
What joyous, health-restoring tidings!
In my joy, I almost stood up, walked, ran,
As if cured.
Rejoice! What liberation, what release!
Rejoice! The army of the Arab nation has torn off the bonds!
O my brethren in God, in blood, in Arabism, in hope,
Arise, for tyrants are laid low,
And light has dispelled the night.
Guard well the Arab revolution
That crushed the "comrades," cast down the oppressors,
For Tammuz, his splendor once stolen by the traitor,[4]
Has arisen, and Iraq is reborn.[5]

Mercifully, perhaps, al-Sayyab died an early death in 1964, still in London. He never had to see what became of his hoped-for revolution.

The Ba'th Party takes its name from an Arabic word that can mean both "renaissance" and "resurrection." That is the promise that it made to the Arab people. But it never delivered on its promise. Instead, it represented an Arab socialism that was bound to destroy the economy of any nation that adopted it, and, like the more famous German national socialism of Adolf Hitler, it created an atmosphere of intense racism and nationalism, of hatred and paranoia directed at non-Arabs. The Kurds, who had fared badly under General Qasim, would do far worse under the Ba'thists.

---

4. Tammuz was an ancient Mesopotamian god of vegetation, who died and was then reborn. Thus, he became a god of resurrection as well. He is mentioned in the Bible at Ezekiel 8:14.

5. Translated in *An Anthology of Modern Arabic Poetry*, edited by Mounah A. Khouri and Hamid Algar (Berkeley: University of California Press, 1975), 91–93.

In 1979, a Ba'thist official by the name of Saddam Hussein established himself as absolute ruler of the country. Having been the second most powerful man in the government since 1968, he now had himself declared president. To consolidate his power, he eliminated the entire governing Revolutionary Command Council—his former close colleagues—within a month of assuming supreme power. (It is said that he shot them himself.) He then launched Iraq on a career of military misadventures that may be without parallel in modern times. He also created a cult of his own personality in which pictures and statues of the Great Leader occupy every public space and many private ones as well.

When Iran's imperial government collapsed in the late 1970s, and a group of theocrats seized power, Saddam saw an opportunity to steal Iranian land and add to his own power. He therefore invaded his neighbor late in 1980, starting a war between Iran and Iraq that would finally end in a virtual stalemate after nearly a decade of fighting and hundreds of thousands of casualties. When that conflict was over, he invaded and occupied nearby Kuwait. And the rest, as they say, is history. Yet despite all his many failures, Saddam retains power. He has maintained that power by being both ruthlessly brutal and cunning. He has managed to create a society in which everyone is under surveillance, and he is willing to kill even his closest friends and associates, if it will serve his purposes. Indeed, he has done so on many occasions.

Most recently, Saddam Hussein has discovered the usefulness of religion as a weapon. His rhetoric during the Gulf crisis drew heavily on the Qur'an and Islamic tradition—something he had never really done before. He prayed on television and invoked the curse of Allah on his Western opponents—but also upon the Kuwaitis and Saudis and Egyptians and Syrians, Muslims all, who formed a part of the coalition against him. Shortly before the war, he "discovered" that he was a descendant of the Prophet. (No doubt a machine gun would have proved his genealogy for anyone who may have been skeptical.) He may have realized that the Ba'th Party, with its secular socialist agenda, was something of a fossil and that he needed to bring it into line with the newly Islamic times. Certainly there is no reason in his past or in the records of his innumerable crimes to suggest that he had the slightest tinge of real religious belief. His cynical use of Islam to further his immoral lust for power was, in fact, an embarrassment both to the religion of Muhammad and to religions in general. Unfortunately, many in the West saw him as a Muslim leader. Anti-Islamic sentiments grew in the United States despite the fact that Saddam's Kuwaiti victims (to say nothing of the Iraqis, who have suffered the most from his ambitions) were themselves Muslims.

Syria, too, is under the control of a wing of the Ba'th Party. It is a hostile faction, however, that despises the Iraq wing of the party and tries to undercut it at every turn. Syria, too, is ruled by a ruthless tyrant. Hafez al-Asad has maintained himself in power since 1970 and is every bit as cruel as Saddam Hussein. But Hafez has a better sense of the way the world works, and he is more adaptable than Saddam. Thus, while Saddam was surprised that the Soviet Union did not back him in his recent conflict in the Gulf, Hafez al-Asad knew that he could no longer rely upon the Soviets as a superpower patron. Although he has hardly become an Arab Gandhi, Hafez now realizes that he must develop a relationship with the only remaining superpower if he is to have any powerful patron at all. And that means that, if not out of conviction then out of policy, he must moderate his behavior. There is some hope, perhaps, for Syria.

On the whole, though, the situation is rather bleak in the Near East. Arab states now have the right, in many instances, to be free from rule by foreign colonialists and to be ruled, instead, by men of their own language and ethnicity—men, unfortunately, whose cruelty and amorality sometimes far exceed anything of which the colonialists ever dreamed. This is the condition in much of the Islamic world. Although he is a Pakistani Urdu poet rather than an Arab, Faiz Ahmad Faiz's poem entitled "Freedom's Dawn" poignantly expresses the disappointment that has been felt by Muslims throughout the world at the outcome of their revolutionary hopes for a better life and a more just society:

> This dawn that's marked and wounded,
> this dawn that night has nibbled on—

It's not the dawn we expected;
it's not the dawn we were looking for...
But what is this we hear?
That all the battles have been fought,
that the destination has been reached!
It's all changed, our leaders' struggling zeal;
celebration is the order of the day, mourning forbidden.
Yet anguish of the heart, unfulfilled desire,
nothing is cured by this false dawn...
The lamp still waits for the morning breeze,
the night weighs on us still.
This is not the moment of our freedom.
Keep moving, keep moving!
We have not arrived![6]

Israel

Early Zionists, coming from Europe, were often unaware—sometimes because they were simply not told—that there already was a people in Palestine who regarded it as home. Their slogan, endlessly repeated, was "The land without a people for the people without a land," as if, alone among all the habitable regions of the world, here was a place that was simply empty. And if there were Arabs there, well, they were Arabs just like other Arabs, indistinguishable. They could live anywhere else just as well. After all, they had the whole Arab world. Golda Meir, the then prime minister of Israel, was once asked in an interview by the London *Sunday Times* about the Palestinians. "They do not exist," she replied simply. In this, her attitude was not so very different from that of many modern Americans, who continue to be puzzled by the notion of Palestinians. "Why," they ask, "don't the Palestinians just go and live in Egypt or in Jordan or the Gulf? They're all Arabs, aren't they?" But to say such things is to overlook the differences of culture and dialect, to miss the peculiar history that links a people to a place after centuries of living there, and to ignore the sheer fact that, to the

---

6. Translated in Mahmood Jamal's anthology entitled *The Penguin Book of Modern Urdu Poetry* (New York: Viking Penguin, 1986), 31.

Palestinians, this is *their land*.[7] I always like to ask these Americans whether, if some foreign power were to take over the United States and expel them, they would be perfectly content to go and live in New Zealand or Scotland. Would they happily give up claim to their property? When the issue is put in such terms, of course, most Americans will begin to understand. It is part of the guilt and shame of some Zionists that, living in Palestine and coming into frequent contact with the Palestinians, they still do not understand.

Not surprisingly, the Palestinian Arabs and the surrounding Arab states all rejected the United Nations proposal to partition Palestine between Arabs and Jews. They felt, with some justification, that Palestine was theirs and that no foreigner had the right to divide up their land and give part of it away to yet another group of foreigners. Furthermore, they felt—mistakenly, as it turned out—that they had the strength to resist such a proposal and to drive the intruders out of their land.

On 14 May 1948, David Ben Gurion proclaimed the independence of a new state of Israel. (It is said that he had not decided whether to call the new country "Israel" or "Zion" until scarcely minutes before he stood up to make his official announcement.) The five Arab states that attacked the new country the next day suffered a humiliating defeat. Indeed, Israel managed not only to defend its territory, but actually seized control of about half of the land that the United Nations had designated for the proposed Palestinian state. That state, of course, never came to be. The portions of its designated territory that had not fallen under Jewish control were divided up between Egypt and Jordan. Egypt took over the Gaza Strip. Jordan seized East Jerusalem and the West Bank of the Jordan River. This changed the character of Jordan in a fundamental way. The Palestinians of the West Bank, along with the Palestinians

---

7. It is significant that, when the Israelis invaded Beirut in September 1982, one of their main targets was the PLO Research Center. This was hardly a military target. The Center was the repository of old photographs of Palestine, old land deeds and other records, books, and pre-1948 maps. Manifestly, the Israelis wanted to eliminate this tangible evidence of the fact that there was another people with a very strong legal claim to Palestine. On this, see Friedman, *From Beirut to Jerusalem*, 159.

who fled from other areas of Palestine that were absorbed into Israel, became subjects first of King Abdullah and then, after his assassination in 1951, of King Hussein, along with the native Bedouins and Jordanians who were already there.

Once again, and not for the last time, the Palestinians emerged as losers. The weak Palestinian nationalism that had been simmering seemed to have lost its chance forever. There was no Palestine any more. Palestinians became refugees among the Egyptians, Jordanians, Lebanese, or Syrians and faced the choice either of assimilation, absorption, or of everlasting confinement to squalid refugee camps. Their situation now was not unlike that which had confronted the Jews themselves, long before. It was the Palestinian *diaspora.* In Israel, the Palestinians became "Israeli Arabs." Though they still yearned for a state of their own, it seemed that the moment of Palestinian nationalism had passed.

On the other hand, the astonishing victory of heroic little Israel, scarcely a few hours old, outnumbered and poorly armed, helped to create a legend of Israel in the West. Clearly, though, the victory was not merely a triumph for Israel; it also could be attributed to revealed corruption and disunity among the five attacking Arab states (a situation which, as pointed out before, still afflicts the Arabs in their dealings with Israel and with one another). Rebellions broke out among the junior officers and common soldiers in several Arab states. As they saw it, they had been betrayed by their generals and politicians, sent out without adequate equipment or ammunition, misled, and abandoned. (Among the officers who began to plot revolt were two Egyptian colonels, Gamal Abdel Nasser and Anwar Sadat.)

The sense of loss among Arabs was powerful and profound. A poem by Abdul Wahab al-Bayati, "The Arab Refugee," gives voice to this. Notice its lament over the lost Arab town of Jaffa, whose orange groves, now in Jewish hands, supply Europe with a substantial proportion of its fruit in the winter. Notice, too, the memory of Arab greatness symbolized by the illustrious anti-Crusader hero, Saladin. This memory is only the more painful because, betrayed and sold by Saladin's corrupt and unworthy successors, it lies so far in the past. I quote a part of the poem:

Ants gnaw his flesh
Crows peck his flesh
The Arab refugee nailed to the cross.

The Arab refugee
Begs and spends his nights in railway stations
Crying his eyes out.
And Jaffa is just a small label
On a box of oranges.

Stop knocking on my door
There's no life left in me.
And Jaffa is just an orange label
It leaves the dead undisturbed.

They've sold the memory of Saladin
They've sold his horse and shield
They've sold the grave of refugees...

Ants gnaw his flesh
Crows peck his flesh
The Arab refugee begging at your door.[8]

Al-Bayati, from Iraq, writes with bitter anger about the sheer humiliation of continuing Arab powerlessness before Israel. Jabra Ibrahim Jabra, on the other hand, is a Palestinian, born at Bethlehem, and his poignant poem about exile is much more gentle than al-Bayati's. Indeed, it seems reminiscent of Jewish yearnings for that same small plot of land, expressed through the centuries of their own *diaspora*, or dispersion from their home. With their wanderings in the desert, portrayed in Jabra's poem, the Palestinians are made to seem a modern equivalent of the children of Israel. "Where," he implicitly asks, "is *their* Moses?"

Spring after spring,
In the deserts of exile,

---

8. Translated by Abdullah al-Udhari, in his collection *Modern Poetry of the Arab World* (New York: Viking Penguin, 1986), 36-37.

What are we doing with our love,
When our eyes are full of frost and dust?

Our Palestine, green land of ours;
Its flowers as if embroidered of women's gowns;[9]
March adorns its hills
With the jewel-like peony and narcissus;
April bursts open in its plains
With flowers and bride-like blossoms;
May is our rustic song
Which we sing at noon,
In the blue shadows,
Among the olive-trees of our valleys,
And in the ripeness of the fields
We wait for the promise of July
And the joyous dance amidst the harvest.

O land of ours where our childhood passed
Like dreams in the shade of the orange-grove,[10]
Among the almond-trees in the valleys—
Remember us now wandering
Among the thorns of the desert,
Wandering in rocky mountains;
Remember us now
In the tumult of cities beyond deserts and seas;
Remember us
With our eyes full of dust
That never clears in our ceaseless wandering.
They crushed the flowers on the hills around us,
Destroyed the houses over our heads,
Scattered our torn remains,
Then unfolded the desert before us,
With valleys writhing in hunger
And blue shadows shattered into red thorns
Bent over corpses left as prey for falcon and crow.

---

9. Traditional women's dresses in Palestine are well known for their embroidery.
10. Again, the nostalgic yearning for the orange groves seized by the Israelis.

> Is it from your hills that the angels sang to the shepherds
> Of peace on earth and goodwill among men?
> Only death laughed when it saw
> Among the entrails of beasts
> The ribs of men,
> And through the guffaw of bullets
> It went dancing a joyous dance
> On the heads of weeping women.
>
> Our land is an emerald,
> But in the deserts of exile,
> Spring after spring,
> Only the dust hisses in our face.
> What then, what are we doing with our love?
> When our eyes and our mouth are full of frost and dust?[11]

Since 1948, of course, there have been other wars, in 1956, in 1967, and 1973, and a state of almost permanent tension and frequent military clashes between Israel and her neighbors. After the fighting of 1948 came to an end, the new Israeli state signed armistice agreements with Syria, Jordan, Lebanon, and Egypt. But the Arab states did not consider the war to be over. In their view, this was merely a lull in the fighting, and they often allowed various Palestinian groups to use their territory as a staging area for raids into Israel. Eventually, in 1964 the Arab states, led by Egypt's Gamal Abdel Nasser, grouped these various Palestinian movements under one umbrella organization, which came to be known as the Palestine Liberation Organization, or PLO. (The May 1964 meeting in which the PLO was formally established was held in the Intercontinental Hotel in what was then Jordanian-held east Jerusalem. This hotel, now known as the Seven Arches, is a landmark familiar to many Holy Land tourists even today.) In its early stages, the PLO was basically a tool of the Arab regimes. It was first and foremost, perhaps, an instrument to control the Palestinians, to prevent them from trying to establish an independent state in Gaza and the West

---

11. This is Jabra's own translation of his poem "In the Deserts of Exile," appearing in Khouri and Algar, *An Anthology of Modern Arabic Poetry*, 225-29.

Bank; only secondarily was it designed to support them in their struggle against the Israeli occupation of their lands.

The war of 1967, often referred to as the "Six Day War," reinforced Israel's image as the almost invincible David who was confronted by a bumbling Arab Goliath. At the same time, it redoubled Arab agony. Arab poets gave anguished voice to the sense of shame and humiliation that seized their people after the Six Day War. I quote from a poem entitled "Footnotes to the Book of the Setback," by the Syrian writer Nizar Qabbani. It attacks the pompous posturing of Arab leaders, backed by no real achievements. It denounces them for taking their immense oil revenues and wasting the money on high living and corruption, rather than using it to fight and to rebuild the Arab nation. (Interestingly, in the early 1970s, in the oil boycott that hurt economies and created waiting lines at gas stations around the world, Arab leaders did eventually begin to use their petroleum resources as an effective weapon.) Qabbani's poem criticizes Arab governments for their disunity, for the incessant bickering that allowed the Israelis to divide them and to conquer them. Not surprisingly, the poem was banned throughout the Arab world. But as a result of that ban, it was secretly printed, smuggled into every Arab country, and committed to memory by thousands of angry Arabs.

> Friends,
> The ancient world is dead.
> The ancient books are dead…
>
> Our poems have gone sour.
> Women's hair, nights, curtains and sofas
> Have gone sour.
> Everything has gone sour.
>
> My grieved country,
> In a flash
> You changed me from a poet who wrote love poems
> To a poet who writes with a knife.
>
> What we feel is beyond words:
> We should be ashamed of our poems.

Stirred
By Oriental bombast,
By Antaric swaggering that never killed a fly,[12]
By the fiddle and the drum,
We went to war
And lost.

Our shouting is louder than our actions,
Our swords are taller than us,
This is our tragedy...

Our enemies did not cross our borders
They crept through our weaknesses like ants.

Friends,...
People take you for a breed of mongrels...

Are we the "Nation by which God blessed mankind"?[13]

Our desert oil could have become
Daggers of flame and fire.
We're a disgrace to our noble ancestors:
We let our oil flow through the toes of whores.

We...
Turn midgets into heroes...

If we hadn't buried our unity
If we hadn't ripped its young body with bayonets
If it had stayed in our eyes
The dogs wouldn't have savaged our flesh.

But Qabbani sees hope for the future, if not for his own generation then at least for the generation growing up. It is a wrathful vision, full of self-contempt.

We want an angry generation
To plough the sky
To blow up history...

---

12. Antar was a great poet and warrior of Arabian tradition.
13. A Qur'anic reference to the Arabs' role in bringing true religion (Islam) to the world.

We want a new generation
That does not forgive mistakes
That does not bend.
We want a generation
Of giants.

Arab children,
Corn ears of the future,
You will break our chains.
Kill the opium in our heads,
Kill the illusions.
Arab children,
Don't read about our windowless generation,
We are a hopeless case.
We are as worthless as water-melon rind.
Don't read about us,
Don't ape us,
Don't accept us,
Don't accept our ideas,
We are a nation of crooks and jugglers.
Arab children,
Spring rain,
Corn ears of the future,
You are the generation
That will overcome defeat.[14]

Qabbani's verses illustrate the new mood of revolutionary anger that the spectacular failure of the Arab regimes in the Six Day War created among the Palestinian people. Those regimes, they felt, were now completely irrelevant, thoroughly discredited. Why, they asked themselves, should they continue to depend upon corrupt and incompetent Arab leaders for their liberation? What had they gained by doing so? From now on, they would rely upon themselves. A coalition of independent, more radical Palestinian guerrilla organizations, the so-called *fedayeen*, seized control of the Palestine Liberation Organization after the war. They were determined to

---

[14] Translated by Abdullah al-Udhari, in *Modern Poetry of the Arab World*, 97-101.

make that organization serve their own interests, the interests of their people as they saw them, rather than the interests of the regimes which had used it but had so often let them down.

Even with all of its many setbacks, Palestinian nationalism was not easily put down. "What Palestinian nationalism?" you are asking yourself. "Didn't I just read that Palestinian nationalism was virtually dead after the disaster of 1948 left the Palestinians and their land parcelled out among various countries facing assimilation?" True. But the 1967 Israeli conquest of Gaza and the West Bank, which realized the long-standing Zionist dream of Jewish control over all of Palestine, also reunited Palestine for the Palestinians. They were one unit once again. And now they did not have to fight for the attractions of life in Jordan in one place and "the flesh pots of Egypt" in another. They had one common enemy, and in that common enemy they again found their nationhood. They were different from Egyptians or Jordanians or Syrians or Lebanese. Those Palestinians who lived under Israeli control were unique among Arabs by that very fact.

The Palestinians under Israeli rule were not faced with assimilation the way they had been under the control of other Arabs or the way their fellow Palestinians were in Lebanon or Jordan. The Israelis spoke a different language. They followed a different religion, when they had one at all, and they certainly had a different history and culture. What is more, they did not *want* to assimilate the Palestinians. Such assimilation would have been a threat to Jewish identity. And the Palestinians did not want to become Jews. Instead, they wanted to show their disdain and to maintain their distinctness. And the distinctness was in being, precisely, Palestinian. But that new sense of Palestinian nationhood could not be expressed under Israeli occupation. The Palestinian flag, for instance, was illegal until the very recent Israeli-PLO peace talks.

In 1969, a civil engineer by the name of Yasir Arafat, who was the leader of the most prestigious group of Palestinian guerrilla fighters, known as Fatah ("Victory," or "Conquest"), was elected chairman of the PLO's executive committee. He stepped into the leadership left by the humiliation of the Six Day War. He made the

PLO into a truly independent Palestinian organization, one which could deal with the Arab states of the region more or less as an equal. With his past experience as a successful engineering contractor, he has managed the PLO's finances relatively well. He has turned it into a multibillion dollar operation that runs radio stations, administers educational programs, gives out scholarships and welfare payments, and maintains a salaried bureaucracy. His role since then has been very much like that of the old bedouin shaykh of pre-Islamic times: He is the ostensible leader over a broad spectrum of organizations, which range from what might be considered the political right to what are definitely radically leftist movements, but his control over them has often been shaky at best, and he is only first among equals. For all these limitations, however, at least some of the credit for the resurrection of Palestinian nationalism, which had seemed dead for a while, must be given to Arafat. He also had help from the Israelis, of course. Their treatment of the Palestinians and their lack of interest in a real solution to the problem played right into Arafat's hands.

Another of Arafat's achievements has been his getting the Palestinian movement to speak mainly with one voice. There had been many factions among the Palestinians. Palestinian Christians mistrusted Palestinian Muslims; residents of one town were suspicious of the residents of other towns. Arafat was able to get them to agree on certain basic propositions. Partly, this was due to his ability to be all things to all people. He was often deliberately vague in what he would say to different factions so that one could read into what he had said what one wanted to hear. This was necessary and very useful in the unifying task he had set for himself. Unfortunately, it meant that he tended to say contradictory things, things that often put him in a bad light with the Israelis when he later wanted to talk with them. They asked, with some plausibility, how they were supposed to take seriously the statements of someone who was so often self-contradictory and so difficult to pin down.

This is particularly the case with regard to what is perhaps the fundamental contradiction within the Palestinian movement. Palestinians today can be divided into two fundamental groups: those who remain within the boundaries of Israel and the occupied territories, and those who live outside of those borders, whether in the Middle East or beyond. These two groups do not necessarily have the same interests. The people of the occupied West Bank and Gaza Strip have to deal with the degrading everyday unpleasantness of Israeli occupation. As they see it, their situation would be vastly improved if the Israelis would simply return to the pre-1967 borders. And the overwhelming majority of them know, from daily contact with the reality of Israel, that this is about as much as they can reasonably expect. Israel is not going to go away. There are too many Israelis, and they are too firmly settled, for the massive Jewish presence in Palestine to simply evaporate. This group of Palestinians would be pleased, for the most part, to have a Palestinian state in the West Bank and Gaza. And they would like that to happen soon. In other words, they are willing to settle for a less than utopian solution, if they can achieve it reasonably quickly.

The other group of Palestinians, however, do not have to deal with the daily reality of Israel and Israeli occupation. They live outside. And those of them who are not in refugee camps—which is to say the leaders of the PLO—have often managed to live in some comfort. Some even travel around the world and are feasted by Arab and other world leaders. They are in no real hurry to settle the problem, and they certainly cannot be satisfied with a partial solution. They are out of Israel in most cases because their farms, their villages, and their shops have been taken over by the Israelis. A Palestinian state in the West Bank and Gaza would not liberate their homes. This segment of the Palestinian population, therefore, has tended to hold out for the most drastic solution to the conflict between itself and Israel—namely, the disappearance (at least in the sense we know it) of the Israeli state.

From his rise to control of the PLO in 1969, and well through the 1970s, it was this latter faction that Yasir Arafat had to keep happy. The population of the West Bank and Gaza was relatively dormant politically and looked to those outside of Palestine for its leadership. The active, combatant Palestinians were those outside. They were the guerrillas. They were the ones actively struggling against Israel. It was their hopes and aspirations that Yasir Arafat had to express if he wanted to maintain himself as leader of the PLO. He could not possibly have survived, politically or even physically, if he had ignored the wishes of his power base and recognized Israel's right to exist. True to his role as a kind of tribal shaykh, he had to embody the consensus of his people; leading them to a position that they would have recoiled from in horror was entirely too dangerous. Arafat had to be a spokesman for the consensus; he could not truly be a leader.

The trouble was, of course, that there is not the slightest chance that Israel will disappear. Thus, the position to which Arafat was irrevocably committed was an absolutely hopeless one. Furthermore, since the Zionists, too, claimed not just a part of Palestine but the whole of it, the PLO's insistence on ruling all of the territory was completely unacceptable to Israel. Neither side was willing to recognize that the other had a legitimate claim to the region. The real problem is that each side has a case—each side has suffered. Neither side has a monopoly on grievances nor a monopoly on virtue. But this simple fact could not be admitted by either party to the dispute. Indeed, since each side saw itself as a victim—the Israelis the victims of Hitler, and now of unfathomable Arab hostility; the Palestinians the victims of yet another instance of Western imperialism, stealing their lands—each side felt justified, especially according to the tribal rules of the region, in whatever vengeance it saw fit to exact.

The newly militant and independent PLO was able to extract considerable amounts of money out of the Arab regimes (who perhaps felt guilty about their own failures but were certainly glad to let someone else fight the battles) and used that money and political support to carry on the struggle against Israel. One way Arafat has been able to get money from the more prosperous Arab states is to argue that they must either support him, or they will have to face an explosion of Palestinian radicalism when he is no longer there to manage some of the wilder factions. (To an extent, then, the PLO still serves to control the Palestinian movement in the interests of the Arab states.) The PLO leadership worked carefully to gain control of

Palestinian refugee camps and used them to stage attacks against Israeli targets in the Middle East and throughout the world. In Jordan and in southern Lebanon, the PLO came very close to establishing sovereign states, beyond the control of the respective national governments. And when the raids they launched brought down upon them, and thus upon Jordanian and Lebanese territory, the violent wrath of the Israelis, it was inevitable that tensions would arise between the Palestinians and their ever more reluctant hosts.

In Jordan, things came to a head in September 1970. In that month, which has ever afterward been known among the Palestinians as "Black September," a group of radical Palestinians flew three hijacked airliners to Jordan and then refused to allow the Jordanian army to rescue the passengers or even to get near the aircraft.[15] This was simply too much for the government of King Hussein and, as events have proved, for many Jordanians. They could see that they were losing control of their own country—the Palestinians were acting as if they were the rulers. King Hussein decided to launch a military offensive against PLO-controlled refugee camps and even against predominantly Palestinian neighborhoods in the capital city of Amman. The Palestinians responded violently, but they were ultimately outmanned and outgunned. Yasir Arafat was obliged to escape from Amman dressed as an Arab woman.

Naturally, he fled to the other chief concentration of PLO power, to Lebanon, where Palestinians had established themselves as a quasi-state in certain parts of Beirut and in the rural south, handily close to Israel. This story will continue with the discussion of Lebanon.

The Six Day War of 1967 caused a crisis for Arab self-respect. It appeared as though they would never be able to climb out of the abyss into which they had fallen. The "October War" of 1973, by contrast, was a great shock to the *Israeli* self-image. Both the government and the military were caught off guard, and Arab forces were able to score a number of early victories in the conflict. Even

---

[15] A prominent Palestinian terrorist organization bears the commemorative title of Black September.

though the Israelis eventually seem to have regained their composure and were pushing toward another victory when a ceasefire was declared, it was the initial Arab success that had immense psychological impact on both sides. At roughly the same time, other things seemed to be going the Arabs' way as well. The rise in oil prices and in Arab oil power in 1974 gave them considerable political clout, and the PLO rode this to a new level of respectability and influence. It is no coincidence that in 1974 Yasir Arafat received an invitation to address the United Nations. Arafat used this new respectability well. It was virtually impossible for any newspaper-reading person in the West to avoid mention of the Palestinian cause. And to make sure that the Palestinians were not forgotten, the PLO undertook terrorist actions in countries throughout the Middle East and abroad.

Prime minister Golda Meir of Israel, criticized for mismanagement of the October War, resigned in 1974. On the Egyptian side, however, Anwar Sadat now felt that he could negotiate from a position of strength and honor, something that was certainly not open to him in the aftermath of the 1967 war. In late 1977, Sadat made his heroic flight to Jerusalem, where his talks with Israeli prime minister Menachem Begin and, later, with Begin and U.S. President Jimmy Carter led to the 1978 Camp David Accords.

Those agreements, signed at the American presidential retreat known as Camp David, included plans for Israel's complete withdrawal from the Sinai Peninsula, which it had occupied in the 1967 war, and for a peace treaty between Israel and Egypt. The peace treaty was signed in 1979, and the Israelis completed their withdrawal from the Sinai in 1982. However, the Accords also called for a five-year period of self-rule, or autonomy, for the Palestinians of the West Bank and the Gaza Strip, after which a final decision would be made about the status of those two areas. But this did not happen (though current developments, begun only since the Israeli-PLO negotiations, may finally lead in that direction). Thus, it is understandable that many Palestinians saw the Camp David Accords as simply one more instance of being abandoned by an Arab state acting in its own self-interest. The Egyptians got a peace treaty, freeing them from the cycle of destructive wars that had drained their economy and killed their sons. They also got back the Sinai. They had long been bitter about what they saw as the disproportionate burden they had been obliged to bear in the struggle against Israel. The Saudis, the Iraqis, the Moroccans, and most other Arab nations were all too willing, as the Egyptians saw it, to fight the Israelis down to the last drop of Egyptian blood. They were relieved to get out of the endless cycle of wars and bloodshed. But what did the Palestinians get? As they see it, nothing. Harun Hashim Rashid speaks for many of his people:

> Palestinian—
> The name pursues me, lives with me;
> Palestinian is my fate,
> Clinging to me, reviving me.
> Palestinian I am,
> Though they trample me and my name;
> Palestinian I am,
> Though they betray me and my cause;
> Palestinian I am,
> Though they sell me in the market
> For what they please,
> For thousands of millions;
> Palestinian I am,
> Though to the gallows they drive me;
> Palestinian I am,
> Though to the walls they bind me...
> Without my name, Palestinian,
> Without a homeland to live for,
> To protect and be protected by:
> I—what am I?
> Answer me, answer me![16]

One of the most pathetic things about the Palestinian-Israeli dispute is the pervasive theme of homelessness. The Jews, an exiled and scattered people, found a renewed homeland in Palestine. But

---

16. From his poem "Palestinian," translated in Khouri and Algar, *An Anthology of Modern Arabic Poetry*, 231-33.

their return has helped to create a new population of refugees. Now, the Palestinians yearn to return to their lost land. But Jews, too, continue to come to Palestine. Despite the uncertainty and stress of life in Israel, approximately two million Jews from around the world have emigrated to the country since its founding in 1948. Israeli law grants the right to settle in the country and to receive Israeli citizenship to any Jew from anywhere in the world—and not merely to any Jew, but to his wife and to any of his descendants for two generations and to any of their wives, whether or not those people are actually Jewish in religion or ethnicity. It can well be imagined that this policy, which grants automatic citizenship to people from Warsaw, Minsk, and Melbourne is irritating to many Palestinian Arabs. They and their families may have been residents of Jerusalem for a score of generations or more, but, unlike the granddaughter-in-law of a Jew from Beverly Hills or Brooklyn, they cannot hope for the right to vote or to participate in government decisions.[17] The rate of immigration, which had been falling, has surged again because of newly lenient Soviet and now Russian emigration policies, which have allowed many Jews to leave who had been harassed and forbidden to do so under earlier Communist rulers. (The pressure to find housing for these immigrants is one of the factors that has led to the building of Israeli settlements on Arab land, which is now one of the chief stumbling blocks to the peace process.)

Religion has less to do with the conflict than many people imagine. The PLO insists that it is not anti-Jewish, just anti-Zionist. Its ranks include nominal Christians as well as Muslims, and it insists that its opposition is solely political and nationalistic. Furthermore, the early Zionists were not religious. Nor, for that matter, are the vast majority of Israelis of today. They are Jewish, but their Judaism is expressed in speaking Hebrew, serving in the Israeli army, and building a Jewish state. They have little connection if any at all to the religion of Judaism. Yet it is inconceivable, in a society (on both sides) where religion is so centrally important, that religion should

---

17. I choose the "granddaughter-in-law" illustration quite deliberately. Even if she is not of Jewish birth, Israeli law will consider her a Jew by reason of her marriage to the grandson of a Jew and will grant her the right of immigration and settlement.

play no role at all. In fact there are religious hostilities between Muslims and Jews. Islam, from the Qur'an forward, has been critical of the Jews, much in the way that Christianity and Christian texts have been critical of them. Furthermore, Islam sees itself as the last revelation of God and views both Christianity and Judaism as apostate and corrupt remnants of earlier revelations. When this fact is coupled with Islam's political orientation, it is not surprising that Muslims have been deeply troubled by Jewish rule over what they regard as Muslim territory—not just any territory, but some of the most sacred on earth. Under Islamic law, Jews and Christians simply do not have the right to rule over Muslims. (This is not unrelated to the early Mormon claim that the governments of the earth were, although worthy of support, ultimately illegitimate usurpers and to the expectation that, someday, he would come "whose right it is to reign.")

I cannot see any easy solution to the problems posed by this situation. Who would want to deny the Jewish people their dream of returning to the Land? Who would turn the Russian Jewish refugees away? What believing Latter-day Saint will deny that it is the Lord's will that the Jews return to Palestine? Yet what honest person can deny that the Palestinian people have also suffered and been wronged? The Holy Land, the land of the "city of peace," has been drenched in tears and blood since the earliest days of human history. Presumably it will continue to be so, even for the righteous, until the day when "God shall wipe away all tears from their eyes; and there shall be no more death, neither sorrow, nor crying, neither shall there be any more pain."[18] In the meantime, the weeping continues on both sides of the conflict.

We have seen that, in pre-Islamic Arabia, mourning and the writing of elegies was the role of women. Assuming that time-honored function, the modern Palestinian poet Salma al-Khadra al-Jayyusi has written an "Elegy to the Martyrs" that offers quite a different view of Palestinian fighters against Israel than we are accustomed to in the West.

---

18. Revelation 21:4.

I know that they died "so the homeland might live,"
Our homeland, the land of the murdered, a field soaked in blood;
I know that freedom is red, and this its price,
Its awesome price, all drenched in sighs;
I know...but the sorrow in my heart's depths knows not.
I weep for every eye that lost the sight of life,
For every soul that breathed its last.

Remember,
O stream of abundant and fertile wealth,
O land of emerald and pearl,
Where mines of turquoise flow in riverbeds,
And pearls of moonlight bathe in the cool of night,
O hoard of yellow golddust,
O waterfall of diamonds in the morning light,
Remember—
The ruby is your most precious jewel,
And remember—
The season of rebirth is your proudest time,
With its thousands of bright springs
That once lost, in an instant, the sheen of life,
Its thousands of generous hands,
And your bounteous gift, once frozen by the snow of death,
And remember—
The river of blood is your most precious river,
It flowed from the veins of your sons—generations of sacrifice—
And into your kind, sweet-scented soil they vanished and dissolved
Who once dispensed life wherever they went.
Each would go drunk along his way
With fresh youth, with verdant hope, with desire,
Some oblivious of the world, others infatuated with its love,
Some planting the seeds of good,
Others reaping, with flower and song,
And some scheming to pluck the red lips' fruit...
They were men like others,
In their weakness and resolve, in their longing,
In manifold hope, in painful yearning,
Then...when the legend of evil shattered their dream,

And a question challenged them, with its echo, abrupt and harsh:
"Shall it be justice and evil's death, or ambition buried alive?
A life in submission, or obstinate refusal?"
They formed their resolve, and the empty tombs
Were filled
With fresh youth, with verdant hope, with desire
With a free life freely given,
Overflowing from the grave's dark pit.

Thus did they die, and others yet follow on their path,
Their dream a fate ineluctable, generation of sacrifice!
A feverish shudder floods my heart, and to my eye comes
A tear of sorrow, and a flash of pride.[19]

Even non-Arab Muslims have been moved to sympathy with what they see as a heroic Palestinian resistance to Israeli and Western oppression. Thus, for example, the late Faiz Ahmad Faiz, an important Pakistani poet, wrote an Urdu poem in tribute "To Those Palestinians Martyred in Foreign Lands":

Sweet earth of Palestine,
wherever I went
carrying the burning scars of your humiliation,
nursing in my heart the longing
to make you proud,
your love, your memories went with me,
the fragrance of your orange groves went with me.[20]

A crowd of unseen friends stood by me
and so many hands clasped mine.
In distant lands, on dark lanes,
in alien cities, on nameless streets,
wherever the banner of my blood unfurled,
I've left a Palestinian flag.
Your enemies destroyed one Palestine;
my wounds created many more.[21]

---

19. Translated in Khouri and Algar, *An Anthology of Modern Arabic Poetry*, 207-9.
20. Yet again, the orange groves.
21. Translated in Jamal, *The Penguin Book of Modern Urdu Poetry*, 32.

This book is basically about the Arabs. It is for that reason that I emphasize here the sufferings of the Palestinians. I also have in mind the fact that, as Westerners and as Latter-day Saints, we have been far more sensitive to the plight of the Jews in recent decades than we have been to the cries of the other displaced people of the area.[22] I certainly do not mean to imply that there have been no injustices perpetrated against the Jews, nor that they have not suffered. If anything should be gained from a consideration of this painfully difficult dispute, it is that there is no easy answer and that both sides will need to give and to forgive, to repent and reform, before Jerusalem shines with the full glory it is destined to have. We must never lose sight of that fact. We must never forget the complexity of the issues.

Plato has Socrates argue that the just man cannot truly be injured; injustice always injures the person committing it, not the person upon whom it is committed. In an eternal sense, he is certainly right. This is one of the reasons that I lament what is happening in Israel. It is not just that injustices are being committed against the Palestinians. They are, of course. But the Palestinians have committed their share of injustices and atrocities too. A noble dream, which Zionism undoubtedly has been and is for many people, is being corrupted. More worrisome still, one of the world's great religions, Judaism, runs the risk of similar corruption, as it is twisted to justify acts of barbarity and cruelty.

I remember a visit to the West Bank town of Hebron in 1978, a city which is now, incidentally, virtually off limits to unarmed civilians. On every roof, it seemed, there were sandbagged machine gun emplacements. The great mosque of Hebron was patrolled by uniformed Israeli troops with automatic weapons slung over their shoulders. The occupation was omnipresent. It reminded me very

---

22. At the time I wrote the first edition of this book, for example, a number of Western hostages were being released in Beirut. Some of them had been held for many years in captivity as pawns in the turbulent politics of the Near East. Such hostage-taking revolted people in the West, as well it should have. Yet one of the obstacles to the return of those hostages was the fact that Israel was holding several hundred Arab hostages in its own jails at the very same time. Little was heard among us about the injustice of *that* act of hostage-taking.

much of films I had seen about the Nazi occupation of Europe. This, I know from conversations with them, is a major concern of many American Jews. There has also been a recent tendency among certain Israelis to dehumanize the Arabs. ("These aren't people," an Israeli soldier told a BYU student who had confronted him in the act of beating two Arab boys with the butt of his rifle. "These are animals.") In the heat of a fierce battle without clear battle lines, it is perhaps understandable that such things would happen. But it remains lamentable. Numerous observers have commented on the striking fact that many Israelis seem unable to distinguish between Palestinians and terrorists. Thus, they can speak with a straight face of "terrorist hospitals."[23]

Crucial issues are involved here. The Israelis are asking themselves today what kind of a country they want Israel to be. Ideally, most of them by far would like it to be both a Jewish state and a democratic one. And they would like it to be located in the biblical homeland of their people. But the big question is whether these dreams are possible, or even mutually compatible. Within the present contours of Israel, including the West Bank and Gaza, it is clear that Israel cannot be simultaneously a Jewish state and a democratic one. To be a Jewish state is to relegate the large Arab population under its control to second-class status. Yet to grant the

---

23. Friedman, *From Beirut to Jerusalem*, 160-66, argues that this helps to explain the abominable behavior of Israeli soldiers and their commanders during the 1982 Sabra and Shatila massacres in Lebanon and their lenient treatment afterwards. Many in the West also think of the word "terrorist" as soon as they hear the term "Palestinian." Some Arabs may think this yet another evil triumph of Israeli propaganda, but it is clear that the Palestinian resistance movement itself bears a large share of the blame. As an acquaintance of mine once had the nerve to put it to Yasir Arafat himself, "If you would shave, wear a suit, and stop carrying a pistol, it would improve your image in the West." Arafat, for the record, replied that he was aware of that fact but also knew that he must preserve his revolutionary image among his people. The Palestinians have always competed with the Israelis for the sympathy of the West under a distinct handicap: The Jews are more like us than are the Arabs. Arabs have, for most of us, unpronounceable names. Israelis might well be named something "normal" like, say, David Levy—the Israeli foreign minister when the first edition of this book was written. Jewish religion and culture is relatively familiar to us; many of us have Jewish neighbors. Islam is relatively foreign, and few of us—certainly until very recent years—have been likely to know any Muslims personally.

Arabs full citizenship in Israel is to put at risk the country's Jewish character.

It must be recalled that the natural population growth rate among Palestinian Arabs is much greater than that among Israeli Jews. Furthermore, many Israeli Jews have chosen to emigrate from Israel to the United States and Europe, and many will no doubt continue to do so because of difficult living conditions and the uncertainties of the region. Inevitably, the proportion of Arabs to Jews in Palestine must increase, until eventually the Arabs will be in the majority. Then, unless it deals with the situation, Israel will be very much in the position of South Africa under apartheid. The recent influx of large numbers of Russian Jews to Israel has merely postponed the day of reckoning. Is it even remotely conceivable that the prime minister of Israel, as it exists today, could someday be named, say, Muhammad? It is not. An Israel led by an Arab Muslim or a Palestinian Christian would not be Israel. The only morally palatable way for the country to maintain itself as both democratic and Jewish is to trim its borders back so that they will enclose a population that is and will remain majority Jewish.[24]

There was a time, early on, when such an option was actually accepted, even if reluctantly, by Israel. When the United Nations offered the Jews a part of Palestine for a Jewish state in 1948—a part even smaller than they eventually obtained in the war that followed their declaration of independence that year—they were willing to accept part of the loaf rather than risk getting nothing at all. The Six Day War of 1967, however, gave them effective control of all of Palestine, which is to say all of the territory that the Zionists had dreamed of for decades. (The fact should not be overlooked, though, that international law and international organizations have not recognized any permanent Israeli right to Gaza and the West Bank.)

---

24. There is another obvious way, and that is to eliminate the Palestinian population, either by driving them out or worse. A nation haunted by a Holocaust can hardly think of such options, although isolated zealots like the late Rabbi Meir Kahane have been willing to do so, and to advocate them as well. It is for such people that the term "Judeo-Nazi" has been invented—by Israeli Jews.

This posed a problem. It is relatively easy to forswear something that you do not have and that you have little realistic prospect of obtaining. It is quite another to give up something that you have yearned for over the course of two thousand years and which is now yours. The territory Israel took in 1967 was the real land of the Zionist dream. Jewish souls had not resonated to the mention of Tel Aviv over the centuries. That city was only founded in the early 1900s. The prayer had always been "Next year in Jerusalem." And it wasn't the pizza shops of West Jerusalem that were mentioned in that prayer. It was the temple mount, the Wailing Wall or Western Wall, the holy places of the Old City, all of which were in Arab East Jerusalem. It was Jericho and Nablus (the biblical Shechem) and Hebron (the burial place of Abraham, Isaac, and Jacob) and the Jordan River and the towns of the West Bank, not the Philistine coastal plain, that formed the core of Jewish history in Palestine. And those places, once held, are very difficult to give up. It might cause a civil war in Israel if someone seriously proposed to do so.

The Israelis were not inclined to give them up. They went to great lengths to incorporate the Gaza Strip and especially the West Bank into the original Israel and to ensure that the Palestinians in those areas could not even establish a basis for independence. They controlled the importation of raw materials for manufactures and the export of finished goods, effectively preventing the Arabs from developing an industrial economy that could compete with Israel's or that would give them any idea that they could survive on their own. The idea was to make the Palestinians dependent upon Israel and, frankly, to keep them poor enough so that their major concern would be economic survival. And, to a large extent, Israeli policy was successful: Many college-educated Palestinians have found that the only jobs available to them have involved laying bricks or sweeping floors. They can be maids or waiters, they can wash the streets or pick up the trash, but they cannot aspire to political equality. An efficient and all-pervasive intelligence network makes it certain that no Palestinian can come close to becoming a leader of the community. Harassment, arrests, and expulsions of prominent Palestinians have become routine. Interrogations are frequently accompanied by torture.

It must be admitted, of course, that the treatment of Palestinians by Israel, although occasionally quite harsh, definitely does not rank among the more oppressive situations in the Middle East. Other Arab regimes in the region, notably Syria and Iraq, have infinitely worse human rights records. Furthermore, it has to be understood that the Israelis are playing for keeps and that their opponents rarely abide by the Geneva conventions. It is not brutality that sets the Israeli-Palestinian relationship apart. The worst and most humiliating aspect of the situation for the Palestinians has been the oppression that has come not from coreligionists, and not even from speakers of Arabic, but from foreigners. Again, we see the tribalism of the Ottoman millet system.

Another obnoxious matter is the hypocrisy. Nobody expects much of Hafez al-Asad in Syria, and certainly nobody expects much of Saddam Hussein in Iraq. We are invited to support Israel because it exists on a higher moral plane than other nations. But it does not. Mormons and other Christians resonate to the idea of a reconstructed Jewish state in the land of the ancient prophets, the land in which our basic moral law has it origins, but too often that state fails to live up to the standards those ancient prophets called for. Israel sometimes seems to want to be judged by other criteria than are normal, wants to claim our support on the basis of a higher moral law, but then objects when it is actually held to that higher standard. (The fact that many now expect little of Israel, and are not surprised when Israel is brutal, is a sad one. To an extent, it represents the loss of a dream.)

This is not only my jaundiced opinion. Thomas Friedman quotes Abba Eban, the great Israeli statesman who, as a young man in 1947, was entrusted with the task of presenting the case for a Jewish state to the United Nations.

> It was not easy to make our case. The entire region rejected us. We were forming a state for people who were not yet here. And we were not a majority in our country. We had to seize the ears of the world. We could not just rely on pure juridicial arguments. We could not argue like Ghana. We had to make ourselves exceptional. So we based our claim on the exceptionality

> of Israel, in terms of the affliction suffered by its people, and in terms of our historical and spiritual lineage. We knew we were basically appealing to a Christian world for whom the biblical story was familiar and attractive, and we played it to the hilt. We are still the victims of our own rhapsodic rhetoric, and our own rhapsodic defense. [But] we chose the line. We chose to emphasize at the beginning of our statehood that Israel would represent the ancient Jewish morality. Some Israelis now complain about being judged by a different standard [from other countries in the Middle East]. But the world is only comparing us to the standard we set for ourselves. You can't go out and declare that we are the descendants of kings and prophets and then come and say, "Why does the world demand that we behave differently from Syria?"[25]

It is not a clear-cut case of good versus evil. My own response to the Arab-Israeli conflict is often either a Shakespearean view ("A plague on both your houses!") or a Book of Mormon one ("It is by the wicked that the wicked are punished"). Of course, that is too simplistic in its own right, because good and innocent people are suffering, on both sides, and it is not just the wicked. So one cannot turn away with a flip answer.

The results of the 1967 war, the expanded borders that Israel obtained by means of fighting, have often been justified as necessary to make the Jewish state truly secure. And it is true that the pre-1967 borders made Israel dangerously narrow at one point—about ten miles from Jordanian Arab territory to the Mediterranean Sea—and horrifically liable to be cut in half by a quick tank thrust.

Certainly there are few today thinking seriously about the prospect that the Jewish state might actually be totally destroyed. (For one thing, it is unthinkable that the United States would simply stand by and allow such a thing to happen.) But it is questionable, from another perspective, whether control of the West Bank and the Gaza Strip has really added to the security of Israel. Where before, the Arab threat was something abstract and manageable on

25. Cited at Friedman, *From Beirut to Jerusalem*, 438-39.

the other side of a clear border and separated from the average Israeli by the fearsome might of the extraordinarily competent Israeli military, today there are Arabs within the practical borders of Israel. They are within, and they are very unhappy. There are no borders behind which the average Israeli can feel wholly safe and secure. The tension in Israel is almost tangible. While many Palestinians continue to live outside of Israel, those within have begun to be the dominant voices of their people. Their profile has risen with the *intifada*.

> Students of Gaza, teach us some of
> what you know, for we have forgotten.
> Teach us to become men, for our men
> have turned into soft clay.
> Crazy people of Gaza, a thousand halloos.
> You freed us from the rotten age of political logic
> and taught us to be crazy, too.[26]

The Arabic root *nfd*, which lies behind the word *intifada*, has to do with the idea of "shaking," or "shaking something off," "ridding oneself of something," "recovering" or "recuperating" from an illness. It occurs in common Arabic phrases meaning "to shake off one's laziness" or "to shake off the dust of something" in the sense of being finished with it, reaching the end of it.[27] Another common use of the root is in phrases meaning "to break with someone," "to dissociate oneself from someone," or "to refuse to have anything to do with someone." All of these senses are relevant to what the term *intifada* means to Palestinians. It has been an act of national repentance, of self-purification. Dormant no longer, a sizeable number of Palestinians now refuse to be part of Israel's economy, to cooperate in Israel's occupation. By slowing down the Israeli economy with strikes, by scaring away the all-important tourist, by filling Israeli prisons to the point of overflowing, these Palestinians are attempting to show Israel that it would be better off without them. The *intifada*

---

26. Nizar Qabbani, "The Angry Ones," cited at Friedman, *From Beirut to Jerusalem*, 366.
27. This seems reminiscent of the argument of Jalal Al-i-Ahmad's *Occidentosis*, cited in the previous chapter.

has also been an act of national self-definition, perhaps the most significant development to date in the crystallization of a real sense of Palestinian nationhood. The word *intifada* itself means "a shaking," "a shiver," "a shudder," or "a tremor." And this is precisely what it has been. The *intifada* has sent a shudder through all of Israeli society.

The *intifada* rose without any command from the PLO, although it saved the PLO from the near irrelevance in which it found itself following its expulsion from Lebanon in the early 1980s. The leadership of the PLO scrambled to get out in front of the situation, so that it might appear to be in command.

The *intifada* has changed the center of gravity within the Palestinian movement from the guerrillas and others outside to the residents of the Gaza Strip and the West Bank. This has had several consequences. Among the Palestinians, these are the people who know the Israelis best. They know the strength of Israel, and they know intimately the many daily humiliations of living under occupation. They are the ones who want a solution now. They would be satisfied with a two-state solution that would end Israeli occupation of their villages. They are now willing to choose the imperfect solution—possession of only part of Palestine rather than the desired whole—because they are realistic enough to take part of the loaf in lieu of no loaf at all. They have also created a new means of resistance which has proven more effective than the international terrorism favored by many of the expatriate Palestinians. For one thing, it is a mode of resistance that the Israelis have found very difficult to counter; while their occupation has been harsh and unpopular, they are simply unwilling to use the overwhelming and devastating force that (in lieu of more saintly alternatives) would be required to definitively end it, and they have not wanted to appear on international television as brutal oppressors. The *intifada* could not have occurred under a totally ruthless regime. Syria or Iraq would simply have annihilated the demonstrators in the streets. (They have in fact done that very thing, on more than one occasion. Similarly, Gandhi's technique of passive resistance could only influence a relatively decent government like that of the British in India;

it could never have moved the Nazis.) Even so, the *intifada* has helped to overcome the terrorist stigma under which the Palestinians have labored for many years and allowed them to claim some of the moral high ground in the conflict. For here, it is the Palestinians who are the victims. Visibly, on American network news, it is unarmed Palestinian children who die under Israeli fire, and it is Palestinian grandmothers who are shot while hanging up their wash. This has been a propaganda coup of major proportions.

It is not surprising that Yasir Arafat became willing in the late 1980s to accept Israel's right to exist. His constituency had changed. If he wished to retain his position at the head of the Palestine Liberation Organization, he had to change with that constituency.

By 1993, things had changed even further. The collapse of the Soviet Union had made it much easier for Russian Jews to emigrate to Israel, and many thousands were doing just that. (The hope of some Palestinians that high Arab fertility rates, coupled with typically small Israeli families and the tendency of many Israelis to seek more comfortable lives abroad, would eventually give them the demographic upper hand was delayed, if not utterly dashed.) The end of the Cold War had made it far less important for the United States and other Western nations to curry the favor of the Arabs and had deprived the Arabs of their powerful Soviet ally. Weary of long and useless conflict, many of the Arab states were now, in fact, beginning to talk with Israel. Furthermore, the PLO's endorsement of the Iraqi invasion of Kuwait had offended not only the West but the conservative Arab governments that funded the Palestinian cause.

But there was and is another problem facing the leadership of the PLO, and it is a very big one. For much of its history, the Palestinian movement has been a rather secular, national affair. Christian Arabs have been well represented in its leadership, and it has sought a local solution and the establishment of a secular state. But Palestinian resistance was caught up in a larger, global change that transcended the Near East: Whereas for years, politics and religion around the world seemed to be drawing further and further apart, and sociologists could confidently speak of a worldwide (and presumably irreversible) tendency towards secularization, things had clearly changed by somewhere in the mid-1970s. (We might take the election of the assertive and anticommunist Pope John Paul II as a sign of this change, along with the Islamic revolution in Iran, the resistance of the Afghan *mujahideen* to the Soviet invasion of their country, the assassination of Anwar Sadat by Islamic militants, and the election of Menachem Begin's Likud government in Israel.) Modernism, it seems, had been unable to create values to replace those lost in the absence of religion. In the capitalist world, people found mere consumerism shallow and unsatisfying; elsewhere, repression, poverty, and dehumanization completely discredited such myths as scientific socialism. It all seemed rather meaningless, and something more (and very different) was wanted. In the Near East, specifically, the continuing failure of the PLO to solve the Palestinian problem led to the birth of radical alternatives such as Islamic Jihad and Hamas. For a while, the Israeli authorities watched the growth of these fundamentalist organizations with some satisfaction, as tending to divide the Palestinians. Indeed, some observers have argued that the Israelis may even have encouraged them.

So, when Yasir Arafat stood on the White House lawn to shake hands with the Israeli prime minister, Yitzhak Rabin, it was in a sense a moment of triumph. But it was also and simultaneously an admission of defeat. Even the *intifada* had failed to end Israel's control of the Palestinians, and the pressure for a solution was growing on Arafat from his own people. Thus, internationally isolated, nearly bankrupt, with nothing to show for nearly thirty years of armed resistance to Israeli occupation, the PLO had little choice. But then, neither did the Israelis. The rapid growth of an expressly *Islamic* Palestinian resistance had begun to worry them, too. Religiously motivated suicide bombers are much more difficult to defend against than the more secular kind of guerrilla who, all things considered, would just as soon survive. And whereas one might be able to negotiate with relatively pragmatic opponents, folks who believe that the will of God demands the abolition of all nation-states and the submission of all peoples to Islam are apt to be a bit stubborn.

A resolution, therefore, has to be found. The Palestinians will not disappear. They do not want to be Israelis, and certainly do not want to be under the thumb of the Israelis. By the same token, Israel will not go away. But the Israelis and the Palestinians have to want peace; they have to be willing to give something up to get it. Nobody can impose it on them from the outside, and neither one of them can impose it upon the other.

A two-state solution seems, therefore, to be the only feasible answer. Leaders on each side have had to recognize that they will not get all that they would ask for if they held all the cards. Pragmatism has come to dominate. Yet Israel has found it difficult to tell its hardline Zionists that they cannot have all they want, and Yasir Arafat has still not managed to finally convince his exile constituency that their homes in Jaffa and the coastal plain are forever beyond their reach. The game is still afoot. No mortal knows precisely how it will turn out.

We should not, however, assume that the problems of the Middle East will all go away when and if the Arab-Israeli dispute is resolved. Those problems are many, and they are deep. It has always been both popular and safe among Arab intellectuals, journalists, and politicians to blame the region's troubles on Israel. They have generally not been free, after all, to criticize their own governments. Thus, the rivalries among the various Arab states, and their internal conflicts and injustices, have tended to be downplayed by both Arab analysts and the Western scholars who follow them. Moreover, for years many Arab governments have managed to divert domestic criticisms onto the ever-useful enemy occupying Palestine and to stigmatize as allies or tools of Zionism those who might dissent. If the Arab-Israeli problem ever goes away, the other fundamental challenges of the Middle East will nonetheless remain. Perhaps no part of the region illustrates this sad fact better than Lebanon.

Lebanon

Because of its mountains and its banks, but perhaps especially because it is a mosaic of different religions and cultures that lived harmoniously together, Lebanon was once known as the Switzerland of the Middle East. It was a symbol of the hope that the various communities of the region could someday learn to live together, peacefully and productively, in other places as well. The collapse of that dream has been painful for many in the Middle East.

Much of what characterizes the area called the "Levant"—a collective name sometimes given to the countries of the eastern Mediterranean—comes from its merchant orientation. Trade ties served, as such ties often do, to open them to new ideas, to make them more tolerant of differences. (This is the tolerance of the free market. After all, nothing should get in the way of a successful deal.) Missionaries, merchants, and diplomats came to the Levant in large numbers during the nineteenth century, bringing with them Western ideas and modes of life, which the intelligent and adaptable merchant class of the region rapidly assimilated. However, various nationalist movements came to power in the region after the close of World War I and the disappearance of the Ottoman Empire. In the same nationalist surge that fed both Palestinian aspirations and the Zionists, the old tolerance and multiculturalism of the Levant disappeared in most of the cities of the area. Minorities were not favored, and they were an affront to the nationalist spirit. It is out of this situation that the famous Turkish massacre of the Armenians ensued. And in the Arab world, cosmopolitan places such as Alexandria were changed forever. The exotic city of Lawrence Durrell's *Alexandria Quartet*, the fascinating Alexandria of the marvelous Greek poet Constantine Cavafy, is now a rather drab, uninteresting, and somewhat dilapidated Arab port. The old Greek *tavernas* are gone, even if their Greek-lettered signs often remain—and inside there is only the usual dull fare of lower-class Egyptian cuisine.

But Beirut remained. Beirut lived on, at least among the upper classes, as an embodiment of the Levantine ideal. Neither the Muslims nor the Christians were strong enough to impose conformity on Lebanon, and they had to cooperate, to a certain extent, in making the place work commercially. Like Hong Kong, it had very few natural resources and had to rely on trade to survive. And, like Hong Kong, it was a kind of island or peninsula, backed up by a vast hinterland in which far less cosmopolitan and far less sophisticated ways were the rule. But those ways were not as foreign to Lebanon as might have appeared to a casual observer. Anyone looking very deeply might have realized that the hinterland was the real Lebanon. Beirut was an aberration, an exception. One of the revelations that came out of the collapse of Beirut and Lebanon was how superficial the Westernization of the country had been. In the countryside and among the lower classes in the cities, hardly a trace of the Levantine spirit seems to have found a permanent place.[28] Like the appearance of parliamentary democracy, the appearance of harmony and Westernization was a mirage.

The Maronites, the Near Eastern Christians in formal communion with the Church of Rome, managed to survive for centuries, even though surrounded by Muslims, by barricading themselves in the rugged terrain of what is known as Mount Lebanon. They shared this difficult area with a religious sect known as the "Druze," who had fled to the mountains for much the same reason that the Maronites had—for refuge and protection.[29] These two groups often did not get along with each other. When Elder Orson Hyde of the Council of the Twelve passed through in 1841, en route to dedicating Palestine for the return of the Jews, he found a situation in Lebanon that seems strikingly similar to the conditions we read about there today. Lebanon, he wrote in a letter to Parley P. Pratt,

> is in a dreadful state—a war of extermination is going on between the Druses and Catholics [Maronites]. At the time I was at Beyroot, a battle was fought in the mountains of Lebanon, near that place, and about 800 killed. Robberies, thefts and murders are daily being committed. It is no uncommon thing to find persons in the streets without heads. An English officer, in going from St. Jean D'Acre to Beyroot, found ten persons murdered in the street,

---

28. This is very much like the situation of ancient Egypt. Alexandria may have been Hellenized, but in the countryside the old language and the old ways persisted. This was true even after the coming of Christianity: In Alexandria, Clement and Origen argued and wrote in Greek; in the hinterlands, as the Gnostic library of Nag Hammadi shows, Coptic—a late form of ancient Egyptian—was the language of Christianity.

29. The Druze are a fairly mysterious offshoot of a Shiite sect of Islam. They cannot really be considered Muslims anymore.

> and was himself taken prisoner, but was rescued by the timely interference of the pasha.[30]

Furthermore, strengthened by the natural sympathy they both felt and received, the Maronites routinely sought help from Western Christians, forging alliances with them from Crusader times on up to the modern period, when France became their special European Christian benefactor.

When the Ottoman Empire collapsed after the end of the First World War, Syria and Lebanon came under French "protection." This was much to the liking of the Lebanese Maronite Christians, who persuaded the French to set up a Lebanese state in which they and their other Christian allies would be the dominant voices. But if the new state had included only the Christian regions of Lebanon, it would never have succeeded economically. This, the Maronites themselves knew. With Maronite encouragement backing up their own greed for more territory, the French included in Lebanon Shiite areas such as south Lebanon and the Bekaa Valley and important coastal cities—the biblical Tyre and Sidon, as well as Tripoli and Beirut—which were largely inhabited by Sunni Muslims. As the borders were drawn, the Maronites were still (barely) in the majority; with their wealth and their Western ties, they were very much in control.[31]

The trouble was, nobody had asked the Druze and the Sunnis and the Shiites whether they wanted to be part of this new and rather artificial Christian-dominated state. And, in fact, the overwhelming majority seem to have resented it from the beginning. They would have preferred to have become part of Syria, a fully Arab and fully Muslim state. Nonetheless, the leaders of the various religious factions eventually worked out an arrangement which left most Lebanese temporarily satisfied. According to that agreement, the so-called National Pact of 1943, the Muslims would give up their desire for union with Syria if the Maronites would cut their ties with

30. Letter from Orson Hyde to P. P. Pratt, dated 22 November 1841, and reproduced in *History of the Church*, 4:454-58. The passage quoted here is found on page 455.
31. The 1932 Lebanese census gave the Maronites 51 percent of the population.

France and accept the notion of Lebanon as an "Arab" country, if not a Muslim one. The Lebanese president would always be a Maronite Christian, the prime minister would always be a Sunni Muslim, and the speaker of the parliament would always be a Shiite. In order to guarantee their predominance, Christians were assured six parliamentary representatives to every five representatives of Muslim background.

This arrangement was probably not entirely unfair at the time it was instituted. But, with the benefit of hindsight, it is hard to deny today that the nation of Lebanon was the product of serious design error. It was probably headed toward civil war from the beginning. For one thing, population figures do not remain static. And while Lebanon's peculiar formula for religious representation was roughly appropriate for a time when Maronite Christians formed a majority of the Lebanese population, they did not retain their majority status. By the 1970s, Christians formed only about a third of the population, while the Muslims and the Druze together represented nearly two-thirds. But when Muslims sought political reforms to bring the National Pact into line with new realities, the Maronites refused. And to make a point, they began to organize private armies, unaffiliated with the state. This was the time, for example, which saw the beginnings of the notorious Phalangist militia, founded by the Gemayel family which still plays a leading role in the politics of Lebanon. In response, the Lebanese Muslims and the Druze organized their own private armies. The situation was now thoroughly polarized, and no democratic government can last long without conciliation and compromise. Lebanon's sad collapse into feudal anarchy was underway.

But the situation was far more complicated than a mere confrontation between the Muslims and the Druze, on the one hand, and the Christians on the other. There were conflicts within conflicts and intrigues within intrigues. The Sunni Muslims had done rather well under the old National Pact. They were the wealthiest, the best educated, the most urbanized of the Lebanese Muslim population. The Shiites, by contrast, were quite poor. Concentrated in the southern countryside, they were relatively unsophisticated and poorly educated. They were the "hewers of wood and drawers of water," the beasts of burden for the more prosperous portions of the population and were accordingly looked down upon by both Maronite and Sunnielites. For years, they did not publicly protest. But this would not last forever.

Furthermore, when Yasir Arafat fled Jordan after "Black September," he was welcomed in Lebanon by the Muslims and the Druze, who saw the PLO as an ally—another private army, and one with considerable battle experience—against their stubborn Maronite Christian opponents. The Maronites, for their part, grew increasingly furious at the fierce retaliation drawn upon Lebanon by PLO-launched raids into the Jewish state. They demanded a Jordanian-style solution to the problem and asked the Lebanese army to commence operations. Unsurprisingly, Muslim leaders refused to cooperate. The result was the near total breakdown of the Lebanese government.

But the private Christian militias—the Phalangists and the Chamoun family's Tigers—were available, and Maronite leaders turned to them for what they could not get from the national government. To their great disappointment, though, they soon learned that their militias were not strong enough to destroy the PLO, much less the PLO's Muslim allies. But neither were the Muslims strong enough to put a definitive end to their Christian attackers. In the ensuing chaos of fatal violence and vengeance, Lebanon dissolved. The civil war had begun. The PLO and various Muslim militias operated out of southern Lebanon—which was conveniently situated for raids into Israel—and western Beirut, while the Christian warlords consolidated their hold on eastern Beirut and their traditional base on Mount Lebanon.

This had negative consequences for the PLO, as Thomas Friedman explains:

> As the PLO got spoiled in Beirut, it turned from an ascetic, authentic, and even courageous young guerrilla organization living primarily in the hardscrabble hills of south Lebanon and trying to lead an armed struggle against Israel, into a rich,

> overweight, corrupt quasi army and state, complete with bagpipe bands, silver Mercedes limousines, and brigades of desk-bound revolutionaries whose paunches were as puffed out as their rhetoric.[32]

The organization gave up its relatively effective guerrilla warfare techniques and tried to convert itself into something like a regular army, complete with ranks and chauffeurs and old Soviet-made T-34 tanks. These were useful, perhaps, for dealing with the other warring militias in Lebanon, but they were useless against the Israelis, whose competent and ultramodern military could beat the PLO in any conventional battle.[33]

In April of 1976, Syria dispatched its army, ostensibly to put an end to the civil war. In fact, they were probably undertaking an effort to restore the boundaries of ancient Greater Syria, which had included modern Lebanon, Jordan, and Israel, as well as the modern state of Syria itself. (Ba'thist ideology sometimes resembles that of Hitler's National Socialists. In the quest for restoration of the more glorious ancient Syria, the Syrian Ba'th leaders were reprising the earlier Nazi quest for Greater Germany.) Syrian forces seized the Bekaa Valley and the northern port city of Tripoli and began to tighten their grip on the rest of the pathetic country of Lebanon.

In order to explain the situation in Beirut, journalist Thomas Friedman cites *Leviathan*, the classic seventeenth-century work of English political philosophy by Thomas Hobbes. Hobbes, who was an advocate of absolute monarchy, argued that the worst of states was anarchy, "the state of nature," in which "every man is enemy to every man…wherein men live without other security than what their own strength and their own invention shall furnish them withal. In such condition," Hobbes continues, "there is no place for

---

32. Friedman, *From Beirut to Jerusalem*, 123.

33. Thomas Friedman discusses this at *From Beirut to Jerusalem*, 123-24. The Palestinians thus furnish yet another instance of the phenomenon of "premature regularization," a persistent error made by guerrilla leaders, which I have discussed elsewhere in connection with the Gadianton robbers. See Daniel C. Peterson, "The Gadianton Robbers as Guerrilla Warriors," in *Warfare in the Book of Mormon*, edited by Stephen D. Ricks and William J. Hamblin (Salt Lake City and Provo: Deseret Book and the Foundation for Ancient Research and Mormon Studies, 1990), 146-73.

industry, because the fruit thereof is uncertain: and consequently no culture of the earth...no arts; no letters; no society; and which is worst of all, continual fear, and danger of violent death; and the life of man, solitary, poor, nasty, brutish, and short."[34]

"I don't know if Beirut is a perfect Hobbesian state of nature," writes Friedman after nearly half a decade living in the midst of Lebanon's civil war, "but it is probably the closest thing to it that exists in the world today."[35] In fact, though, however true the rest of Hobbes's prediction may be, the people of Beirut and Lebanon have done all within their power to avoid being solitary. As the larger Lebanese society has broken down, other community bonds have come to the fore. People have become more and more closely linked to their families, their clans, their religious denominations, and their neighborhoods. These alternate communities have prevented them from feeling completely solitary, utterly alone in the horrifying chaos that their country has become. However, these clan and religious loyalties were a major cause of the Lebanese problem in the first place, and, while they indisputably help people cope with a hellish situation, they also serve to prolong that situation. Lebanese Druze find it difficult to relate to Lebanese Maronites, and Lebanese Shiites find it difficult to relate to Lebanese Sunnis, because the concept of "Lebanon" or "Lebanese" has ceased to have real meaning. The Druze therefore have little in common with the Maronites, or the Shiites with the Sunnis, except for their shared rivalry. And these old distinctions have become barriers to communication and cooperation. Each faction has necessarily become self-sufficient and justifiably suspicious of every other faction. The Lebanese people have, in fact, fallen back in many instances into a perfectly tribal existence. It is a situation well depicted in the Book of Mormon.

"Beirut's enduring lesson for me," writes Thomas Friedman, "was how thin is the veneer of civilization, how easily the ties that bind can unravel, how quickly a society that was known for generations as the Switzerland of the Middle East can break apart into a

---

34. Thomas Hobbes, *Leviathan: Or, Matter, Form, and Power of a Commonwealth Ecclesiastical and Civil*, 1:13.
35. Friedman, *From Beirut to Jerusalem*, 30.

world of strangers."[36] This too is a lesson taught by the Book of Mormon and one reason why it can be said that that volume is increasingly relevant to the situation in which mankind finds itself today. Fortunately, the Book of Mormon also teaches us the path we must take to avoid such situations as those of the Nephites, the Jaredites, and the unfortunate people of Beirut.

When the Israelis invaded Lebanon in 1982, they did so in order to put an end to Palestinian raids into the north of Israel. Yasir Arafat and his men had too many weapons there for them to feel entirely comfortable. But in the twelve months leading up to the invasion, there had only been one Israeli death inflicted by Palestinians operating out of Lebanon. The Israelis plainly had other things to think about, other concerns that moved them to launch the invasion when they did. It is not unreasonable to conclude that they were worried about the quasi-state that Yasir Arafat and his men had built up in Lebanon and about Arafat's new role as a kind of statesman (based upon his new role as a Lebanese warlord), which was giving him too much international respectability for their liking.

Unfortunately, the Israelis did not understand Lebanon. Not at all. They invaded to come to the aid of the Maronite Christians of the country, who were locked in a war with the Sunni Muslims (among whom were the PLO) and with the Druze. The Israelis tended to see the Maronites as much like themselves, representatives of Western civilization getting no gratitude from backward Arab Muslims despite all the good they were trying to do. It seemed to the Israelis that Lebanon was, or was supposed to be, a Christian society, just as Israel was a Jewish society, and that each was afflicted with a troublesome bunch of Islamic primitives.

This view was simply not true. As Thomas Friedman puts it, the then Israeli prime minister, Menachem Begin, and other Israelis

> did not notice that these "Christians" they were going to save in Lebanon were not a group of hooded monks living in a besieged monastery but, rather, a corrupt, wealthy, venal collection of

---

[36] Friedman, *From Beirut to Jerusalem*, 47.

> mafia-like dons, who favored gold chains, strong cologne, and Mercedeses with armor plating. They were Christians like the Godfather was a Christian.[37]

I have seen television advertisements in which conservative Protestants appeal to their audience to donate money to help the suffering and persecuted Christians of Lebanon. There is absolutely no question that innocent Christians are suffering in Lebanon, but to portray the struggle there as one between virtuous followers of Jesus who want only to be left alone and evil anti-Christian Muslims is utterly misleading. The soulful eyes of the children shown on such advertisements are genuinely moving, but they could as easily be the eyes of Muslim children, for there are innocent Muslims suffering there as well. The battle is not so much about faith as it is about control of insurance rackets and smuggling and, now, about vengeance for past wrongs. It is the ancient Arab principle of blood vengeance come back to life. But that principle is pagan Arab, not Christian.

One quite unintended consequence of the Israeli invasion of Lebanon was the energizing of the largest of the country's ethnic factions, the Shiites, who had been relatively docile. The way in which this was done is a tribute to the awesome power of ignorance and misunderstanding. (Another factor, of course, was the emergence of a militant Shiite state in Iran, under the leadership of the Ayatollah Khomeini. Many Lebanese Shiite religious leaders had been trained in Iran, and the rise of the Islamic Republic gave them a new pride, a new fire.) It will be recalled that the PLO had set itself up in South Lebanon for the purpose of raiding into Israel and had turned itself into a kind of quasi-state. They had turned the south into a battleground in which the Shiites often took most of the casualties, and they were prone to liberate any item—up to and including homes and cars—that took their revolutionary fancy. Many of the Shiites fled into the cities, most notably into Beirut, where they continued to serve as the menials of the upper classes (if they found work at all) and where they did not share at all in the

---

37. Friedman, *From Beirut to Jerusalem*, 137.

Levantine high life of sophisticated Lebanon. It is not surprising, then, that the first reaction of the Shiites in the south was to welcome the Israeli invaders as liberators from PLO oppression.

But the Shiites had not expected the Israelis to stay forever, and they were not pleased when the Israelis turned to Lebanese Christian militiamen to help them rule the area. Furthermore, the Israelis, many of whom have not the slightest personal religious experience,[38] were grotesquely insensitive to Shiite religious feelings. (There are virtually no Shiite Muslims in Israel.) Stories are told by various authors of Israeli desecrations of mosques and of the Qur'an, done ham-handedly in the course of routine searches. The most spectacular instance of this occurred on 16 October 1983, in the town of Nabatiyya, when an Israeli military convoy decided to drive through a crowd of between 50,000 and 60,000 Shiites who were celebrating the most important of their holidays, Ashura, which commemorates the martyrdom of Husayn, the Prophet's grandson, at the hands of the unjust Umayyad tyranny. This is a holy day, a day during which the worshipers work themselves up to an emotional pitch and even go so far as to bloody themselves with whips. When the Israeli convoy ran into difficulty getting through the crowd, it began to honk horns and demand that people clear out of the way.

"It was the equivalent," says Thomas Friedman, "of someone turning on a ghetto blaster in a synagogue on Yom Kippur, the Jewish Day of Atonement."[39] The crowd began to throw rocks and bottles, and in the ensuing chaos some of the Israeli vehicles were overturned. The Israelis panicked and opened fire on the worshipers.

This incident brought the sleeping Shiite population to life. They began to fight against the Israelis with sniper ambushes, bombs packed with nails, wandering donkeys set to explode, ambulances packed with dynamite. There were the suicide bombers, too. With a religious faith virtually based on the idea of martyrdom,

---

38. Friedman, *From Beirut to Jerusalem*, 475, tells an interesting anecdote to illustrate his claim that the majority of Israelis don't even know what to do inside a synagogue. How, then, could they be expected to know much of *mosque* etiquette?
39. Friedman, *From Beirut to Jerusalem*, 180.

they were willing, indeed almost happy, to die.[40] It is extremely difficult to defend oneself against such an opponent. Strict Israeli measures such as travel and trade restrictions, car searches, and checkpoints only managed to irritate the Shiites more.

Misunderstanding was also the problem when the American Marines were sent to Lebanon in 1982. The United States thought, as well it might, that it was sending the troops in to prop up the legitimate government of Lebanon and to help it reestablish its control over the entire countryside. What the Americans did not realize was that the government of Lebanon was controlled by the Maronite Christians, largely for their own benefit, and that it really was simply one among the many warring factions of the country, with little more claim to legitimacy than any other of the country's warlords. In fact, the government of Lebanon called in the Americans to help in its battle against other sectors of the population, most particularly against the Druze with whom the Maronites shared the Shouf Mountains. The American problem was that it was reading the Lebanese situation in the light of its own concepts and experience. It was deceived by the appearance of parliamentary democracy and republican presidency that Lebanon had copied so well from its contacts with the West. The Lebanese, too, would read the Americans in the light of their own experience. To many of them, the American Marines would come to be merely one more of the nation's private militias, one that happened to be in the pay and control of the Maronites. Thus, to the Shiites and the Sunnis and the Druze, the Americans became the enemy. The United States had entered a tribal conflict on behalf of one of the tribes and did not even know it. (This case ought, by itself, to illustrate the imperative need for more knowledge of foreign countries and cultures among our policymakers.)[41] That is why the American

---

40. One of the most striking pieces of testimony about the suicide attack on the Marine barracks in Beirut, which occurred about a week after the incident in Nabatiyya, is that the driver of the bomb-laden truck *smiled* at the guard as he hurtled past to his death.

41. Certain writers, notable among them Frances Fitzgerald, have made a compelling case that a sometimes spectacular American failure to understand Vietnamese culture played a major role in producing the military disaster that occurred there.

Marines were blown up. It was an act that seemed full of irrational hatred to most in the West. Within the framework of Lebanese history and society, it had a certain logic.

By the mid-1980s, the Shiites had emerged to dominate Beirut. Their fiery religious absolutism, a far cry from the old and rather decadent tolerance of the Levant, had fundamentally changed the atmosphere of the city.

It is into this Near East, surging with passions and boiling with a newly reenergized Islam, that the Church must someday bring the restored gospel of Jesus Christ. The time is clearly not yet. Nevertheless, because of our own deep interest in the region, and because of our mandate to preach the gospel to all mankind, we are in the area now. Indeed, although it is little known among the Saints, we have been in the area for quite some time. The next and final chapter of this book will sketch the history of Latter-day Saint contacts with the Near East and will attempt to outline the direction the future of the gospel will take there.

After a great deal of opposition and controversy, Brigham Young University's Jerusalem Center for Near Eastern Studies took its prominent place on the city's Mount Scopus, near the campus of the Hebrew University.

The Church in the Near East

When leadership of The Church of Jesus Christ of Latter-day Saints fell to the Quorum of the Twelve Apostles after the martyrdom of Joseph Smith, they faced one crisis after another. The Prophet was dead. Many of the Saints wondered what this meant and what it portended for the future of the Church. They would have been less than human if, for at least a moment, doubts had not crossed their minds. Enemies from the communities around Nauvoo were pressuring the Saints, often violently, to leave. Property held by the Mormons would have to be abandoned, and those who could get it cheap would enjoy huge advantages. Plans were underway to move thousands of people through hostile wilderness, across the plains and the Rocky Mountains to an essentially unknown land beyond the current borders of the United States. To make matters worse, militant anti-Mormons, who had already shown what they were capable of, were threatening the freedom and the physical safety of the apostles themselves, making orderly planning very difficult.

In the midst of all this, the Twelve issued a proclamation to the world, which testified, among other things,

> that the Jews among all nations are... commanded, in the name of the Messiah, to prepare to return to Jerusalem in Palestine, and to rebuild that city and temple to the Lord. And also to organize and establish their own political government, under their own rulers, judges and governors, in that country. For be it

> known unto them that *we* now hold the keys of the priesthood and kingdom which are soon to be restored unto them. Therefore let them also repent, and prepare to obey the ordinances of God.[1]

The process by which this commandment has begun to be fulfilled has been a long and complicated one, far beyond the scope of the present book. I have already offered a brief discussion of the Zionist movement and of the return of the Jews to Palestine. My intention in this chapter is to survey, again in a brief and inadequate way, the involvement of the Church in the gathering of the Jews and in the Near East in general. However, I intend to glance not merely at past history in the region, but to attempt to discern, through the scattered scriptural and other clues that have been given to us, something of the future of the Church and the Near East in the divine plan. This is an ambitious undertaking, and a risky one. It must be stressed again that what I say here represents only my own reading of the information available.[2]

The Latter-day Saints and their leaders never lost the deep interest in the Near East, and especially in Palestine, that had been with them from the beginning. Even as they abandoned their temple in Illinois, they saw themselves as a modern-day Camp of Israel, led by an American Moses. However, this was no mere daydream or literary fancy. It was a reality of daily dirt and grit. Hard work required almost all their attention if they were to succeed in establishing Zion in the tops of the Rocky Mountains. Amid the demands of a forced exodus from Nauvoo, an historic and difficult trek westward, and the colonization of the Great Basin in the West, their energies were largely devoted to their own concerns. Hundreds of communities had to be established. Irrigation systems needed to be built. Sometimes, it was a matter of simple survival. Still, they remembered Palestine and the Near East, and that remembrance is

---

1. Printed in England and bound with *The Latter-day Saints' Millennial Star* 6 (1845).
2. I must repeat that, for information on the history of the Church in the Holy Land and in the Near East generally, I have been heavily (though not entirely) dependent upon Baldridge, *Grafting In*, and Barrett, *The History of the Mormons in the Holy Land*.

illustrated in the names they chose for many of their settlements and for the physical features of their new home in the western desert. When they saw a river that connected a fresh water lake to a vast lake of salt water, it was inevitable that they would call that river the "Jordan." Towns bearing names like Enoch, Ephraim, Hebron, Jericho, Jerusalem, Little Zion,[3] Manasseh, Moab, Ophir, and Salem sprang up throughout areas of Mormon settlement. Mountains received names like Canaan, Carmel, Gog and Magog, Nebo, and Pisgah. In Sevier County, the settlers named a prominent rock formation "Solomon's Temple." In the southern part of Utah, a particularly spectacular area came to be known as Zion Canyon. But even though they remembered the land of Palestine, and continued to dream of its glorious future and to draw inspiration from events in its past, there was, for a long time, little that the Latter-day Saints could do about the area in a practical way. For more than thirty years after Orson Hyde's dedicatory prayer, Mormon activity was absent from the Holy Land.

When they were able to free themselves from the day-to-day demands of colonization and survival, however, the leaders of the Church acted to reestablish contact between the new capital city of God's people in the New World and the ancient city of His people in the Old. In October of 1872, another apostolic mission was sent to Palestine, with the assignment of rededicating the Holy Land for the return of Judah. President George A. Smith, first counselor to Brigham Young, was selected to lead the group. He was accompanied by two members of the Quorum of the Twelve, Elders Lorenzo Snow and Albert Carrington, and by several other Latter-day Saints, including the poet and Relief Society leader Eliza R. Snow. The group's journey to the Holy Land and back occupied eight months, considerably less time than Orson Hyde's journey had required. (Improved transportation, including the newly completed transcontinental railroad in North America, played a major role in this.)

---

3. For a number of years after Brigham Young visited this Washington county settlement in 1870 and, upon inspection, declared that it was "not Zion," the town was actually called Not Zion. See John W. Van Cott, *Utah Place Names* (Salt Lake City: University of Utah Press, 1990), 230-31.

Officially traveling as tourists rather than as missionaries, the company was able to enter countries from which Latter-day Saints had previously been barred.

Their travels took them to England, Holland, Belgium, France, Bavaria and other parts of Germany, Austria, Russia, Greece, Egypt, Turkey, and Syria. The journey was strenuous, but the little party of Latter-day Saint tourists seems to have retained a sense of humor. In Egypt, their Coptic Christian guide took them to an area near the modern city of Heliopolis, the biblical On, where he showed them an ancient sycamore tree. This, he informed them, was the very tree under which Mary, Joseph, and the infant Jesus had camped during their flight into Egypt. Mary had bathed in the nearby well and, although it had only given brackish and undrinkable water before, from that time forward its water had become sweet and good. President Smith tasted it and agreed that the water was excellent, reminding him of "the big spring at Saint George." There was just one thing lacking, to his taste. "I remarked to the man I really wished she had made it cold while she was about it, for a drink of cold water would have been very refreshing just then. This cost me one franc."[4]

In Palestine itself, the apostolic party visited the traditional home of Simon the Tanner in Jaffa, where the Apostle Peter had received his important vision of the sheet let down from heaven that opened the way for the preaching of the gospel to the Gentiles. While there, they asked the Arab caretaker of the house whether Peter had been a Muslim. Yes, he replied, pointing to a *mihrab* niche in the wall of the building as the place where the apostle had prayed.[5] They saw the beautiful orange groves in the vicinity of Jaffa. They spent a night at the monastery of Mar Saba near Bethlehem, and, in that town itself, they went to the Grotto of the Nativity, which local tradition identifies as the precise spot of Christ's birth. They were struck by the remarkable similarity between the Dead Sea and their own Great Salt Lake. They noted that Palestine's Jordan River was smaller than Utah's and rather barren in its surroundings. "We

---

4. *Journal of Discourses* 16:91.
5. *Journal of Discourses* 16:92.

used to sing about the flowery banks of Jordan," said President Smith, "but it takes off the romance to go and see them."[6] Lorenzo Snow especially liked the Arab town of Nablus. He was attracted to its setting in a relatively verdant and well-watered valley, surrounded by olive trees, fruit orchards, and various gardens, as well as by its white domes, its mosques, and its many minarets. But the hilly scenery, while picturesque, made for difficult travel. "I have seen a good many rough roads in Utah in the mountains," recalled President Smith, "but of all the rough horseback riding I ever did see, I think that Palestine has the premium."[7] Still, beyond all the discomforts of touring in the Holy Land, there was the marvelous sense, felt by hundreds of thousands of pilgrims before and since, of walking in the very footsteps of Jesus and the personalities of the Bible. "I cannot communicate...to any extent," President Smith later remarked,

> the impressions I felt at the time. I had no doubt that I passed over the grounds where the Savior and his Apostles, and the Prophets, kings and nobles of Israel had lived, although I did not believe a great deal about the identical spots set down by the monks, yet I was satisfied that I was in the localities in which the great events of scripture took place.[8]

On Sunday morning, 2 March 1873, President Smith arranged with their guide to take a tent, a table, several chairs, and a carpet up onto the Mount of Olives. He and his companions rode up the slope on horseback. When all was ready, and after Elder Carrington had offered an invocation, President Smith led them in a prayer

---

6. *Journal of Discourses* 16:100. Mark Twain was similarly unimpressed by Palestinian geography. "When I was a boy," he recalled in his travel memoir *The Innocents Abroad*, "I somehow got the impression that the river Jordan was four thousand miles long and thirty-five miles wide. It is only ninety miles long, and so crooked that a man does not know which side of it he is on half the time... It is not any wider than Broadway in New York. There is the Sea of Galilee and this Dead Sea– neither of them twenty miles long or thirteen wide. And yet when I was in Sunday school I thought they were sixty thousand miles in diameter." See Mark Twain, *The Innocents Abroad/Roughing It* (New York: Literary Classics of the United States, 1984). We have many misconceptions about the region. Every Christmas, Latter-day Saints sing of a sacred event that took place, "Far, Far Away on Judea's Plains." But Judea is hill country, with hardly a flat spot in it.

7. *Journal of Discourses* 16:98.

8. *Journal of Discourses* 16:100.

rededicating the land of Palestine for the return of the Jews. "When on the Mount of Olives with our faces bowed toward Jerusalem," he later reported to the Saints back in Utah,

> we lifted our prayers to God that he would preserve you and confound your enemies. We felt in our hearts that Zion was onward and upward, and that no power could stay her progress; that the day was not far distant when Israel would gather, and those lands would begin to teem with a people who would worship God and keep his commandments; that plenty and the blessings of eternity would be poured out bounteously upon that desert land, and that all the prophecies concerning the restoration of the house of Israel would be fulfilled.[9]

After President Smith's prayer, the other brethren prayed in turn, confirming and repeating his supplications for themselves and on behalf of scattered Judah. Their assigned task completed, the party then returned to the mountains of North America. The memories of their visit to Palestine remained with them, however. As a recent biographer of Lorenzo Snow has put it:

> Lorenzo's words and conduct during the quarter of a century of life that was to remain after his Palestine tour reflected the lasting impression this trip had made upon him. The experience transformed him into a man more sensitive to the reality of Jesus' earthly life and ministry... Thereafter, his sermons that developed themes of biblical history or doctrine would have greater depth of meaning because of his direct exposure to the ancient land of the prophets and the patriarchs... But, more germane to his highest role as a special witness of Jesus Christ, were the spiritual assurances and illuminations he had received of the Savior's divinity and Godhood that had come to him as he had visited the historic places where the great Messianic drama had been enacted. These would ever be in his heart and his mind's eye in the years ahead as he served and bore testimony of the Master.[10]

---

9. *Journal of Discourses* 16:102.
10. Francis M. Gibbons, *Lorenzo Snow: Spiritual Giant, Prophet of God* (Salt Lake City: Deseret Book, 1982), 138, 148.

This was, however, not the last time that apostles of the Lord would visit Palestine in this dispensation to dedicate the land for the return of the Jews. Altogether, there seem to have been at least ten separate dedications of the Holy Land under apostolic authority. (No clearer illustration could possibly be provided than this of the urgent interest with which the prophets and apostles of this dispensation have watched events in the Holy Land.) Elder Anthon H. Lund of the Quorum of the Twelve, in company with Ferdinand F. Hintze of the Turkish Mission, rededicated the land from the Mount of Olives on 8 May 1898. Francis M. Lyman, then president of the Twelve, dedicated the land on three separate occasions and at three different sites during March of 1902. Elder David O. McKay, passing through Palestine on his world tour of missions, climbed with his companion Hugh J. Cannon to the top of the Mount of Olives and offered a prayer of thanksgiving and praise to God on 3 November 1921. Elder James E. Talmage rode with President Joseph W. Booth to the top of Mount Carmel, near Haifa, and rededicated the land for the redemption of Judah on 18 October 1927. Finally, in May of 1933, Elder John A. Widtsoe, accompanied by his wife and by President Badwagon Piranian of the Palestine Syria Mission, climbed the Mount of Olives to dedicate the land one more time. (He had offered an earlier prayer of dedication from high on Mount Carmel, overlooking the blue of the Mediterranean Sea.)

The actual preaching of the gospel to the inhabitants of Palestine and the Near East—although notably not to the Jews—began in 1884. During that year, an Armenian living in Istanbul, who had somehow heard of the Mormons, wrote to the president of the European Mission and asked him to send a representative of the Church to introduce the gospel into Turkey. The choice fell upon a Swiss convert to Mormonism by the name of Jacob Spori. When he arrived at Istanbul—where he was able to baptize the Armenian and his family—he became the first Latter-day Saint missionary ever to serve in the Near East.

A second missionary, Joseph Tanner, arrived during the last month of 1885. In the spring of 1886, Francis M. Lyman, Jr., came to Istanbul and then accompanied Elder Tanner on a journey through the Middle East and Palestine. In the city of Haifa, they ran across a colony of devout German Christians who had settled in the Holy Land to await the second coming of Jesus. Impressed by the cleanliness and order of this colony, and remembering past contact with another member of the group who had joined the Church in Berlin, Elder Tanner persuaded his priesthood superiors that permanent missionaries should be sent to work with the Germans in Haifa. It was hoped that such missionary labor, besides being valuable in and of itself, would one day serve as a stepping stone to proselyting among the Palestinian Arabs.

As things turned out, only one available missionary had both the funds and the language capacity to go to Haifa and work among the German colonists there. That was Jacob Spori. Fortunately, he was granted a vision before his departure in which he saw a black-bearded man in Haifa, a blacksmith, who, he was told, would be prepared to receive him and his message when he arrived. This vision was precisely fulfilled. Upon reaching Haifa in late July of 1886, Elder Spori made his way to the street that he had seen in his vision and found the blacksmith's shop just as he had expected it to be. The blacksmith, in turn, seeing Jacob Spori outside, dropped his tools and ran out into the street, crying after the missionary. He had, he said, seen Elder Spori in a dream the night before and knew that he had a divine message for him.

Not surprisingly, the blacksmith, a man named Johan Georg Grau, was converted along with his family. They became the nucleus of the Haifa Branch, the first organized unit of the Church in Palestine since ancient times. Even when Elder Spori returned to Istanbul, and then to Switzerland and then on to Utah, the Grau family and subsequent converts kept the flame of the gospel alive in Palestine. Joseph Tanner replaced Elder Spori, working for five months in Haifa and down the coast in Jaffa. He baptized thirteen converts of Russian and German descent, as well as an Arab who was the first of his lineage to join the Church in this dispensation. Other missionaries came, too. Among them was Janne M. Sjodahl, a Danish convert who would later become a prominent writer on Mormon subjects in Utah. A former Baptist minister, he labored for nine months in Palestine, spending most of his time in and around Jaffa. He sensed deeply the magnitude of the task before him. In a letter to Wilford Woodruff, he wrote:

> When I came here to Palestine, I was soon made aware of the fact, that I was placed face to face with millions of human beings, to whom the latter-day message has never sounded. I mean the Arabian speaking nations, who are scattered all over Syria, Arabia, Egypt, and a large part of Africa. And my prayer to God was that He would lead me and make an opening by which the light of His gospel might shine through.[11]

At first it appeared that Elder Sjodahl's prayer would be abundantly answered. He did have some success among the Arabs. However, sickness cut short his mission in the Near East, and he was obliged to return to Switzerland. There were other setbacks, too. In 1888, Magdalena Grau, the blacksmith's wife, died and was buried in the old German cemetery in Haifa at the foot of Mount Carmel, where her grave can still be seen. Her husband emigrated to Utah for a few years, but returned to Haifa in the late nineties as a missionary to his old German friends in the colony there. For some years, he served the branch in Haifa as its president. Meanwhile, in 1890, Elder Edgar D. Simmons became the first Latter-day Saint missionary to die in the Near East when he succumbed to smallpox and was buried at Aintab, Turkey (modern-day Gaziantep). Another, Elder Adolph Haag of Payson, Utah, died of typhus fever at Haifa on 3 October 1892 and was buried not far from Magdalena Grau in the city's little German cemetery.

This was sad, but the work went on. Elder Haag's companion, President Musser of the Turkish Mission, kept himself busy preaching the gospel in both English and German, as well as studying Arabic in order to expand the scope of his missionary service yet further. He visited Jerusalem on several occasions, working among the Arabs. He was astonished by their customs, which to him were completely exotic. He was also deeply impressed by the Dome of

---

11. Cited by Barrett, *The Story of the Mormons in the Holy Land*, 41.

the Rock, the Muslim shrine on the temple mount. By the time he left, there were three small branches of the Church in the Near East: at Aleppo in Syria, at Aintab, Turkey, and at Haifa. In 1895, however, yet another missionary, serving the Lord in a far off and very foreign land, died of smallpox. Elder John A. Clark was buried near the grave of Adolph Haag, again in the German cemetery at Haifa—a place that, for more than one Latter-day Saint visitor to the Near East, has now taken on something of the character of holy ground. Yet the graveyard is not entirely a melancholy place, and not only because we know of the glorious promises made to those who give their lives in the faithful service of the Lord. It demonstrates, as eloquently as anything can, the interest that The Church of Jesus Christ of Latter-day Saints has long had in the land of Palestine and the high price that members of the Church have been willing to pay for that interest and that faith.[12]

The earliest Mormon missionaries in the Near East dreamed of a Latter-day Saint presence in the Holy Land, something more than a few scattered elders and something larger than the graves of a few faithful Saints. They envisioned a Latter-day Saint colony in Palestine. Ferdinand F. Hintze, the first president of the Turkish Mission, wrote to his wife as early as 1889 that he was trying to get a colony started somewhere near Jerusalem. Such a colony, he felt, would serve as a base from which the message of the gospel could go forth. Living together, the Saints would find strength in numbers and would be less prone to fall away through sheer isolation not only from the center of the Church but from one another. Furthermore, it would allow the Saints to become temporally independent as they gained greater understanding of the practical arts and sciences, much as the Saints in Utah were building their own commonwealth in the semiarid lands of the American West. Near

12. It has been claimed that, many years later when the question arose of official recognition for the Church in the nation of Israel (previously Palestine), the graves of Elders Haag and Clark in Haifa served to demonstrate that the Church had been actively established in the land prior to the partition of Palestine and the organization of the State of Israel, which was a condition required for recognition. See Baldridge, *Grafting In*, 7. Unfortunately, recent research has cast doubt on that claim, and it cannot be substantiated at the present time.

Eastern missionaries had seen what the industry and discipline of the German colonists had been able to accomplish in Haifa. Could the Saints not do even better, blessed as they were by the companionship of the Holy Ghost?

In 1873, President George A. Smith had reported much the same feeling after his visit to Palestine. "I was often asked," he recalled to an audience of Saints assembled in the new tabernacle at Salt Lake City, "if we were going to settle in Palestine. I replied that we were not, but I could take a thousand 'Mormons,' go up the Jordan, put in a dam to take out the water, and irrigate several thousand acres."[13] Although President Smith died in 1875, it appears that his confidence about the abilities of the Latter-day Saints to deal with the difficult terrain of Palestine was shared by his brethren. At any rate, when the idea of a Mormon colony in the Holy Land was presented to the leaders of the Church, they were positively inclined toward it. They even saw the possibility of sending colonists from the American Zion to Jerusalem to put their colonizing skills to work in that land. Late in 1897, the First Presidency called Elder Anthon H. Lund of the Council of the Twelve to accompany Brother Hintze on a tour of the region to see if land for a Latter-day Saint colony could be secured. Suitable land was indeed found in the Jezreel Valley along the banks of the Kishon River. Unfortunately, the Church was in precarious financial health in 1898 and simply had no money with which to pursue the project. The dream had to be deferred. (This was the financial crisis that led to President Lorenzo Snow's famous revelation on tithing, received in the tabernacle at St. George.)

A resident of Alpine, Utah, by the name of Joseph Wilford Booth was called to serve as the eleventh president of the Turkish Mission in August 1903. Elder Booth had previously served as a missionary in the same mission for almost four years, having only been released from his labors in April of the previous year. Already, he was headed back. This time, however, he was accompanied by his wife, Mary Reba, who would become the first "mission mother"

---

[13] *Journal of Discourses* 16:100.

in the history of the modern Near East. Her presence was important because, in the conservative and gender-segregated culture of the region, she could gain access to women in a way that was utterly impossible for the elders. The Booths worked side by side in Turkey and throughout the Near East until, because of political unrest, the Turkish Mission was shut down in 1909 and they and their missionaries were withdrawn.

For more than ten years, Church headquarters in Utah sent no representatives to the Middle East. When Joseph W. Booth returned in 1921, much was changed, including the name of the mission. In recognition of the group among whom most of the Church's limited proselyting success had occurred, it was now to be called the "Armenian Mission." Some changes, though, were clearly for the worse. The Haifa Branch had long since disappeared—the victim of emigration to Utah. But other units of the Church were in trouble as well. Where there had been more than a hundred members in the branch at Aintab in 1909, there were now only thirty-five. The First World War, the Turkish massacres of the Armenians, and the revolutionary unrest that accompanied the end of the Ottoman Empire had taken their terrible toll. "Aintab, the beautiful city of so many years of my missionary experiences, is now in ruins," President Booth lamented, "and perhaps two thirds of the Christian population and a big percent of the Moslems have been slain in this awful struggle the past few years."[14]

Late in 1921, Elder David O. McKay of the Quorum of the Twelve arrived at Jerusalem, along with his traveling companion Hugh J. Cannon. They were delighted to be there. Jerusalem, Elder McKay exclaimed, was "the most historic place in the world!" One of his assignments from the First Presidency was to leave an apostolic blessing on the land. He soon saw how desperately such a blessing was needed. Looking at the silver and gold decorations in the Grotto of the Nativity, the purported place of the birth of Jesus, Elder McKay felt them to be "desecrations." Worse, with his own eyes he saw examples of the fatal violence that had begun to boil

---

14. Cited by Barrett, *The Story of the Mormons in the Holy Land*, 57.

between Jews and Arabs in the so-called City of Peace. His own Arab Christian guide was vehement that the Jews would never be allowed to rule over Palestine. Elder McKay could not allow this to pass without contradiction.

"Michael," he declared, "standing here on the street of David, this 2nd of November, 1921, I want to tell you something to remember. No matter how much the Mohammedans and the Greek Christians oppose the Jews' coming back to Palestine, the Jews are coming and will possess this land."

"Never," Michael cried out, bitterly. "The streets will flow with blood first!"

"The streets may and undoubtedly will flow with blood," replied the apostle, "but that will not prevent the Jews possessing their land. Don't you believe your Bible?"

Elder McKay's guide admitted that the Bible did foretell the rebuilding of Jerusalem. "But," he insisted, "the time hasn't come yet."

"Yes," Elder McKay corrected him, "the time has come."[15]

The other mission entrusted by the First Presidency to Elders McKay and Cannon was, somehow, to get in contact with President Joseph W. Booth. They needed to reorganize the surviving members of the Church in the region, and without his language skills and his knowledge of the areas and the members, it would be virtually impossible for them to do so. They absolutely had to find him. Yet this was a very difficult proposition. President Booth was always in motion, and they had no idea whatsoever of how to get in touch with him. They contacted the U.S. consul at Aleppo, Syria, but this did not seem to help much. A cable from European Mission headquarters told them that President Booth was somewhere en route to Aleppo, but this meant that he could still be anywhere. Nonetheless, after a series of inspired changes in plan, the two representatives from Salt Lake City literally ran into President Booth on a train bound for Haifa. Their mission had been a success.

---

15. See Clare Middlemiss, ed., *Cherished Experiences from the Writings of President David O. McKay* (Salt Lake City: Deseret Book, 1976), 95.

Among the steps upon which the Church leaders agreed was the removal of the entire branch at Aintab to the safer city of Aleppo during the last two months of 1922. For the next five years, President Booth would devote himself to caring for the needs of these members, with little or no time left over for proselyting. He still dreamed of a Latter-day Saint colony in the Near East, and perhaps he consoled himself that his work with the Saints at Aleppo was at least a step in that direction. Even that dream, however, was soon to die. In early 1927, Dr. Franklin S. Harris arrived in the Near East on assignment from the First Presidency, with specific instructions to evaluate the feasibility of establishing a Mormon colony in the Holy Land. His report was not encouraging. He found that only twenty of nearly two hundred members of the Church in Palestine were able to support themselves. Furthermore, those who were productively employed had industrial skills, rather than the agricultural skills that would be necessary to create the kind of Mormon settlement that had long been envisioned. Dr. Harris could not in good conscience recommend that the project be pursued any further. The dream of an agricultural colony for Latter-day Saints in Palestine was dead.

In October 1927, Elder James E. Talmage of the Council of the Twelve, who was serving as president of the European Mission at the time, arrived at Aleppo to work for a season with President Booth. Together, they purchased a mission home in Haifa, on the corner of Carmel and Allenby Streets. American missionaries, President Booth was directed, should establish themselves in respectable quarters in Haifa rather than living, as they had been, like refugees in the relatively backward city of Aleppo. A new focus for the work was in order. Syria and Turkey had simply failed to produce the number and quality of self-supporting converts that had been expected, and it was felt that a transfer of the missionaries to Haifa would allow for greater emphasis on work within Palestine and among the better-educated European population there.

A brief return trip to Aleppo to check on the condition of the Saints in the branch there was a great disappointment to President Booth. He found them to be, in his view, disobedient, selfish, and unworthy of the blessings they were receiving from the Lord through their knowledge of the restored gospel. In November, he went back again to Aleppo. Along the way, he stopped off in Beirut and Damascus, as well, to see how the few Mormons in those cities were doing. One of his tasks while there was to arrange for the shipment of rugs to Utah. The Church, interested in bettering the material situation of its Armenian members, had begun to invest in their oriental carpet manufacturing and to sell the carpets through ZCMI, its department store in Salt Lake City. Though the idea of a Mormon agricultural settlement had come to nothing, the traditional Latter-day Saint mix of temporal and spiritual things was still very much evident in the Near East.

Nonetheless, it could not truly be said that the cause of the Restoration was flourishing in the region. Just prior to his departure from Haifa, President Booth summarized the status of the Church in the Near East in a message that was later published in the Church magazine, the *Improvement Era*:

> Our past and present status may be briefly told by counting up to ten; thus: One lady missionary, two workers in the field today, three cities have served as our headquarters, four elders have died in the field, five nationalities have been baptized, six languages are needed to teach them, seven apostles have been here, eight cities now claim one or more of our members, and nine out of ten are in poverty.[16]

It was not, as it must have seemed to him, much to show for the years of care and labor he had devoted to his stewardship. "Your humble servant," he wrote to the brethren, "has had the pleasure and honor of seventeen years total in the mission field. The task at times has been a difficult one—almost like trying to tear away old Timpanogos with a tooth brush while a man with a team and scraper endeavors to pile it up again."[17] After nearly eighteen years of missionary service among the peoples of the Near East, he continued to

---

[16] See Joseph W. Booth, "The Armenian Mission," in *Improvement Era* 31 (October 1928), 1048–52. The quotation occurs on pp. 1048–49.

[17] Booth, "The Armenian Mission," 1050.

see members who were not living up to the standards they knew to be right, who were still dependent in far too many cases upon foreign missionaries, not only for their spiritual development but for their financial welfare as well.

President Booth managed to express both his deep sense of isolation and his desire for fellow laborers to help him fulfill the monumental task that he well knew stretched out before him. "Besides Sister Booth and Elder Snell, the writer, since he left London, October 2, 1921, has seen on an average only one face from Zion in 202 days, so you may be sure of a warm welcome if you come to do missionary work." Elder Talmage had promised him that three pairs of missionaries would be sent from the European Mission to work with him and his wife. By the time he left for his trip to Aleppo, however, they had still not arrived. But a note from Elder Talmage had come, containing the reassuring words, "You may think we have forgotten you, but we have not." Upon receiving these words of comfort, Joseph W. Booth, still working alone with only his wife as a companion in a faraway land of many languages and exotic customs, exclaimed, "In heaven's name who would not proselyte for such [a] cause, where the harvest is so great and the laborers are so few?"[18]

President Booth's mission, however, was finished. He was worn out, exhausted. He died of a heart attack on 5 December 1928, unaware that his release, signed by the First Presidency, was in the mail. The Church, grateful for the services he had rendered, erected a large headstone over his burial place in the sandy and desolate foreigners' cemetery on the outskirts of Aleppo. Nearly five years later, Elder John A. Widtsoe dedicated his grave.

Joseph Wilford Booth was certainly the greatest missionary of The Church of Jesus Christ of Latter-day Saints yet to serve in the Near East. Yet he has been virtually forgotten. That is why I have chosen to dedicate this book to his memory and to his example of devoted and competent service among the peoples of the eastern Mediterranean.

18. Both quotations occur at Booth, "The Armenian Mission," 1052.

President Booth's sudden death did not end missionary work in the Near East. No new mission president was called until 1933, however, when an Armenian by the name of Badwagon Piranian was appointed to preside over what would now be called the Palestine-Syrian Mission. He rented a new mission home, at 25 Garden Street in Haifa, and immediately went to work. Unfortunately, a substantial portion of the work that he had to do involved cleansing the portion of the Church that was under his charge. Following directions from Elder Widtsoe, President Piranian began an attempt to wean the members from dependence on Church welfare and the dole, to which many had become addicted during the troubled times of the 1920s. Such assistance had helped them greatly and in some cases had perhaps even saved their lives. But it had now become an obstacle to the development of their own character and self-reliance. Nearly a hundred of the never-very-numerous Near Eastern Saints were excommunicated, many at their own request, and a number of them chose to move to the Soviet Union, hoping to live in the new earthly utopia promised by communism. It was a depressing and difficult experience for the missionaries.

In many respects, things grew even worse for President Piranian's successor. Joseph Jacobs, a Salt Lake City school teacher, was called to preside over the Palestine-Syrian Mission in August 1937. This was a time of mounting violence by Arabs against Jews and by Jews against Arabs. He was spared some of this, as he spent his first two years working in peaceful Beirut. However, during a visit to Jerusalem in the summer of 1939 he intended to survey conditions for missionary work there and learned that a bomb had gone off in Haifa and had killed seventeen Arabs and wounded many more. In Jerusalem, the streets were funereal and nearly deserted. Tension was everywhere. The day after his arrival in the city, an Arab coffee shop was destroyed by a bomb, which left two dead and a number of others wounded. As one man explained the situation to him, "Jerusalem is a holy city with unholy people living in it." Not surprisingly, President Jacobs decided that the time was not right for opening missionary work in Jerusalem.

Unfortunately, conditions were hardly ideal anywhere. It was, after all, 1939. Hitler and Nazi Germany were moving the world toward a brutal war. On 1 September 1939, German forces invaded Poland. On 17 September, Soviet forces attacked that same unfortunate country from the east. The war had begun. Not long after his return to Beirut, President Jacobs was withdrawn to the United States and the Palestine-Syrian Mission was closed.

In September of 1947, two years after the end of the Second World War, the Palestine-Syrian Mission was reopened, again under the experienced leadership of Badwagon Piranian and his wife, who had previously presided over it during the years from 1933 to 1937. Things had changed a great deal. Two branches of the Church still existed within the mission, one in Aleppo and the other in Beirut, with a few members scattered in Damascus and Jerusalem. Altogether, the membership within the mission was less than seventy. Thus, the mission president and the elders who worked with him decided to concentrate their efforts on proselyting. At the first, they worked mostly with Armenians. Gradually, however, they began to work with the English and French-speaking populations in Beirut and Tripoli, including a large number of Palestinian Arab refugees. One technique that was used to gain publicity for the Church was the organization of a missionary basketball team. Even when they lost, as in a game against the Syrian Olympic team in 1949, they won friends. Their star was a missionary by the name of Carlos E. Asay, who later went on to tour throughout the Middle East as a member of the Lebanese National Basketball Team. Today, Elder Asay serves in the First Quorum of the Seventy.

With the changing political conditions in the region, which made it impossible to preach the gospel in either Syria or Israel/ Palestine, the Palestine-Syrian Mission was rechristened as the Near East Mission. Unfortunately, by the close of 1950 it had become evident that the disturbed conditions of the region made any kind of missionary work impossible in most areas. The mission was therefore closed, and the missionaries were transferred to different fields of labor in Europe and elsewhere. President Piranian was sent to Fresno, California, to continue his service among the large Armenian immigrant population in that area. The few members remaining in Beirut and Aleppo were placed under the jurisdiction of the Switzerland Mission. A few missionaries, sent from Switzerland, continued to labor in Beirut.

Over a hundred years of intermittent missionary labor in the Near East have produced only scanty results. The golden age of conversions came in the 1890s. Most converts were Armenian Christians, with a fair number of Germans also figuring in the totals. Some Greeks and Bulgarians joined the Church, along with a very small number of Arabs and Turks. Efforts among these latter groups were limited by the fact that very few missionaries ever became proficient in the languages that were necessary in order to reach them. Foreign customs, political restrictions and instabilities, and, of course, Islam itself all served as further barriers to the success of the missionaries. (I have not even mentioned the Church's short-lived mission in Iran, which had to be abandoned when the Islamic revolution turned that country into a xenophobic religious tyranny.)

However, while the missionary efforts of the Church in the Near East were winding down or entirely absent, its presence in the Holy Land began to grow in the late 1960s and early 1970s. A study group from Brigham Young University first came to Israel in the winter and spring of 1968. David B. Galbraith, a Canadian Latter-day Saint, arrived in Israel in 1969 with his Dutch-born wife, Frieda, in order to pursue a doctorate at the Hebrew University of Jerusalem. In February 1972, the first of what would be a regular series of BYU study groups arrived, and the growth of an LDS presence in Israel began perceptibly to accelerate. Already by April of 1972, hopes for a memorial to Orson Hyde and for a Latter-day Saint visitors' center were under discussion among ambitious members of the Church there. From the beginning, however, an unofficial, nonlegal ban on proselyting in Israel was closely observed by the Saints, both residents and visiting students.

In the fall of 1972, President Harold B. Lee, accompanied by Elder Gordon B. Hinckley of the Council of the Twelve and by President Edwin Q. Cannon of the Switzerland Zurich Mission, became the first president of the Church to visit the Holy Land since the days of the first Christian apostles. While there, at a meeting at the Garden Tomb on 20 September 1972, President Lee organized the Jerusalem Branch, calling David B. Galbraith and setting him apart as branch president. John A. Tvedtnes, a graduate student in ancient Near Eastern studies at the Hebrew University, was set apart by Elder Hinckley as first counselor. During this historic visit, the matter of a visitors' center and the question of a memorial monument to Orson Hyde were again subjects of conversation. (Jerusalem mayor Teddy Kollek himself had independently suggested an Orson Hyde monument some time before.)

Another upshot of President Lee's visit to Jerusalem was his eventual approval of the members' custom, already established there, of holding their church meetings on Saturday, the Jewish sabbath. For many reasons, this seemed the practical thing to do, and President Lee signalled his approval of it by letter after his return to the United States. This was a striking demonstration of the Church's flexibility, under prophetic leadership and divine authority, in adapting to new situations without compromising on basic principles. The letter also authorized branches in Muslim countries to hold their meetings on Fridays, in keeping with the practices of the societies in which they are located.

The idea of an Orson Hyde monument continued to be discussed as time went on, although some—notably Elder Howard W. Hunter of the Quorum of the Twelve Apostles—worried that it might compromise Church efforts among the Arabs.[19] Finally, on 24 October 1979, the anniversary of Elder Hyde's momentous prayer, an Orson Hyde Memorial Garden, more than five landscaped acres on the slope of the Mount of Olives, was dedicated by President Spencer W. Kimball. The Prophet was accompanied by his first counselor, N. Eldon Tanner, as well as by Elder Howard W. Hunter. President Ezra Taft Benson of the Quorum of the Twelve came separately, as did Elders LeGrand Richards and Marvin J. Ashton, also of the Twelve. This was beyond doubt the densest concentration of

19. On Elder Hunter's view, see Baldridge, *Grafting In*, 26.

apostles in Jerusalem since ancient times. Today, although it has been overshadowed by more recent developments involving the Church in Israel, the Orson Hyde Memorial Garden remains a symbol of Latter-day Saint interest in, and concern for, the remarkable past, present, and future of the land of Jerusalem. When political conditions permit, the garden serves as an occasional meeting place for the Saints, especially for sunrise services on Easter and for the annual commemoration of Elder Hyde's prayer on 24 October.

Meanwhile, the Church continued to grow within Israel. Branches or groups began to appear in Tel Aviv, Haifa, and the Galilee. Most of the growth came from immigration, but there were also new members converted either within Israel or abroad. (Still, it must be stressed, there was no proselyting among the Jews.) One of these new members allowed the Jerusalem Branch to mark a major milestone: Suheil Abu Hadid, a Palestinian convert, became the first Arab from Jerusalem to be called on a mission in this dispensation when he accepted an assignment to serve in the Utah Salt Lake City South Mission. Later, an Israeli Arab named Ehab Abu Nuwara, who had investigated the Church in Israel but had been baptized while a student at BYU, was called to serve in the England London Mission.

The dedication of the Orson Hyde Memorial Garden represented the fulfillment of a long-standing dream for many members of the Church. But another dream remained. That was the construction of a visitors' center in Israel, probably to be combined with facilities for the growing number of students who came year after year to participate in BYU's study programs in Jerusalem. Although it was fully realized that proselyting, as such, was not a viable option under current Israeli conditions, many still thought that, as long as there were no actual missionaries going from door to door, and as long as the Mormons were not actually seeking people out, some more low-key method of making the gospel known within Israel might nonetheless be acceptable.

However, it soon became clear that any plan to teach the gospel to the Jews, however inoffensive it might seem to the aggressively missionary-minded Latter-day Saints, would have to be given up.

Israeli sensitivities were simply too acute. Many Israeli Jews were willing to say that the loss of any Jew to another religion was equivalent, in its threat to the survival of Judaism as a whole, to the loss of a Jew in Hitler's Holocaust. (The clear implication of this popular formula was, of course, that those who sought to proselyte the Jews were like Nazis in at least one respect: Both aimed at the "destruction" of Judaism.) Thus, when in March 1981 plans were submitted to the Israeli government for the building of a BYU Center for Near Eastern Studies, they included neither a formal visitors' center nor, despite the fact that LDS services were intended to be held there, a baptismal font.

The proposed building was approved by the government in early 1984. A small ground-breaking ceremony was held on 21 August of that year, and construction was soon underway. Also underway since late May, however, was a campaign to stop the building of the center. A Jewish antimissionary organization known as Yad L'Achim protested the construction of the center as soon as it found out about it, citing the Latter-day Saints' indisputable missionary zeal as a threat to Judaism. Several steps were taken by the Church to counter public fears. The special representative couples who were serving at the time in various areas of Israel were reassigned to other fields of labor. Newspaper advertisements offering LDS literature to anybody interested were cancelled. English and Hebrew-language pamphlets about the Church were destroyed. Sales of the Hebrew edition of the Book of Mormon were stopped, and no reprinting was authorized. It was, for the present, the end of any hope of teaching the gospel to Israeli Jews.

Such attempts at conciliation did not, however, pacify the most militant opponents of the center. Throughout its three years of construction, hysterical articles appeared in local newspapers and in the American Jewish press about the Mormon "threat" to Judaism and to the holy city of Jerusalem. (During one period lasting somewhat less than three weeks, 345 articles appeared in the Israeli press about the Latter-day Saints and their building.) The center, it was alleged, was merely a front for LDS missionaries. The students enrolled in its programs would not be real students, but undercover agents of the Mormon Church. Some of the allegations were actually flattering, in a twisted sort of way. For example, the Latter-day Saints were said to be dispatching "beautiful blonde women"—apparently BYU coeds—to Israel in order to lure Jewish boys away from their religious upbringing. They were also conspiring, with their Saudi Arabian allies, to create a vast and dangerous international financial empire. Other charges were harder to read in a positive light. It was argued by some that the Mormons were "desecrating" Mount Scopus, the hill upon which the center was to stand. For a while, a number of agitators claimed that the site was actually an ancient Jewish cemetery; repeated denials of that claim by the Israeli archaeologist assigned to the site excavations were only gradually able to allay the concerns it had aroused.

Jerusalem's Mayor Teddy Kollek was personally vilified for his support of the Mormons and was even accused of accepting bribes from them as the price for his alleged betrayal of the Jewish people. Orthodox Jews demonstrated and prayed in front of the homes of David Galbraith and other Church and university leaders. Anonymous callers threatened prominent Mormons over the telephone and even tapped their phones, hoping perhaps to discover the sordid truth that lurked behind the Saints' seemingly innocent faces. Thousands of Orthodox Jews demonstrated at the so-called Wailing Wall. Drives were organized to raise funds and to gather signatures on petitions designed to "fight the Mormons." Anti-Mormon bumper stickers appeared on autos and trucks throughout Israel. Handwritten anti-Mormon slogans appeared on Israeli currency. Vandals damaged the place where the Jerusalem Branch held its sabbath meetings. Demonstrations near the center on Mount Scopus included the singing of such heart-warming lyrics, addressed to the Latter-day Saints, as "You better run for your life/Back to Utah overnight." Even Ed Decker, the professional apostate who founded Ex-Mormons for Jesus and created the notorious pseudo-documentary film *The God Makers*, brought his traveling show to the city.

As the center came under attack it was clearly the Church that was being assaulted. The LDS claim that this was a university building, an academic facility, rather than a mission home or a church, was almost universally brushed aside as a smoke screen. Still, many people in and out of Israel rose to their defense. Mayor Kollek did not back down from his support of the center, but defended its construction now as a matter of religious freedom, pluralism, and human rights. Furthermore, he solicited from David Galbraith a carefully-crafted statement promising on behalf of the Church that students and staff of the center would engage in neither overt nor covert proselyting. The statement was published in the *Jerusalem Post*. Leading newspapers throughout Israel pointed to the Mormons' excellent record of abstaining from missionary activities during the more than fifteen years that they had been operating programs in Israel. The rabbi of Salt Lake City wrote a letter in support of the center. New York's Jewish Anti-Defamation League endorsed the center's continued construction, as did the Arizona Regional Board of the National Conference of Christians and Jews and the Jewish Genealogical Society of New York. Former American president Gerald Ford sent a personal letter of support to Prime Minister Shimon Peres. One hundred and fifty-four members of the United States Congress signed a letter of endorsement that was distributed to all members of the Knesset, the Israeli parliament.

Still the attacks on the Church continued. In November 1985, the announcement was made that Brigham Young University had retained a prominent Israeli public relations firm in order to help in presenting a more positive image of the university, the center, and the Church to the Israeli public. The truth had to be heard above the clamor of voices denouncing the Mormons. The firm immediately took out advertisements in a number of leading Israeli newspapers in order to explain Mormons and Mormonism to an audience that knew very little about them and to clarify the purpose and projected function of the Jerusalem Center for Near Eastern Studies. Perhaps even more effective was a program, broadcast just after Christmas on Israeli television, which featured the Galbraith family. At one point in the program, Professor Galbraith played portions of a cassette tape on which he had recorded some of the threatening telephone calls he and his family had received. When the audience heard things like "This is your last warning; we're bloodthirsty. If you don't leave Israel we're going to kill all of you, one by one," there was an immediate response of outrage and of sympathy for the Galbraiths. More to the issue, there was a surge of support for the center itself, and it would probably be fair to describe this television broadcast as a turning point in the story.

Many moderate Israeli and American Jews realized that, in fundamental ways, the dispute was not really about the Latter-day Saints at all. It was primarily a battle about the nature of Israeli society and the Israeli state. In a sense, they themselves were the targets of this ultra-Orthodox agitation. Was Israel really to be a Jewish state? What, then, would be the status of non-Jews within it? And what would be the status of nonreligious Jews, or of Jews who did not live according to the strict rules favored by the ultra-Orthodox? Should Judaism be enforced by law? The issues involved are much the same as those faced by many contemporary Muslims.

Judaism, like Islam, finds a major source of its religious authority and practice in the past. But modern values like democracy, equal rights, and religious toleration have come into general acceptance only since the time in which the fundamental documents of the two religions were composed or revealed. Consequently, they do not directly figure in the sacred texts upon which the two faiths are based. How, then, are they to be incorporated into modern Jewish and Islamic practice? Or should they be incorporated at all? Two easy solutions present themselves to the question of how to harmonize an ancient heritage with modern insights, values, and ways of thought: Either the ancient heritage can be abandoned, and all modern ideas embraced without exception (the secularist solution), or the modern age can be ignored (the fundamentalist solution). The difficult thing is to find a middle ground that preserves the best features of both. Not only is it difficult to find such a middle ground, but even if someone does manage to position himself in the middle, he thereby opens himself to attacks from both extremes. To the fundamentalists, he is an apostate; to the secularists, he is either a fundamentalist himself or a coward, caving in to pressure from reactionaries and fanatics. This was an unmistakable aspect of the struggle over the building of the Jerusalem Center for Near Eastern Studies.

Gradually, however, it dawned on even the most die-hard enemies of the center that the building was going to be completed and that the government would not stop its construction. And, gradually, the campaign of harassment, distortion, and vilification against the Latter-day Saints began to wind down. There were still occasional flare-ups. Late in the construction process, for instance, local and general officers of the Church were requested to sign documents promising that neither the center, nor the university, nor the Church itself would engage in any proselyting of Jews in Israel—ever. This was to be in addition to promises already made by BYU officials and leaders of the Church that the center would not be used for missionary purposes and that Latter-day Saints would not proselyte in Israel so long as such activity was not allowed by the government.

Mormon leaders refused to sign. As Elder James E. Faust, then of the Council of the Twelve, put it during a visit to Israel in January 1987, "We will never say never." This most recent demand touched on a matter of fundamental importance, a matter beside which even the expensive and long-dreamed-of building on Mount Scopus was relatively unimportant. Latter-day Saints obey the law. This is a matter of principle and religious belief, enshrined in their Articles of Faith. They are willing to limit their missionary efforts when the law demands it. But they make no secret of another principle of their faith, namely that it is their ultimate goal and duty to take the gospel to all nations of the earth, including the Jews. They cannot renounce this principle and certainly will not do so merely to satisfy the excessive demands of any human government. The Church stood firm, and those making the demand backed down.

On 4 March 1987, occupancy permits were issued for the not-quite-completed center and, on the recommendation of both the Church's legal staff and its local lawyers, students and faculty immediately moved into the twenty-million-dollar structure. On the eighteenth of May in the following year, President Jeffrey Holland of

Brigham Young University signed a forty-nine year lease for the land on which the building sits, with a renewal option for another forty-nine years beyond that. He again committed the university and the Church to refrain from any kind of proselyting "as long as such activity is not allowed by the government of Israel."

Not all critics of the center and the Latter-day Saints were silenced by the fact that students had actually occupied the building. They are still on the lookout for any sign of missionary activity on the part of students, faculty, or staff at the center. Students are required to sign a pledge that they will not engage in such activity. They are even told to refer people who ask questions to generally available encyclopedia articles rather than to engage themselves in conversations on religion. For one thing, the person inquiring might be some kind of provoçateur seeking to create an incident. An oversight committee of Israeli officials, created as part of the agreement that permitted the construction of the center, must approve concerts, organ recitals, and public lectures in the building, after screening them for any evidence of secret missionary agendas. (The committee's jurisdiction extends only to nonacademic functions in the center; university and Church officials insisted that purely academic matters remain internal.)

The limitations within which the Church and its members have agreed to work in Israel (and occasionally elsewhere in the Near East) sometimes create ironic situations. It is only in the Near East that I have been taught, and have taught others, that it is part of a Latter-day Saint's religious duty not to proselyte and, indeed, to avoid speaking on religious subjects with the local population. An illustration of the kind of awkwardness of which I speak occurred in my own personal experience. When, a few years ago, some of us at Brigham Young University were laying the groundwork for an intensive Arabic language program to be conducted at the Jerusalem Center, we were not yet certain that there would be enough interested students on our own campus to make the program worthwhile. It would be necessary, we thought then, to recruit superior students from other universities as well. So we tentatively decided that we would circulate advertisements for our program to appropriate departments at other schools and place them in several journals dealing with Near Eastern studies. But, someone suddenly exclaimed, what if a *Jewish* student applies to participate? Many of the best students of Arabic in the United States at any given time are, after all, Jewish. They have a natural reason for interest in Near Eastern fields and often have a head start on the study of other Semitic languages because of a knowledge of Hebrew. Our critics in Israel, however, would not be any the less upset with us if we seemed to be "proselyting" among American Jews instead of Israelis. Well, it was suggested, perhaps we could screen out people with "Jewish" names. But another person pointed out that such screening was illegal in the United States and probably wasn't completely effective anyway. Some American Jews don't have obviously Jewish names. And what if, someday, it came to somebody's attention that we had systematically turned down Jewish applicants even when they had excellent credentials? I myself suggested that maybe, at the bottom of our ad, we could have a small eagle and a swastika, along with a note in German that no Jews need apply. Obviously, we were caught between discriminating against Jews, which was not only wrong but illegal in the United States, and not discriminating against Jews, which would eventually get us into horrible trouble in Israel. The irony that Israeli policies encouraged us to discriminate against American Jews was every bit as rich as the irony of devoutly nonproselyting Mormons. Eventually, though, we decided that the risks of recruiting students elsewhere were simply too great and gave up the idea.

No matter how careful we are, some new and usually rather ridiculous charge still surfaces. One amusing instance of this was the accusation published by an Orthodox Jewish newspaper in both Jerusalem and New York during October 1987 that the nefarious Mormons were using their building's highly visible location to impose a large illuminated cross on the nighttime horizon of Jerusalem. And it was true! (Sort of.) At night, when all the rooms on the sixth level had their lights burning, and when the lights were on in the stairway that runs down the center of the building, an imaginative person could make out a kind of electric cross. Denials that the appearance of a cross was intentional carried no weight with the critics, needless to say. Nor did it help to point out that, in contrast to other Christian groups, the cross plays no role in Latter-day Saint architecture or liturgy—a fact for which we are routinely assailed and assaulted by Protestant anti-Mormons. Finally, officials of the center simply had to make sure that lights on the sixth level were either turned out or that the windows were covered when they were on.

But these little skirmishes mean little. The battle had been won. The building had been completed, despite intense opposition. What does it mean? Perhaps no one fully knows. Sitting on slightly more than four acres and with a total floor space of 103,420 square feet, Brigham Young University's Jerusalem Center for Near Eastern Studies is among the most beautiful buildings in Jerusalem and is certainly one of the most visible. (Indeed, it has itself become a tourist attraction that draws thousands of Israelis.) Like a waterfall, it flows down the slope of Mount Scopus. Its many levels are adorned with Italian marble and Burmese teakwood. Its Danish-built organ is one of the finest in the Middle East. From its upper auditorium, where sabbath services are now held for students enrolled in its academic programs, a breathtaking panoramic view of the Old City of Jerusalem can be seen through three walls of plate-glass windows. Through them, too, the sadness and strife of occupied East Jerusalem can also often be seen, as, behind the pulpit, clouds of tear gas and smoke arise from the ongoing conflicts that rend the City of Peace.

A community of Latter-day Saints now exists in the Holy Land. It is not a community of agriculturalists and canal-builders, as our ancestors had pictured, but a community of scholars, teachers, and students. In a very real sense, I believe it fulfills the dreams and aspirations of the early missionaries who labored so faithfully in the Near East to build outposts of the kingdom of God in that historic but tortured land. What role the Jerusalem Center for Near Eastern Studies will play in the future of the Church and in the future of the Near East remains to be seen. Perhaps, if we prove worthy of the blessings we have received, it will someday serve the region as a city on a hill, a candle held high to give light to those around it.[20] Whatever benefit it may prove to others, however, it is certainly benefiting us. We can already confidently say that it is building up a new generation of Latter-day Saints to whom the land of Palestine is familiar and for whom the stories of the Bible and the events of the area's history live in a way they have never lived for our people in the past. If even a small proportion of those who administer and enjoy the programs and courses of the center come away from their experience at Jerusalem with something of the impact that others such as Lorenzo Snow have received, the spiritual life of the Church can only grow in depth and devotion. If even a few return from Palestine with a clearer understanding of our Muslim and Jewish brothers and sisters, our capacity to carry out the mission entrusted to us by the Lord can only increase.

The Future

At the beginning of this book, I said that we would treat the question of whether Orson Hyde's mission to the Near East had been a success. The answer, I think, should by now be completely beyond dispute. It is clear that many portions of Elder Hyde's inspired prayer have at least begun to be fulfilled.

> (1) Judah's scattered remnants have indeed begun to gather back to Palestine, according to the predictions of the holy prophets. (Nowhere in scripture are we told what number of Jews need to return to the Holy Land, nor are we told what percentage of the world's Jews need to be involved.) Large ships have returned them from virtually every corner of the earth.
>
> (2) Many foreign governments have gone to unusual lengths to assist Israel and to aid in the emigration of Jews to Palestine.
>
> (3) Israeli ingenuity and industry have reclaimed large tracts of desert land and restored them to fertility.
>
> (4) Jerusalem has been built up again. It is a beautiful city, with modern buildings, hospitals, a great university, museums, a philharmonic orchestra, and a vibrant commercial and cultural

20. See Matthew 5:14-16.

life. At the same time, much of its ancient and medieval character has been preserved. And, although many nations (including the United States) do not officially recognize its status, Jerusalem functions today as the capital of a Jewish state.

But it is just as clear that certain portions of Elder Hyde's prayer remain yet to be fulfilled.

(1) No divinely authorized temple has yet been built in Jerusalem.

(2) No Davidic king presides over the gathered Jews.

(3) The returning Jews have not, for the most part, come home with "a spirit of grace and supplication." Many of them are thoroughly secular, Jews only in a cultural sense. Their unbelief has not yet been conquered and subdued. From the perspective of the restored gospel, their hearts remain stony.

So where do we stand? I think we are in the middle of a process that has been underway for some time but that still has a considerable distance to go. The Lord is not in the same kind of hurry that we anxious mortals often are. He has time. I think that early Latter-day Saints imagined that the events previous to the Second Coming of the Lord would happen quickly, but they have not. That is not to say that those events have not commenced or that the Lord is not acting. Clearly, he is. It seems to be the clear teaching of the Book of Mormon that the true gathering of the Jews will commence after, and not before, they come to a knowledge of the true gospel.

> And after they have hardened their hearts and stiffened their necks against the Holy One of Israel, behold, the judgments of the Holy One of Israel shall come upon them. And the day cometh that they shall be smitten and afflicted. Wherefore... they shall be scattered, and smitten, and hated; nevertheless, the Lord will be merciful unto them, that when they shall come to the knowledge of their Redeemer, they shall be gathered together again to the lands of their inheritance.[21]

---

[21] 2 Nephi 6:10–11.

> When the day cometh that they shall believe in me, that I am Christ, then have I covenanted with their fathers that they shall be restored in the flesh, upon the earth, unto the lands of their inheritance.[22]

> And I will remember the covenant which I have made with my people; and I have covenanted with them that I would gather them together in mine own due time, that I would give unto them again the land of their fathers for their inheritance, which is the land of Jerusalem, which is the promised land unto them forever, saith the Father. And it shall come to pass that the time cometh, when the fulness of my gospel shall be preached unto them; and they shall believe in me, that I am Jesus Christ, the Son of God, and shall pray unto the Father in my name... Then will the Father gather them together again, and give unto them Jerusalem for the land of their inheritance.[23]

Does this mean that the remarkable return of hundreds of thousands of Jews from around the world to Palestine is not, in the fullest sense, the promised gathering? I think it does. Does it mean that it has nothing to do with the gathering? No, I think a positive answer to that question is inconceivable. And the scriptures do not commit us to it. Rather, they clearly teach that unbelieving Jews will be upon the land of Palestine when the Lord returns.

> And then shall the Lord set his foot upon this mount, and it shall cleave in twain... And then shall the Jews look upon me and say: What are these wounds in thine hands and in thy feet? Then shall they know that I am the Lord; for I will say unto them: These wounds are the wounds with which I was wounded in the house of my friends. I am he who was lifted up. I am Jesus that was crucified. I am the Son of God. And then shall they

---

22. 2 Nephi 10:7. Notable here is the emphasis on the literal reality of the return to Palestine. It is not merely a metaphor or a spiritual abstraction, but will occur "in the flesh, upon the earth." Professor Stephen D. Ricks addresses this issue on purely biblical grounds in his article "The Prophetic Literality of Tribal Reconstruction," in Avraham Gileadi, ed., *Israel's Apostasy and Restoration: Essays in Honor of Roland K. Harrison* (Grand Rapids: Baker Book House, 1988), 273-81. The entire book is of interest in this regard.

23. 3 Nephi 20:29-31, 33.

> weep because of their iniquities; then shall they lament because they persecuted their king.[24]

In 1875, Elder Orson Pratt offered the clarification that some of the Jews gathering to Palestine would have already accepted the gospel. "Some of them," he said,

> will believe in the true Messiah, and thousands of the more righteous, whose fathers did not consent to the shedding of the blood of the Son of God, will receive the gospel before they gather from among the nations. Many of them, however, will not receive the gospel... They will have their synagogues, in which they will preach against Jesus of Nazareth, "that impostor," as they call him, who was crucified by their fathers.[25]

Perhaps, indeed, the physical return of the Jews to Palestine is designed to play a central role in the advent of a belief in Christ.

> Wherefore, he will bring them again out of captivity, and they shall be gathered together to the lands of their inheritance; and they shall be brought out of obscurity and out of darkness; and they shall know that the Lord is their Savior and their Redeemer, the Mighty One of Israel.[26]

I like to think of the current state of Israel, and of the Jewish immigration that gave rise to it and continues to sustain it, as a kind of preparatory gathering. It does not seem to meet the Book of Mormon's requirements for being the "gathering" in the full sense of the word. This full sense was expressed by the late Elder Bruce R. McConkie, of the Council of the Twelve, as follows: "Now I call your attention to the facts, set forth in these scriptures, that the gathering of Israel consists of joining the true Church, of coming to a knowledge of the true God and of his saving truths, and of worshiping him in the congregations of the Saints in all nations and among all peoples."[27]

---

24. Doctrine and Covenants 45:48, 51–53.
25. *Journal of Discourses* 18:64.
26. 1 Nephi 22:12.
27. Bruce R. McConkie, in Official Report of the First Mexico and Central America Area General Conference (Salt Lake City: The Church of Jesus Christ of Latter-day Saints, 1973), 45.

But the return of the Jews to Palestine is an astonishing thing, something that manifestly cannot be disconnected from the events that will ultimately occur in that area. Indeed, we need only think for a moment about the sheer improbability of the whole thing to begin to see its miraculous character. What other nation has ever come back into existence as a sovereign state more than two thousand years after its disappearance? The empire of the pharaohs is gone. Nobody thinks seriously of resurrecting the ancient Babylonian Empire (although Saddam Hussein likes to strut about as if he were some sort of Babylonian monarch). Mussolini tried to resuscitate the glories of the Roman Empire but ended his career hanging upside down, revealed to all as a tyrant and a buffoon. And Hitler's "Third Reich," claiming to restore the lost Roman Empire itself along with the Holy Roman Empire of Charlemagne, was supposed to last a thousand years. It managed, though, to survive only twelve—and those twelve years were cruel, barbarous, and utterly fraudulent.

But little Israel, the footpath of the ancient world, walked over and trodden down by every army that moved along the King's Highway, deprived for many years of self-rule and then finally scattered to the four corners of the globe, persecuted and butchered as perhaps no other people in human history, little Israel maintained itself as a people and is now reborn as a state. What is more, its ancient language, Hebrew, has come back to life as a language of literature, business, and science. (Ancient languages are not always so easily maintained. In Ireland, attempts to keep the old Gaelic tongue alive are failing even as I write.) The mere fact that Israel is a commonplace subject of newspapers, magazines, and television news should not be allowed to obscure for us the miraculous fact of its sheer existence.

With all of this, however, there still remain steps toward the Second Coming that we are not yet authorized to take. Leaders of The Church of Jesus Christ of Latter-day Saints have consistently taught that the time to take the gospel to the Jews has not arrived. "Jerusalem," said Brigham Young in 1854, "is not to be redeemed by the soft still voice of the preacher of the gospel of peace." Why? Because, he said, the Jews had rejected Christ and Christ's gospel as it was taught by the early apostles and prophets and were now destined to be "the last of all the seed of Abraham to have the privilege of receiving the New and Everlasting Covenant... It is impossible to convert the Jews, until the Lord God Almighty does it."[28] Speaking in 1857, Wilford Woodruff recalled the many times during his travels when he had seen Jews pray for their return to Jerusalem and for the coming of their Messiah. "When I have seen this," that great missionary said,

> my soul has been filled with a desire to proclaim unto them the word of God unto eternal life, but I knew I could not do this, the time had not come, I could not preach to them... They do not believe in Jesus Christ; there is an unbelief resting upon them, and will until they go home and rebuild Jerusalem and their temple more glorious than at the beginning, and then by and by, after this Church and kingdom has arisen up in its glory, the Saviour will come to them and show the wounds in his hands and side...and then their eyes will begin to open...and they will for the first time receive Jesus Christ as their Saviour, they will begin to comprehend where they have been wandering for the space of two thousand years.[29]

It is at least partly this sense that the time has not yet come for the preaching of the gospel to the Jewish people that underlies the Church's promises made in connection with Brigham Young University's Jerusalem Center for Near Eastern Studies.

There are other things that have yet to occur with regard to Palestine or Israel. The ancient King David lost his exaltation as a result of transgression, so his blessings and role are to be given to another. "The Priesthood that he received," said the Prophet Joseph Smith, "and the throne and kingdom of David is to be taken from him and given to another by the name of David in the last days, raised up out of his lineage."[30] Several of the ancient prophets seem to have known of this important figure. "Alas!" wrote Jeremiah,

---

28. *Journal of Discourses* 2:142.
29. *Journal of Discourses* 4:232.
30. *History of the Church* 6:253; compare Doctrine and Covenants 132:39.

> For that day is great, so that none is like it: it is even the time of Jacob's trouble; but he shall be saved out of it. For it shall come to pass in that day, saith the Lord of hosts, that I will break his yoke from off thy neck, and will burst thy bonds, and strangers shall no more serve themselves of him: But they shall serve the Lord their God, and David their king, whom I will raise up unto them.[31]

> Behold, the days come, saith the Lord, that I will raise unto David a righteous Branch, and a King shall reign and prosper, and shall execute judgment and justice in the earth. In his days Judah shall be saved, and Israel shall dwell safely.[32]

The prophet Zechariah used a man by the name of Joshua, the son of Josedech, as a visual aid to make his point:

> Behold the man whose name is The BRANCH...and he shall build the temple of the Lord: Even he shall build the temple of the Lord; and he shall bear the glory, and shall sit and rule upon his throne; and he shall be a priest upon his throne.[33]

Hosea appears to have known of a Davidic king who would follow a period of apostasy, a period in which the Israelites would have neither a functioning state nor a functioning priesthood.

> For the children of Israel shall abide many days without a king, and without a prince, and without a sacrifice, and without an image, and without an ephod, and without teraphim: Afterward shall the children of Israel return, and seek the Lord their God, and David their king; and shall fear the Lord and his goodness in the latter days.[34]

The prophet Ezekiel, writing from Babylonian exile, knew a great deal about this figure of the latter days.

> Thus saith the Lord God; Behold, I will take the children of Israel from among the heathen, whither they be gone, and will

---

31. Jeremiah 30:7-9.
32. Jeremiah 23:5-6.
33. Zechariah 6:12-13; compare 3:8.
34. Hosea 3:4-5.

> gather them on every side, and bring them into their own land: And I will make them one nation in the land upon the mountains of Israel; and one king shall be king to them all...[I] will cleanse them: so shall they be my people, and I will be their God. And David my servant shall be king over them; and they all shall have one shepherd: they shall also walk in my judgments, and observe my statutes, and do them. And they shall dwell in the land that I have given unto Jacob my servant, wherein your fathers have dwelt; and they shall dwell therein, even they, and their children, and their children's children for ever: and my servant David shall be their prince for ever. Moreover I will make a covenant of peace with them; it shall be an everlasting covenant with them: and I will place them, and multiply them, and will set my sanctuary in the midst of them for evermore. My tabernacle also shall be with them: yea, I will be their God, and they shall be my people. And the heathen shall know that I the Lord do sanctify Israel, when my sanctuary shall be in the midst of them for evermore.[35]

The emphasis on unity is noteworthy. "Ephraim shall not envy Judah," writes Isaiah, "and Judah shall not vex Ephraim." "They shall be no more two nations," declares Ezekiel, "neither shall they be divided into two kingdoms any more at all."[36]

Another development that needs to be achieved, as most Latter-day Saints know, is the construction of a temple in Jerusalem. The prophet Ezekiel saw a vision of a great latter-day temple and its rituals and recorded that vision in chapters 40–47. Joseph Smith taught that, although the entire law of Moses would not be restored, the rituals of sacrifice would be restored and carried out in that temple at Jerusalem.[37] Little more than a year prior to his death, at the April 1843 general conference, Joseph prophesied that

> Judah must return, Jerusalem must be rebuilt, and the temple, and water come out from under the temple, and the waters of the Dead Sea be healed. It will take some time to rebuild the

35. Ezekiel 37:21–28.
36. Isaiah 11:13; Ezekiel 37:22.
37. See *History of the Church* 4:211–12.

> walls of the city and the temple...and all this must be done before the Son of Man will make His appearance.[38]

Two months later, on 11 June 1843, the Prophet taught a very important historical principle to the Saints at Nauvoo, one that has application to the future as well. "What was the object," he asked,

> of gathering the Jews, or the people of God in any age of the world?... The main object was to build unto the Lord a house whereby He could reveal unto His people the ordinances of His house and the glories of His kingdom, and teach the people the way of salvation; for there are certain ordinances and principles that, when they are taught and practiced, must be done in a place or house built for that purpose. It was the design of the councils of heaven before the world was, that the principles and laws of the priesthood should be predicated upon the gathering of the people in every age of the world.[39]

What kind of a temple will this be? That question is closely linked to the question of precisely who will participate in its construction. "Who do you think is going to build it?" Elder Orson Pratt asked at a special conference in Logan in 1877. "You may think that it will be the unbelieving Jews who rejected the Savior." However, Elder Pratt could not accept that notion. "The Temple at Jerusalem will undoubtedly be built," he declared, "by those who believe in the true Messiah."[40] Certainly we can conclude that valid and authorized ordinances revealed in connection with the restored gospel will be practiced there, since Jerusalem is one of the places designated in the Doctrine and Covenants for the performance of vicarious baptisms for the dead.[41]

Construction of the temple raises a very serious question, though. Charles W. Penrose, speaking before his call to the Council

---

38. *History of the Church* 5:337. The prophecy of the healing of the waters of the Dead Sea echoes that of Ezekiel 47:1-10. Incidentally, the very ancient notion that the waters of life are to be found at the base of the mountain of the Lord's house reappears in the location of baptismal fonts in or near the basements of Latter-day Saint temples.
39. *History of the Church* 5:423.
40. *Journal of Discourses* 19:20.
41. Doctrine and Covenants 124:36.

of the Twelve and, later, to the First Presidency, remarked that "the gathering of the Jews to their own land" was in process in order "that they may build it up as it was in former times; that the temple may be rebuilt and the mosque of the Moslem which now stands in its place may be moved out of the way; that Jerusalem may be rebult [*sic*] upon its original site; that the way may be prepared for the coming of the Messiah."[42] I am glad that Brother Penrose was not yet an apostle when he made this statement because I hope it is partially wrong. Let me clarify what I mean. Many Latter-day Saints look with positive pleasure to the day when the Dome of the Rock will be cleared off the temple mount and the site will be ready for the construction there of the great latter-day temple. I do not. I love the Dome of the Rock, which has to be ranked as one of the world's truly great, interesting, and beautiful buildings. (Perhaps, I sometimes daydream, it will be possible to incorporate the Dome into the design of the new temple.) Furthermore, I am aware that the Dome of the Rock and the adjacent mosque of al-Aqsa are among the most holy shrines in the world of Islam. Any deliberate injury to them will almost certainly provoke terrible bloodshed. I cannot see why anybody would look forward to such a thing.

Unfortunately, though, we can be quite confident that terrible bloodshed will come. According to the Revelation of John, a horrific war of the evil nations against Israel will occur in the valley of Armageddon—also known as Esdraelon. This is a triangle-shaped plain situated about sixty miles north of Jerusalem, a place associated with a number of decisive ancient battles. The most traumatic of the conflicts that occurred there, from the point of view of ancient Israel—or, more precisely, ancient Judah—was the one in which pharaoh Necho, going up against Assyria, was intercepted by the righteous king Josiah. Josiah did not appreciate the Egyptians' unauthorized transit through his territory and went out to stop them. Unfortunately, he was killed.[43] So the place already had strong and melancholy associations in the minds of Jews. But, looking into the future, John saw

---

42. *Journal of Discourses* 24:215.
43. Judges 23:29. See also Judges 5:19; 2 Kings 9:27; Zechariah 12:11.

> spirits of devils, working miracles,...go forth unto the kings of the earth and of the whole world, to gather them to the battle of that great day of God Almighty... And he gathered them together into a place called in the Hebrew tongue Armageddon.[44]

The prophet Joel apparently also knew about this titanic struggle.

> For, behold, in those days, and in that time, when I shall bring again the captivity of Judah and Jerusalem [i.e., when I shall bring the captives back], I will also gather all nations, and will bring them down into the valley of Jehoshaphat... Proclaim ye this among the Gentiles; prepare war, wake up the mighty men, let all the men of war draw near; let them come up: Beat your plowshares into swords, and your pruninghooks into spears...[45] Assemble yourselves, and come, all ye heathen... Let the heathen be wakened, and come up to the valley of Jehoshaphat: for there will I sit to judge all the heathen round about. Put ye in the sickle, for the harvest is ripe: come, get you down; for the press is full, the fats [i.e., vats] overflow; for their wickedness is great. Multitudes, multitudes in the valley of decision: for the day of the Lord is near in the valley of decision.[46]

Armed and bloody conflict seems inevitable. Does that mean that we as Latter-day Saints and as citizens of our respective nations should simply sit back and let it happen? Does it mean that we have no responsibility as citizens of the world, or, it may be, even as government officials to try to make an unpleasant prophecy fail? I cannot imagine that our Heavenly Father would have us draw such a conclusion. "Therefore," the Lord directs us, "renounce war and proclaim peace, and seek diligently to turn...the hearts of the Jews unto the prophets, and the prophets unto the Jews; lest I come and smite the whole earth with a curse, and all flesh be consumed before me."[47]

---

44. Revelation 16:14, 16.
45. This is a direct contrast to Isaiah 2:4 and Micah 4:3.
46. Joel 3:1-2, 9-14.
47. Doctrine and Covenants 98:16-17.

I have made the statement as my opinion—though I think it is an opinion firmly grounded in the scriptures—that only a partial or preliminary gathering of the Jews has occurred thus far. What practical conclusions can we draw from this, if it is true? One conclusion to be drawn is that Latter-day Saints are not obliged to give a blank check of unqualified approval to the government of Israel. Israel as it exists in the Near East is a nation-state much like other nation-states of the region and the world. It is not to be identified with Israel as the people of God. There may perhaps be some overlap, there may be—as I believe there is—a link between political Israel and spiritual Israel in the eternal purposes of God, but they are not one and the same. "For," as the apostle Paul says, "they are not all Israel, which are of Israel."[48] I have occasionally heard Western Christians, including some Latter-day Saints, talk as if we must support every action and every policy of the government of Israel because that government is the leadership of God's chosen people. This is false. Worse, I believe it is idolatrous. We are not obligated to give such complete and abject loyalty to any political institution on the face of the earth—not to our own government and certainly not to the government of Israel. We are under no obligation to be more supportive of whatever Israeli prime minister happens to be in power than are the Israeli opposition parties themselves. (And there is sometimes fierce dissent in the Israeli Knesset.)

Our sympathy for Israel—and, as I read the prophecies and the scriptures, we cannot fail to have such sympathy—must not blind us to the fact that Zion and the Jerusalem of the last days must be built upon the principles of the gospel and on the basis of the ethical teachings of the Hebrew and other prophets sent by the Lord. And those principles are rather clear.

> Wherewith shall I come before the Lord, and bow myself before the high God? shall I come before him with burnt offerings, with calves of a year old? Will the Lord be pleased with thousands of rivers of oil?... He hath shewed thee, O man, what is

---

48. Romans 9:6.

> good; and what doth the Lord require of thee, but to do justly, and to love mercy, and to walk humbly with thy God?[49]

> I hate, I despise your feast days, and I will not smell in your solemn assemblies. Though ye offer me burnt offerings, and your meat offerings, I will not accept them: neither will I regard the peace offerings of your fat beasts. Take thou away from me the noise of thy songs; for I will not hear the melody of thy viols. But let judgment [justice] run down as waters, and righteousness as a mighty stream.[50]

> And I will turn my hand upon thee, and purely purge away thy dross, and take away all thy tin: And I will restore thy judges as at the beginning: afterward thou shalt be called, The city of righteousness, the faithful city. Zion shall be redeemed with judgment [justice], and her converts with righteousness.[51]

The scriptures even offer guidance on the troubling problem of how Israel should treat the Palestinians who live under its control.

> And if a stranger sojourn with thee in your land, ye shall not vex him. But the stranger that dwelleth with you shall be unto you as one born among you, and thou shalt love him as thyself; for ye were strangers in the land of Egypt: I am the Lord your God.[52]

When injustices are perpetrated by any side in the Near East, we must be clear-sighted enough to recognize them and honest enough to condemn them wherever they occur and whoever is responsible. "Speak for justice," the Qur'an says, "even if it affects your own kinsmen."[53]

> For the vineyard of the Lord of hosts is the house of Israel, and the men of Judah his pleasant plant: and he looked for judgment [justice], but behold oppression; for righteousness, but behold a cry.[54]

---

49. Micah 6:6-8.
50. Amos 5:21-24.
51. Isaiah 1:25-27.
52. Leviticus 19:33-34.
53. 6:152.
54. Isaiah 5:7.

> How is the faithful city become an harlot! it was full of judgment [justice]; righteousness lodged in it; but now murderers.[55]

The ancient prophets of Israel were willing to condemn injustices committed by their people within the Holy Land itself. Indeed, they were more concerned about injustice and unrighteousness among the chosen people than with similar offenses committed elsewhere because they held Israel to a higher standard. "For of him unto whom much is given much is required; and he who sins against the greater light shall receive the greater condemnation."[56] It was because the prophets loved Israel that they sought to make it better. We ourselves can do no less, for ourselves and for the rest of the house of Israel. It will not suffice for us to choose sides, to pick a team in the way the world does, and then to pretend not to notice the outrages and injustices committed by our alleged allies. Leaders of the Church have repeatedly reminded us that the Church as such takes absolutely no position on the Arab-Israeli conflict. President Howard W. Hunter put this quite clearly while yet a member of the Council of the Twelve:

> We do not need to apologize nor mitigate any of the prophecies concerning the Holy Land. We believe them and declare them to be true. But this does not give us justification to dogmatically pronounce that others of our Father's children are not children of promise.
>
> Elder Hunter admonished
>
> members of the Church who give the impression that we favor only the aims of the Jews. The Church has an interest in all of Abraham's descendents... Both the Jews and the Arabs are children of our Father. They are both children of promise, and as a church we do not take sides.[57]

---

55. Isaiah 1:21.
56. Doctrine and Covenants 82:3.
57. Howard W. Hunter, "All Are Alike Unto God," *Ensign* 9 (June 1979), 72-72. Compare also the statements of Elders Hunter, William R. Bradford, and W. Grant Bangerter, recorded respectively at Baldridge, *Grafting In*, i; 57; and Barrett, *The Story of the Mormons in the Holy Land*, 102. David B. Galbraith, first president of the Jerusalem Branch and holder of a doctorate in political science from the Hebrew University of Jerusalem, makes much the same point at Baldridge, *Grafting In*, 65.

There is no such thing, in this terribly complex matter, as "the Lord's side." Neither side is without sin, and neither side is without just cause. As a Church, we must attempt to steer a neutral course between the various factions. As Latter-day Saints, we must hold ourselves and everyone who would seek our support to the standards of justice and charity that the gospel mandates. It is only after a purging and a cleansing that Israel will be truly worthy of all the blessings that the Lord is willing to grant. "Then shall Jerusalem be holy."[58]

> In that day shall the branch of the Lord be beautiful and glorious, and the fruit of the earth shall be excellent and comely for them that are escaped of Israel. And it shall come to pass, that he that is left in Zion, and he that remaineth in Jerusalem, shall be called holy, even everyone that is written among the living in Jerusalem: When the Lord shall have washed away the filth of the daughters of Zion, and shall have purged the blood of Jerusalem from the midst thereof by the spirit of judgment, and by the spirit of burning.[59]

The Lord's justice and mercy extend to all peoples of the earth. Every human individual of every race is his child and the object of his love. Our task as individuals is to emulate that divine love. Our mission as members of The Church of Jesus Christ of Latter-day Saints is to work toward the day when all the nations "shall even go up from year to year to worship the King, the Lord of hosts, and to keep the feast of tabernacles."[60]

The prophet Isaiah foretold such a time, when the example of God's people would draw all the world's attention and make many from all nations desire to know more of what the Saints have.

> And it shall come to pass in the last days, that the mountain of the Lord's house shall be established in the top of the mountains, and shall be exalted above the hills; and all nations shall flow unto it. And many people shall go and say, Come ye, and let us go up

---

[58]. Joel 3:17.
[59]. Isaiah 4:2–4.
[60]. Zechariah 14:16.

> to the mountain of the Lord, to the house of the God of Jacob, and he will teach us of his ways, and we will walk in his paths: for out of Zion shall go forth the law, and the word of the Lord from Jerusalem. And he shall judge among the nations, and shall rebuke many people: and they shall beat their swords into plowshares, and their spears into pruninghooks: nation shall not lift up sword against nation, neither shall they learn war any more.[61]

The prophet Micah gives almost precisely the same words, but then adds, "But they shall sit every man under his vine and under his fig tree; and none shall make them afraid: for the mouth of the Lord of hosts hath spoken it. For all people will walk every one in the name of his god, and we will walk in the name of the Lord our God for ever and ever."[62] As the prophets have consistently taught, there will be differences of religious opinion on the earth even during the Millennium. What will be missing at that day is the hostility and the lack of respect that too often characterizes our relationships with those who disagree with us now. If we are serious about working for the establishment of Zion, we will do all we can to drive those characteristics out of our lives.

There is common ground between us, the Jews, and the Muslims. We should seek both to identify it and to build upon it. Indeed, we may have a special calling and responsibility to do so. "A cabinet minister of Egypt once told me," Elder Hunter recalled, "that if a bridge is ever built between Christianity and Islam it must be built by the Mormon Church."[63] We also have common enemies. Materialism and immorality are denounced from the pulpit of the Tabernacle just as they are denounced by Muslim observers of the West. We both seek to build a society that will be pleasing to God. We call it Zion, a name that presently has offensive connotations for Muslims. But what we mean by "Zion" is something that they would find not at all offensive. It is a society that would embody

---

61. Isaiah 2:2-4.
62. Micah 4:4-5.
63. Hunter, "All Are Alike Unto God," 74.

many of the deepest values of the Qur'an, including care of orphans, widows, and the poor; worship of the one God; a religion that permeates all aspects of life and serves as the basis for our commercial, cultural, and social activities; and a desire to please God by action, by faith, and works.

So long as we are separated from the Muslims by a wall of mutual incomprehension, and by a mutual hostility that has been centuries in construction, so long as we mistrust each other's motives, we will find it very hard to communicate any of the things that matter most to us. Generations of Christian missionaries have testified to the difficulty of bringing Muslims to an acceptance of the divinity of Christ. When once we have established that basis of mutual respect and mutual sympathy, however, I am convinced that it will be possible to share the gospel with Muslims. It may take a very long time to do so, but "the worth of souls is great" and abundantly merits our investment. Furthermore, the Lord promises success in that venture. Someday, he says, his blessings will rest upon Egypt and Iraq, as well as upon Israel. The three nations, no more divided by the violent political hatreds that have crippled the region for centuries, will be united in God's service. And, most astonishing of all, a temple will someday stand on the banks of the Nile.

> In that day shall there be an altar to the Lord in the midst of the land of Egypt, and a pillar at the border thereof to the Lord. And it shall be for a sign and for a witness unto the Lord of hosts in the land of Egypt: for they shall cry unto the Lord because of the oppressors, and he shall send them a saviour, and a great one, and he shall deliver them. And the Lord shall be known to Egypt, and the Egyptians shall know the Lord in that day, and shall do sacrifice and oblation; yea, they shall vow a vow unto the Lord, and perform it. And the Lord shall smite Egypt: he shall smite and heal it: and they shall return even to the Lord, and he shall be intreated of them, and shall heal them. In that day shall there be a highway out of Egypt to Assyria, and the Assyrian shall come into Egypt, and the Egyptian into Assyria, and the Egyptians shall serve with the Assyrians. In that day

> shall Israel be the third with Egypt and with Assyria, even a blessing in the midst of the land: Whom the Lord of hosts shall bless, saying, Blessed be Egypt my people, and Assyria the work of my hands, and Israel mine inheritance.[64]

This is a remarkable prospect. It will take all our ability, all our learning, all our sensitivity, all our devotion and commitment to make it come true. But, with the blessing of God, someday it most surely will.

64. Isaiah 19:19-25.

Further reading

It hardly needs to be said that there is a vast literature on the Near East in all periods of its history. I will suggest here just a few of the books and articles that I think would be of interest to readers of the present volume.

Wanderings: Chaim Potok's History of the Jews (New York: Fawcett Crest, Ballantine, 1983) will please readers who have already come to love Potok's novels, which include such titles as *The Chosen*, *The Promise*, and *My Name Is Asher Lev.* As might be expected, this history, which is available in paperback, is written with a novelist's flair. But Potok has genuine credentials to write it. He holds a doctorate in philosophy and is an ordained rabbi. More detailed but still very readable is Paul Johnson's *A History of the Jews* (New York: Harper and Row, 1987). It too is available in paperback. Johnson is a brilliant writer, a personal favorite of mine, whose *Modern Times* and *Intellectuals* and *History of Christianity* I recommend to anyone who will listen. Pushing the very limits of what can be published in paperback is *A History of the Jewish People*, edited by H. H. Ben-Sasson (Cambridge: Harvard University Press, 1976), a very learned one-volume work produced by leading historians at the Hebrew University of Jerusalem.

The Arabs in History, by Bernard Lewis, 4th ed. (London: Hutchinson, 1966), is a fine, brief introduction to the subject and is available in paperback. Albert Hourani's *A History of the Arab Peoples*

(Cambridge: Harvard University Press, 1991) represents the life's work of one of the very greatest modern Arab historians. Marshall G. S. Hodgson's *The Venture of Islam: Conscience and History in a World Civilization*, 3 vols. (Chicago and London: The University of Chicago Press, 1974), carries the story of Islam beyond the history of the Arabs, who, although they are indisputably the foremost ethnic group within the Islamic community, still represent only a part of it. Hodgson's work is difficult, but richly worth the trouble for those who really want to understand Islamic civilization. A more recent attempt to synthesize all of Islamic history into one volume is *A History of Islamic Societies*, by Ira M. Lapidus of the University of California at Berkeley (Cambridge: Cambridge University Press, 1988).

There are few serious Latter-day Saint works on the Arabs or Islam. Hugh Nibley's "Islam and Mormonism-A Comparison," in *Ensign* 2 (March 1972), 55-64, emphasizes the contrasts, whereas I have attempted here to focus on similarities and points of contact between our own faith and that of the Muslims. Still, it is a worthwhile article by a remarkable scholar. James B. Mayfield wrote a very sympathetic piece entitled "Ishmael, Our Brother," which appeared in the *Ensign* 9 (June 1979), 24-32. Arnold H. Green and Lawrence P. Goldrup examined a specific but very important issue in their article on "Joseph Smith, An American Muhammad? An Essay on the Perils of Historical Analogy," in *Dialogue: A Journal of Mormon Thought* 6 (Spring 1971), 46-58. The most sustained work on the subject is Spencer J. Palmer, ed., *Mormons and Muslims: Spiritual Foundations and Modern Manifestations* (Provo: Religious Studies Center, Brigham Young University, 1983). The product of a symposium held at Brigham Young University, this volume is somewhat uneven, but contains several quite interesting papers.

Index